Commentary on the Gospel of John

❖c❖

Chapters 6–12

THOMAS AQUINAS IN TRANSLATION

EDITORIAL BOARD

Kevin White, The Catholic University of America, *Editorial Director*

John F. Boyle, University of St. Thomas, St. Paul

Jude P. Dougherty, The Catholic University of America

Thérèse-Anne Druart, The Catholic University of America

David M. Gallagher

Jorge J. E. Gracia, State University of New York at Buffalo

R. E. Houser, University of St. Thomas, Houston

Timothy Noone, The Catholic University of America

John F. Wippel, The Catholic University of America

David J. McGonagle, The Catholic University of America Press

ST. THOMAS AQUINAS

Commentary on the Gospel of John

Translated by
†Fabian Larcher, O.P., and
†James A. Weisheipl, O.P.

With introduction and notes by
Daniel Keating and Matthew Levering

Chapters 6–12

The Catholic University of America Press
Washington, D.C.

Copyright © 2010
The Catholic University of America Press
All rights reserved
The paper used in this publication meets the minimum requirements
of American National Standards for Information Science—Permanence
of Paper for Printed Library materials, ANSI Z39.48-1984.
∞

Library of Congress Cataloging-in-Publication Data
Thomas, Aquinas, Saint, 1225?–1274.
[Super Evangelium S. Joannis lectura. English]
Commentary on the Gospel of John / St. Thomas Aquinas ;
translated by Fabian Larcher and James A. Weisheipl ;
with introduction and notes by Daniel Keating and Matthew Levering.
p. cm. — (Thomas Aquinas in translation)
Includes bibliographical references and index.
ISBN 978-0-8132-1723-9 ((first vol.) paper : alk. paper) —
ISBN 978-0-8132-1733-8 ((second vol.) paper : alk. paper) —
ISBN 978-0-8132-1734-5 ((third vol.) paper : alk. paper)
1. Bible. N.T. John I, 1–18—Commentaries.
I. Larcher, Fabian R. (Fabian Richard), 1914–
II. Weisheipl, James A.   III. Keating, Daniel A.
IV. Levering, Matthew, 1971–   V. Title.   VI. Series.
BS2615.53.T5513 2010
226.5'07—dc22   2010005230

CONTENTS

Abbreviations for Patristic and Medieval Sources	vii
Chapter 6	1
Chapter 7	60
Chapter 8	99
Chapter 9	156
Chapter 10	183
Chapter 11	220
Chapter 12	260
Index	309

ABBREVIATIONS FOR PATRISTIC AND MEDIEVAL SOURCES

Alcuin

Comm. in S. Ioannis Evang.   *Commentaria in sancti Ioannis Evangelium*

Ambrose

Comm. in ep. ad Cor. primam   *Commentaria in epistolam ad Corinthios primam*
Expos. Evang. sec. Luc.   *Expositio Evangelii secundum Lucam*
Hex.   *Hexaemeron*

Anselm

Mon.   *Monologion*

Augustine

Conf.   *Confessiones*
Con. Faust.   *Contra Faustum*
De agon. chris.   *De agone christiano*
De bapt. parv.   *De baptismo parvulorum*
De bono conj.   *De bono conjugali*
De civ. Dei   *De civitate Dei*
De cons. Evang.   *De consensu Evangelistarum*
De div. quaest. 83   *De diversis quaestionibus octaginta tribus liber unus*
De Gen. ad litt.   *De Genesi ad litteram libri XII*
De nat. boni   *De natura boni*
De oper. mon.   *De opere monachorum*
De praed. sanct.   *De praedestinatione sanctorum*

De Symb.	De Symbolo
De Trin.	De Trinitate
Ep.	Epistolae
Enarr. in Ps.	Enarrationes in Psalmos
Enchir.	Enchiridion de fide, spe et caritate
Quaest. ex Novo Test.	Quaestiones ex Novo Testamento
Quaest. in Evang. sec. Matt	Quaestionum septemdecim in Evangelium secundum Matthaeum
Quaest. vet. et novi Test.	Quaestiones veteris et novi Testamenti
Serm. de Scrip.	Sermones de Scripturis
Serm. de symb. ad catechum.	Sermo de symbolo ad catechumenos
Serm. supposit.	Sermones suppositii
Tract. in Io.	Tractatus in evangelium Ioannis

Bede

Hom. XIII in dom. sec. post Epiphan.	Homilia XIII in dominica secunda post Epiphaniam
In S. Ioannis Evang. expos.	In S. Joannis Evangelium expositio
In S. Matthaei Evang. expos.	In S. Matthaei Evangelium expositio

Chrysostom

Hom. in Io.	Homiliae in Ioannem
Comm. ad Gal.	Commentarius in Epistolam ad Galatas

Cyprian

De unit. Eccl.	De unitate Ecclesiae

Didymus

De Spir. Sanc.	Interpretatio libri Didymi de Spiritu Sancto

Dionysius

De coel. hier.	De coelesti hierarchia
De div. nom.	De divinis nominibus

De ecc. hier.	*De ecclesiastica hierarchia*
De myst. theol.	*De mystica theologia*
Ep.	*Epistolae*

Erigena

Comm. in S. Evang. sec. Io.	*Comm. in S. Evangelium secundum Ioannem*
Hom. in prol. Evang. sec. Io.	*Homilia in prologum S. Evangelii secundum Ioannem*

Eusebius

HE	*Historia ecclesiastica*

Gregory the Great

XL hom. in Evang.	*XL homilia in Evangelia*
Ep. V ad Theoc.	*Epistola V ad Theoctistam*
Hom. in Ezech.	*Homiliarum in Ezechielem*
Mor.	*Librorum moralium*
Reg. pastor. liber	*Regulae pastoralis liber*

Hilary

De Trin.	*De Trinitate*
Liber de Syn.	*Liber de Synodis*

Jerome

Comm. in Matt.	*Commentaria in Evangelium S. Matthaei*
Expos. in quat. Evang.	*Expositio in quatuor Evangeliorum*
In Evang. sec. Ioan.	*In Evangelium secundum Ioannem*
Praef. in Pent.	*Praefatio in Pentateuchum*

John of Damascus

De fide orth.	*De fidei orthodoxae*

Leo the Great

Serm.   *Sermones*

Origen

Comm. in Io.   *Commentaria in Evangelium Ioannis*
Comm. in Matt.   *Commentaria in Evangelium secundum Matthaeum*
De Prin.   *De Principiis*

Peter Lombard

Collect. in Epist. Pauli   *Collectanea in Epistolas S. Pauli*
In Ep. I ad Tim.   *In Epistolam I ad Timothaeum*

Theophylact

Enar. in Evang. S. Ioannis   *Enarratio in Evangelium Ioannis*

Thomas Aquinas

Expos. in Ps.   *Expositio in Psalmos*
Expos. super Job   *Expositio super Job ad litteram*
Sent.   *Scriptum super Sententiis*
ST   *Summa Theologiae*
Super Eph.   *Super Epistolam B. Pauli ad Ephesios lectura*
Super Rom.   *Super Epistolam B. Pauli ad Romanos lectura*

Commentary on the Gospel of John

Chapters 6–12

CHAPTER 6

LECTURE 1

1 After this Jesus went across the Sea of Galilee, which is that of Tiberias. 2 And a great multitude followed him because they saw the miracles he worked on those who were sick. 3 Jesus therefore went up a mountain, and there sat down with his disciples. 4 Now the Passover was near, a festival day of the Jews. 5 Then, when Jesus lifted his eyes and saw that a great multitude had come to him, he said to Philip, "Where shall we buy bread that these may eat?" 6 He said this, however, to test him, for he knew what he would do. 7 Philip replied, "Two hundred denarii worth of bread would not suffice for each to have a little bit." 8 One of his disciples, Andrew, the brother of Simon Peter, said to him, 9 "There is a boy here who has five barley loaves and two fishes, but what are these for so many?" 10 Jesus then said, "Make the people recline." There was much grass in the place. Therefore the men reclined, in number about five thousand. 11 Jesus then took the bread, and when he had given thanks, he distributed it to those reclining; he did likewise with the fish, as much as they wanted. 12 When they had their fill, he said to his disciples, "Gather up the fragments that are left over, lest they be wasted." 13 They therefore gathered and filled twelve baskets with the leftovers, from the five barley loaves and the two fishes, that remained after all had eaten.[1]

838. The Evangelist has presented the teaching of Christ on the spiritual life, by which he gives life to those who are born again. He now tells us of the spiritual food by which Christ sustains those to whom he has given life. First, he describes a visible miracle, in which Christ furnished bodily food. Secondly, he considers spiritual food (6:26). He does two things about the first. First, he describes the visible miracle. Secondly, he shows the effect this miracle had (6:14). He tells us two things about this miracle. First, its circumstances, secondly, about its actual accomplishment (v. 5). As to the first he does three things. First he describes the crowd that Jesus fed, secondly, the place; thirdly, the time (v. 4). As to the first he does three things. First, he identifies the place where the crowd followed Jesus; secondly, the people who followed him; and thirdly, he tells why they followed him.

839. The Evangelist describes the place to which the crowd followed

---

1. St. Thomas refers to Jn 6:9–11 in *ST* III, q. 74, a. 3, obj. 1.

our Lord when he says, **After this Jesus went across the Sea of Galilee**, i.e., after the mysterious words Jesus had spoken concerning his power. This Sea of Galilee is mentioned frequently in various places in Scripture. Luke calls it a lake (Lk 5:1) because its water is not salty, but was formed from the waters flowing in from the Jordan. Yet it is still called a "Sea," because in Hebrew all bodies of water are called "seas": "God called the waters 'seas'" (Gen 1:10). It is also called Gennesaret because of the character of its location: for this water is tossed about a great deal, being buffeted by the winds that come from the vapors rising from its surface. Thus in Greek the word "Gennesaret" means "wind forming." It is called the Sea of Galilee from the province of Galilee in which it is located. Again, it is called the Sea of Tiberias from the city of Tiberias: this city was situated on one side of the sea, facing Capernaum on the opposite side. The city of Tiberias was formerly called Chinnereth, but later, when it was rebuilt by Herod the Tetrarch, it was renamed as Tiberias in honor of Tiberius Caesar.

840. The literal reason why Jesus crossed the sea is given by Chrysostom:[2] to give ground to the anger and agitation which the Jews felt against Christ because of the things he had said about them. As Chrysostom says: just as darts strike a hard object with great force if they meet it, but pass on and soon come to rest if nothing is in their way, so also the anger of defiant men increases when they are resisted, but if we yield a little, it is easy to keep their fury within bounds. So Christ, by going to the other side of the sea, was able to soften the anger of the Jews, caused by what he had said. He thus gives us an example to act in the same way: "Do not be provoked by one who speaks evil of you" (Sir 8:14).

841. In the mystical sense, the sea signifies this present troubled world: "This great sea, stretching wide" (Ps 103:25). Our Lord crossed over this sea when he assumed the sea of punishment and death by being born, trod it under foot by dying, and then crossing over it by his rising, arrived at the glory of his resurrection. We read of this crossing: "Jesus knew that his time had come to leave this world for the Father" (below 13:1). A great crowd, composed of both peoples, has followed him in this crossing, by believing in him and imitating him: "Your heart will be full of wonder and joy, when the riches of the sea will be given to you" (Is 60:5); "Rise up, O Lord, you who demand that justice be done; and the people will gather round you" (Ps 7:7).

842. The crowd that followed him is described as large, **And a great multitude followed him.**

843. The reason why they followed him is because he was performing miracles, hence he says, **because they saw the miracles he worked on those who were sick.** We should point out that some followed Christ

---

2. *Hom. in Io.* 42. 1; PG 59, col. 239; cf. *Catena aurea*, 6:1–14.

because of his teachings, that is, those who were better disposed. But there were others, i.e., those who were less perfect and less perceptive, who followed him because they were attracted by visible miracles; "Signs were given to unbelievers, not to believers" (1 Cor 14:22). Still others followed him out of devotion and faith, those, namely, whom he had cured of some bodily defect: for our Lord had so healed their body that they were also completely healed in soul: "The works of God are perfect" (Dt 32:4). This is clear, because he expressly said to the paralytic, "Do not sin again" (above 5:14), and in Matthew (9:2) he says, "Son, your sins are forgiven"; and these remarks concern the health of the soul rather than that of the body.

844. We might remark that although the Evangelist had mentioned only three miracles (the one at the marriage reception, the son of the official, and the paralytic), he says here in a general way, **the miracles he worked**. He does this to indicate that Christ worked many other miracles that are not mentioned in this book, as he will say below (21:25). For his main object was to present the teaching of Christ.

845. Then he gives the location of the miracle, on a mountain; hence he says: **Jesus therefore went up a mountain**, i.e., privately, **and there sat down with his disciples**. Now a mountain is a place well suited for refreshment, for according to the Psalm a mountain signifies the perfection of justice: "Your justice is like the mountains of God" (Ps 35:7). And so, because we cannot be satisfied by earthly things—indeed, "Whoever drinks this water will be thirsty again" (above 4:13)—but spiritual things will satisfy us, our Lord leads his disciples to a higher place to show that full satisfaction and the perfection of justice are found in spiritual realities. We read of this mountain: "The mountain of God is a rich mountain" (Ps 67:16). Thus he also exercised his office of teacher there, sitting with his disciples; for he is the one who teaches every man.[3]

846. The time is mentioned when he says, **Now the Passover was near**. This time was also well suited for their refreshment, for "Passover" means "passage": "It is the Passover of the Lord, that is, his passage" (Ex 12:11). We understand from this that anyone who desires to be refreshed by the bread of the divine Word and by the body and blood of the Lord must pass from vices to virtues: "Our Passover, Christ, has been sacrificed, and so let us feast with the unleavened bread of sincerity and truth" (1 Cor 5:7). And again, divine Wisdom says: "Pass over to me, all who desire me" (Sir 24:26).

This is the second Passover the Evangelist has mentioned. However, our Lord did not go to Jerusalem this time, as the law commanded. The reason for this being that Christ was both God and man: as man he was subject to the law, but as God he was above the law. So, he ob-

---

3. See *ST* III, q. 42.

served the law on certain occasions to show that he was a man, but he also disregarded the law at other times to show that he was God. Further, by not going he indicated that the ceremonies of the law would end gradually and in a short time.

847. Then he considers the miracle itself (v. 5). First, why it was needed. Secondly, its accomplishment. We can see the need for this miracle from our Lord's question to his disciple, and the disciple's answer. First, our Lord's question is given; and then the answer of his disciple (v. 7). He does three things about the first. First, the occasion for the question is given; secondly, we have the question itself (v. 5b); thirdly, we are told why Christ asked this question (v. 6).

848. The occasion for Christ's question was his sight of the crowd coming to him. Hence he says, **Then, when Jesus**, on the mountain with his disciples, i.e., with those who were more perfect, **lifted his eyes and saw that a great multitude had come to him.** Here we should note two things about Christ. First, his maturity: for he is not distracted by what does not concern him, but is appropriately concerned with his disciples. He is not like those spoken of in Proverbs (30:13): "A generation whose eyes are proud." And, "A man's dress, and laughter, and his walk, show what he is" (Sir 19:27). Secondly, we should note that Christ did not sit there with his disciples out of laziness; he was looking right at them teaching them carefully and attracting their hearts to himself: "Then he lifted his eyes to his disciples (Lk 6:20). Thus we read: **Then, when Jesus lifted his eyes.** In the mystical sense, our Lord's eyes are his spiritual gifts; and he lifts his eyes on the elect, i.e., looks at them with compassion, when he mercifully grants these gifts to them. This is what the Psalm asks for: "Look upon me, O Lord, and have mercy on me" (Ps 85:16).

849. Our Lord's question concerns the feeding of the crowd, so he said to Philip: **Where shall we buy bread that these may eat?** He assumes one thing and asks about another. He assumes their poverty, because they did not have food to offer this great crowd; and he asks how they might obtain it, saying, **Where shall we buy bread that these may eat?**

Here we should note that every teacher is obliged to possess the means of feeding spiritually the people who come to him. And since no man possesses of himself the resources to feed them, he must acquire them elsewhere by his labor, study, and persistent prayer: "Hurry, you who have no money, and acquire without cost wine and milk" (Is 55:1). And there follows: "Why do you spend your money," i.e., your eloquence, "for what is not bread," i.e., not the true wisdom which refreshes—"Wisdom will feed him with the bread of life and understanding" (Sir 15:5)—"and why do you work for what does not satisfy you," i.e., by learning things that drain you instead of filling you?[4]

---

4. See *ST* II-II, qq. 166–67.

850. Our Lord's intention is given when he says, **He said this, however, to test him**. Here the Evangelist raises one difficulty in answering another. For we could wonder why our Lord asked Philip what to do, as though our Lord himself did not know. The Evangelist settles this when he says, **for he knew what he would do**. But it seems that the Evangelist raises another difficulty when he says, **to test him**. For to test is to try out; and this seems to imply ignorance.

I answer that one can test another in various ways in order to try him out. One man tests another in order to learn; the devil tests a man in order to ensnare him: "Your enemy, the devil, as a roaring lion, goes about seeking whom he can devour" (1 Pt 5:8). But Christ (and God) does not test us in order to learn, because he sees into our hearts; nor in order to ensnare us, for as we read in James (1:13): "God does not test [i.e., tempt] anyone." But he does test us that others might learn something from the one tested. This is the way God tested Abraham: "God tested Abraham" (Gen 22:1); and then it says (v. 12): "Now I know that you fear God," i.e., I have made it known that you fear the Lord. He tests Philip in the same way: so that those who hear his answer might be very certain about the miracle to come.

851. Now we have the answer of the disciples. First, the answer of Philip; then that of Andrew (v. 8).

852. With respect to the first, note that Philip was slower in learning than the others, and so he asks our Lord more questions: "Lord, show us the Father, and that will be enough for us" (below 14:8). Here, according to the literal sense, Andrew is better disposed than Philip, for Philip does not seem to have any understanding or anticipation of the coming miracle. And so he suggests that money is the way by which they could feed all the people, saying: **Two hundred denarii worth of bread would not suffice for each to have a little bit**. And since we do not have that much, we cannot feed them. Here we see the poverty of Christ, for he did not even have two hundred denarii.[5]

853. Andrew, however, seems to sense that a miracle is going to take place. Perhaps he recalled the miracle performed by Elisha with the barley loaves, when he fed a hundred men with twenty loaves (2 Kg 4:42). And so he says, **There is a boy here who has five barley loaves**. Still, he did not suspect that Christ was going to perform a greater miracle than Elisha: for he thought that fewer loaves would be miraculously produced from fewer, and more from a larger number. But in truth, he who does not need any material to work with could feed a crowd as easily with few or many loaves. So Andrew continues: **but what are these for so many?** As if to say: Even if you increased them in the measure that Elisha did, it still would not be enough.

854. In the mystical sense, wisdom is a symbol for spiritual refresh-

---

5. See *ST* III, q. 40, a. 3.

ment. One kind of wisdom was taught by Christ, the true wisdom: "Christ is the power of God, and the wisdom of God" (1 Cor 1:24). Before Christ came, there were two other teachings or doctrines: one was the human teachings of the philosophers; the other was the teachings found in the written law. Philip mentions the first of these when he speaks of buying: *Two hundred denarii worth of bread would not suffice*, for human wisdom must be acquired.[6] Now the number one hundred implies perfection. Thus two hundred suggests the twofold perfection necessary for this wisdom: for there are two ways one arrives at the perfection of human wisdom, by experience and by contemplation. So he says, *Two hundred denarii worth of bread would not suffice*, because no matter what human reason can experience and contemplate of the truth, it is not enough to completely satisfy our desire for wisdom: "Let not the wise man glory in his wisdom, nor the strong man in his strength, nor the rich man in his riches. But let him who glories glory in this: that he knows and understands me" (Jer 9:23).[7] For the wisdom of no philosopher has been so great that it could keep men from error; rather, the philosophers have led many into error.[8]

It is Andrew who mentions the second kind of teaching [that of the law]. He does not want to buy other bread, but to feed the crowd with the loaves of bread they had, that is, those contained in the law. And so he was better disposed than Philip. So he says: *There is a boy here who has five barley loaves*. This boy can symbolize Moses, because of the imperfection found in the state of the law: "The law brought nothing to perfection" (Heb 7:19);[9] or the Jewish people, who were serving under the elements of this world (Gal 4:3).

This boy had five loaves, that is, the teaching of the law: either because this teaching was contained in the five books of Moses, "The law was given through Moses" (above 1:17); or because it was given to men absorbed in sensible things, which are made known through the five senses. These loaves were of barley because the law was given in such a way that what was life-giving in it was concealed under physical signs: for the kernel in barley is covered with a very firm husk. Or, the loaves were of barley because the Jewish people had not yet been rubbed free of carnal desire, but it still covered their hearts like a husk: for in the Old Testament they outwardly experienced hardships because of their ceremonial observances: "A yoke, which neither our fathers nor we were able to bear" (Acts 15:10). Further, the Jews were engrossed in material things and did not understand the spiritual meaning of the law: "A veil is over their hearts" (2 Cor 3:15).

The two fishes, which gave a pleasant flavor to the bread, indicate the teachings of the Psalms and the prophets. Thus the Old Law not only had five loaves, i.e., the five books of Moses, but also two fishes,

6. See *ST* I-II, q. 57, a. 2.
8. See *ST* II-II, q. 2, a. 4.
7. See *ST* I, q. 1, a. 6.
9. See *ST* I-II, q. 98, a. 1.

that is, the Psalms and the prophets. So the Old Testament writings are divided into these three: "The things written about me in the law of Moses, and in the prophets and in the Psalms" (Lk 24:44). Or, according to Augustine,[10] the two fishes signify the priests and kings who ruled the Jews; and they prefigured Christ, who was the true king and priest.[11]

But what are these for so many? for they could not bring man to a complete knowledge of the truth: for although God was known in Judea, the Gentiles did not know him.

855. Next (v. 10), the miracle is presented. First, we see the people arranged; secondly, the miracle itself; and thirdly, the gathering of the leftovers. He does two things about the first. First, he shows Christ directing the disciples to have the people recline; secondly, why this was appropriate; and thirdly, he tells us the number of people present.

856. Our Lord told his disciples to arrange the people so that they could eat; thus Jesus says, **Make the people recline**, i.e., to eat. For as mentioned before, in former times people took their meals lying on couches; consequently, it was the custom to say of those who sat down to eat that they were reclining. In the mystical sense, this indicates that rest which is necessary for the perfection of wisdom. Again, the people are prepared by the disciples because it is through the disciples that the knowledge of the truth has come to us: "Let the mountains receive peace for the people" (Ps 71:3).[12]

857. The character of the place shows why it was convenient that they recline, for **There was much grass in the place**. This is the literal meaning. In the mystical sense, grass indicates the flesh: "All flesh is grass" (Is 40:6). In this sense it can refer to two things. First, to the teachings of the Old Testament, which were given to a people resting in things of the flesh and wise according to the flesh: "If you are willing, and listen to me, you will eat the good things of the land" (Is 1:19); "The posterity of Jacob dwells in a land of grain, wine and oil" (Dt 33:28). Or, it can refer to one who perceives true wisdom, which cannot be attained without first abandoning the things of the flesh: "Do not imitate this world" (Rom 12:2).[13]

858. There was a great number of people; thus he says, **the men reclined, in number about five thousand**. The Evangelist counted only the men, according to the custom in the law, for as mentioned in Numbers (1:3), Moses counted the people who were twenty years and older, without including the women. The Evangelist does the same, because only men can be completely instructed: "We speak wisdom to those who are mature" (1 Cor 2:6); "Solid food is for the mature" (Heb 5:14).

---

10. *De div. quaest. 83*, q. 61. 2; PL 40; col. 48–49; cf. *Catena aurea*, 6:1–14; see also *Tract. in Io*. 24. 5; PL 35, col. 1595.
11. See *ST* III, q. 31, a. 2. 12. See *ST* III, q. 42, a. 4.
13. See *ST* II-II, q. 182, a. 1.

859. Then (v. 11), the Evangelist presents the feeding of the crowd. First, we see the attitude of Christ; secondly, the food used; thirdly, that the people were satisfied. As to the attitude of Jesus, both his humility and his giving of thanks are mentioned.

860. We see his humility because he took the bread and gave it to the people. Now although in this miracle Christ could have fed the people with bread created from nothing, he chose to do so by multiplying bread that already existed.[14] He did this, first, to show that sensible things do not come from the devil, as the Manichean error maintains. For if this were so, our Lord would not have used sensible things to praise God, especially since "The Son of God appeared to destroy the works of the devil" (1 Jn 3:8). He did it, secondly, to show that they are also wrong in claiming that the teachings of the Old Testament are not from God but from the devil. Thus, to show that the doctrine of the New Testament is none other than that which was prefigured and contained in the teachings of the Old Testament, he multiplied bread that already existed, implying by this that he is the one who fulfills the law and brings it to perfection: "I have not come to destroy the law, but to fulfill it," as we read in Matthew (5:17).[15]

861. We see that he gave thanks, **when he had given thanks**. He did this to show that whatever he had, he had from another, that is, from his Father.[16] This is an example for us to do the same. More particularly, he gave thanks to teach us that we should thank God when we begin a meal: "Nothing is to be rejected if it is received with thanksgiving" (1 Tim 4:4); "The poor will eat and be satisfied; and they will praise the Lord" (Ps 21:27). Again, he gave thanks to teach us that he was not praying for himself, but for the people who were there, for he had to convince them that he had come from God. Accordingly, he prays before he works this miracle before them, in order to show them that he is not acting against God, but according to God's will.

We read in Mark (6:41) that Christ had the apostles distribute the bread to the people. It says here that he distributed it because in a way he himself does what he does by means of others. In the mystical sense, both statements are true: for Christ alone refreshes from within, and others, as his ministers, refresh from without.[17]

862. Their food was bread and fish, about which enough has been said above.

Finally, those who ate were completely satisfied, because they took **as much as they wanted**. For Christ is the only one who feeds an empty soul and fills a hungry soul with good things: "I will be satisfied when your glory appears" (Ps 16:15). Others perform miracles through having grace in a partial manner; Christ, on the other hand, does so with

---

14. See *ST* III, q. 44, a. 4.
16. See *ST* III, q. 21.
15. See *ST* I-II, q. 107, a. 3.
17. See *ST* III, q. 64.

unlimited power, since he does all things superabundantly.[18] Hence it says that the people *had their fill*.

863. Now we see the leftovers collected (v. 12). First, Christ gives the order; secondly, his disciples obey.

864. The Evangelist says that after the people had eaten their fill, Christ said to his disciples: **Gather up the fragments that are left over**. This was not pretentious display on our Lord's part; He did it to show that the miracle he accomplished was not imaginary, since the collected leftovers kept for some time and provided food for others. Again, he wanted to impress this miracle more firmly on the hearts of his disciples, whom he had carry the leftovers: for most of all he wanted to teach his disciples, who were destined to be the teachers of the entire world.

865. His disciples obeyed him faithfully; hence he says, **They therefore gathered and filled twelve baskets with the leftovers**. Here we should note that the amount of food that remained was not left to chance, but was according to plan: for as much as Christ willed was left over, no more and no less. This is shown by the fact that the basket of each apostle was filled. Now a basket is reserved for the work of peasants. Therefore, the twelve baskets signify the twelve apostles and those who imitate them, who, although they are looked down upon in this present life, are nevertheless filled with the riches of spiritual sacraments. There are twelve because they were to preach the faith of the Holy Trinity to the four parts of the world.

LECTURE 2

14 Now when these people saw that Jesus had worked a miracle, they said: "This is truly the Prophet who is to come into the world." 15 So Jesus, knowing that they would come to seize him and make him king, fled again into the mountains, alone. 16 When evening came, his disciples went down to the sea. 17 After they got into the boat, they set out across the sea to Capernaum. It was already dark, and Jesus had not yet come to them. 18 The sea became rough, agitated by a great wind. 19 After they had rowed twenty-five or thirty stadia [three or four miles], they saw Jesus walking on the water, coming toward the boat, and they were afraid. 20 But he said to them: "It is I. Do not be afraid." 21 They then wanted to take him into the boat; and suddenly the boat was on the land toward which they were going.

866. Above, the Evangelist told us of the miracle of the loaves and fishes. Now he shows the threefold effect this miracle had on the peo-

---

18. See *ST* III, q. 43, a. 2.

ple. First, its effect on their faith; secondly, on their plans to honor Jesus; thirdly, how it led them (and the disciples) to search for Jesus.

867. With respect to the first, we should note that the Jews said in the Psalm: "We have not seen our signs; there is now no prophet" (Ps 73:9). For it was customary in earlier days for the prophets to work many signs; so, when these signs were absent, prophecy seemed to have ended.[19] But when the Jews see such signs, they believe that prophecy is returning. Accordingly, the people were so impressed by this miracle they just saw that they called our Lord a prophet. Thus we read, **Now when these people**, who had been filled with the five loaves, **saw that Jesus had worked a miracle, they said: This is truly the Prophet**. However, they did not yet have perfect faith, for they believed that Jesus was only a prophet, while he was also the Lord of the prophets. Yet, they were not entirely wrong, because our Lord called himself a prophet.

868. Here we should remark that a prophet is called a seer: "He who is now called a prophet was formerly called a seer" (1 Sam 9:9). Further, seeing pertains to the cognitive power. Now in Christ there were three kinds of knowledge. First of all, there was sense knowledge. And in this respect he had some similarity to the prophets, insofar as sensible species could be formed in the imagination of Christ to present future or hidden events. This was especially due to his passibility, which was appropriate to his state as a "wayfarer." Secondly, Christ had intellectual knowledge; and in this he was not like the prophets, but was even superior to all the angels: for he was a "comprehensor" in a more excellent way than any creature. Again, Christ had divine knowledge, and in this way he was the one who inspired the prophets and the angels, since all knowledge is caused by a participation in the divine Word.[20]

Still, these people seemed to realize that Christ was a superior prophet, for they said: **This is truly the Prophet**. For although there had been many prophets among the Jews, they were waiting for a particular one, according to: "The Lord your God will raise up a prophet for you" (Dt 18:15). This is the one they are speaking of here; thus it continues: **who is to come into the world**.

869. Next, we see the second effect of Christ's miracle: the honor the people planned for Christ, which he refused. First, we have the attempt by the people; secondly, Christ's flight from them.

870. The attempt of the people is mentioned when he says, **they would come to seize him and make him king**. A person or thing is seized if it is taken in a way that one does not will or is not opportune.

---

19. See *ST* II-II, q. 171, a. 1.
20. See *ST* III, q. 9, aa. 1–2.

Now it is true that God's plan from all eternity had been to establish the kingdom of Christ; but the time for this was not then opportune. Christ had come then, but not to reign in the way we ask for his reign when we say, "Your kingdom come" (Mt 6:10); at that time he will reign even as man. Another time was reserved for this: after the judgment of Christ, when the saints will appear in glory.[21] It was about this kingdom the disciples asked when they said: "Lord, will you restore the kingdom to Israel at this time?" (Acts 1:6).

So the people, thinking he had come to reign, wanted to make him their king. The reason for this is that men often want as their ruler someone who will provide them with temporal things. Thus, because our Lord had fed them, they were willing to make him their king: "You have a mantle, be our ruler" (Is 3:6). Chrysostom[22] says: "See the power of gluttony. They are no longer concerned about his breaking the Sabbath; they are no longer zealous for God. All these things are set in the background now that their bellies are full. Now he is regarded as a prophet among them, and they want to set him on the royal throne as their king."

871. We see Christ's flight when he says that he *fled again into the mountains, alone.* We can see from this that when our Lord had first seen the crowd of people he came down from the mountain and fed them in the valley, for we would not read that he went again into the mountains if he had not come down from them.

Why did Christ flee from the people, since he really is a king? There are three reasons for this. First, because it would have detracted from his dignity to have accepted a kingdom from men: for he is so great a king that all other kings are kings by participating in his kingship: "It is by me that kings rule" (Pr 8:15).[23] Another reason is that it would have been harmful to his teaching if he had accepted this dignity and support from men; for he had worked and taught in such a way that everything was attributed to divine power and not to the influence of men: "Praise from men I do not need" (above 5:41). The third reason was to teach us to despise the dignities of this world: "I have given you an example that as I have done to you, so you should do also" (below 13:15); "Do not seek dignity from men" (Sir 7:4). And so, he refused the glory of this world, but still endured its punishment of his own will: "Jesus endured the cross, despising the shame, for the joy set before him" (Heb 12:2).[24]

872. Matthew seems to conflict with this, for he says that "Jesus went up the mountain alone, to pray" (Mt 14:23). However, in the

---

21. See *ST* III, q. 59, a. 5.
22. *Hom. in Io.* 42. 3; PG 59, col. 243; cf. *Catena aurea,* 6:15–21.
23. See *ST* III, q. 59, a. 4, ad 1.
24. See *ST* III, q. 47, a. 2.

opinion of Augustine,[25] there is no conflict here, because he had reason both to flee and to pray. For our Lord is teaching us that when a reason for flight draws near, there is great reason to pray.

In the mystical sense, Christ went up into the mountain when the people he had fed were ready to subject themselves to him, because he went up into heaven when the people were ready to subject themselves to the truth of the faith, according to: "A congregation of people will surround you. Return above for their sakes" (Ps 7:8), i.e., return on high so a congregation of people may surround you.[26]

He says that Christ fled, to indicate that the people could not understand his grandeur: for if we do not understand something, we say that it flees or eludes us.

873. Now he considers the third effect of Christ's miracle, the search for Christ. First, by his disciples; secondly, by the people. As to the first, he does two things. First, he tells of the eagerness of the disciples; and secondly, enlarges upon this (v. 17b). He does two things about the first. First, he tells that they went down to the shore. Secondly, he tells of their journey across the sea (v. 17).

874. Note, about the first, that Christ went up into the mountain without the knowledge of his disciples. So, they waited there until evening came, for they expected that he would come back to them. But their love was so great that when evening came they just had to go looking for him. Thus he says, **When evening came, his disciples went down to the sea**, looking for Jesus.

In the mystical sense, "evening" signifies our Lord's passion or his ascension. For as long as the disciples enjoyed Christ's physical presence, no trouble disturbed them and no bitterness vexed them: "Can the friends of the groom mourn as long as the groom is with them?" (Mt 9:15). But when Christ was away, then they "went down to the sea," to the troubles of this world: "This great sea, stretching wide" (Ps 103:25).

875. He adds that they crossed, saying, **After they got into the boat, they set out across the sea to Capernaum**, for the love that burned within them could not endure our Lord's absence for very long.

876. Now (17b), he enlarges upon what he had already said in summary fashion. First, on their going down to the sea; secondly, on their crossing (v. 18).

877. As to the first, he says, **It was already dark, and Jesus had not yet come to them**. The Evangelist does not tell us this without a reason, for it shows the intensity of their love, since not even night or evening could stop them.

---

25. *De cons. Evang.* 2. 47. 100; PL 34, col. 1127–28; cf. *Catena aurea*, 6:15–21; see also *Tract. in Io.* 25. 4; PL 35, col. 1598.
26. See *ST* III, q. 57, a. 1.

In the mystical sense, the "dark" signifies the absence of love; for light is love, according to: "He who loves his brother dwells in the light" (1 Jn 2:10). Accordingly, there is darkness in us when Jesus, "the true light" (above 1:9) does not come to us, because his presence repels all darkness.

Jesus left his disciples alone for this length of time so that they might experience his absence; and they did indeed experience it during the storm at sea: "Know and realize, that it is evil and bitter for you to have left the Lord" (Jer 2:19). He left them, in the second place, so that they might look for him more earnestly: "Where has your beloved gone, most beautiful of women? We will search for him with you" (Sg 5:17).

878. As for their crossing, first we see the storm at sea; then Christ coming to them, and the time; and thirdly, the effect this had.

879. The storm was caused by a rising wind; thus he says: ***The sea became rough, agitated by a great wind.*** This wind is a symbol for the trials and persecutions which would afflict the Church due to a lack of love. For as Augustine[27] says, when love grows cold the waves of the sea begin to swell and danger threatens the boat. Still, these winds and the storm, darkness, did not stop the progress of the boat or so batter it that it broke apart: "He who perseveres to the end will be saved" (Mt 24:13); and again: "And the rains fell, and the floods came, and the house did not collapse," as we read in Matthew (7:25).

880. Christ did not appear to them when the storm first began, but only some time later; thus he says, ***After they had rowed twenty-five or thirty stadia, they saw Jesus.*** We see from this that our Lord allows us to be troubled for a while so our virtue may be tested; but he does not desert us in the end, but comes very close to us: "God is faithful, and will not allow you to be tested beyond your strength" (1 Cor 10:13).[28]

According to Augustine,[29] the twenty-five stadia they rowed are the five books of Moses. For twenty-five is the square of five, since five times five is twenty-five. But a number that is multiplied in this way keeps the meaning of its root. Thus, just as five signifies the Old Law, so twenty-five signifies the perfection of the New Testament. Thirty, however, signifies that perfection of the New Testament which was lacking in the law: for thirty is the result of multiplying five by six, which is a perfect number. So, Jesus comes to those who row twenty-five or thirty stadia, i.e., to those who fulfill the law or the perfection taught by the Gospel; and he comes treading under foot all the waves of pride and the dignities of this present world: "You rule the might of the sea and calm its waves" (Ps 88:10). And then we will see Christ near our boat, because divine help is close: "The Lord is near to all who fear

---

27. *Tract. in Io.* 25. 5–6; PL 35, col. 1598–99; cf. *Catena aurea*, 6:15–21.
28. See *ST* I-II, q. 109, a. 10; II-II, q. 137, a. 4.
29. *Tract. in Io.* 25. 6; PL 35, col. 1599; cf. *Catena aurea*, 6:15–21.

him" (Ps 144:18). Thus it is clear that Christ is near to all those who seek him rightly. Now the apostles loved Christ very keenly: this is obvious because they tried to go to him despite the darkness, the stormy sea, and the distance to shore. Consequently, Christ was with them.

881. Now we see the effect of Christ's appearance. First, the interior effect; secondly, the exterior effect (v. 21b).

882. The interior effect of Christ's appearance was fear; and he mentions the fear of the disciples at the sudden appearance of Christ when he says, *and they were afraid*. This was a good fear, because it was the effect of humility: "Do not be proud; rather fear" (Rom 11:20); or it was an evil fear, because "they thought it was a ghost" (Mk 6:49), "They trembled with fear" (Ps 13:5): for fear is especially appropriate to the carnal, because they are afraid of spiritual things.[30]

Secondly, we see Christ encouraging them against two dangers. First, they are encouraged against the danger to the faith in their intellect when he says, *It is I*, to eliminate their doubts: "Look at my hands and my feet! It is really me" (Lk 24:39). Secondly, Christ encourages them against the danger of fear in their emotions, saying, *Do not be afraid*: "Do not be afraid when they are present" (Jer 1:8); "The Lord is my light and my salvation; whom shall I fear" (Ps 26:1).[31]

Thirdly, we see the reaction of the disciples, for *They then wanted to take him into the boat*. This signifies that we receive Christ by love and contemplation after servile fear has been taken out of our hearts: "I stand at the door and knock. If any one opens it for me, I will enter" (Rev 3:20).[32]

883. There were two exterior effects: the storm abated, and their boat suddenly landed, although it had just been at a distance from the shore, for our Lord gave them a calm journey, without danger. He himself did not enter the boat because he wished to accomplish a greater miracle. So here we have three miracles: the walking on the sea, the quick calming of the storm, and the sudden arrival of the boat on the land although it had been far away. We learn from this that the faithful, in whom Christ is present, put down the swelling pride of this world, tread under their feet its waves of tribulation, and cross quickly to the land of the living; "Your good spirit will lead me to land" (Ps 142:10).

884. There are a number of difficulties here. The first concerns the literal sense: Matthew (14:22) seems to conflict with our present account for he says that the disciples were told by Christ to go to the shore, while here it says the disciples went there to search for him. Another difficulty is that Matthew (14:34) says that the disciples crossed over to Gennesaret, while we read here that they came to Capernaum.

---

30. See Aquinas, *Super Rom.*, chap. 8, lec. 3, nos. 638–43; *ST* II-II, q. 19.
31. See *ST* II-II, q. 125, a. 1.
32. See *ST* II-II, q. 19, a. 6.

The third difficulty is that Matthew (14:32) says that Christ got into the boat, but here he did not.

Chrysostom[33] settles these difficulties quite briefly by saying that the two accounts do not deal with the same miracle. For, as he says, Christ frequently miraculously walked upon the sea in front of his disciples, but not for the people, lest they think he did not have a real body. But, according to Augustine,[34] and this is the better opinion, John and Matthew are describing the same miracle. Augustine answers the first difficulty by saying it makes no difference that Matthew says the disciples went down to the shore because our Lord told them to. For it is possible that our Lord did so, and they went believing that he would sail with them. And that is why they waited until night, and when Christ did not come, they crossed by themselves.

There are two answers to the second difficulty. One is that Capernaum and Gennesaret are neighboring towns on the same shore. And perhaps the disciples landed at a place near both, so that Matthew mentions one and John the other. Or, it might be said that Matthew does not say that they came to Gennesaret immediately; they could have come first to Capernaum and then to Gennesaret. [The answer to the third difficulty is not given.]

LECTURE 3

22 On the next day, the crowd that stood on the other side of the sea saw that there was no second boat there, but only one, and that Jesus had not gone into the boat, but only his disciples had gone. 23 But other boats arrived from Tiberias, near the place where they had eaten the bread, after having given thanks to God. 24 When therefore the people saw that Jesus was not there, nor his disciples, they got into the boats and set off for Capernaum, looking for Jesus. 25 When they found him on the other side of the sea, they said: "Rabbi, when did you come here?" 26 Jesus replied and said: "Amen, amen, I say to you: you seek me not because you have seen miracles, but because you have eaten of the bread and have been filled. 27 Do not work for the food that perishes, but for that which endures to eternal life, which the Son of Man will give you, for on him has God the Father set his seal." 28 Then they said to him: "What must we do that we may perform the works of God?" 29 Jesus replied and said to them: "This is the work of God, that you believe in him whom he sent." 30 They then said to him: "What sign then are you going to give that we may see and believe you? What

---

33. *Hom. in Io.* 43. 1; PG 59, col. 245–46; cf. *Catena aurea,* 6:15–21.
34. *De cons. Evang.* 2. 47. 100; PL 34, col. 1127–28; cf. *Catena aurea,* 6:15–21.

work do you perform? 31 Our fathers ate manna in the desert, as it is written: 'He gave them bread from heaven to eat.'"[35]

885. After having described how the disciples searched for Christ, the Evangelist now shows the people looking for him. First, he states their motive; secondly, the occasion; and thirdly, the search itself (v. 24).

886. The crowd of people was looking for Christ because of the miracle mentioned above, that is, because he had crossed the sea without using any boat. They realized this because the other evening he had not been on the shore near where he had performed the miracle of the bread, and where there had been only one boat which had left for the opposite shore with the disciples, but without Christ. So that morning, when they could not find Christ on this side, since he was already on the other side although there was no other boat he could have used, they suspected that he had crossed by walking upon the sea. And this is what he says: **On the next day**, following the one on which he had worked the miracle of the bread, **the crowd that stood on the other side of the sea**, where he had performed this miracle, **saw that there was no second boat there, but only one**, because the day before that was the only one there, and they had seen **that Jesus had not gone into the boat, but only his disciples had gone.** This one ship signifies the Church, which is one by its unity of faith and sacraments: "One faith, one baptism" (Eph 4:5).[36] Again, our Lord's absence from his disciples signifies his physical absence from them at the ascension: "After the Lord Jesus spoke to them, he was taken up into heaven" (Mk 16:19).[37]

887. It was the arrival of other boats from the opposite side of the sea that gave the people the opportunity to look for Christ; they could cross on these and search for him. He says: **But other boats arrived**, from the other side, that is, **from Tiberias, near the place where they had eaten the bread, after having given thanks to God.**

These other boats signify the various sects of heretics and of those who seek their own profit, and not the good of Jesus Christ: "You seek me ... because you have eaten of the bread and have been filled" (v. 26). These groups are either separated in faith, as are the heretics, or in the love of charity, as are the carnal, who are not properly in the Church, but next to it, insofar as they have a feigned faith and the appearance of holiness: "They have the appearance of devotion, but deny its power" (2 Tim 3:5); "Do not be surprised if the ministers of Satan disguise themselves" (2 Cor 11:14).[38]

888. The people were eager to find Christ. First, he shows how they

---

35. St. Thomas refers to Jn 6:31 in *ST* III, q. 33, a. 3, ad 3.
36. See *ST* III, q. 61, a. 1.
37. See *ST* III, q. 57.
38. See *ST* II-II, q. 11, aa. 1–2.

looked for him; secondly, how they questioned him after they found him (v. 25).

889. He says, **When the people saw that Jesus was not there, nor his disciples, they got into the boats**, which had come from Tiberias, **looking for Jesus**; and this is praiseworthy: "Search for the Lord while he can be found" (Is 55:6); "Seek the Lord, and your soul will have life" (Ps 68:33).

890. Once they found him, they questioned him. **When they**, the people, **found him**, Christ, **on the other side of the sea**, they asked him: **Rabbi, when did you come here?** This can be understood in two ways. In the first way, they were asking about the time only. And then, Chrysostom[39] says, they should be rebuked for their rudeness, because, after such a miracle, they did not ask how he crossed without a boat, but only when he did so. Or, it can be said that by asking when, they wanted to know not just the time, but the other circumstances connected with this miraculous crossing.

891. Note that now, after they have found Christ, they do not wish do make him their king, while before, after he had fed them, they did. They wanted to make him their king then because they were emotionally excited with the joy of their meal; but such emotions quickly pass. So it is that things that we plan according to our emotions do not last; but matters that we arrange by our reason last longer: "A wise man continues on in his wisdom like the sun; a fool changes like the moon" (Sir 27:12); "The work of the wicked will not last" (Pr 11:18).

892. Then (v. 26), our Lord begins to mention a food that is spiritual. First, he states a truth about this spiritual food. In the second place, he clears up a misunderstanding (6:41). As to the first he does three things. First, he presents a truth about this spiritual food; secondly, he mentions its origin; and thirdly, he tells them how this spiritual food is to be acquired (6:34). He does two things about the first. First, he explains this spiritual food and its power; in the second place, he tells what this food is (v. 28). As to the first, he does two things. First, he rebukes them for their disordered desires; in the second place, he urges them to accept the truth (v. 27).

893. He says, **Amen, amen, I say to you**, that although you seem to be devout, **you seek me not because you have seen miracles, but because you have eaten of the bread and have been filled**. As if to say: You seek me, not for the sake of the spirit, but for the sake of the flesh, because you hope for more food. As Augustine[40] says, these people represent those who seek Jesus not for himself, but in order to gain certain worldly advantages: as those engaged in some business call on clerics and prelates, not for the sake of Christ, but so that through their

---

39. *Hom. in Io.* 43. 2; PG 59, col. 246; cf. *Catena aurea*, 6:22–27.
40. *Tract. in Io.* 25. 10; PL 35, col. 1600; cf. *Catena aurea*, 6:22–27.

intervention they might be advanced into the ranks of those who are important: and like those who hurry to the churches, not for Christ, but because they have been urged to do so by those who are more powerful; and like those who approach our Lord for sacred orders not because they desire the merits of the virtues, but because they are looking for the satisfactions of this present life, as wealth and praise, as Gregory says in his *Moralia*.[41] This is obvious: for to perform miracles is a work of divine power, but to eat loaves of bread which have been multiplied is temporal. Accordingly, those who do not come to Christ because of the power they see in him, but because they eat his bread, are not serving Christ but their own stomachs, as we see from Philippians (3:19); and again, "He will praise you when you are good to him," as we read in the Psalm (48:19).[42]

894. He leads them back to the truth by calling their attention to spiritual food, saying, **Do not work for the food that perishes but for that which endures to eternal life.** First, he mentions its power; secondly, that it comes from him, **which the Son of Man will give you.**

895. The power of this food is seen in the fact that it does not perish. In this respect we should point out that material things are likenesses of spiritual things, since they are caused and produced by them; and consequently they resemble spiritual things in some way. Now just as the body is sustained by food, so that which sustains the spirit is called its food, whatever it might be. The food that sustains the body is perishable, since it is converted into the nature of the body; but the food that sustains the spirit is not perishable, because it is not converted into the spirit; rather, the spirit is converted into its food. Hence Augustine says in his *Confessions*:[43] "I am the food of the great; grow and you will eat me. But you will not change me into yourself, as you do bodily food, but you will be changed into me."[44]

So our Lord says: **work,** i.e., seek by your work, or merit by your works, **not for the food that perishes,** i.e., bodily food: "Food is for the stomach, and the stomach for food, but God will destroy both" (1 Cor 6:13), because we will not always need food; but **work for that which,** that is, the spiritual food, **endures to eternal life.** This food is God himself, insofar as he is the Truth which is to be contemplated and the Goodness which is to be loved, which nourish the spirit: "Eat my bread" (Pr 9:5); "Wisdom will feed him with the bread of life and understanding" (Sir 15:5).[45] Again, this food is the obedience to the divine commands: "My food is to do the will of him who sent me"

41. *Mor.* 23. 25; PL 76, col. 282; cf. *Catena aurea*, 6:22–27. See also *ST* II-II, q. 185, a. 1.
42. See Aquinas, *Expos. in Ps.* 48, no 10.
43. *Conf.,* VII, chap. 10. 16; PL 32, col. 742.
44. See *ST* III, q. 79, a. 1.
45. See *ST* II-II, q. 180, a. 4.

(above 4:34).⁴⁶ Also, it is Christ himself: "I am the bread of life" (6:35); "My flesh truly is food and my blood is drink (6:56): and this is so insofar as the flesh of Christ is joined to the Word of God, which is the food by which the angels live.⁴⁷ The difference between bodily and spiritual food which he gives here, is like the one he gave before between bodily and spiritual drink: "Whoever drinks this water will be thirsty again, but whoever drinks the water that I give, will never be thirsty again" (4:13). The reason for this is that bodily things are perishable, while spiritual things, and especially God, are eternal.

896. We should note that according to Augustine, in his work, *On the Labor of Monks*,⁴⁸ that certain monks misunderstood our Lord's saying, **Do not work for the food that perishes**, and claimed that spiritual men should not perform physical work. But this interpretation is false because Paul, who was most spiritual, worked with his hands; as we read in Ephesians, there he says (4:28): "Let him who stole, steal no longer; rather let him work with his hands." The correct interpretation, therefore, is that we should direct our work, i.e., our main interest and intention, to seeking the food that leads to eternal life, that is, spiritual goods. In regard to temporal goods, they should not be our principal aim but a subordinate one, that is, they are to be acquired only because of our mortal body, which has to be nourished as long as we are living this present life.⁴⁹ So the Apostle speaks against this opinion, saying: "If any one will not work, neither let him eat" (2 Thes 3:10); as if to say: those who maintain that physical work is not to be done should not eat, since eating is physical.

897. Next (v. 27), he mentions the one who gives this spiritual food. First, we see the author of this food; secondly, the source of his authority to give us this food. Christ is the author of this spiritual food, and the one who gives it to us. Thus he says, **which**, that is, the food that does not perish, **the Son of Man will give you**. If he had said, "the Son of God," it would not have been unexpected; but he captures their attention by saying that **the Son of Man** gives this food. Yet the Son of Man gives this food in a spiritual way, because human nature, weakened by sin, found spiritual food distasteful, and was not able to take it in its spirituality. Thus it was necessary for the Son of Man to assume flesh and nourish us with it: "You have prepared a table before me" (Ps 22:5).⁵⁰

898. He adds the source of his authority to give us this food when he says, **for on him has God the Father set his seal**. As if to say: the Son of Man will give us this food because he surpasses all the sons of

---

46. See *ST* III, q. 47, a. 2.
47. See *ST* III, q. 73, a. 1; III, q. 80, a. 2.
48. *De oper. mon.*; PL 40, col. 547–82.   49. See *ST* II-II, q. 182, a. 1.
50. See *ST* III, q. 61, a. 1.

men by his unique and preeminent fullness of grace.[51] Thus he says, *on him*, i.e., on the Son of Man, *has God the Father set his seal*, i.e., he has significantly distinguished him from others: "God, your God, has anointed you with the oil of gladness above your fellows" (Ps 44:8).

Hilary[52] explains it this way. *God set his seal*, i.e., impressed with a seal. For when a seal is impressed on wax, the wax retains the entire figure of the seal, just as the Son has received the entire figure of the Father. Now the Son receives from the Father in two ways. One of these ways is eternal, and *set his seal* does not refer to this way, because when something is sealed the nature receiving the seal is not the same as the nature impressing the seal. Rather these words should be understood as referring to the mystery of the Incarnation, because God the Father has impressed his Word on human nature; this Word who is "the brightness of his glory, and the figure of his substance" (Heb 1:3).

Chrysostom[53] explains it this way. God the Father has *set his seal*, i.e., God the Father specifically chose Christ to give eternal life to the world: "I came that they may have life" (below 10:10). For when someone is chosen to perform some great task, he is said to be sealed for that task: "After this, the Lord appointed (*designo*, appoint; *signo*, seal, mark) seventy other disciples" (Lk 10:1).

Or, it could be said that God the Father *set his seal*, i.e., Christ was made known by the Father, by his voice at Christ's baptism, and by his works, as we saw in the fifth chapter.

899. Next (v. 28), we see the nature of spiritual food. First, the Jews pose their question; in the second place, we have the answer of Jesus Christ (v. 29).

900. Concerning the first, we should note that the Jews, since they had been taught by the law, believed that only God was eternal.[54] So when Christ said that his food would endure to eternal life, they understood that it would be a divine food. Thus when they question Christ, they do not mention this food, but rather the work of God, saying: *What must we do that we may perform the works of God?* Indeed, they were not far from the truth since spiritual food is nothing else than performing and accomplishing the works of God: "What shall I do to gain eternal life?" (Lk 18:18).

901. The Lord's answer is given when he says: *This is the work of God, that you believe in him whom he sent*. Here we should reflect that in Romans (4:2), the Apostle distinguished faith from works, saying that Abraham was justified by his faith, not by his works. If this is so,

---

51. See *ST* III, q. 7.
52. *De Trin.* 8. 44; PL 10, col. 269B; cf. *Catena aurea*, 6:22–27.
53. *Hom. in Io.* 44. 1; PG 59, col. 250; cf. *Catena aurea*, 6:22–27.
54. See *ST* I-II, q. 98, a. 4; I-II, q. 101, a. 3.

why does our Lord say here that to have faith, i.e., to believe, is a work of God? There are two answers to this. One is that the Apostle is not distinguishing faith from absolutely all works, but only from external works. External works, being performed by our body, are more noticeable and so the word "works" ordinarily refers to them. But there are other works, interior works, performed within the soul, and these are known only to the wise and those converted in heart.

From another point of view, we can say that to believe can be regarded as included in our external works, not in the sense that it is an external work, but because it is the source of these works.[55]

Thus he significantly says: **that you believe in him** (*in illum*). Now it is one thing to say: "I believe God" (*credere Deum*), for this indicates the object. It is another thing to say: "I believe God" (*credere Deo*), for this indicates the one who testifies. And it is still another thing to say: "I believe in God" (*in Deum*), for this indicates the end.[56] Thus God can be regarded as the object of faith, as the one who testifies, and as the end, but in different ways. For the object of faith can be a creature, as when I believe in the creation of the heavens. Again, a creature can be one who testifies, for I believe Paul (*credo Paulo*) or any of the saints. But only God can be the end of faith, for our mind is directed to God alone as its end. Now the end, since it has the character of a good, is the object of love. Thus to believe in God (*in Deum*) as in an end is proper to faith living through the love of charity. Faith, living in this way, is the principle of all our good works; and in this sense to believe is said to be a work of God.

902. But if faith is a work of God, how do men do the works of God? Isaiah (26:12) gives us the answer when he says: "You have accomplished all our works for us." For the fact that we believe, and any good we do, is from God: "it is God who is working in us, both to will and to accomplish" (Phil 2:13).[57] Thus he explicitly says that to believe is a work of God in order to show us that faith is a gift of God, as Ephesians (2:8) maintains.

903. Next, we see the origin of this food. First, we have the question asked by the Jews; secondly, the answer of Christ (v. 32). Three things are done about the first: first, the Jews look for a sign; secondly, they decide what it should be; and thirdly, they bring in what is narrated in Scripture.

904. They look for a sign by asking Christ: **What sign then are you going to give that we may see and believe you?** This question is explained differently by Augustine and by Chrysostom. Chrysostom[58]

---

55. See *ST* II-II, q. 4, a. 5.
56. See *ST* II-II, q. 2, a. 2.
57. See *ST* II-II, q. 6, a. 1; II-II, q. 109, a. 2.
58. *Hom. in Io.* 45. 1; PG 59. col. 251–52; cf. *Catena aurea*, 6:28–34.

says that our Lord was leading them to the faith. But the evidence that leads one to the faith are miracles: "Signs were given to unbelievers" (1 Cor 14:22). And so the Jews were looking for a sign in order to believe, for it is their custom to seek such signs: "For Jews demand signs" (1 Cor 1:22). So they say: *What sign then are you going to give*?

But it seems foolish to ask for a miracle for this reason, for Christ had just performed some in their presence which could lead them to believe, as multiplying the bread and walking on the water. What they were asking was that our Lord always provide them with food. This is clear because the only sign they mention is the one given by Moses to their ancestors for forty years, and they ask in this way that Christ always provide food for them. Thus they say: *Our fathers ate manna in the desert*. They did not say that God provided their ancestors with the manna, so that they would not seem to be making Christ equal to God. Again, they did not say that Moses fed their ancestors, so they would not seem to be preferring Moses to Christ, trying in this way to influence our Lord. We read of this food: "Man ate the bread of angels" (Ps 77:25).

905. According to Augustine,[59] however, our Lord had said that he would give them food that would endure to eternal life. Thus, he seemed to put himself above Moses. The Jews, on the other hand, considered Moses greater than Christ; so they said: "We know that God spoke to Moses, but we do not know where this man is from" (below 9:29). Accordingly, they required Christ to accomplish greater things than Moses; and so they recall what Moses did, saying: *Our fathers ate manna in the desert*. As if to say: What you say about yourself is greater than what Moses did, for you are promising a food that does not perish, while the manna that Moses gave became wormy if saved for the next day. Therefore, if we are to believe you, do something greater than Moses did. Although you have fed five thousand men once with five barley loaves, this is not greater than what Moses did, for he fed all the people with manna from heaven for forty years, and in the desert too: "He gave them the bread of heaven" (Ps 77:24).

LECTURE 4

32 Jesus therefore said to them: "Amen, amen, I say to you: Moses did not give you bread from heaven, but my Father gives you true bread from heaven. 33 For the true bread is that which descends from heaven, and gives life to the world." 34 They then said to him: "Lord, give us this bread always." 35 But Jesus said to them: "I am the bread

---

59. *Tract. in Io.* 25. 12; PL 35, col. 1602; cf. *Catena aurea*, 6:28–34.

CHAPTER 6

of life. Whoever comes to me shall not hunger; and whoever believes in me shall never thirst. 36 But I have told you that you have both seen me and do not believe. 37 All that the Father gives me shall come to me; and the one who comes to me I will not cast out, 38 because I have come down from heaven, not to do my own will, but the will of him who sent me. 39 Now it is the will of him who sent me, the Father, that of all that he has given me I should lose nothing, but raise it up on the last day. 40 For this is the will of my Father, who sent me, that every one who sees the Son and believes in him, should have eternal life. And I will raise him up on the last day."

906. Having told us the question the Jews had asked Christ, the Evangelist now gives his answer. First, Christ tells us of the origin of this spiritual food; secondly, he proves what he has just said (v. 33).

907. Concerning the first, we should note that the Jews had mentioned two things to Christ concerning the bodily food which had been given to their ancestors: the one who gave this food, Moses, and the place, that is, from heaven. Accordingly, when our Lord tells them about the origin of spiritual food, he does not mention these two, for he says that there is another who gives this food and another place. He says: **Amen, amen, I say to you: Moses did not give you bread from heaven**. There is another who gives to you, that is, my Father; and he gives, not just bodily bread, but **the true bread from heaven**.

908. But was it not true bread that their ancestors had in the desert? I answer that if you understand "true" as contrasted with "false," then they had true bread for the miracle of the manna was a true miracle. But if "true" is contrasted with "symbolic," then that bread was not true, but was a symbol of spiritual bread, that is, of our Lord Jesus Christ whom that manna signified, as the Apostle says: "All ate the same spiritual food" (1 Cor 10:3).

909. When the Psalm (77:24) says, "He gave them the bread of heaven," this seems to conflict with, **Moses did not give you bread from heaven**. I answer that the word "heaven" can be understood in three ways. Sometimes it can mean the air, as in "The birds of heaven ate them" (Mt 13:4), and also in, "The Lord thundered from heaven" (Ps 17:14). Sometimes "heaven" means the starry sky, as in, "The highest heaven is the Lord's" (Ps 113:24), and in, "The stars will fall from heaven" (Mt 24:19). Thirdly, it can signify goods of a spiritual nature, as in "Rejoice and be glad, because your reward is great in heaven" (Mt 5:12). So the manna was said to be from heaven, not the heaven of the stars or of spiritual food, but from the air. Or, the manna was said to be from heaven insofar as it was a symbol of the true bread from heaven, our Lord Jesus Christ.

910. When he says, **For the true bread is that which descends from heaven, and gives life to the world**, he proves that it is from heaven

by its effect. For the true heaven is spiritual in nature, and has life by its own essence; therefore, of itself, it gives life: "It is the spirit that gives life" (below 6:64). Now God himself is the author of life. Therefore, we know that this spiritual bread is from heaven when it produces its proper effect, if it gives life. That bodily bread used by the Jews did not give life, since all who ate the manna died. But this [spiritual] bread does give life; so he says: **the true bread**, not that symbolic bread, **is that which descends from heaven**. This is clear, because it **gives life to the world**: for Christ, who is the true bread, gives life to whom he wills: "I came that they may have life" (below 10:10). He also descended from heaven: "No one has gone up to heaven except the One who came down from heaven" (above 3:13). Thus Christ the true bread, gives life to the world by reason of his divinity, and he descends from heaven by reason of his human nature, for as we said on the prior text, he came down from heaven by assuming human nature: "He emptied himself, taking the form of a servant" (Phil 2:7).

911. Now he considers the acquisition of this spiritual food. First, we see the Jews asking for it; secondly, he shows the way it is acquired (v. 35).

912. We should note with respect to the first, that the Jews understood what Christ said in a material way; and so, because they desired material things, they were looking for material bread from Christ. Hence they said to him, **Lord, give us this bread always**, which physically nourishes us. The Samaritan woman also understood what our Lord said about spiritual water in a material way, and wishing to slake her thirst, said, "Give me this water" (above 4:15). And although these people understood what our Lord said about food in a material way, and asked for it this way, we are expected to ask for it as understood in a spiritual way: "Give us this day our daily bread" (Mt 6:11), because we cannot live without this bread.

913. Then, he shows how this bread is acquired. First, he shows what this bread is; secondly, how to obtain it (v. 37). Concerning the first, he does three things. First, he explains what this bread is; **I am the bread of life**; secondly, he gives the reason for this, **Whoever comes to me shall not hunger**; thirdly, he shows why this had to be explained (v. 36).

914. Jesus said to them: **I am the bread of life**, for as we saw above, the word of wisdom is the proper food of the mind, because the mind is sustained by it: "He fed him with the bread of life and understanding" (Sir 15:3). Now the bread of wisdom is called the bread of life to distinguish it from material bread, which is the bread of death, and which serves only to restore what has been lost by a mortal organism; hence material bread is necessary only during this mortal life. But the bread of divine wisdom is life-giving of itself, and no death can affect it. Again, material bread does not give life, but only sustains for a time

a life that already exists. But spiritual bread actually gives life: for the soul begins to live because it adheres to the word of God: "For with you is the fountain of life," as we see in the Psalm (35:10). Therefore, since every word of wisdom is derived from the Only Begotten Word of God—"The fountain of wisdom is the Only Begotten of God" (Sir 1:5)—this Word of God is especially called the bread of life. Thus Christ says, **I am the bread of life**. And because the flesh of Christ is united to the Word of God, it also is life-giving. Thus, too, his body, sacramentally received, is life-giving: for Christ gives life to the world through the Mysteries which he accomplished in his flesh. Consequently, the flesh of Christ, because of the Word of the Lord, is not the bread of ordinary life, but of that life which does not die. And so the flesh of Christ is called bread: "The bread of Asher is rich" (Gen 49:20).[60]

His flesh was also signified by the manna. "Manna" means "What is this?" because when the Jews saw it they wondered, and asked each other what it was. But nothing is more a source of wonder than the Son of God made man, so that everyone can fittingly ask, "What is this?" That is, how can the Son of God be the Son of Man? How can Christ be one person with two natures? "His name will be called Wonderful" (Is 9:6). It is also a cause for wonder how Christ can be present in the sacrament.

915. Next (v. 35), he gives the reason for this from the effect of this [spiritual] bread. When material bread is eaten, it does not permanently take away our hunger, since it must be destroyed in order to build us up; and this is necessary if we are to be nourished. But spiritual bread, which gives life of itself, is never destroyed; consequently, a person who eats it once never hungers again. Thus he says: **Whoever comes to me shall not hunger; and whoever believes in me shall never thirst**.

According to Augustine,[61] it is the same thing to say, **whoever comes**, as to say, **whoever believes**: since it is the same to come to Christ and to believe in him, for we do not come to God with bodily steps, but with those of the mind, the first of which is faith. To eat and to drink are also the same: for each signifies that eternal fullness where there is no want: "Blessed are they who hunger and thirst for what is right, for they will be filled" (Mt 5:6); so that food which sustains and that drink which refreshes are one and the same.

One reason why temporal things do not take away our thirst permanently is that they are not consumed altogether, but only bit by bit, and with motion, so that there is always still more to be consumed. For this reason, just as there is enjoyment and satisfaction from what has been consumed, so there is a desire for what is still to come. Another reason is that they are destroyed; hence the recollection of them

---

60. See *ST* III, q. 79, a. 2.
61. *Tract. in Io.* 25. 14; PL 35, col. 1603; cf. *Catena aurea*, 6:35–40.

remains and generates a repeated longing for those things. Spiritual things, on the other hand, are taken all at once, and they are not destroyed, nor do they run out; and consequently the fullness they produce remains forever: "They will neither hunger nor thirst" (Rev 7:16); "Your face will fill me with joy; the delights in your right hand (i.e., in spiritual goods) will last forever," as the Psalm (15:11) says.

916. Then (v. 36), we see why Christ had to explain these things. For someone could say: We asked for bread; but you did not answer, "I will give it to you," or "I will not." Rather, you say, *I am the bread of life*; and so your answer does not seem to be appropriate. But our Lord shows that it is a good answer, saying, *I have told you that you have both seen me and do not believe.* This is the same as a person having bread right in front of him without his knowing it, and then being told: Look! The bread is right before you. And so Christ says: *I have told you (I am the bread of life) that you have both seen me and do not believe*, i.e., you want bread, and it is right before you; and yet you do not take it because you do not believe. In saying this he is censuring them for their unbelief: "They have seen and hated both me and my Father" (below 15:24).

917. Then (v. 37), he shows how this bread is acquired. First, he mentions the way to acquire it; secondly, the end attained by those who come to him (v. 37b); thirdly, he enlarges on this (v. 38).

918. Concerning the first, we should note that the very fact that we believe is a gift of God to us: "You are saved by grace, through faith; and this is not due to yourself, for it is the gift of God" (Eph 2:8); "It has been granted to you not only to believe in him, but also to suffer for him" (Phil 1:2).[62] Sometimes, God the Father is said to give those who believe to the Son, as here: All that the Father gives me shall come to me. At other times, the Son is said to give them to the Father, as in 1 Corinthians (15:24): "He will hand over the kingdom to God and the Father." We can see from this that just as the Father does not deprive himself of the kingdom in giving to the Son, neither does the Son in giving to the Father. The Father gives to the Son insofar as the Father makes a person adhere to his Word: "Through whom (that is, the Father) you have been called into the fellowship of his Son" (1 Cor 1:9). The Son, on the other hand, gives to the Father insofar as the Word makes the Father known: "I have made known your name to those you have given me" (below 17:6). Thus Christ says: All that the Father gives me shall come to me, i.e., those who believe in me, whom the Father makes adhere to me by his gift.

919. Perhaps some might say that it is not necessary for one to use God's gift: for many receive God's gift and do not use it. So how can he say: *All that the Father gives me shall come to me*? We must say to this

---

62. See also Aquinas, *Super Eph.*, chap. 2, lec. 3, no. 93; *ST* II-II, q. 6, a. 1.

that in this giving we have to include not only the habit which is faith, but also the interior impulse to believe. So, everything which contributes to salvation is a gift of God.

920. There is another question. If everything which the Father gives to Christ comes to him, as he says, then only those come to God whom the Father gives him. Thus, those who do not come are not responsible, since they are not given to him. I answer that they are not responsible if they cannot come to the faith without the help of God. But those who do not come are responsible, because they create an obstacle to their own coming by turning away from salvation, the way to which is of itself open to all.[63]

921. Then (v. 37b), the end attained by those who come is mentioned. For some might say, "We will come to you, but you will not receive us." To exclude this he says, **the one who comes to me**, by steps of faith and by good works, **I will not cast out**. By this he lets us understand that he is already within, for one must be within before one can be sent out. Let us consider, therefore, what is interior, and how one is cast out from it.

We should point out that since all visible things are said to be exterior with respect to spiritual things, then the more spiritual something is the more interior it is. What is interior is twofold. The first is the most profound and is the joy of eternal life. According to Augustine,[64] this is a sweet and most interior retreat, without any weariness, without the bitterness of evil thoughts, and uninterrupted by temptations and sorrows. We read of this: "Share the joy of your Lord" (Mt 25:21); and, "You will hide them in the secret of your face," that is, in the full vision of your essence (Ps 30:21). From this interior no one is cast out: "He who conquers, I will make him a pillar in the temple of the living God: and he will no longer leave it" (Rev 3:12), because "the just will go to everlasting life," as we see from Matthew (25:46).[65] The other interior is that of an upright conscience; we read of this: "When I enter into my house I will enjoy repose" (Wis 8:16); and "The king has brought me into his storerooms" (Sg 1:3). It is from this interior that some are cast out.

So, when our Lord says, **the one who comes to me I will not cast out**, we can understand this in two ways. In one way, those who come to him are those who have been given to him by the Father through eternal predestination. Of these he says: **the one who comes to me**, predestined by the Father, **I will not cast out**: "God has not rejected his people, the people he chose" (Rom 11:2).[66] In a second way, those who do go out are not cast out by Christ; rather, they cast themselves out,

---

63. See *ST* I, q. 23, a. 3; I, q. 49, a. 2.
64. *Tract. in Io.* 25. 14; PL 35, col. 1603; cf. *Catena aurea*, 6:35–40.
65. See *ST* I-II, q. 5, a. 4.
66. See *ST* I, q. 23, a. 6.

because through their unbelief and sins they abandon the sanctuary of an upright conscience. Thus we read: *I will not cast out* such; but they do cast themselves out: "You are the burden, and I will cast you aside, says the Lord" (Jer 23:33). It was in this way that the man who came to the wedding feast without wedding clothes was cast out (Mt 22:13).

922. Next (v. 38), he gives the reason for what he just said. First, he mentions his intention to accomplish the will of the Father; secondly, he states what the will of the Father is (v. 39); and thirdly, he shows the final accomplishment of this will (v. 40b).

923. Concerning the first, we should note that this passage can be read in two ways: either as Augustine does, or following the interpretation of Chrysostom. Augustine[67] understands it this way: **the one who comes to me I will not cast out**; and this is because the one who comes to me imitates my humility. In Matthew (11:29), after our Lord said, "Come to me, all you who labor," he added, "Learn from me, for I am gentle and humble of heart." Now the true gentleness of the Son of God consists in the fact that he submitted his will to the will of the Father. Thus he says, **the one who comes to me I will not cast out, because I have come down from heaven, not to do my own will, but the will of him who sent me.** Since a soul abandons God because of its pride, it must return in humility, coming to Christ by imitating his humility; and this humility of Christ was in not doing his own will, but the will of God the Father.[68]

Here we should note that there were two wills in Christ. One pertains to his human nature, and this will is proper to him, both by nature and by the will of the Father. His other will pertains to his divine nature, and this will is the same as the will of the Father. Christ subordinated his own will, that is, his human will, to the divine will, because, wishing to accomplish the will of the Father, he was obedient to the Father's will: "My God, I desired to do your will" (Ps 39:9).[69] We ask that this will be accomplished in our regard when we say, "Your will be done" (Mt 6:10). Thus, those who do the will of God, not their own will, are not cast out. The devil, who wanted to do his own will out of pride, was cast from heaven; and so too the first man was expelled from paradise.[70]

Chrysostom[71] explains the passage this way. The reason I do not cast out one who comes to me is because I have come to accomplish the will of the Father concerning the salvation of men. So, if I have become incarnate for the salvation of men, how can I cast them out? And this is what he says: I will not cast out one who comes, **because I**

---

67. *Tract. in Io.* 25. 15–17, col. 1603–5; cf. *Catena aurea*, 6:35–40.
68. See *ST* III, q. 1, a. 2; III, q. 20, a. 1.
69. See *ST* III, q. 18, a. 5.
70. See *ST* I, q. 63, a. 3; II-II, q. 163, a. 1; II-II, q. 164, a. 2.
71. *Hom. in Io.* 45. 3; PG 59, col. 254–55; cf. *Catena aurea*, 6:35–40.

have come down from heaven, not to do my own will, my human will, so as to obtain my own benefit, *but the will of him who sent me*, that is, the Father, "He desires the salvation of all men" (1 Tim 2:4). And therefore, so far as I am concerned, I do not cast out any person: "For if, when we were enemies, we were reconciled to God by the death of his Son, now much more, having been reconciled, we will be saved by his life" (Rom 5:10).[72]

924. Then (v. 39), he shows what the Father wills; and next, why he wills it (v. 40).

925. He says: I will not cast out those who come to me, because I have taken flesh in order to do the will of the Father: **Now it is the will of him who sent me, the Father**, that those who come to me **I will not cast out**; and so I will not cast them out, "This is the will of God, your sanctification" (1 Thes 4:3). Therefore he says that it is the will of the Father **that of all that he**, the Father, **has given me I should lose nothing**, i.e., that I should lose nothing until the time of the resurrection. At this time some will be lost, the wicked; but none of those given to Christ through eternal predestination will be among them: "The way of the wicked will perish" (Ps 1:6). Those, on the other hand, who are preserved until then, will not be lost.

Now when he says, *lose*, we should not understand this as implying that he needs such people or that he is damaged if they perish. Rather, he says this because he desires their salvation and what is good for them, which he regards as his own good.

926. What John later reports Christ as saying seems to conflict with this: "None of them," that is, of those you have given me, "have been lost except the son of perdition" (below 17:12). Thus, some of those given to Christ through eternal predestination are lost. Accordingly, what he says here, **that of all that he has given me I should lose nothing**, is not true. We must say to this that some are lost from among those given to Christ through a present justification; but none are lost from among those given to him through eternal predestination.[73]

927. Now he gives the reason for the divine will (v. 40). The reason why the Father wills that I lose nothing of all that he has given me is that the Father wills to bring men to life spiritually, because he is the fountain of life.[74] And since the Father is eternal, he wills, absolutely speaking, that every one who comes to me should have eternal life. And this is what he says: **For this is the will of my Father, who sent me, that every one who sees the Son and believes in him, should have eternal life**. Note that he said above: "Whoever hears my voice and believes in him who sent me, possesses eternal life" (above 5:24), while

---

72. See *ST* I, q. 23, a. 3; III, q. 49, a. 3.
73. See *ST* I, q. 23, a. 6.
74. See *ST* I, q. 18, aa. 3–4.

here he says: *every one who sees the Son and believes in him*. We can understand from this that the Father and the Son have the same divine nature; and it is the vision of this, through its essence, that is our ultimate end and the object of our faith.[75] When he says here, *sees the Son*, he is referring to the physical sight of Christ which leads to faith, and not to this vision through essence which faith precedes. Thus he expressly says, *every one who sees the Son and believes in him*: "Whoever believes in him . . . will not encounter judgment, but has passed from death to life" (above 5:24); "These things are written that you may believe that Jesus Christ is the Son of God, and that believing you may have life in his name" (below 20:31).

928. This will of the Father will also be accomplished. So he adds: *And I will raise him up on the last day,* for he wills that we have eternal life not just in our soul alone, but also in our body, as Christ did at his resurrection: "Many of those who sleep in the dust of the earth will awake: some to an everlasting life, and others to everlasting shame" (Dn 12:2); "Christ, having risen from the dead, will not die again" (Rom 6:9).[76]

LECTURE 5

41 *The Jews therefore grumbled about him because he had said, "I am the living bread that has come down from heaven." 42 And they said: "Is he not the son of Joseph? Do we not know his father and mother? How then can he say that he has come down from heaven?" 43 Jesus responded and said to them: "Stop grumbling among yourselves. 44 No one can come to me unless the Father, who sent me, draws him. And I will raise him up on the last day. 45 It is written in the prophets: 'They shall all be taught by God.' Every one who has heard the Father and has learned, comes to me. 46 Not that any one has seen the Father, except the one who is from God—he has seen the Father."*[77]

929. Those opinions that conflict with the above teaching of Christ are now rejected. First, those of the people who were discontented; secondly, those of the disciples who were in a state of doubt (v. 61). He does two things about the first. First, we see the people grumble about the origin of this spiritual food; secondly, we see Christ check the dispute which arose over the eating of this spiritual food (v. 53). As to the first he does two things. First, he mentions the grumbling of the

75. See *ST* II-II, q. 3, a. 8.
76. See *ST* III, q. 53, a. 1.
77. St. Thomas quotes Jn 6:44 in *ST* I-II, q. 109. a. 6, *sed contra*; and Jn 6:45 in *ST* I, q. 43, a. 5, ad 2; I-II, q. 112, a. 2, ad 2; I-II, q. 112, a. 3; I-II, q. 113, a. 3, *sed contra*; II-II, q. 2, a. 3; II-II, q. 8, a. 5, *sed contra*; III, q. 69, a. 5, ad 2.

people; secondly, how it was checked (v. 43). As to the first he does two things. First, he shows the occasion for this complaining; secondly, what those complaining said (v. 42).

930. He continues that some of the people were grumbling over what Christ had said, that is, because Christ had said, *I am the living bread that has come down from heaven*, a spiritual bread they did not understand or desire. And so they grumbled because their minds were not fixed on spiritual things. They were following in this case the custom of their ancestors: "They grumbled in their tents" (Ps 105:25); "Do not grumble, as some of them did" (1 Cor 10:10). As Chrysostom[78] says, they had not complained till now because they still hoped to obtain material food; but as soon as they lost that hope, they began to grumble, although they pretended that it was for a different reason. Yet they did not contradict him openly due to the respect they had for him arising from his previous miracle.

931. He says those who complained said: *Is he not the son of Joseph?* For since they were earthly minded, they only considered Christ's physical generation, which hindered them from recognizing his spiritual and eternal generation. And so we see them speaking only of earthly things, "He who is of earth is earthly and speaks of earthly things" (above 3:31), and not understanding what is spiritual. Thus they said: *How then can he say that he has come down from heaven?* They called him the son of Joseph as this was the general opinion, for Joseph was his foster father: "the son of Joseph (as was supposed)" (Lk 3:23).

932. Next (v. 43), the grumbling of the people is checked. First, Christ stops this complaining, secondly, he clears up their difficulty (v. 47). As to the first he does two things. First, he checks their complaining, secondly, he tells why they were doing it (v. 44).

933. Jesus noticed that they were grumbling and checked them, saying, *Stop grumbling among yourselves*. This was good advice, for those who complain show that their minds are not firmly fixed on God; and so we read in Wisdom (1:11): "Keep yourselves from grumbling, for it does no good."

934. The reason for their grumbling was their unbelief, and he shows this when he says, *No one can come to me....* First, he shows that if one is to come to Christ, he has to be drawn by the Father. Secondly, he shows the way one is drawn (v. 45). As to the first he does three things. First, he mentions that coming to Christ surpasses human ability; secondly, the divine help we receive for this; and thirdly, the end or fruit of this help.

That we should come to Christ through faith surpasses our human ability; thus he says, *No one can come to me*. Secondly, divine help is effective in helping us to this; thus he says, *unless the Father, who*

---

78. *Hom. in Io.* 46. 1; PG 59, col. 257; cf. *Catena aurea*, 6:41–46.

sent me, draws him. The end or fruit of this help is the very best, so he adds, *And I will raise him up on the last day.*

935. He says first: It is not unexpected that you are grumbling, because my Father had not yet drawn you to me, for *No one can come to me*, by believing in me, *unless the Father, who sent me, draws him.*

There are three questions here. The first is about his saying: *unless the Father draws him.* For since we come to Christ by believing, then, as we said above, to come to Christ is to believe in him. But no one can believe unless he wills to. Therefore, since to be drawn implies some kind of compulsion, one who comes to Christ by being drawn is compelled.

I answer that what we read here about the Father drawing us does not imply coercion, because there are some ways of being drawn that do not involve compulsion.[79] Consequently, the Father draws men to the Son in many ways, using the different ways in which we can be drawn without compulsion. One person may draw another by persuading him with a reason. The Father draws us to his Son in this way by showing us that he is his Son. He does this in two ways. First, by an interior revelation, as in: "Blessed are you, Simon Bar-Jonah, for flesh and blood has not revealed this to you (that is, that Christ is the Son of the living God), but it was done so by my Father" (Mt 16:17). Secondly, it can be done through miracles which the Son has the power to do from the Father: "The very works which my Father has given me to perform . . . they bear witness to me" (above 5:36).

Again, one person draws another by attracting or captivating him: "She captivated him with her flattery" (Pr 7:21). This is the way the Father draws those who are devoted to Jesus on account of the authority of the paternal greatness. For the Father, i.e., the paternal greatness, draws those who believe in Christ because they believe that he is the Son of God. Arius—who did not believe that Christ was the true Son of God, nor begotten of the substance of the Father—was not drawn in this way. Neither was Photinus—who dogmatized that Christ was a mere man. So, this is the way those who are captivated by his greatness are drawn by the Father. But they are also drawn by the Son, through a wonderful joy and love of the truth, which is the very Son of God himself. For if, as Augustine[80] says, each of us is drawn by his own pleasure, how much more strongly ought we to be drawn to Christ if we find our pleasure in truth, happiness, justice, eternal life: all of which Christ is! Therefore, if we would be drawn by him, let us be drawn through love for the truth, according to: "Take delight in the Lord, and he will give you the desires of your heart" (Ps 36:4). And so

---

79. See *ST* I-II, q. 113, aa. 3–5.
80. *Tract. in Io.* 26. 4; PL 35, col. 1608; cf. *Catena aurea*, 6:41–46.

in the Song of Solomon, the bride says: "Draw me after you, and we will run to the fragrance of your perfume" (1:4).

An external revelation or an object are not the only things that draw us. There is also an interior impulse that incites and moves us to believe. And so the Father draws many to the Son by the impulse of a divine action, moving a person's heart from within to believe: "It is God who is working in us, both to will and to accomplish" (Phil 2:13); "I will draw them with the cords of Adam, with bands of love" (Hos 11:4); "The heart of the king is in the hand of the Lord; he turns it wherever he wills" (Pr 21:1).[81]

936. The second problem is this. We read that it is the Son who draws us to the Father: "No one knows the Father but the Son, and he to whom the Son wishes to reveal him" (Mt 11:26); "I have made your name known to those you have given me" (below 17:6). So how can it say here that it is the Father who draws us to the Son? This can be answered in two ways: for we can speak of Christ either as a man, or as God. As man, Christ is the way: "I am the way" (below 14:6); and as the Christ, he leads us to the Father, as a way or road leads to its end. The Father draws us to Christ as man insofar as he gives us his own power so that we may believe in Christ: "You are saved by grace, through faith; and this is not due to yourself, for it is the gift of God" (Eph 2:8). Insofar as he is Christ, he is the Word of God and manifests the Father. It is in this way that the Son draws us to the Father. But the Father draws us to the Son insofar as he manifests the Son.[82]

937. The third problem concerns his saying that no one can come to Christ unless the Father draws him. For according to this, if one does not come to Christ, it is not because of himself, but is due to the one who does not draw him. I answer and say that, in truth, no one can come unless drawn by the Father. For just as a heavy object by its nature cannot rise up, but has to be lifted by someone else, so the human heart, which tends of itself to lower things, cannot rise to what is above unless it is drawn or lifted. And if it does not rise up, this is not due to the failure of the one lifting it, who, so far as lies in him, fails no one; rather, it is due to an obstacle in the one who is not drawn or lifted up.

In this matter we can distinguish between those in the state of integral nature, and those in the state of fallen nature. In the state of integral nature, there was no obstacle to being drawn up, and thus all could share in it. But in the state of fallen nature, all are equally held back from this drawing by the obstacle of sin; and so, all need to be drawn.[83] God, in so far as it depends on him, extends his hand to ev-

---

81. See *ST* I-II, q. 113, aa. 3–5.
82. See *ST* I, q. 43, a. 4; III, q. 39, a. 8; III, q. 45, a. 4.
83. See *ST* I-II, q. 109, a. 3.

ery one, to draw every one; and what is more, he not only draws those who receive him by the hand, but even converts those who are turned away from him, according to: "Convert us, O Lord, to yourself, and we will be converted" (Lam 5:21); and "You will turn, O God, and bring us to life," as one version of the Psalm (84:7) puts it. Therefore, since God is ready to give grace to all, and draw them to himself, it is not due to him if someone does not accept; rather, it is due to the person who does not accept.[84]

938. A general reason can be given why God does not draw all who are turned away from him, but certain ones, even though all are equally turned away. The reason is so that the order of divine justice may appear and shine forth in those who are not drawn, while the immensity of the divine mercy may appear and shine in those who are drawn. But as to why in particular he draws this person and does not draw that person, there is no reason except the pleasure of the divine will. So Augustine[85] says: "Whom he draws and whom he does not draw, why he draws one and does not draw another, do not desire to judge if you do not wish to err. But accept and understand: If you are not yet drawn, then pray that you may be drawn." We can illustrate this by an example. One can give as the reason why a builder puts some stones at the bottom, and others at the top and sides, that it is the arrangement of the house, whose completion requires this. But why he puts these particular stones here, and those over there, this depends on his mere will. Thus it is that the prime reason for the arrangement is referred to the will of the builder. So God, for the completion of the universe, draws certain ones in order that his mercy may appear in them; and others he does not draw in order that his justice may be shown in them.[86] But that he draws these and does not draw those, depends on the pleasure of his will. In the same way, the reason why in his Church he made some apostles, some confessors, and others martyrs, is for the beauty and completion of the Church. But why he made Peter an apostle, and Stephen a martyr, and Nicholas a confessor, the only reason is his will.[87] We are now clear on the limitations of our human ability, and the assistance given to us by divine help.

939. He follows with the end and fruit of this help when he says, **And I will raise him up on the last day**, even as man; for we obtain the fruit of the resurrection through those things which Christ did in his flesh: "For as death came through a man, so the resurrection of the dead has come through a man" (1 Cor 15:21). So **I**, as man, **will raise him up**, not only to a natural life, but even to the life of glory; and this on the last day. For the Catholic Faith teaches that the world will be

---

84. See *ST* I, q. 19, a. 9; I, q. 23, a. 3; I, q. 49, a. 2; III, q. 49, a. 3.
85. *Tract. in Io.* 26. 2; PL 35, col. 1607.
86. See *ST* I, q. 21, a. 4.
87. See *ST* I, q. 19, a. 5; I, q. 23, a. 5.

made new: "Then I saw a new heaven and a new earth" (Rev 21:1), and that among the changes accompanying this renewal we believe that the motion of the heavens will stop, and consequently, time.[88] "And the angel I saw standing on the sea and on the land, raised his hand to heaven" (Rev 10:5), and then it says that he swore that "time will be no more" (v. 6). Since at the resurrection time will stop, so also will night and day, according to "There will be one day, known to the Lord, not day and night" (Zec 14:7). This is the reason he says, *And I will raise him up on the last day*.

940. As to the question why the motion of the heavens and time itself will continue until then, and not end before or after, we should note that whatever exists for something else is differently disposed according to the different states of that for which it exists. But all physical things have been made for man; consequently, they should be disposed according to the different states of man. So, because the state of incorruptibility will begin in men when they arise—according to "What is mortal will put on incorruption," as it says in 1 Corinthians (15:54)—the corruption of things will also stop then. Consequently, the motion of the heavens, which is the cause of the generation and corruption of material things, will stop. "Creation itself will be set free from its slavery to corruption into the freedom of the children of God" (Rom 8:21).

So, it is clear that the Father must draw us if we are to have faith.

941. Then (v. 45), he considers the way we are drawn. First, he states the way; secondly, its effectiveness (v. 45b), and thirdly, he excludes a certain way of being drawn (v. 46).

942. The manner in which we are drawn is appropriate, for God draws us by revealing and teaching; and this is what he says: **It is written in the prophets: They shall all be taught by God.** Bede[89] says that this comes from Joel. But it does not seem to be there explicitly, although there is something like it in: "O children of Zion, rejoice and be joyful in the Lord your God, because he will give you a teacher of justice" (Jl 2:23). Again, according to Bede, he says, **in the prophets**, so that we might understand that the same meaning can be gathered from various statements of the prophets. But it is Isaiah who seems to state this more explicitly: "All your children will be taught by the Lord" (Is 54:13). We also read: "I will give you shepherds after my own heart, and they will feed you with knowledge and doctrine" (Jer 3:15).

943. **They shall all be taught by God** can be understood in three ways. In one way, so that *all* stands for all the people in the world; in another way, so that it stands for all who are in the Church of Christ,

---

88. See *ST* I, q. 10, a. 4.

89. According to the French edition of Aquinas's *Commentary on John*, ed. M.-D. Philippe, *Commentaire sur l'évangile de Saint Jean* (Paris:Les Éditions du Cerf, 1998), 405, n. 6, these comments cannot be found in the extant works of Bede.

and in a third way, so it means all who will be in the kingdom of heaven.

If we understand it in the first way, it does not seem to be true, for he immediately adds, **Every one who has heard the Father and has learned, comes to me**. Therefore, if every one in the world is taught [by God], then every one will come to Christ. But this is false, for not every one has faith. There are three answers to this. First, one could say, as Chrysostom[90] does, that he is speaking of the majority: **all**, i.e., very many shall be taught, just as we find in Matthew: "Many will come from the East and the West" (Mt 8:11). Secondly, it could mean, **all**, so far as God is concerned, shall be taught, but if some are not taught, that is due to themselves. For the sun, on its part, shines on all, but some are unable to see it if they close their eyes, or are blind. From this point of view, the Apostle says: "He desires the salvation of all men, and that all come to the knowledge of the truth" (1 Tim 2:4). Thirdly, we could say, with Augustine,[91] that we must make a restricted application, so that **They shall all be taught by God**, means that all who are taught, are taught by God. It is just as we might speak of a teacher of the liberal arts who is working in a city: he alone teaches all the boys of the city, because no one there is taught by anyone else. It is in this sense that it was said above: "He was the true light, which enlightens every man coming in to this world" (1:9).

944. If we explain these words as referring to those who are gathered into the Church, it says: **They shall all**, all who are in the Church, **be taught by God**. For we read: "All your children will be taught by the Lord" (Is 54:13). This shows the sublimity of the Christian faith, which does not depend on human teachings, but on the teaching of God.[92] For the teaching of the Old Testament was given through the prophets; but the teaching of the New Testament is given through the Son of God himself. "In many and various ways (i.e., in the Old Testament) God spoke to our fathers through the prophets; in these days he has spoken to us in his Son" (Heb 1:1); and again in (2:3): "It was first announced by the Lord, and was confirmed to us by those who heard him." Thus, all who are in the Church are taught, not by the apostles nor by the prophets, but by God himself. Further, according to Augustine,[93] what we are taught by men is from God, who teaches from within: "You have one teacher, the Christ" (Mt 23:10). For understanding, which we especially need for such teaching, is from God.

945. If we explain these words as applying to those who are in the kingdom of heaven, then **They shall all be taught by God**, because they

---

90. *Hom. in Io.* 46. 1; PG 59, col. 258; cf. *Catena aurea*, 6:41–46.
91. *De praed. sanct.* 8. 14; PL 44, col. 971; cf. *Catena aurea*, 6:41–46.
92. See *ST* I-II, q. 106, a. 1.
93. *Tract. in Io.* 26. 7; PL 35, col. 1610; cf. *Catena aurea*, 6:41–46.

will see his essence without any intermediary: "We shall see him as he is" (1 Jn 3:2).[94]

946. This drawing by the Father is most effective, because, *Every one who has heard the Father and has learned, comes to me*. Here he mentions two things: first, what relates to a gift of God, when he says, *has heard*, that is, through God, who reveals; the other relates to a free judgment, when he says, *and has learned*, that is, by an assent. These two are necessary for every teaching of faith. *Every one who has heard the Father*, teaching and making known, *and has learned*, by giving assent, comes to me.

He comes in three ways: through a knowledge of the truth; through the affection of love; and through imitative action. And in each way it is necessary that one hear and learn. The one who comes through a knowledge of the truth must hear, when God speaks within: "I will hear what the Lord God will speak within me" (Ps 84:9); and he must learn, through affection, as was said. The one who comes through love and desire—"If any one thirsts, let him come to me and drink" (below 7:37)—must hear the word of the Father and grasp it, in order to learn and be moved in his affections. For that person learns the word who grasps it according to the meaning of the speaker. But the Word of the Father breathes forth love.[95] Therefore, the one who grasps it with eager love, learns. "Wisdom goes into holy souls, and makes them prophets and friends of God" (Wis 7:27).[96] One comes to Christ through imitative action, according to: "Come to me, all you who labor and are burdened, and I will refresh you" (Mt 11:28). And whoever learns even in this way comes to Christ: for as the conclusion is to things knowable, so is action to things performable. Now whoever learns perfectly in the sciences arrives at the conclusion; therefore, as regards things that are performable, whoever learns the words perfectly arrives at the right action: "The Lord has opened my ear: and I do not resist" (Is 50:5).

947. To correct the thought that some might have that every one will hear and learn from the Father through a vision, he adds: *Not that any one has seen the Father*, that is, a person living in this life does not see the Father in his essence, according to: "Man will not see me and live" (Ex 33:20), *except the one*, that is the Son, *who is from God—he has seen the Father*, through his essence.[97] Or, *Not that any one has seen the Father*, with a comprehensive vision: neither man nor angel has ever seen or can see in this way; *except the one who is from God*, i.e., the Son: "No one knows the Father except the Son" (Mt 11:27).[98]

The reason for this, of course, is that all vision or knowledge comes

---

94. See *ST* I, q. 12, a. 5.
95. See *ST* I, q. 36, a. 2.
96. See *ST* II-II, q. 4, a. 3.
97. See *ST* I, q. 12, a. 11.
98. See *ST* I, q. 12, a. 7.

about through a likeness: creatures have a knowledge of God according to the way they have a likeness to him.[99] Thus the philosophers say that the intelligences know the First Cause according to this likeness which they have to it. Now every creature possesses some likeness to God, but it is infinitely distant from a likeness to his nature, and so no creature can know him perfectly and totally, as he is in his own nature.[100] The Son, however, because he has received the entire nature of the Father perfectly, through an eternal generation, sees and comprehends totally.

948. Note how the words used are appropriate: for above, when he was speaking of the knowledge others have, he used the word "heard"; but now, in speaking of the Son's knowledge, he uses the word "seen," for knowledge which comes through seeing is direct and open, while that which comes through hearing comes through one who has seen. And so we have received the knowledge we have about the Father from the Son, who saw him. Thus, no one can know the Father except through Christ, who makes him known; and no one can come to the Son unless he has heard from the Father, who makes the Son known.

LECTURE 6

47 "Amen, amen, I say to you: Whoever believes in me has eternal life. 48 I am the bread of life. 49 Your fathers ate manna in the desert, and they are dead. 50 This is the bread that comes down from heaven, so that if anyone eats of this [bread], he will not die. 51 I am the living bread that has come down from heaven. 52 If anyone eats of this bread, he will live forever. And the bread which I will give is my flesh, for the life of the world."[101]

949. After our Lord quieted the grumbling of the Jews, he now clears up the doubt they had because of his saying, "I am the bread that has come down from heaven." He intends to show here that this is true. This is the way he reasons: The bread which gives life to the world descended from heaven; but I am the bread that gives life to the world: therefore, I am the bread which descended from heaven. He does three things concerning this. First, he presents the minor premise of his reasoning, that is, I am the bread of life. In the second place,

---

99. See *ST* I, q. 13, a. 5.
100. See *ST* I, q. 4, a. 3.
101. St. Thomas refers to Jn 6:50 in *ST* III, q. 79, a. 4, obj. 3; III, q. 79, a. 6, *sed contra*; III, q. 79, a. 8, obj. 1; III, q. 80, a. 3, *sed contra*; to Jn 6:51 in *ST* I-II, q. 102, a. 3, ad 12; I-II, q. 102, a. 4, ad 6; and to Jn 6:52 in *ST* III, q. 79, a. 1, *sed contra*; III, q. 79, a. 2, *sed contra*.

he gives the major premise, that is, that the bread that descended from heaven ought to give life (v. 49). Thirdly, we have the conclusion (v. 51). As to the first he does two things. First, he states his point; secondly, he expresses it as practically proved (v. 48).

950. His intention is to show that he is the bread of life. Bread is life-giving insofar as it is taken. Now one who believes in Christ takes him within himself according to: "Christ dwells in our hearts through faith" (Eph 3:17). Therefore, if he who believes in Christ has life, it is clear that he is brought to life by eating this bread. Thus, this bread is the bread of life. And this is what he says: **Amen, amen, I say to you: Whoever believes in me**, with a faith made living by love, which not only perfects the intellect but the affections as well (for we do not tend to the things we believe in unless we love them), **has eternal life**.

Now Christ is within us in two ways: in our intellect through faith so far as it is faith; and in our affections through love, which informs or gives life to our faith: "He who abides in love, abides in God, and God in him" (1 Jn 4:16).[102] So he who believes in Christ so that he tends to him, possesses Christ in his affections and in his intellect. And if we add that Christ is eternal life, as stated in "that we may be in his true Son, Jesus Christ. This is the true God and eternal life" (1 Jn 5:20), and in "In him was life" (above 1:4), we can infer that whoever believes in Christ has eternal life. He has it, I say, in its cause and in hope, and he will have it at some time in reality.

951. Having stated his position, he expresses it as, **I am the bread of life**, which gives life, as clearly follows from the above. We read of this bread: "The bread of Asher will be rich, he will furnish choice morsels," of eternal life, "to kings" (Gen 49:20).

952. Then when he says, **Your fathers ate manna in the desert, and they are dead**, he gives the major premise, namely, the bread that descended from heaven ought to have the effect of giving life. First, he explains this; secondly, he draws his point (v. 50).

953. He explains his meaning through a contrasting situation. It was said above (909) that Moses gave the Jews bread from heaven, in the sense of from the air. But bread that does not come from the true heaven cannot give adequate life. Therefore, it is proper to the heavenly bread to give life. So, the bread given by Moses, in which you take pride, does not give life. And he proves this when he says, **Your fathers ate manna in the desert, and they are dead**.

In this statement he first reproaches them for their faults, when he says, **Your fathers**, whose sons you are, not only according to the flesh, but also by imitating their actions, because you are grumblers just as "they grumbled in their tents" (Ps 105:25); this was why he said to

---

102. See *ST* II-II, q. 4, a. 3.

them: "Fill up, then, the measure of your fathers," as we read in Matthew (23:32). As Augustine[103] says, this people is said to have offended God in no matter more than by grumbling against God. Secondly, he mentions for how short a time this was done, saying, *in the desert*: for they were not given manna for a long period of time; and they had it only while in the desert, and not when they entered the promised land (Jos 5:12). But the other bread [from the true heaven] preserves and nourishes one forever. Thirdly, he states an inadequacy in that bread, that is, it did not preserve life without end; so he says, *and they are dead*. For we read in Joshua (chap. 5) that all who grumbled, except Joshua and Caleb, died in the desert. This was the reason for the second circumcision, as we see here, because all who had left Egypt died in the desert.

954. One might wonder what kind of death God is speaking of here. If he is speaking of physical death, there will be no difference between the bread the Jews had in the desert and our bread, which came down from heaven, because even Christians who share the latter bread die physically. But if he is speaking of spiritual death, it is clear that both then among the Jews and now among the Christians, some die spiritually and others do not. For Moses and many others who were pleasing to God did not die, while others did. Also those who eat this bread [of the Christians] unworthily, die spiritually: "He who eats and drinks unworthily, eats and drinks judgment upon himself" (1 Cor 11:29).[104]

We may answer this by saying that the food of the Jews has some features in common with our spiritual food. They are alike in the fact that each signifies the same thing: for both signify Christ. Thus they are called the same food: "All ate the same spiritual food" (1 Cor 10:3). He calls them the same because each is a symbol of the spiritual food. But they are different because one [the manna] was only a symbol; while the other [the bread of the Christians] contains that of which it is the symbol, that is, Christ himself. Thus we should say that each of these foods can be taken in two ways. First, as a sign only, i.e., so that each is taken as food only, and without understanding what is signified; and taken in this way, they do not take away either physical or spiritual death. Secondly, they may be taken in both ways, i.e., the visible food is taken in such a way that spiritual food is understood and spiritually tasted, in order that it may satisfy spiritually. In this way, those who ate the manna spiritually did not die spiritually. But those who eat the Eucharist spiritually, both live spiritually now without sin, and will live physically forever.[105] Thus, our food is greater than their food, because it contains in itself that of which it is the symbol.

---

103. *Tract. in Io.* 26. 11; PL 35, col. 1611; cf. *Catena aurea*, 6:47–51.
104. See *ST* III, q. 80, a. 4.
105. See *ST* III, q. 79, a. 2; III, q. 80, a. 1.

955. Having presented the argument, he draws the conclusion: ***This is the bread that comes down from heaven***. He says, ***This***, the Gloss[106] says, to indicate himself. But our Lord does not understand it this way as it would be superfluous, since he immediately adds, ***I am the living bread that has come down from heaven***. So we should say that our Lord wants to say that the bread which can do this, i.e., give life, comes from heaven; but I am that bread: thus, I am that bread that comes down from heaven. Now the reason why that bread which comes down from heaven gives a life which never ends is that all food nourishes according to the properties of its nature; but heavenly things are incorruptible: consequently, since this food is heavenly, it is not corrupted, and as long as it lasts, it gives life. So, he who eats it, will not die. Just as if there were some bodily food which never corrupted, then in nourishing it would always be life-giving. This bread was signified by the tree of life in the midst of Paradise, which somehow gave life without end: "He must not be allowed to stretch out his hand and take from the tree of life and eat, and live forever" (Gen 3:22). So if the effect of this bread is that anyone who eats it will not die, and I am such, then [anyone who eats of me will not die].

956. He does two things concerning this. First, he speaks of himself in general; secondly, in particular, ***And the bread which I will give is my flesh***. In regard to the first, he does two things: first, he mentions his origin; secondly his power (v. 52).

957. He said, ***I am the living bread***; consequently, I can give life. Material bread does not give life forever, because it does not have life in itself; but it gives life by being changed and converted into nourishment by the energy of a living organism. ***That has come down from heaven***: it was explained before [467] how the Word came down.[107] This refuted those heresies which taught that Christ was a mere man, because according to them, he would not have come down from heaven.

958. He has the power to give eternal life; thus he says, ***If anyone eats of this bread***, i.e., spiritually, ***he will live***, not only in the present through faith and justice, but ***forever***. "Everyone who lives and believes in me, will never die" (below 11:26).

959. He then speaks of his body when he says, ***And the bread which I will give is my flesh***. For he had said that he was the living bread; and so that we do not think that he is such so far as he is the Word or in his soul alone, he shows that even his flesh is life-giving, for it is an instrument of his divinity. Thus, since an instrument acts by virtue of the agent, then just as the divinity of Christ is life-giving, so too his flesh gives life (as Damascene[108] says) because of the Word to which

---

106. *Glossa ordinaria Evang. Ioan.*; PL 114, col. 384C.
107. See *ST* III, q. 2, a. 6.
108. See John of Damascus, *De fide orth*. 3. 15–17; PG 94, col. 1047–72. See also *ST* III, q. 79, a. 2.

it is united. Thus Christ healed the sick by his touch. So what he said above, *I am the living bread*, pertained to the power of the Word; but what he is saying here pertains to the sharing in his body, that is, to the sacrament of the Eucharist.[109]

960. We can consider four things about this sacrament: its species, the authority of the one who instituted it, the truth of this sacrament, and its usefulness.

As to the species of this sacrament: *This is the bread*; "Come, and eat my bread" (Pr 9:5). The reason for this is that this is the sacrament of the body of Christ; but the body of Christ is the Church, which arises out of many believers forming a bodily unity: "We are one body" (Rom 12:5). And so because bread is formed from many grains, it is a fitting species for this sacrament.[110] Hence he says, *And the bread which I will give is my flesh*.

961. The author of this sacrament is Christ: for although the priest confers it, it is Christ himself who gives the power to this sacrament, because the priest consecrates in the person of Christ.[111] Thus in the other sacraments the priest uses his own words or those of the Church, but in this sacrament he uses the words of Christ: because just as Christ gave his body to death by his own will, so it is by his own power that he gives himself as food: "Jesus took bread, he blessed it and broke it, and gave it to his disciples, saying: 'Take and eat it, this is my body'" (Mt 26:26).[112] Thus he says, *which I will give*; and he says, *will give*, because this sacrament had not yet been instituted.

962. The truth of this sacrament is indicated when he says, *is my flesh*. He does not say, "This signifies my flesh," but it *is my flesh*, for in reality that which is taken is truly the body of Christ: "Who will give us his flesh so that we may be satisfied?" as we read in Job (31:31).[113]

Since the whole Christ is contained in this sacrament, why did he just say, this *is my flesh*? To answer this, we should note that in this mystical sacrament the whole Christ is really contained: but his body is there by virtue of the conversion; while his soul and divinity are present by natural concomitance.[114] For if we were to suppose what is really impossible, that is, that the divinity of Christ is separated from his body, then his divinity would not be present in this sacrament. Similarly, if someone had consecrated during the three days Christ was dead, his soul would not have been present there [in the sacrament], but his body would have been, as it was on the cross or in the tomb.[115] Since

---

109. See *ST* III, q. 79, a. 1.
110. See *ST* III, q. 74, a. 1.
111. See *ST* III, q. 22, a. 4; III, q. 82, a. 1.
112. See *ST* III, q. 78, a. 1.
113. See *ST* III, q. 75, a. 1; III, 76, a. 1.
114. See *ST* III, q. 76, aa. 2, 4.
115. See *ST* III, q. 81, a. 4.

this sacrament is the commemoration of our Lord's passion—according to "As often as you eat this bread and drink this cup, you proclaim the death of the Lord" (1 Cor 11:26)—and the passion of Christ depended on his weakness according to "He was crucified through weakness" (2 Cor 13:4) he rather says, *is my flesh*, to suggest the weakness through which he died, for "flesh" signifies weakness.

963. The usefulness of this sacrament is great and universal. It is great, indeed, because it produces spiritual life within us now, and will later produce eternal life, as was said. For as is clear from what was said, since this is the sacrament of our Lord's passion, it contains in itself the Christ who suffered. Thus, whatever is an effect of our Lord's passion is also an effect of this sacrament. For this sacrament is nothing other than the application of our Lord's passion to us. For it was not fitting for Christ to be always with us in his own presence; and so he wanted to make up for this absence through this sacrament.[116] Hence it is clear that the destruction of death, which Christ accomplished by his death, and the restoration of life, which he accomplished by his resurrection, are effects of this sacrament.[117]

964. The usefulness of this sacrament is universal because the life it gives is not only the life of one person, but, so far as concerns itself, the life of the entire world: and for this the death of Christ is fully sufficient. "He is the offering for our sins; and not for ours only, but also for those of the entire world" (1 Jn 2:2).[118]

We should note that this sacrament is different from the others: for the other sacraments have individual effects: as in baptism, only the one baptized receives grace. But in the immolation of this sacrament, the effect is universal: because it affects not just the priest but also those for whom he prays, as well as the entire Church, of the living and of the dead.[119] The reason for this is that it contains the universal cause of all the sacraments, Christ. Nevertheless, when a lay person receives this sacrament it does not benefit others *ex opere operato* [by its own power] considered as a receiving. However, due to the intention of the person who is acting and receiving, it can be communicated to all those to whom he directs his intention. It is clear from this that lay persons are mistaken when they receive the Eucharist for those in purgatory.

LECTURE 7

53 The Jews therefore disputed among themselves, saying: "How can this man give us his flesh to eat?" 54 Jesus then said to them:

---

116. See *ST* III, q. 73, a. 5.
118. See *ST* III, q. 49, a. 3.
117. See *ST* III, q. 79, aa. 1–2.
119. See *ST* III, q. 79, a. 7.

"Amen, amen, I say to you, unless you eat the flesh of the Son of Man, and drink his blood, you will not have life in you. 55 Whoever eats my flesh and drinks my blood has eternal life; and I will raise him up on the last day. 56 For my flesh truly is food, and my blood truly is drink. 57 He who eats my flesh and drinks my blood abides in me, and I in him. 58 Just as the living Father has sent me, and I live because of the Father, so whoever eats me, he also will live because of me. 59 This is the bread that has come down from heaven. Unlike your fathers who ate manna and are dead, whoever eats this bread shall live forever." 60 These things he said teaching in the synagogue at Capernaum.[120]

965. Above, our Lord checked the grumbling of the Jews over the origin of this spiritual food; here, he stops their dispute over the eating of this same food. First, we see their dispute; secondly, our Lord stops it (v. 54); thirdly, the Evangelist mentions the place where all this happened (v. 60).

966. As to the first, note that the Evangelist brings in the dispute among the Jews in the form of a conclusion, saying, **The Jews therefore disputed among themselves.** And this is fitting: for according to Augustine,[121] our Lord had just spoken to them about the food of unity, which makes into one those who are nourished on it, according to, "Let those who are just feast and rejoice before God," and then it continues, according to one reading, "God makes those who agree to live in one house" (Ps 67:4). And so, because the Jews had not eaten the food of harmony, they argued with each other: "When you fast, you argue and fight" (Is 58:4). Further, their quarreling with others shows that they were carnal: "For while you are envious and quarreling, are you not carnal?" (1 Cor 3:3). Therefore, they understood these words of our Lord in a carnal way, i.e., as meaning that our Lord's flesh would be eaten as material food. Thus they say, **How can this man give us his flesh to eat?** As if to say: This is impossible. Here they were speaking against God just as their fathers did: "We are sick of this useless food" (Nm 21:5).

967. Our Lord stops this argument. First, he states the power that comes from taking this food; secondly, he amplifies on it (v. 55). As to the first he does three things. First, he states why it is necessary to eat this flesh; secondly, its usefulness; and thirdly, he adds something about its truth (v. 56).

968. Jesus said: **Amen, amen, I say to you, unless you eat the flesh**

---

120. St. Thomas refers to Jn 6:54 in *ST* III, q. 65, a. 1; III, q. 65, a. 4, obj. 2; III, q. 73, a. 3 obj. 1; III, q. 75, a. 1, obj. 1; III, q. 80, a. 9, ad 3; III, q. 80, a. 11, *sed contra*; III, q. 83, a. 4, ad 2; to Jn 6:56 in *ST* III, q. 73, a. 2; III, q. 76, a. 1, obj. 2; III, q. 76, a. 1, ad 2; III, q. 79, a. 1; III, q. 79, a. 2; to Jn 6:57 in *ST* III, q. 75, a. 1; III, q. 77, a. 7, obj. 3; and to Jn 6:58 in *ST* III, q. 79, a. 1.

121. *Tract. in Io.* 26. 14; PL 35, col. 1613; cf. *Catena aurea*, 6:52–54.

of the Son of Man and drink his blood, you will not have life in you. As if to say: You think it is impossible and unbecoming to eat my flesh. But it is not only possible, but very necessary, so much so that *unless you eat the flesh of the Son of Man and drink his blood, you will not have,* i.e., you will not be able to have, *life in you,* that is, spiritual life. For just as material food is so necessary for bodily life that without it you cannot exist—"They exchanged their precious belongings for food" (Lam 1:11); "Bread strengthens the heart of man" (Ps 103:15)—so spiritual food is necessary for the spiritual life to such an extent that without it the spiritual life cannot be sustained: "Man does not live by bread alone, but by every word which comes from the mouth of God" (Dt 8:3).[122]

969. We should note that this statement can refer either to eating in a spiritual way or in a sacramental way.[123] If we understand it as referring to a spiritual eating, it does not cause any difficulty. For that person eats the flesh of Christ and drinks his blood in a spiritual way who shares in the unity of the Church; and this is by the love of charity: "You are one body, in Christ" (Rom 12:5). Thus, one who does not eat in this way is outside the Church, and consequently, without the love of charity.[124] Accordingly, such a one does not have life in himself: "He who does not love, remains in death" (1 Jn 3:14).

But if we refer this statement to eating in a sacramental way, a difficulty appears. For we read above: "Unless one is born again of water and the Holy Spirit, he cannot enter the kingdom of God" (3:5). Now this statement was given in the same form as the present one: *Unless you eat the flesh of the Son of Man.* Therefore, since baptism is a necessary sacrament, it seems that the Eucharist is also.[125] In fact, the Greeks think it is; and so they give the Eucharist to newly baptized infants. For this opinion they have in their favor the rite of Dionysius,[126] who says that the reception of each sacrament should culminate in the sharing of the Eucharist, which is the culmination of all the sacraments. This is true in the case of adults, but it is not so for infants, because receiving the Eucharist should be done with reverence and devotion, and those who do not have the use of reason, as infants and the insane, cannot have this. Consequently, it should not be given to them at all.[127]

We should say, therefore, that the sacrament of baptism is necessary for everyone, and it must be really received because without it no one is born again into life. And so it is necessary that it be received in reality, or by desire in the case of those who are prevented from the former.

---

122. See *ST* III, q. 73, a. 3.
123. See *ST* III, q. 80, a. 1.
124. See *ST* II-II, q. 23, a. 1.
125. See *ST* III, q. 73, a. 3.
126. *De ecc. hier.* III. 1; PG 3, col. 424B–25A.
127. See *ST* III, q. 80, a. 9.

For if the contempt within a person excludes a baptism by water, then neither a baptism of desire nor of blood will benefit him for eternal life.[128] However, the sacrament of the Eucharist is necessary for adults only, so that it may be received in reality, or by desire, according to the practices of the Church.[129]

970. But even this causes difficulty: because by these words of our Lord, it is necessary for salvation not only to eat his body, but also to drink his blood, especially since a repast of food is not complete without drink. Therefore, since it is the custom in certain Churches for only the priest to receive Christ's blood, while the rest receive only his body, they would seem to be acting against this.[130]

I answer that it was the custom of the early church for all to receive both the body and blood of Christ; and certain Churches have still retained this practice, where even those assisting at the altar always receive the body and blood. But in some Churches, due to the danger of spilling the blood, the custom is for it to be received only by the priest, while the rest receive Christ's body. Even so, this is not acting against our Lord's command, because whoever receives Christ's body receives his blood also, since the entire Christ is present under each species, even his body and blood. But under the species of bread, Christ's body is present in virtue of the conversion, and his blood is present by natural concomitance; while under the species of wine, his blood is present in virtue of the conversion, and his body by natural concomitance.[131]

It is now clear why it is necessary to receive this spiritual food.

971. Next, the usefulness of this food is shown: first, for the spirit or soul; secondly, for the body, and *I will raise him up on the last day*.

972. There is great usefulness in eating this sacrament, for it gives eternal life; thus he says, **Whoever eats my flesh and drinks my blood has eternal life**. For this spiritual food is similar to material food in the fact that without it there can be no spiritual life, just as there cannot be bodily life without bodily food, as was said above. But this food has more than the other, because it produces in the one who receives it an unending life, which material food does not do: for not all who eat material food continue to live. For, as Augustine[132] says, it can happen that many who do take it die because of old age or sickness, or some other reason. But one who takes this food and drink of the body and blood of our Lord **has eternal life**. For this reason it is compared to the tree of life: "She is the tree of life for those who take her" (Pr 3:18); and so it is called the bread of life: "He fed him with the bread of life and understanding" (Sir 15:3). Accordingly, he says, **eternal life** be-

---

128. See *ST* III, q. 66, a. 10.
129. See *ST* III, q. 65, a. 4.
130. See *ST* III, q. 80, a. 12.
131. See *ST* III, q. 76, a. 2.
132. *Tract. in Io.* 26. 15; PL 35, col. 1613–14; cf. *Catena aurea*, 6:52–54.

cause one who eats this bread has within himself eternal life," as John says (1 Jn 5:20).[133]

Now one has eternal life who eats and drinks, as it is said, not only in a sacramental way, but also in a spiritual way. One eats and drinks sacramentally or in a sacramental way, if he receives the sacrament; and one eats and drinks spiritually or in a spiritual way, if he attains to the reality of the sacrament.[134] This reality of the sacrament is twofold: one is contained and signified, and this is the whole Christ who is contained under the species of bread and wine. The other reality is signified but not contained, and this is the mystical body of Christ, which is in the predestined, the called, and the justified.[135] Thus in reference to Christ as contained and signified, one eats his flesh and drinks his blood in a spiritual way if he is united to him through faith and love, so that one is transformed into him and becomes his member: for this food is not changed into the one who eats it, but it turns the one who takes it into itself, as we see in Augustine,[136] when he says: "I am the food of the robust. Grow and you will eat me. Yet you will not change me into yourself, but you will be transformed into me." And so this is a food capable of making man divine and inebriating him with divinity.[137] The same is true in reference to the mystical body of Christ, which is only signified [and not contained], if one shares in the unity of the Church. Therefore, one who eats in these ways has eternal life. That this is true of the first way, in reference to Christ, is clear enough. In the same way, in reference to the mystical body of Christ, one will necessarily have eternal life if he perseveres: for the unity of the Church is brought about by the Holy Spirit: "One body, one Spirit . . . the pledge of our eternal inheritance" (Eph 4:4; 1:14). So this bread is very profitable, because it gives eternal life to the soul; but it is so also because it gives eternal life to the body.[138]

973. And therefore he adds, *and I will raise him up on the last day*. For as was said, one who eats and *drinks in a spiritual way* shares in the Holy Spirit, through whom we are united to Christ by a union of faith and love, and through him we become members of the Church. But the Holy Spirit also merits the resurrection: "He who raised Jesus Christ our Lord from the dead, will raise our mortal bodies because of his Spirit, who dwells in us" (Rom 8:11). And so our Lord says that he will raise up to glory whoever eats and drinks; to glory, and not to condemnation, as this would not be for their benefit. Such an effect is fittingly attributed to this sacrament of the Eucharist because, as Augus-

---

133. See *ST* III, q. 79, a. 2.
134. See *ST* III, q. 80, a. 1.
135. See *ST* III, q. 60, a. 3, *sed contra*.
136. *Conf.* VII. 10. 16; PL 32, col. 742. See also *ST* III, q. 75, a. 1.
137. See *ST* III, q. 79, a. 1, ad 2.
138. See *ST* III, q. 79, a. 2.

tine[139] says and as was said above, it is the Word who raises up souls, and it is the Word made flesh who gives life to bodies. Now in this sacrament the Word is present not only in his divinity, but also in the reality of his flesh; and so he is the cause of the resurrection not just of souls, but of bodies as well: "For as death came through a man, so the resurrection of the dead has come through a man" (1 Cor 15:21).[140] It is now clear how profitable it is to take this sacrament.

974. We see its truth when he says, *For my flesh truly is food*. For some might think that what he was saying about his flesh and blood was just an enigma and a parable. So our Lord rejects this, and says, *my flesh truly is food*. As if to say: Do not think that I am speaking metaphorically, for my flesh is truly contained in this food of the faithful, and my blood is truly contained in this sacrament of the altar: "This is my body . . . this is my blood of the new covenant," as we read in Matthew (26:26).[141]

Chrysostom explains this statement in the following way. Food and drink are taken for man's refreshment. Now there are two parts in man: the chief part is the soul, and the second is the body. It is the soul which makes man to be man, and not the body; and so that truly is the food of man which is the food of the soul.[142] And this is what our Lord says: *my flesh truly is food*, because it is the food of the soul, not just of the body. The same is true of the blood of Christ. "He has led me to the waters that refresh" (Ps 22:2). As if to say: this refreshment is especially for the soul.

Augustine[143] explains these words this way. A thing is truly said to be such and such a thing if it produces the effect of that thing. Now the effect of food is to fill or satisfy. Therefore, that which truly produces fullness is truly food and drink. But this is produced by the flesh and blood of Christ, who leads us to the state of glory, where there is neither hunger nor thirst: "They will neither hunger nor thirst" (Rev 7:16). And so he says: *For my flesh truly is food, and my blood truly is drink*.

975. Now our Lord proves that this spiritual food has such power, that is, to give eternal life. And he reasons this way: Whoever eats my flesh and drinks my blood is united to me; but whoever is united to me has eternal life: therefore, whoever eats my flesh and drinks my blood has eternal life. Here he does three things: first, he gives his major premise; secondly, the minor premise, which he proves (v. 58); and thirdly, he draws his conclusion: *This is the bread that has come down from heaven*.

139. *Tract. in Io.* 19. 16; PL 35, col. 1553; cf. *Catena aurea*, 6:52–54.
140. See *ST* III, q. 56, aa. 1–2.
141. See *ST* III, q. 75, a. 1.
142. See *ST* I, q. 75, a. 4; I, q. 76, a. 1.
143. *Tract. in Io.* 26. 17; PL 35, col. 1614; cf. *Catena aurea*, 6:55–59.

CHAPTER 6

976. We should note, with respect to the first, that if his statement, *He who eats my flesh and drinks my blood abides in me, and I in him*, is referred to his flesh and blood in a mystical way, there is no difficulty. For, as was said, that person eats in a spiritual way, in reference to what is signified only, who is incorporated into the mystical body through a union of faith and love. Through love, God is in man and man is in God: "He who abides in love abides in God, and God in him" (1 Jn 4:16). And this is what the Holy Spirit does; so it is also said, "We know that we abide in God and God in us, because he has given us his Spirit" (1 Jn 4:13).

If these words are referred to a sacramental reception, then whoever eats this flesh and drinks this blood abides in God. For, as Augustine[144] says, there is one way of eating this flesh and drinking this blood such that he who eats and drinks abides in Christ and Christ in him. This is the way of those who eat the body of Christ and drink his blood not just sacramentally, but really. And there is another way by which those who eat do not abide in Christ nor Christ in them. This is the way of those who approach [the sacrament] with an insincere heart: for this sacrament has no effect in one who is insincere.[145] There is insincerity when the interior state does not agree with what is outwardly signified. In the sacrament of the Eucharist, what is outwardly signified is that Christ is united to the one who receives it, and such a one to Christ. Thus, one who does not desire this union in his heart, or does not try to remove every obstacle to it, is insincere. Consequently, Christ does not abide in him nor he in Christ.

977. Now he presents his minor premise, that is, whoever is united to Christ has life. He mentions this to show the following similarity: the Son, because of the unity he has with the Father, receives life from the Father; therefore one who is united to Christ receives life from Christ. And this is what he says: *Just as the living Father has sent me, and I live because of the Father*. These words can be explained in two ways about Christ: either in reference to his human nature, or in reference to his divine nature.

If they are explained as referring to Christ the Son of God, then the "as" implies a similarity of Christ to creatures in some respect, though not in all respects, which is, that he exists from another. For to be from another is common to Christ the Son of God and to creatures.[146] But they are unlike in another way: the Son has something proper to himself, because he is from the Father in such a way that he receives the entire fullness of the divine nature, so that whatever is natural to the

---

144. *Serm. de Scrip.* 71. 11. 17; PL 38, col. 453; *De civ. Dei* 21. 25, no. 4; PL 41, col. 742; cf. *Catena aurea*, 6:55–59.
145. See *ST* III, q. 80, a. 4.
146. See *ST* III, q. 3, a. 8.

Father is also natural to the Son.[147] Creatures, on the other hand, receive a certain particular perfection and nature. "Just as the Father possesses life in himself, so he has given it to the Son to have life in himself" (above 5:26). He shows this because, when speaking of his procession from the Father, he does not say: "As I eat the Father and I live because of the Father," as he said, when speaking of sharing in his body and blood, **whoever eats me, he also will live because of me**. This eating makes us better, for eating implies a certain sharing. Rather, Christ says that he lives because of the Father, not as eaten, but as generating, without detriment to his equality.[148]

If we explain this statement as applying to Christ as man, then in some respect the "as" implies a similarity between Christ as man and us: that is, in the fact that as Christ the man receives spiritual life through union with God, so we too receive spiritual life in the communion or sharing in this Sacrament. Still, there is a difference: for Christ as man received life through union with the Word, to whom he is united in person; while we are united to Christ through the sacrament of faith.[149] And so he says two things: **sent me** and **Father**. If we refer these words to the Son of God, then he is saying, **I live because of the Father**, because the Father himself is living. But if they are referred to the Son of Man, then he is saying, **I live because of the Father**, because the Father **has sent me**, i.e., made me incarnate. For the sending of the Son is his Incarnation: "God sent his Son, made from a woman" (Gal 4:4).

978. According to Hilary,[150] this is a rejection of the error made by Arius. For if we live because of Christ, because we have something of his nature (as he says, "Whoever eats my flesh and drinks my blood has eternal life"), then Christ too lives because of the Father, because he has in himself the nature of the Father (not a part of it, for it is simple and indivisible). Therefore, Christ has the entire nature of the Father.[151] It is because of the Father, therefore, that the Son lives, because the Son's birth did not involve another and different nature [from that of the Father].

979. Next (v. 59), he presents his two conclusions. For they were arguing about two things: the origin of this spiritual food and its power. The first conclusion is about its origin; the second is about its power: **whoever eats this bread shall live forever**.

980. With respect to the first, we should note that the Jews had been troubled because he had said, "I am the living bread that has come down from heaven" (v. 51). Therefore, in opposition to them,

---

147. See *ST* I, q. 34, a. 3. 148. See *ST* I, q. 42, aa. 1–2.
149. See *ST* III, q. 23, aa. 1, 4.
150. See *De Trin.* 3. 15–16; PL 10, col. 85; cf. *Catena aurea*, 6:55–59.
151. See *ST* I, q. 27, a. 2.

he arrives at this same conclusion again, from his statement, "I live because of the Father," when he says, *This is the bread that has come down from heaven*. For to come down from heaven is to have an origin from heaven; but the Son has his origin from heaven, since he lives because of the Father: therefore, Christ is the one who has come down from heaven. And so he says, *This is the bread that has come down from heaven*, i.e., from the life of the Father. Come down, in relation to his divinity; or *come down* even in his body, so far as the power that formed it, the Holy Spirit, was from heaven, a heavenly power. Thus, those who eat this bread do not die; as our fathers died, who ate the manna that was neither from heaven, nor was living bread, as was said above. How those who ate the manna died is clear from what has been mentioned before.

981. The second conclusion, concerning the power of this bread, is given when he says, *whoever eats this bread shall live forever*. This follows from his statement, "He who eats my flesh and drinks my blood abides in me, and I in him" (v. 57). For whoever eats this bread abides in me, and I in him. But I am eternal life. Therefore, *whoever eats this bread*, as he ought, *shall live forever*.

982. Jesus said this in the synagogue, in which he was teaching at Capernaum. He used to teach in the temple and in the synagogues in order to attract many, so that at least some might benefit: "I have proclaimed your justice in the great assembly" (Ps 39:10).[152]

LECTURE 8

61 On hearing this, many of his disciples said: "This is a hard saying! Who can accept it?" 62 But Jesus, knowing fully that his disciples were grumbling about this, said to them: "Does this scandalize you? 63 What if you should see the Son of Man ascending to where he was before? 64 It is the spirit that gives life; flesh profits nothing. The words that I have spoken to you are spirit and life. 65 But there are some of you who do not believe." For Jesus knew from the beginning those who would believe in him, and who it was that would betray him. 66 And he said: "This is why I said to you, that no one can come to me, unless it he given him by my Father." 67 From this time on, many of his disciples turned back, and no longer walked with him. 68 Jesus then said to the Twelve: "Do you too wish to leave?" 69 Simon Peter replied: "Lord, to whom shall we go? You have the words of eternal life. 70 We have come to believe and to know that you are the Christ, the Son of God." 71 Jesus answered him: "Did I not choose you Twelve? And one of you

---

152. See *ST* III, q. 42, a. 3.

is a devil." 72 Now he was talking about Judas, son of Simon Iscariot, who would betray him, since he was one of the Twelve. [153]

983. After our Lord put an end to the complaining and arguing among the Jews, he now removes the scandal given to his disciples. First, we see the scandal of those disciples who left him; secondly, the devotion of those who remained with him (v. 68). Concerning the first, he does three things: first, we see the scandal given to his disciples; secondly, the kindly way Christ takes it away (v. 62); and thirdly, the stubbornness and unbelief of those who leave him (v. 67).

984. We should note, with respect to the first, that there were many Jews who adhered to Christ, believed him and followed him.[154] And although they had not left all things as the Twelve did, they were still all called his disciples. It is of these that he says, *many*, that is, many of the people who believed him, *on hearing this*, what he had said above, said, *This is a hard saying!* We read of these: "They believe for a while, and in the time of testing fall away" (Lk 8:13). He says, many, because "The number of fools is infinite" (Ecc 1:15); and, "Many are called but few are chosen" (Mt 20:16).

They said: *This is a hard saying!* Now that is said to be hard which is difficult to divide, and which offers resistance. Accordingly, a saying is hard either because it resists the intellect or because it resists the will, that is, when we cannot understand it with our mind, or when it does not please our will. And this saying was hard for them in both ways. It was hard for their intellects because it exceeded the weakness of their intellects: for since they were earthly minded, they were incapable of understanding what he said, namely, that he would give them his flesh to eat. And it was hard for their wills, because he said many things about the power of his divinity: and although they believed him as a prophet, they did not believe that he was God. Consequently, it seemed to them that he was making himself greater than he was. "His letters are strong" (2 Cor 10:10); "Wisdom is exceedingly unpleasant to the unlearned" (Sir 6:21). And so it reads on, *Who can accept it?* They said this as an excuse: for since they had given themselves to him, they should have accepted what he said. But because he was not teaching them things that were pleasing to them, they were waiting for an occasion to leave him: "A fool does not accept words of wisdom unless you tell him what he desires" (Pr 18:2).

985. Next (v. 62), we see the kindly way Christ dispelled their diffi-

---

153. St. Thomas refers to Jn 6:61 in *ST* I-II, q. 12, a. 1 *sed contra*; III, q. 75, a. 1, obj. 1; to Jn 6:63 in *ST* II-II, q. 183, a. 2, ad 3; to Jn 6:64 in *ST* III, q. 75, a. 1, obj. 1; III, q. 75, a. 4; III, q. 80, a. 1, obj. 1; to Jn 6:70 in *ST* I, q. 24, a. 2, obj. 3; and to Jn 6:71 in *ST* III, q. 47, a. 3, obj. 3.

154. See *ST* III, q. 42, a. 2.

culty. First, he takes notice of it; secondly, he removes its cause (v. 63); and thirdly, he mentions what the cause was (v. 65).

986. He had noticed that they were scandalized because they had said, although privately, so he could not hear, ***This is a hard saying!*** But Christ, who in virtue of his divinity knew that they had said this, mentions it.[155] And this is what he says: ***But Jesus, knowing in himself***, what they said within themselves, that is, ***that his disciples were grumbling about this***—"He did not need anyone to give him testimony about men. He was well aware of what was in man's heart" (above 2:25); "God searches into the hearts and loins of men" (Ps 7:10)—said to them, ***Does this scandalize you?*** As if to say: You should not be scandalized at this. Or, it can be understood less strongly, as meaning: I know that you are scandalized at this. "He will be our sanctification," i.e., those who believe in Christ, but "a stumbling-stone to the two houses of Israel" (Is 8:14), to the grumbling disciples and the crowds.

987. But since teachers should avoid creating difficulties for those who are listening to them, why did our Lord mention those things that would upset the people and have them leave?[156] I answer that Christ had to mention such things because his teaching required it. For they had pleaded with him for material food, when he had come to strengthen their desire for spiritual food; and so he had to make known to them his teaching on spiritual food.

Nevertheless, their difficulty was not caused by any defect in what Christ was teaching, but by their own. For if they had not understood what our Lord was saying, because of their own earthly mindedness, they could have questioned him, as the apostles had done in similar circumstances. According to Augustine,[157] however, our Lord purposely permitted this situation, to give teachers a reason for consolation and patience with those who belittle what they say, since even the disciples presumed to disparage what Christ said.

988. Then (v. 63), he takes away the occasion of their scandal so far as concerns the person speaking and what he said, as Chrysostom[158] says. First, he deals with the person who was speaking; secondly, with what he said (v. 64).

989. The occasion for their scandal was when they heard our Lord say divine things about himself. And so, because they believed that he was the son of Joseph, they were upset at what he said about himself. God takes away this reason by showing them his divinity more openly, and says: You are upset over the things I have said about myself; ***What if you should see the Son of Man ascending to where he was be-***

---

155. See *ST* III, q. 10, a. 2.
156. See *ST* III, q. 42, a. 2.
157. *Tract. in Io.* 27. 8; PL 35, col. 1619.
158. *Hom. in Io.* 47. 2; PG 59, col. 264; cf. *Catena aurea*, 6:60–71.

fore? What would you say then? As if to say: You can never deny that I came down from heaven, or that I am the one who gives and teaches eternal life. He did the same thing before with Nathanael. When Nathanael said to him, "You are the King of Israel" our Lord, wanting to lead him to more perfect knowledge, answered him: "You will see greater things than this" (above 1:50). And here too, our Lord reveals to them something greater about himself which would happen in the future, saying, **What if you should see the Son of Man ascending to where he was before?** Indeed, he did ascend into heaven in the sight of his disciples (Acts 1:9). If, therefore, he does ascend to where he was before, then he was in heaven before: "No one has gone up to heaven except the one who came down from heaven" (above 3:13).

990. Let us note that Christ is one person: the person of the Son of God and the person of the Son of Man being the same person. Still, because of his different natures, something belongs to Christ by reason of his human nature, that is, to ascend, which does not belong to him by reason of his divine nature, according to which he does not ascend, since he is eternally at the highest summit of things, that is, in the Father. It is according to his human nature that it belongs to him to ascend **to where he was before**, that is, to heaven, where he had not been in his human nature. (This is in opposition to the teaching of Valentinus, who claimed that Christ had assumed a heavenly body). Thus, Christ ascended in the sight of his apostles to where he was before according to his divinity; and he ascended, by his own power, according to his humanity: "I came forth from the Father, and I have come into the world. Now I am leaving the world and am going to the Father" (below 16:28).[159]

991. Augustine[160] understands this passage differently. He said that the disciples were scandalized when our Lord said that he would give him them his flesh to eat because they understood this in a material-minded way, as if they were literally to eat this flesh, just like the flesh of an animal. Our Lord rejected this interpretation and said, **What if you should see the Son of Man ascending**, with his entire body, **to where he was before**? Would you say that I intended to give you my flesh to eat like you do the flesh of an animal?

992. Then (v. 64), he settles the offense they took at what he said. And, as Chrysostom[161] says, he distinguished two ways in which his words could be understood. And secondly, he showed which way was appropriate here (v. 64b).

With respect to the first, we should note that Christ's words can be understood in two senses: in a spiritual way, and in a material way.

---

159. See *ST* III, q. 2, a. 2; III, q. 57, a. 2.
160. *Tract. in Io.* 27. 3; PL 35, col. 1616; cf. *Catena aurea*, 6:60–71.
161. *Hom. in Io.* 47. 2; PG 59, col. 264.

Thus he says, *It is the spirit that gives life*, that is, if you understand these words according to their spiritual meaning, they will give life. *Flesh profits nothing*, that is, if you understand them in a material way, they will be of no benefit to you, they will, rather, be harmful, for "If you live according to the flesh you will die" (Rom 8:13).

What our Lord said about eating his flesh is interpreted in a material way when it is understood in its superficial meaning, and as pertaining to the nature of flesh. And it was in this way that the Jews understood them. But our Lord said that he would give himself to them as spiritual food, not as though the true flesh of Christ is not present in this sacrament of the altar, but because it is eaten in a certain spiritual and divine way.[162] Thus the correct meaning of these words is spiritual, not material. So he says: *The words that I have spoken to you*, about eating my flesh, *are spirit and life*, that is, they have a spiritual meaning, and understood in this way they give life. And it is not surprising that they have a spiritual meaning, because they are from the Holy Spirit: "It is the Spirit who tells mysteries" (1 Cor 14:2). And therefore, the mysteries of Christ give life: "I will never forget your justifications, because through them you have brought me to life" (Ps 118:93).

993. Augustine[163] explains this passage in a different way, for he understands the statement, *flesh profits nothing*, as referring to the flesh of Christ. It is obvious that the flesh of Christ, as united to the Word and to the Spirit, does profit very much and in every way; otherwise, the Word would have been made flesh in vain, and the Father would have made him known in the flesh in vain, as we see from 1 Timothy (chap. 4). And so we should say that it is the flesh of Christ, considered in itself, that profits nothing and does not have any more beneficial effect than other flesh. For if his flesh is considered as separated from the divinity and the Holy Spirit, it does not have different power than other flesh. But if it is united to the Spirit and the divinity, it profits many, because it makes those who receive it abide in Christ, for man abides in God through the Spirit of love:"We know that we abide in God and God in us, because he has given us his Spirit" (1 Jn 4:13).[164] And this is what our Lord says: the effect I promise you, that is, eternal life, should not be attributed to my flesh as such, because understood in this way, *flesh profits nothing*. But my flesh does offer eternal life as united to the Spirit and to the divinity. "If we live by the Spirit, let us also walk by the Spirit" (Gal 5:25). And so he adds, *The words that I have spoken to you are spirit and life*, i.e., they must be understood of the Spirit united to my flesh; and so understood they are life, that is, the life of the soul. For as the body lives its bodily life

---

162. See *ST* III, q. 76, a. 7.
163. *Tract. in Io.* 27. 5; PL 35, col. 1617–18; cf. *Catena aurea*, 6:60–71.
164. See *ST* III, q. 76, a. 1.

through a bodily spirit, so the soul lives a spiritual life through the Holy Spirit: "Send forth your Spirit, and they will be created" (Ps 103:30).

994. Then (v. 65), he indicates the reason why they were upset, that is, their unbelief. As if to say: the cause of your difficulty is not the hardness of what I have just said, but your own unbelief. And so first, he mentions their unbelief; secondly, he excludes an incorrect interpretation; and thirdly, he gives the reason for their unbelief.

995. Our Lord indicated their unbelief when he said, **But there are some of you who do not believe**. He did not say, "who do not understand." He did more than this, for he gave the reason why they did not understand: they did not understand because they did not believe. "If you do not believe, you will not understand," as we read in another version of Isaiah (7:9). He said, *some*, in order to exclude his disciples: "All do not have faith" (2 Thes 3:2); "All do not obey the Gospel" (Rom 10:16); "They did not believe what he said" (Ps 105:24).

996. The Evangelist then rejects an incorrect interpretation when he adds, **For Jesus knew**. As if to say: Jesus did not say, *there are some of you who do not believe*, because he just recently learned it, but because **Jesus knew from the beginning**, i.e., of the world, **those who would believe in him, and who it was that would betray him**. "All things are naked and open to his eyes" (Heb 4:13); "All things were known to the Lord God before they were created," as we read in Sirach (23:29).

997. Our Lord next mentioned the cause of their unbelief which was the withdrawal of attracting grace. Thus he said: **This is why I said to you**. As if to say: Thus it was necessary to tell you what I told you before: that no one can come to me, i.e., through faith, unless it be given him by my Father. It follows from this, according to Augustine,[165] that the act of believing itself is given to us by God.[166] Why it is not given to everyone we discussed above, where our Lord used almost the same words (6:44). They are repeated here for two reasons. First, to show that Christ received them in the faith more for their advantage and benefit than for his own: "It has been granted to you to believe in him" (Phil 1:29). As if to say: It is good for you to believe. Thus Augustine[167] says: "It is a great thing to believe; rejoice, because you have believed." Secondly, to show that Christ was not the son of Joseph, as they thought, but of God; for it is God the Father who draws men to the Son, as is clear from what has been said.

998. Then (v. 67), we see the stubbornness of the disciples: for although our Lord had rebuked them and had taken away the cause of their difficulty so far as it concerned himself, they still would not believe. Thus he says, **From this time on, many of his disciples turned**

---

165. *Tract. in Io.* 27. 7; PL 35, col. 1618; cf. *Catena aurea*, 6:60–71; see also *ST* I, q. 111, a. 1, ad 1; *Super Eph.*, chap. 2, lec. 3, no. 95.

166. See *ST* II-II, q. 6, a. 1.

167. *Tract. in Io.* 27. 7; PL 35, col. 1618; cf. *Catena aurea*, 6:60–71.

back. He did not say, "they left," but that they **turned back**, i.e., from the faith, which they had in a virtuous way; and cut off from the body of Christ, they lost life, because perhaps they were not in the body, as Augustine[168] says. There are some who turn back in an absolute way, that is, those who follow the devil, to whom our Lord said, "Go back, Satan" (Mt 4:10). We also read of certain women that "Some turned back after Satan" (1 Tim 5:15). But Peter did not turn back in this way; he rather turned after Christ: "Follow after me, Satan" (Mt 16:23). But the others followed after Satan.[169]

Then follows: **they no longer walked with him**, that is, even though we are required to walk with Jesus: "I will show you man what is good," and then it continues on, "to walk attentively with your God" (Mic 6:8).

999. Then (v. 68), our Lord examined those disciples who remained with him. First, we see this in the question he asked them; secondly, Peter's answer shows the devotion of those who remained; and thirdly, our Lord corrects Peter's answer (v. 71).

1000. Our Lord examined the Twelve who remained as to their willingness to stay on; and so he said **to the Twelve**, that is, to the apostles, **Do you too wish to leave?** He asked them this for two reasons. First, so that they would not take pride, thinking it was due to their own goodness, in the fact that they stayed on while the others left, and think that they were doing Christ a favor. And so he showed that he did not need them by holding them off, but still giving them strength: "If you live rightly, what do you give him or what does he receive from your hand?" (Jb 35:7). Secondly, it sometimes happens that a person would really prefer to leave another but is kept from doing so by shame or embarrassment. Our Lord did not want them to stay with him because they were forced to do so out of embarrassment (because to serve unwillingly is not to serve at all), and so he took away any embarrassment in their leaving or necessity for their staying, and left it to their own judgment whether they wanted to stay with him or leave, because "God loves a cheerful giver" (2 Cor 9:7).

1001. Then, from Peter's answer, we see the devotion of those who did not leave. For Peter—who loved the brethren, who guarded his friendships, and had a special affection for Christ—answered for the whole group, and said, **Lord, to whom shall we go? You have the words of eternal life**. Here he did three things. First, he extolled the greatness of Christ; secondly, he praised his teaching; and thirdly, he professed his faith.

1002. He extolled the greatness of Christ when he said, **Lord, to whom shall we go?** As if to say: Are you telling us to leave you? Give

---

168. Ibid., 27. 8, col. 1619; cf. *Catena aurea*, 6:60–71.
169. See *ST* II-II, q. 10, a. 3.

us someone better to whom we can go. But then, "There is no one like you among the strong, O Lord" (Ex 15:11); "Who is like God" (Ps 88:7). And so you will not tell us to go. "Where can I go that is away from your spirit?" (Ps 138:7). Further, according to Chrysostom,[170] Peter's words show great friendship; for to him, Christ was more worthy of honor than father or mother.

1003. He praised his teaching when he said, **You have the words of eternal life.** Now Moses, and the prophets, also spoke the words of God; but they rarely had the words of eternal life. But you are promising eternal life. What more can we ask? "Whoever believes in me has eternal life" (above 6:47); "Whoever believes in the Son has eternal life" (above 3:36).

1004. He professed his faith when he said, **We have come to believe and to know that you are the Christ, the Son of God.** For in our faith there are two things above all that must be believed: the mystery of the Trinity, and the Incarnation.[171] And these two Peter professed here. He professed the mystery of the Trinity when he said, *you are the Son of God*: for in calling Christ the Son of God he mentioned the person of the Father and that of the Son, along with the person of the Holy Spirit, who is the love of the Father and of the Son, and the bond or nexus of both. He professed the mystery of the Incarnation when he said, *you are the Christ*: for in Greek, the word "Christ" means "anointed"; anointed, that is, with the invisible oil of the Holy Spirit. He was not anointed according to his divine nature, because one who is anointed by the Holy Spirit is made better by that anointing. But Christ, so far as he is God, is not made better. Thus, Christ was anointed as man.

He said, **We have come to believe and to know**, because believing comes before knowing. And therefore, if we wanted to know before believing, we would neither know nor be able to believe, as Augustine[172] says, and as in that other version of Isaiah: "If you do not believe, you will not understand" (Is 7:9).

1005. Our Lord corrected Peter's answer when he said, **Did I not choose you Twelve? And one of you is a devil.** First, we have our Lord's reply; secondly, the Evangelist's explanation of it (v. 72).

1006. Because Peter was great-hearted and included all in his answer, **We have come to believe and to know that you are the Christ, the Son of God**, it seemed that all of them would arrive at eternal life. And so our Lord excluded Judas from this community of believers. This trust was commendable in Peter, who did not suspect any evil in his companions; but we must also admire the wisdom of our Lord, who saw what was hidden. Thus he says, **Did I not choose you Twelve? And one of you is a devil**; not by nature, but by imitating the devil's malice:

170. *Hom. in Io.* 47. 3; PG 59, col. 266; cf. *Catena aurea*, 6:60–71.
171. See *ST* II-II, q. 2, aa. 7–8.
172. *Tract. in Io.* 27. 9; PL 35, col. 1619; cf. *Catena aurea*, 6:60–71.

"Death came into the world by the envy of the devil; his disciples imitate him" (Wis 2:24); "After the morsel, Satan entered into him" (below 13:27), because Judas became like him in malice.[173]

1007. But if Christ chose Judas, who was later to become evil, it seems that our Lord made a mistake in choosing him. First, we might answer this as Chrysostom[174] does, and say that this choice was not for predestination, but for some task, and in reference to a condition of present justice. Sometimes a person is chosen this way, not in relation to the future, but according to present realities; for being chosen in this way does not destroy one's free choice or the possibility of sinning: hence we read, "Let him who thinks that he stands, take heed so he will not fall" (1 Cor 10:12). And so our Lord did choose Judas, but not as evil at that time; and being so chosen did not take away his possibility of sinning. Secondly, we could answer with Augustine,[175] who said that our Lord did choose Judas as evil. And although he knew that he was evil, because it is characteristic of a good person to use evil for good, God made good use of this evil in allowing himself to be betrayed in order to redeem us. Or, we could say that the choice of the Twelve does not refer here to the persons, but rather to the number; as if to say: I have chosen Twelve. For this number is fittingly set apart for those who would preach the faith of the Holy Trinity to the four corners of the world. And indeed, this number did not pass away, because Matthias was substituted for the traitor. Or, according to Ambrose,[176] Jesus chose Judas as evil so that when we read that our Lord and Master was betrayed by his disciple, we might be consoled if sometimes our friends betray us.

1008. We could ask here why the disciples did not say anything after our Lord said, **one of you is a devil**; for later on, when he says, "One of you will betray me" (below 13:21), they reply, "Is it I, Lord?" (Mt 26:22). I answer that the reason for this is that our Lord was speaking here in a general way when he said that one of them was a devil; for this could mean any kind of malice, and so they were not disturbed. But later on, when they heard of such a great crime, that their Master would be betrayed, they could not keep quiet. Or, we could say that when our Lord said this, each of them had confidence in his own virtue, and so none feared for himself; but after he said to Peter, "Follow after me, Satan" (Mt 16:23), they were afraid, and realized their own weakness. That is why they asked in that indecisive way, "Is it I, Lord?"

1009. Finally, what our Lord had just said privately is explained by the Evangelist when he says, **he was talking about Judas**, as events proved and which will be clear below (chap. 13).

---

173. See *ST* I-II, q. 78, a. 4.
174. *Hom. in Io.* 47. 3; PG 59, col. 267; cf. *Catena aurea*, 6:60–71.
175. *Tract in Io.* 27. 10; PL 35, col. 1619–20; cf. *Catena aurea*, 6:60–71.
176. *Expos. Evang. sec. Luc.* 5. 45; PL 15, col. 1648.

CHAPTER 7

LECTURE 1

1 After this, Jesus walked about in Galilee, for he did not want to walk in Judea because the Jews sought to kill him. 2 Now it was close to the Jewish feast of Tabernacles. 3 So his brethren said to him: "Leave this place, and go to Judea, so that your disciples also may see your works which you perform. 4 Surely, no one works in secret if he wants to be publicly renowned. If you do these things, reveal yourself to the world." 5 For not even his brethren believed in him. 6 Jesus therefore said to them: "My time has not yet come, but your time is always here. 7 The world cannot hate you, but me, it hates, because I bear witness against it, for its works are evil. 8 You yourselves go up for this feast. I, however, will not go up for this festival, because my time is not yet completed."

1010. After our Lord considered the spiritual life and its food, he now treats of his instruction or teaching, which, as mentioned above, is necessary for those who are spiritually reborn. First, he shows the origin of his teaching; secondly, its usefulness (chap. 8 and onwards). As to the first, he does three things. First, he mentions the place where he revealed the origin of his teaching; secondly, the occasion for revealing this (v. 11); and thirdly, his actual statement is given (v. 16). Three things are done about the first. First, we see Christ invited to go to the place where he revealed the origin of his teaching; secondly, we see our Lord refuse (v. 6); and thirdly, how Jesus finally did go (v. 9). As to the first, he does two things. First, he gives the reasons why they encouraged Christ to go to Judea; secondly, he adds their exhortation (v. 3). They were influenced by three things to encourage Christ to go to Judea: first, by his lingering on [in Galilee], secondly, by his intention [not to travel in Judea]; and thirdly, by the appropriateness of the time.

1011. They were influenced by Christ's lingering on in Galilee, which showed that he wanted to stay there. Thus he says, **After this**, after teaching in Capernaum, **Jesus walked about in Galilee**, i.e., he set out from Capernaum, a city of Galilee, with the intention to journey throughout this region. Our Lord lingered on so often in Galilee to show us that we should pass from vices to virtues: "So you, son of man, prepare your belongings for exile, and go during the day in their sight" (Ez 12:13).

1012. Then they were influenced by Christ's intention, which he perhaps told them; hence he says, *for he did not want to walk in Judea*, the reason being, *because the Jews sought to kill him*. "The Jews tried all the harder to kill him, because he not only broke the Sabbath rest, but even called God his own Father, making himself equal to God" (above 5:18).

But could not Christ still have gone among the Jews without being killed by them, as he did after (chap. 8)? Three answers are given to this question. The first is given by Augustine,[1] who says that Christ did this because the time would come when some Christians would hide from those who were persecuting them. And so they would not be criticized for this, our Lord wanted to console us by setting a precedent himself in this matter. He also taught this in word, saying: "If they persecute you in one town, flee to another" (Mt 10:23). Another answer is that Christ was both God and man. By reason of his divinity, he could prevent his being injured by those persecuting him. Yet, he did not want to do this all the time, for while this would have shown his divinity, it might have cast doubt on his humanity.[2] Therefore, he showed his humanity by sometimes fleeing, as man, those who were persecuting him, to silence all those who would say that he was not a true man. And he showed his divinity by sometimes walking among them unharmed, thus refuting all those who say he was only a man. Thus, Chrysostom[3] has another text, which reads: "He could not, even if he wanted to, walk about Judea." This is expressed in our human way, and is the same as saying: Due to the danger of treachery, a person cannot go anywhere he might wish. The third answer is that it was not yet the time for Christ's passion. The time would come when Christ would suffer, at the feast of the Passover, when the lamb was sacrificed, so that victim would succeed victim: "Jesus knew that his time had come to leave this world for the Father" (below 13:1).[4]

1013. They were also influenced by the suitableness of the time, for it was a time for going to Jerusalem. *Now it was close to the Jewish feast of Tabernacles* (*scenopegia*). *Scenopegia* is a Greek word, composed of *scenos*, which means "shade," or "tent," and *phagim*, which means "to eat." As if to say: It was the time in which they used to eat in their tents. For our Lord (Lev 23:41) had ordered the children of Israel to stay in their tents for seven days during the seventh month, as a reminder of the forty years they had lived in tents in the desert. This was the feast the Jews were then celebrating. The Evangelist mentions this in order to show that some time had already passed since the pre-

---

1. *Tract. in Io.* 28. 2; PL 35, col. 1622; cf. *Catena aurea*, 7:1–8.
2. See *ST* III, q. 14, aa. 1–2; III, q. 47, a. 1.
3. *Hom. in Io.* 48. 1; PG 59, col. 269.
4. See *ST* III, q. 73, a. 6.

vious teaching about spiritual food. For it was near the Passover when our Lord performed the miracle of the loaves, and this feast of Tabernacles is much later. The Evangelist does not tell us what our Lord did in the intervening five months. We can see from this that although Jesus was always performing miracles, as the last chapter says, the Evangelist was mainly concerned with recording those matters over which the Jews argued and with which they disagreed.

1014. Then (v. 3), our Lord is urged on by his brethren. First, we are given their advice; secondly, the reason for it (v. 3b); and thirdly, the Evangelist mentions the cause of this reason (v. 5).

1015. As to the first, the ones who urge Christ are mentioned; hence he says, **So his brethren said to him**. These were not brothers of the flesh or of the womb, as the blasphemous opinion of Helvidius would have it. It is, indeed, offensive to the Catholic faith that the most holy virginal womb, which bore him who was God and man, should later bear another mortal man. Thus, they were his brothers or brethren in the sense of relatives, because they were related by blood to the Blessed Virgin Mary.[5] For it is the custom in Scripture to call relatives "brothers," as in Genesis (13:8): "Let us not quarrel, for we are brothers," although Lot was the nephew of Abraham. And, as Augustine[6] says, just as in the tomb in which our Lord's body had been placed no other body was placed either before or after, so the womb of Mary conceived no other mortal person either before or after Christ. Although some of the relatives of the Blessed Virgin were apostles, such as the sons of Zebedee, and James [son] of Alphaeus, and some others, we should not think that these were among those who were urging Christ; this was done by other relatives who did not love him.

Secondly, we see their advice when they say: **Leave this place**, that is, Galilee, **and go to Judea**, where you will find Jerusalem, a sacred place, well-suited to teachers. "Seer, go, flee to the land of Judah. There eat your bread and there prophesy" (Am 7:12).

1016. They give their reason when they say: *so that your disciples also may see your works which you perform*. Here they show, first, that they are hungry for an empty glory; secondly, they are suspicious; and thirdly, do not believe [in our Lord].

They show that they are hungry for an empty glory when they say, *so that your disciples also may see your works which you perform*. For they allowed something human to Christ and wanted to share the glory of the human honor that the people would show him. And so, they urged him to perform his works in public: for it is a characteristic of one who is seeking human glory to want publicly known whatever of his own or of his associates can bring glory. "They like to pray at street

---

5. See *ST* III, q. 28, a. 3.
6. *Tract. in Io.* 28. 3; PL 35, col. 1623; cf. *Catena aurea*, 7:1–8.

corners, so people can see them" (Mt 6:5). We read of such people: "For they loved the glory of men, more than the glory of God" (below 12:43).[7]

They reveal that they themselves are suspicious, and first of all remark on Christ's fear, saying: *Surely, no one works in secret*. As if to say: You say that you are performing miracles. But you are doing them secretly because of fear; otherwise you would go to Jerusalem and do them before the people. Nevertheless, our Lord says below: "I have said nothing secretly" (below 18:20).

Secondly, they refer to his love of glory, saying: *if he wants to be publicly renowned*. As if to say: You want glory because of what you are doing, yet you are hiding because you are afraid. Now this attitude is characteristic of those who are evil: to think that other people are experiencing the same emotions as they are. Notice the disrespect with which the prudence of the flesh reproached the Word made flesh. Job says against them: "You reproach him who is not like you, and say what you should not" (Jb 4:3).

They show they do not believe when they say: *If you do these things, reveal yourself to the world*, doubting whether he did perform miracles. "He who does not believe is unfaithful" (Is 21:2).

1017. The Evangelist tells why they said this when he says, *For not even his brethren believed in him*. For sometimes blood relatives are very hostile to one of their own, and are jealous of his spiritual goods. They may even despise him. Thus Augustine[8] says: "They could have Christ as a relative, but in that very closeness they refused to believe in him." "A man's enemies are in his own house" (Mic 7:6); "He has put my brethren far from me and my acquaintances, like strangers, have gone from me. My relatives have left me, and those who knew me have forgotten me" (Jb 19:13).

1018. Then (v. 6), Christ's answer is given. First, he mentions that the time was not appropriate for going to Jerusalem; secondly, the reason for this (v. 7); and thirdly, we see Christ deciding not to go (v. 8).

1019. We should note that all of the following text is explained differently by Augustine and by Chrysostom. Augustine[9] says that the brethren of our Lord were urging him to a human glory. Now there is a time, in the future, when the saints do acquire glory; a glory they obtain by their sufferings and troubles. "He has tested them like gold in a furnace, and he accepted them as the victim of a holocaust. At the time of their visitation they will shine" (Wis 3:6). And there is a time, the present, when the worldly acquire their glory. "Let not the flowers of the time pass us by; let us crown ourselves with roses before

---

7. See *ST* II-II, q. 132.
8. *Tract. in Io.* 28. 4; PL 35, col. 1623; cf. *Catena aurea*, 7:1–8.
9. Ibid., 28. 5, col. 1623–24; cf. *Catena aurea*, 7:1–8.

they wither" (Wis 2:7). Our Lord, therefore, wanted to show that he was not looking for the glory of this present time, but that he wanted to attain to the height of heavenly glory through his passion and humiliation. "It was necessary for Christ to suffer, and so enter into his glory" (Lk 24:26).[10] So Jesus says to them, i.e., his brethren: *My time*, i.e., the time of my glory, **has not yet come**, because my sorrow must be turned into joy: "The sufferings of this present time are not worthy to be compared with the glory to come, which will be revealed in us" (Rom 8:18); *but your time*, i.e., the time of the glory of this world, *is always here*.

1020. He gives the reason why these times are different when he says, **The world cannot hate you, but me, it hates**. The reason why the time for the glory of the worldly is here is that they love the same things the world loves, and they agree with the world. But the time for the glory of the saints, who are looking for a spiritual glory, is not here, because they want what is displeasing to the world, that is, poverty, afflictions, doing without food, and things like that.[11] They even disparage what the world loves; in fact, they despise the world: "The world has been crucified to me, and I to the world" (Gal 6:14). And so he says, **The world cannot hate you**. As if to say: Thus, the time of your glory is here, because the world does not hate you, who are in agreement with it; and every animal loves its like. **But me, it hates**, and so my time is not always here. And the reason it hates me is *because I bear witness against it*, that is, the world, *for its works are evil*; that is, I do not hesitate to reprimand those who are worldly, even though I know that they will hate me for it and threaten me with death. "They," that is, those who love evil, "hate the one who rebukes at the city gate" (Am 5:10); "Do not rebuke one who mocks, lest he hate you" (Pr 9:8).[12]

1021. But cannot a person of the world be hated by the world, i.e., by another person of the world? I answer that, in a particular case, one worldly person can hate another insofar as the latter has what the first wants, or prevents him from obtaining what relates to the glory of this world. But precisely insofar as a person is of the world, the world does not hate him. The saints, however, are universally hated by the world because they are opposed to it. And if anyone of the world does love them, it is not because he is of the world, but because of something spiritual in him.

1022. Our Lord refuses to go when he says, **You yourselves go up for this feast. I, however, will not go up for this festival**. For just as there are two kinds of glory, so there are two different feasts. Worldly people have temporal feasts, that is, their own enjoyments and ban-

10. See *ST* III, q. 49, a. 6.
11. See *ST* II-II, q. 184, a. 3.
12. See *ST* II-II, q. 33.

quets and such exterior pleasures. "The Lord called for weeping and mourning . . . and look at the rejoicing and gladness" (Is 22:12); "I hate your feasts" (Is 1:14). But the saints have their own spiritual feasts, which consist in the joys of the spirit: "Look upon Zion, the city of your feasts" (Is 33:20). So he says: *You yourselves*, who are looking for the glory of this world, *go up for this feast*, i.e., to the feasts of temporal pleasure; *I, however, will not go up for this festival*, for I will go up to the feast of an eternal celebration. I am not going up now *because my time*, that is, the time of my true glory, which will be a joy that lasts forever, an eternity without fatigue, and a brightness without shadow, *is not yet completed*.

1023. Chrysostom[13] keeps the same division of the text, but explains it this way. He says that these brethren of our Lord joined with the Jews in plotting the death of Christ. And so they urged Christ to go to the feast, intending to betray him and hand him over to the Jews. That is why he says: *My time*, that is, the time for my cross and death, *has not yet come*, to go to Judea and be killed. *But your time is always here*, because you can associate with them without danger. And this is because they cannot hate you: you who love and envy the same things they do. *But me, it hates, because I bear witness against it, for its works are evil.* This shows that the Jews hate me, not because I broke the sabbath, but because I denounced them in public. *You yourselves go up for this feast*, that is, for its beginning (for it lasted seven days, as was said); *I, however, will not go up for this festival*, that is, with you, and when it first begins: *because my time is not yet completed*, when I am to suffer, for he was to be crucified at a future Passover. Accordingly, he did not go with them then in order to remain out of sight, and so forth.

LECTURE 2

9 When he had said this, he remained in Galilee. 10 However, after his brethren had gone up, he himself went up for the feast, not publicly, but as it were in secret. 11 The Jews looked for him at the feast, and they asked: "Where is he?" 12 There was much whispering among the people concerning him, for some were saying that he was a good man, while others said, "On the contrary, he leads people astray." 13 Nevertheless, no one spoke openly about him for fear of the Jews. 14 Now when the festival was half over, Jesus went into the temple, and he taught. 15 The Jews were amazed, saying, "How did this man get his learning, since he never studied?" 16 Jesus answered and said: "My

---

13. *Hom. in Io.* 48. 2; PG 59, col. 271; cf. *Catena aurea*, 7:1–8.

doctrine is not mine, but his who sent me. 17 If anyone wants to do his will, he will know whether this doctrine is from God, or whether I am speaking on my own. 18 Whoever speaks on his own [authority] seeks his own glory. But the one who seeks the glory of him who sent him is truthful, and there is no injustice in him. 19 Did not Moses give you the law? And yet none of you obey the law. 20 Why do you want to kill me?" The crowd replied and said: "You have a demon within you! Who wants to kill you?" 21 Jesus answered and said to them: "I performed one work, and you are all amazed. 22 Therefore, Moses gave you circumcision (not that it originated with Moses, but with the patriarchs) and you circumcise on the sabbath day. 23 If a man receives circumcision on the sabbath day, so that the law of Moses may not be broken, why are you indignant with me because I healed a whole man on the sabbath? 24 Judge not by the appearances, but with a just judgment."[14]

1024. After the Evangelist mentioned how our Lord's relatives urged him to go to Judea, and what Christ replied to them, he then tells us of his journey. First, of his delay in going into Judea; secondly, of the order of the events; and thirdly, the way Christ went up.

1025. He mentions our Lord's delay in going when he says, **When he had said this**, in answer to his relatives, **he remained in Galilee**, and did not go to the feast with them. He did this to keep to his word: "I, however, will not go up for this festival." As we read in Numbers (23:19): "God is not like man, a liar."

1026. He gives the order of events when he says, **However, after his brethren**, that is, his relatives, **had gone up, he himself went up for the feast**. This seems to conflict with what he had said before: "I will not go up", for the Apostle says, "Jesus Christ, whom we preached among you ... was not 'Yes' and 'No,' but only 'Yes'" (2 Cor 1:19).

I answer, first, that the festival of Tabernacles lasted for seven days, as was mentioned. Now our Lord first stated, "I, however, will not go up for this festival," that is, for its beginning. When it says here that **he himself went up for the feast**, we should understand this to refer to the middle of the feast. This is why we read a little further on: "Now, when the festival was half over" (v. 14). So it is clear that Christ was not breaking his word. Secondly, as Augustine says, his relatives wanted him to go to Jerusalem to try for a temporal glory. So he said to them: "I however will not go up this festival," for the purpose you want me to. But he did go to the festival to teach the people and to tell them

---

14. St. Thomas refers to Jn 7:15 in *ST* III, q. 9, a. 4, obj. 1; to Jn 7:22 in *ST* I-II, q. 103, a. 1, ad 3; and to Jn 7:23 in *ST* II-II, q. 6, a. 2, obj. 3; II-II, q. 40, a. 4; II-II, q. 122, a. 4, ad 3; III, q. 40, a. 4, ad 1; III, q. 44, a. 3, ad 3; III, q. 52, a. 8, obj. 3; III, q. 70, a. 3, ad 3.

about an eternal glory. Thirdly, as Chrysostom[15] says, our Lord said, "I, however, will not go up for this festival," to suffer and die as they wished; but he did go, not in order to suffer, but to teach others.

1027. The way he went was **not publicly, but as it were in secret**. There are three reasons for this. The first, given by Chrysostom[16] is so that he would not call more attention to his divinity, and so perhaps make his Incarnation less certain, as was said above: and so that those who are virtuous would not be ashamed to hide from those who are persecuting them when they cannot openly restrain them. Thus he says, **in secret**, to show that this was done according to plan: "Truly, you are a hidden God" (Is 45:15). Augustine[17] gives us another reason: to teach us that Christ was hidden in the figures of the Old Testament: "I will wait for the Lord, who has hidden his face (i.e., clear knowledge) from the house of Jacob" (Is 8:17); so, "Even to this day ... a veil is over their hearts" (2 Cor 3:15). Thus, everything that was said to this ancient people was a shadow of the good things to come, as we see from Hebrews (10:1). So our Lord went up in secret to show that even this feast was a figure. *Scenopegia*, as we saw, was the feast of Tabernacles; and the one who celebrates this feast is the one who understands that he is a pilgrim in this world. Another reason why our Lord went up in secret was to teach us that we should conceal the good things we do, not looking for human approval or desiring the applause of the crowd: "Take care not to perform your good actions in the sight of men, in order to be seen by them" (Mt 6:1).

1028. Then (v. 11), he mentions the opportunity Christ had to show the origin of his spiritual teaching. He mentions two such opportunities: one was due to the disagreement among the people: the other to their amazement (v. 15). The people disagreed in what they thought of Christ. He does three things concerning this. First, he shows what they had in common; secondly, how they differed (v. 12); and thirdly, whose opinion prevailed (v. 13).

1029. What they had in common was that they **looked for him at the feast, and they asked: Where is he?** It is obvious that they did not even want to mention his name because of their hatred and hostility: "They hated him and could not speak civilly to him" (Gen 37:4).

1030. They differed, however, because some looked for him because they wished to learn: "Seek him, and your soul will live" (Ps 68:33); others were looking for him in order to harm him: as in the Psalm (39:15): "They seek my soul to carry it away." And so **there was much whispering among the people concerning him**, because of their disagreements. And although "whispering" (*murmur*) is neuter in gender,

---

15. *Hom. in Io.* 49. 1; PG 59, col. 273–74; cf. *Catena aurea*, 7:9–13.
16. Ibid., 48. 2, col. 271; cf. *Catena aurea*, 7:9–13.
17. *Tract. in Io.* 28. 9; PL 35, col. 1626; cf. *Catena aurea*, 7:9–13.

Jerome makes it masculine (*murmur multus*) because he was following the custom of the older grammarians, or else to show that divine Scripture is not subject to the rules of Priscian.[18]

There was disagreement: for **some** of the people, that is, those who were right in heart, **were saying**, of Christ, **that he was a good man**. "How good God is to Israel, to those whose heart is right" (Ps 72:1); "The Lord is good to those who hope in him, to the one who seeks him" (Lam 3:25). **While others**, that is, those who were badly disposed, **said: On the contrary**, i.e., he is not a good man. We can see from this that it was the people who thought that he was a good person, while he was considered evil by the chief priests; so they say, **he leads people astray**: "We found this man leading our people astray" (Lk 23:2); "We have remembered that that seducer said . . . " (Mt 27:63).

1031. Here we should note that to seduce is to lead away. Now a person can be led away either from what is true or from what is false. And in either way a person can be called a seducer: either because he leads one away from the truth, and in this sense it does not apply to Christ, because he is the truth (below chap. 8); or because he leads one away from what is false, and in this sense Christ is called a seducer: "You seduced me, O Lord, and I was seduced. You were stronger than I, and you have won" (Jer 20:7). Would that all of us were called and were seducers in this sense, as Augustine[19] says. But we call a person a seducer primarily because he leads others away from the truth and deceives them: because a person is said to be led away if he is drawn from the common way. But the common way is the way of truth; heresies, on the other hand, and the way of the wicked, are detours.

1032. It was the opinion of the evil, that is, of the chief priests, that finally won out. Thus he continues, **Nevertheless, no one spoke openly about him**. This was because the people were held back by their fear of the chief priests, for as stated below (9:22): "if any one should profess him to be the Christ, he would be put out of the synagogue." This reveals the wickedness with which the leaders plotted against Christ; and it shows that those who were subject to them, i.e., the people, were not free to say what they thought.

1033. Next (v. 15), we see the second opportunity Christ had to present his teaching, that is, the amazement of the people. First, we see the object of their amazement; secondly, their amazement itself, and thirdly, the reason why they were amazed.

1034. The object of their amazement is the doctrine or teaching of Christ.[20] Both the time and the place of this teaching are given. The

18. Priscian was a Latin grammarian who flourished about the year 500 in Constantinople. His work, *Institutiones grammaticae*, became the standard textbook for Latin grammar in the Middle Ages.
19. *Tract. in Io.* 29. 1; PL 35, col. 1628; cf. *Catena aurea*, 7:9–13.
20. See *ST* III, q. 42, a. 4.

time is mentioned when he says, *Now when the festival was half over*, that is, when as many days were left of the feast as had passed. Thus, since the feast lasted some seven days, this took place on the fourth day. As we said, when Christ hid himself, it was a sign of his humanity, and an example of virtue for us. But when he did come before them, and they could not suppress him, this showed his divinity. Further, our Lord went when the feast was half over, because at the beginning everyone would be occupied with matters relating to the feast: the good, with the worship of God, and others with trivialities and financial profit; but when it was half over, and such matters had been settled, the people would be better prepared to receive his teaching. Thus our Lord did not go to the first several days of the feast so that he would find them more attentive and better prepared for his teaching. Similarly, Christ's going to the feast at this time paralleled the arrangement of his teaching: for Christ came to teach us about the kingdom of God, not at the beginning of the world, nor at its ending, but during the intervening time "You will make it known in the intervening years" (Hab 3:2).[21]

The place where our Lord taught is mentioned when he says, *into the temple*. He taught there for two reasons. First, to show that he was teaching the truth, which they could not deprecate, and which was necessary for all: "I have said nothing secretly" (below 18:20).[22] Secondly, because the temple, since it was a sacred place, was appropriate for the very holy teaching of Christ: "Come! Let us go up the mountain of the Lord, and to the house of the God of Jacob. And he will teach us his ways, and we will walk in his steps," as we read in Isaiah (2:3).[23]

The Evangelist does not mention what Christ taught, for, as was said, the Evangelists do not report everything our Lord did and said, but those which excited the people or produced some controversy. And so here he mentions the excitement his teaching produced in the people: that is, that those who had said before, "he leads people astray," were now amazed at his teaching.

1035. He mentions this amazement when he says, *The Jews were amazed*. And this is not surprising, for "Your testimony is wonderful" (Ps 118:129). For the words of Christ are the words of divine wisdom.

He adds the reason why they were amazed when he says, *How did this man get his learning, since he never studied?* For they knew that Jesus was the son of a poor woman and he was considered the son of a carpenter; as such, he would be working for a living and devoting his time, not to study, but to physical work, according to "I am poor, and have labored since my youth" (Ps 87:16). And so when they hear him teach and debate, they are amazed, and say, *How did this man get his*

---

21. See *ST* III, q. 1, aa. 5–6.
23. See *ST* I-II, q. 102, a. 4, ad 6.

22. See *ST* III, q. 42, a. 3.

70   COMMENTARY ON THE GOSPEL OF JOHN

learning, since he never studied? Much the same is said in Matthew (13:54): "Where did he acquire this wisdom, and these great works? Isn't he the son of the carpenter?"[24]

1036. Having been told of the place and opportunity which Christ had to reveal the origin of his spiritual teaching, we now see the origin of this teaching. First, he shows them that God is the source of this spiritual teaching; secondly, he invites them to accept it (v. 37). As to the first, he does two things. First, he shows the origin of this teaching; secondly, the origin of the one teaching it (v. 25). He does two things about the first. First, he shows the origin of this teaching; secondly, he answers an objection (v. 19). In regard to the first he does two things. First, he shows the origin of this teaching; secondly, he proves that it comes from God (v. 17).

1037. He says, *Jesus answered and said*. As if to say: You are wondering where I gained my knowledge; but I say, *My doctrine is not mine*. If he had said: "The doctrine that I am presenting to you is not mine," there would be no problem. But he says: *My doctrine is not mine*; and this seems to be a contradiction. However, this can be explained, for this statement can be understood in several ways. Our Lord's doctrine can in some sense be called his own, and in some sense not his own. First, we can understand Christ as the Son of God. Then, since the doctrine of anyone is nothing else than his word, and the Son of God is the Word of God, it follows that the doctrine of the Father is the Son himself. But this same Word belongs to himself through an identity of substance. "What does belong to you, if not you yourself?" However, he does not belong to himself through his origin. As Augustine[25] says: "If you do not belong to yourself (because you are from another), what does?" This seems to be the meaning, expressed in summary fashion, of: *My doctrine is not mine*. As if to say: I am not of myself. This refutes the Sabellian heresy, which dared to say that the Son is the Father.[26]

Or, we could understand it as meaning that *My doctrine*, which I proclaim with created words, *is not mine, but his who sent me*, i.e., it is the Father's; that is, my doctrine is not mine as from myself, but it is from the Father: because the Son has even his knowledge from the Father through an eternal generation. "All things have been given to me by my Father" (Mt 11:27).

Secondly, we can understand Christ as the Son of Man. Then he is saying: *My doctrine*, which I have in my created soul, and which my lips proclaim, *is not mine*, i.e., it is not mine as from myself, but from God: because every truth, by whomever spoken, is from the Holy Spirit.

24. See *ST* III, q. 9, a. 3.
25. *Tract. in Io.* 29. 3; PL 35, col. 1629; cf. *Catena aurea*, 7:14–18.
26. See *ST* I, q. 27, a. 1.

Thus, as Augustine says in *The Trinity*,[27] our Lord called this doctrine his own from one point of view, and not his own from another point of view. According to his form of God, it was his own; but according to his form of a servant, it was not his own. This is an example for us, that we should realize that all our knowledge is from God, and thank him for it: "What do you have which you have not been given? And if you have been given it, why do you glory as if you have not been given it?" (1 Cor 4:7).[28]

1038. Then (v. 17), he proves that his doctrine is from God. And he does this in two ways: first, from the judgment of those who correctly understand such matters; and secondly, from his own intention (v. 18).

1039. With respect to the first, we should note that when there is a question whether someone is performing well in some art, this is decided by one who has experience in that art; just as the question whether someone is speaking French well should be decided by one who is well versed in the French language. With this in mind, our Lord is saying: The question whether my doctrine is from God must be decided by one who has experience in divine matters, for such a person can judge correctly about these things. "The sensual man does not perceive those things that pertain to the Spirit of God. The spiritual man judges all things" (1 Cor 2:14). Accordingly, he is saying: Because you are alienated from God, you do not know whether a doctrine is from God.[29] **If anyone wants to do his will**, that is, the will of God, he can know whether this doctrine is from God, **or whether I am speaking on my own** (*a meipso*). Indeed, one who is speaking what is false is speaking on his own, because "When he lies, he speaks on his own," as we read below (8:44).

Chrysostom[30] explains this text in another way. The will of God is our peace, our love, and our humility; thus Matthew (5:9) says: "Happy are the peacemakers, because they will be called sons of God." But the love of controversy often distorts a person's mind to such an extent that he thinks that what is really true is false. Thus, when we abandon the spirit of controversy, we possess more surely the certitude of truth.[31] "Answer, I entreat you, without contention, and judge, speaking what is just" (Jb 6:29). So our Lord is saying: If anyone wishes to judge my doctrine correctly, let him do the will of God, i.e., abandon the anger, the envy and the hatred which he has for me without reason. Then, nothing will prevent him from knowing **whether this doc-**

---

27. *De Trin.* 1. 12. 27; PL 42, col. 839; cf. *Catena aurea*, 7:14–18.
28. See *ST* I, q. 16, a. 6.
29. See *ST* III, q. 42, a. 2.
30. *Hom. in Io.* 49. 1; PG 59, col. 274–75; cf. *Catena aurea*, 7:14–18; see also Thomas Aquinas, *Expos. super Job* 6. 29.
31. See *ST* II-II, q. 39.

trine is from God, or whether I am speaking on my own, i.e., whether I am speaking the words of God.

Augustine[32] explains it this way. It is the will of God that we know his works, just as it is the will of a head of a household that his servants do his works. The work of God is that we believe in him whom he has sent: "This is work of God, that you believe in him whom he sent" (above 6:29). Thus he says: ***If anyone wants to do his will***, that is, God's will, which is to believe in me, ***he will know whether this doctrine is from God***: "If you do not believe, you will not understand," as that other version of Isaiah (7:9) says.

1040. Then when he says, ***Whoever speaks on his own seeks his own glory***, he proves the same thing from his intention. And he presents two intentions through which we can recognize the two sources of a doctrine. Some are said to speak on their own [*a se*] and others not on their own. Now whoever strives to speak the truth does not speak on his own. All our knowledge of the truth is from another: either from instruction, as from a teacher; or from revelation, as from God; or by a process of discovery, as from things themselves, for "the invisible things of God are clearly known by the things that have been made" (Rom 1:20). Consequently, in whatever way a person acquires his knowledge, he does not acquire it on his own. That person speaks on his own who takes what he says neither from things themselves, nor from any human teaching, but from his own heart: "They proclaim a vision taken out of their own hearts" (Jer 23:16); "Woe to those foolish prophets who prophesy out of their own hearts" (Ez 13:3). Accordingly, when a person devises a doctrine on his own he does it for the sake of human glory: for, as we see from Chrysostom,[33] a person who wishes to present his own private doctrine does so for no other purpose than to acquire glory. And this is what our Lord says, proving that his doctrine is from God: ***Whoever speaks on his own***, about a certain knowledge of the truth, which is really from another, ***seeks his own glory***. It is for this reason, and because of pride, that various heresies and false opinions have arisen.[34] And this is a characteristic of the antichrist "who opposes and is exalted above all that is called God, or is worshipped" (2 Thes 2:4).

But the one who seeks the glory of him who sent him, as I do—"I do not seek my own glory" (below 8:50)—***is truthful, and there is no injustice in him***. I am truthful because my doctrine contains the truth; there is no injustice in me because I do not appropriate the glory of another. As Augustine[35] says: "He gave us a magnificent example of

---

32. *Tract. in Io.* 29. 6; PL 35, col. 1630; cf. *Catena aurea*, 7:14–18.
33. *Hom. in Io.* 49. 2; PG 59, col. 275; cf. *Catena aurea*, 7:14–18.
34. See *ST* II-II, q. 39, a. 2.
35. *Tract. in Io.* 29. 8; PL 35, col. 1631; cf. *Catena aurea*, 7:14–18.

CHAPTER 7

humility when, in the form of a man, he sought the glory of the Father, and not his own. O man, you should do the same! When you do something good, you seek your glory; when you do something evil, you insult God." It is obvious that he was not looking for his own glory, because if he had not been an enemy of the chief priests, he would not have been persecuted by them. So Christ, and everyone who is looking for the glory of God, has knowledge in his intellect, "Master, we know that you are truthful" (Mt 22:16): thus he says, he *is truthful*. And he has the correct intention in his will: thus he says, *and there is no injustice in him*. For a person is unjust when he takes for himself what belongs to another; but glory is proper to God alone; therefore, he who seeks glory for himself is unjust.[36]

1041. Then (v. 19), he answers an objection. For someone could tell Christ that his doctrine was not from God because he broke the sabbath, according to, "This man is not from God, for he does not keep the sabbath" (below 9:16). This is what he intends to answer; and he does three things. First, he clears himself, by arguing from the actions of those who are accusing him; secondly, we see their vicious reply (v. 20); and thirdly, he vindicates himself with a reasonable explanation (v. 21).

1042. He says: Even granting, as you say, that my doctrine is not from God because I do not keep the law, breaking the sabbath, nevertheless, you do not have any reason to accuse me since you do the same thing. Thus he says: *Did not Moses give you the law*? i.e. did he not give it to your people? *And yet none of you obey the law*. "You received the law through the angels, and have not kept it" (Acts 7:53). This is why Peter says: "A yoke, which neither our fathers nor we were able to bear" (Acts 15:10). Therefore, if you do not keep the law, why do you want to kill me for not keeping it? You are not doing this because of the law, but out of hatred.[37] If you were acting out of devotion for the law, you would keep it yourselves. "Let us lie in wait for the just man, because he is unfavorable to us, and against our works, and he reproaches us for breaking the law" (Wis 2:12); and a little further on we read: "Let us condemn him to a most shameful death" (Wis 2:20).

Or, it could be explained this way: You do not keep the law that Moses gave you; and this is obvious from the fact that you want to kill me, which is against the law: "You shall not kill" (Ex 20:13). Another explanation, following Augustine,[38] is: You do not keep the law because I myself am included in the law: "If you believed Moses, you would perhaps believe me as well, for it was about me that he wrote" (above 5:46). But you want to kill me.

---

36. See *ST* II-II, q. 132, a. 1.
37. See *ST* II-II, q. 34, aa. 1, 6.
38. *Tract. in Io.* 30. 2; PL 35, col. 1633; cf. *Catena aurea*, 7:19–24.

1043. Then we see the vicious reply of the crowd, when he says, *The crowd replied and said: You have a demon within you!* As Augustine says, their reply indicates disorder and confusion, rather than any order: for they are saying that the one who casts out devils has one himself (Mt chap. 12).

1044. Then when he says, *I performed one work, and you are all amazed*, our Lord, at peace in his own truth, answers them, and justifies himself with a reasonable explanation. First, he recalls the incident that is troubling them; secondly, he shows that this should not bother them (v. 22); and thirdly, he shows the way to a judgment that is just (v. 24).

1045. Jesus answered them: *I performed one work, and you are all amazed.* He does not trade one insult for another, nor rebuff it, because "When he was derided, he did not deride in return" (1 Pet 2:23). He rather recalls for them his cure of the paralytic, which was the cause of their amazement. But their amazement was not one of devotion, as in "Your heart will be amazed and expanded" (Is 60:5), but a kind of agitation and disturbance, as in "Those who see it will be afflicted with terrible fear, and will be amazed" (Wis 5:2). So, if you are amazed over one of my works, i.e., if you are disturbed and troubled, what would you do if you saw all of my works? For, as Augustine[39] says, his works were those which they saw in the world: even all the sick are healed by him. "He sent his word, and healed them" (Ps 106:20); "It was neither a herb nor a poultice that healed them, but Your word, O Lord, which heals all" (Wis 16:12). Thus, the reason why you are disturbed is that you have seen only one of my works, and not all of them.[40]

1046. Then (v. 22), he shows that there is no reason why they should be disturbed. First, he recalls the command given to them by Moses; secondly, he states their customary behavior; and thirdly, he presents an argument based on the first two.

1047. The command of Moses was about circumcision; so he says: *Therefore*, i.e., to signify my works, *Moses gave you circumcision*. For circumcision was given as a sign, as we read, "It will be a sign of the covenant between me and you" (Gen 17:11). For it signified Christ. This is the reason why it was always done on the genital organ, because Christ was to descend, in his human nature, from Abraham; and Christ is the one who spiritually circumcises us, i.e., both in mind and body. Or, it was done to the genital organ because it was given in opposition to original sin.

We do not find it explicitly stated that Moses gave circumcision, unless in Exodus (12:44): "Every slave who is bought shall be circumcised." And although Moses did tell them to circumcise, he was not the

---

39. Ibid., 30. 3, col. 1633–34; cf. *Catena aurea*, 7:19–24.
40. See *ST* III, q. 44, a. 3.

one who established this practice, because he was not the first one to receive the command to circumcise; this was Abraham, as we see from Genesis (17:10).[41]

1048. Now it was the custom among the Jews to circumcise on the sabbath. And this is what he says: you circumcise on the sabbath day. They did this because Abraham was told that a boy should be circumcised on the eighth day: "He circumcised him on the eighth day, as God had commanded him" (Gen 21:4). On the other hand, they were told by Moses not to do any work on the sabbath. But it sometimes happened that the eighth day was a sabbath. And so, in circumcising a boy on that day, they were breaking a command of Moses for a command of the patriarchs.

1049. Our Lord is arguing from those facts when he says: *If a man receives circumcision on the sabbath day, so that the law of Moses may not be broken, why are you indignant with me because I healed a whole man on the sabbath?*

We should note here that three things make this argument effective: two of these are explicit, and the other implied. First, although the command given to Abraham [about circumcision] was the first to be given, it was not canceled by the command given to Moses concerning observing the sabbath. "I say that the covenant, confirmed by God, is not canceled by the law, which came four hundred and thirty years later" (Gal 3:17). And so Christ is arguing from this: Although when dealing with human laws, the later ones cancel the earlier laws, in the case of divine laws, the earlier ones have greater authority. And so the command given to Moses about observing the sabbath does not cancel the command which was given to Abraham concerning circumcision. Therefore, much less does it interfere with me, who am only doing what was decided by God, before the creation of the world, for the salvation of mankind; and this salvation was symbolized by the sabbath.[42]

Another point is that the Jews were commanded not to work on the sabbath; yet they did do things that were related to the salvation of the individual. So Christ is saying: If you people, who were commanded not to work on the sabbath, circumcise on that day (and this concerns the salvation of the individual, and thus it was done to an individual organ) and you do this *so that the law of Moses may not be broken* (from which it is clear that those things that pertain to salvation should not be omitted on the sabbath), it follows with greater reason that a man should do on that day those things that pertain to the salvation of everyone. Therefore, you should not be indignant with me *because I healed a whole man on the sabbath.*

---

41. See *ST* III, q. 70, aa. 1–2.
42. See *ST* I, q. 73, a. 1; I-II, q. 100, a. 5, ad 2; III, q. 40, a. 4, ad 1.

The third point is that each command was a symbol: for "all these things happened to them in symbol" (1 Cor 10:11). Thus, if one symbol, i.e., the command to observe the sabbath, does not cancel the other symbol, i.e., the command to circumcise, much less does it cancel the truth. For circumcision symbolized our Lord, as Augustine[43] says.

Finally, he says, *a whole man*, because, since God's works are perfect, the man was cured so as to be healthy in body, and he believed so as to be healthy in soul.

1050. Then when he says, *Judge not by the appearances, but with a just judgment*, he guides them to a fair consideration of himself, so that they do not judge him according to appearances, but give a judgment which is just. There are two ways in which one is said to judge according to appearances. First, a judge may reach his decision relying on the allegations: "Men see the things that are evident" (1 Kgs 15:7). But this way can lead to error; thus he says, *Judge not by the appearances*, i.e., by what is immediately evident, but examine the matter diligently: "I diligently investigated the stranger's cause" (Jb 29:16); "He will not judge by appearances" (Is 11:3). In the second way, *Judge not by the appearances*, i.e., do not show partiality or favoritism in your judgment: for all judges are forbidden to do this. "You will not show favoritism when judging a person who is poor" (Ex 23:6); "You have shown partiality in your judgment" (Mal 2:9). To show partiality in a judgment is not to give a judgment that is just because of love, or deference, or fear, or the status of a person, which things have nothing to do with the case.[44] So he says: *Judge not by the appearances, but with a just judgment*, as if to say: Just because Moses is more honored among you than I am, you should not base your decision on our reputations, but on the nature of the facts: because the things I am doing are greater than what Moses did.

But it should be noted, according to Augustine,[45] that one who loves all equally does not judge with partiality. For when we honor men differently according to their rank, we must beware of showing partiality.

LECTURE 3

25 Some of the inhabitants of Jerusalem then said: "Is he not the man they want to kill? 26 Look, he is speaking publicly, and they say nothing to him! Could it be that the rulers really know that he is the Christ? 27 We know where this man comes from; but when the Christ

43. *Tract. in Io.* 30. 5; PL 35, col. 1635; cf. *Catena aurea*, 7:19–24.
44. See *ST* II-II, q. 63, aa. 1, 4.
45. *Tract. in Io.* 30. 8; PL 35, col. 1636; cf. *Catena aurea*, 7:19–24.

comes, no one will know where he comes from." 28 So as Jesus was teaching in the temple, he cried out and said: "You do indeed know me, and you know where I come from. And I have not come of my own accord. But the one who sent me is truthful, whom you do not know. 29 I know him. And if I were to say that I do not know him, I would be like you, a liar. But I do know him, because I am from him, and he sent me." 30 They therefore wanted to seize him, but no one laid a hand on him, because his hour had not yet come. 31 Many of the people, however, believed in him, and they said: "When the Christ comes, will he work more wonders than this man has done?" 32 The Pharisees heard the people saying these things about him, so the rulers and Pharisees sent officers to apprehend Jesus.[46]

1051. Having considered the origin of his doctrine, he now tells us about the origin of its teacher. First, Christ shows his source, from which he comes, secondly, he shows his end, to which he goes (v. 33). He does three things concerning the first. First, we see the doubt of the people about his origin; secondly, we have Christ's teaching concerning his origin (v. 28); and thirdly, we see the effect this teaching had (v. 30). He does two things about the first. First, we see the amazement of the people; secondly, their conjecture (v. 26). The people were amazed over two things: at the unjust statements of their leaders, and at the public teaching of Christ (v. 25).

1052. As we said before, Christ went up to this feast in secret to show the weakness of his human nature; but he publicly taught in the temple, with his enemies being unable to restrain him, to show his divinity. And so, as Augustine[47] remarks, what was thought to be a lack of courage turned out to be strength. Accordingly, **Some of the inhabitants of Jerusalem then said**, in amazement, for they knew how fiercely their leaders were looking for him, as they lived with them in Jerusalem. Thus Chrysostom[48] says: "The most pitiable of all were they who saw a very clear sign of his divinity and, leaving everything to the judgment of their corrupt leaders, failed to show Christ reverence." "As the ruler of a city is, so are its inhabitants" (Sir 10:2). Yet they were amazed at the power he had which kept him from being apprehended. So they said: **Is he not the man they**, i.e., their leaders, **want**? This agrees with what was said before: "For reasons like this the Jews began to persecute Jesus, because he performed such works on the sabbath" (above 5:16); "Evil has come out of the elders of the people, who ruled them" (Dn 13:5). This also shows that Christ spoke the truth, while what their leaders said was false. For above, when our Lord asked them: "Why do you want to kill me?" they denied it

---

46. St. Thomas refers to Jn 7:31 in *ST* III, q. 47, a. 5.
47. *Tract. in Io.* 31. 1; PL 35, col. 1636–37; cf. *Catena aurea,* 7:25–30.
48. *Hom. in Io.* 50. 1; PG 59, col. 277–78; cf. *Catena aurea,* 7:25–30.

and said: "You have a demon within you! Who wants to kill you?" But here, what their leaders had denied, these others admit when they say, **Is he not the man they want to kill?** Accordingly, they are amazed, considering the evil intentions of their leaders.

1053. Again, they were amazed that Christ was openly teaching; so they said: **Look, he is speaking publicly**, i.e., Christ was teaching, an indication of the secure possession of the truth, "I have spoken publicly" (below 18:20), **and they say nothing to him**, held back by divine power.[49] For it is a characteristic of God's power that he prevents the hearts of evil men from carrying out their evil plans. "When the Lord is pleased with the way a man is living he will make his enemies be at peace with him" (Pr 16:7); and again, "The heart of the king is in the hand of the Lord; he turns it wherever he wills" (Pr 21:1).

1054. We see their conjecture when he says, **Could it be that the rulers really know that he is the Christ?** As if to say: Before, they sought to kill him; but now that they have found him, they do not say anything to him. Still, the leaders had not changed their opinion about Christ: "If they had known, they would never have crucified the Lord of glory" (1 Cor 2:8), but were restrained by divine power.

1055. Their objection to this conjecture is then added: **We know where this man comes from.** As if to argue: The Christ should have a hidden origin; but the origin of this man is known; therefore, he is not the Christ. This shows their folly, for granted that some of their leaders believed Christ, they did not follow their opinion, but offered another, which was false. "This is Jerusalem; I have set her in the midst of the nations" (Ez 5:5). For they knew that Christ took his origin from Mary, but they did not know the way this came about: "Isn't Joseph his father, and Mary his mother?" as we read in Matthew (13:55).

1056. Why did they say, **when the Christ comes, no one will know where he comes from**, since it says in Micah (5:2): "Out of you [Bethlehem-Ephrathah] will come a leader, who will rule my people Israel."? I answer that they took this opinion from Isaiah, who said: "Who will make known his origin?" (53:8).[50] Thus, they knew from the prophets where he was from, according to his human origin; and they also knew from them that they did not know it, according to his divine origin.

1057. Then (v. 28), he shows his origin. First, he shows in what sense his origin is known, and in what sense it is not known; in the second place, he shows how we can acquire a knowledge of his origin (v. 29). He does two things about the first. First, he shows what they knew about his origin; secondly, what they did not know about it (v. 28b).

1058. They did know the origin of Jesus; and so he says of Jesus that

---

49. See *ST* III, q. 42, a. 3.
50. See *ST* III, q. 35, a. 7.

he cried out. Now a cry comes from some great emotion. Sometimes it indicates the upheaval of a soul in interior distress; and in this sense it does not apply to Christ: "He will not cry out" (Is 42:2); "The words of the wise are heard in silence" (Ecc 9:17). Sometimes it implies great devotion, as in, "In my trouble I cried to the Lord" (Ps 119:1). And sometimes, along with this, it signifies that what is to be said is important, as in, "The Seraphim cried to each other and said: 'Holy, holy, holy, is the Lord God of hosts'" (Is 6:3); and in, "Does not wisdom cry out?" (Pr 8:1). This is the way preachers are encouraged to cry out: "Cry out, do not stop! Raise you voice like a trumpet" (Is 58:1). This is the way Christ cried out here, **teaching in the temple**.

And he said: **You do indeed know me**, according to appearances, **and you know where I come from**, that is, as to my bodily existence: "After this he was seen on earth" (Bar 3:38). For they knew that he was born from Mary in Bethlehem, and brought up in Nazareth; but they did not know about the virgin birth, and that he had been conceived through the Holy Spirit, as Augustine says.[51] With the exception of the virgin birth, they knew everything about Jesus that pertained to his humanity.

1059. They did not know his hidden origin; and so he says: **And I have not come of my own accord**. First, he gives his origin: and secondly, he shows that it is hidden from them.

His origin is from the Father, from eternity. And so he says: **I have not come of my own accord**, as if to say: Before I came into the world through my humanity, I existed according to my divinity: "Before Abraham came to be, I am" (below 8:58). For he could not have come unless he already was. And although I have come, **I have not come of my own accord** [*a me ipso*], because the Son is not of himself [*a se*], but from the Father. "I came from the Father and have come into the world" (below 16:28).[52] Indeed, his origin was foretold by the Father, who promised to send him: "I beg you, O Lord, send him whom you are going to send" (Ex 4:13); "I will send them a Savior and a defender, to free them" (Is 19:20). And so he says: **the one who sent me is truthful**, as if to say: I have not come from another but from him who promised and kept his promise, as he is truthful: "God is truthful" (Rom 3:4). Consequently, he teaches me to speak the truth, because I have been sent by one who is truthful. But they do not know this, because they do not know him who sent me; and so he says: **whom you do not know**.

1060. But since every man, although born in a bodily condition, is from God, it seems that Christ could say that he is from God; and con-

---

51. *Tract. in Io.* 31. 3; PL 35, col. 1637; cf. *Catena aurea*, 7:25–30. See also *ST* III, q. 28, a. 1; III, q. 32, a. 1.
52. See *ST*, I, q. 43, a. 1.

sequently, that they do know where he comes from. I answer, according to Hilary, that the Son is *a* (from) God in a different way than others: for he is from God in such a way that he is also God; and so God is his consubstantial principle.[53] But others are *a* (from) God, but in such a way that they are not *ex* (from) him. Thus, it is not known where the Son is from because the nature *ex* (from) which he is, is not known. But where men are from is not unknown: for if something exists *ex* (from) nothing, where it is from cannot be unknown.

1061. Then when he says, *I know him*, he teaches us how to know him from whom he is. For if a thing is to be learned, it must be learned from one who knows it. But only the Son knows the Father. And so he says: If you wish to know him who sent me, you must acquire this knowledge from me, because I alone know him. First, he shows that he knows him; secondly, he shows the perfection of his knowledge; and thirdly, the nature of his knowledge.

1062. He shows that he knows him when he says, *I know him*. Now it is true that "All men see him" (Jb 36:25), but they do not see him in the same way, for in this life we see him through the intermediary of creatures: "The invisible things of God are clearly known through the things that have been made" (Rom 1:20). Thus we read: "Now we see in a mirror, in an obscure manner" (1 Cor 13:12).[54] But the angels and the blessed in heaven see him through his essence: "Their angels in heaven always see the face of my Father, who is in heaven" (Mt 18:10); "We shall see him as he is" (1 Jn 3:2). The Son of God, on the other hand, sees him in a more excellent way than all, that is, with a comprehensive or all-inclusive vision: "No one has ever seen God," i.e., in a comprehensive way; "it is the Only Begotten Son, who is in the bosom of the Father, who has made him known" (above 1:18); "No one knows the Father but the Son" (Mt 11:27). It is of this vision that he is speaking of here, when he says: *I know him*, with a comprehensive knowledge.[55]

1063. He shows the perfection of his knowledge when he says: And if I were to say *that I do not know him, I would be like you, a liar*. This is mentioned for two reasons. Intellectual creatures do know God, though from a distance and imperfectly, for "All men see him, from a distance" (Jb 36:2). For divine truth transcends all our knowledge: "God is greater than our hearts" (1 Jn 3:20). Therefore whoever knows God can say without lying: "I do not know him," because he does not know him to the full extent that he is knowable. But the Son knows God the Father most perfectly, just as he knows himself most perfectly. Thus he cannot say: I do not know him.

Again, because our knowledge of God, especially that which comes

---

53. See *ST* I, q. 27, a. 2.
55. See *ST* I, q. 12, a. 1.

54. See *ST* I, q. 2, a. 1.

through grace, can be lost—"They forgot God, who saved them" (Ps 105:21)—men can say, *I do not know him*, as long as they are in this present life: because no one knows whether he deserves love or hatred.[56] The Son, on the other hand, has a knowledge of the Father that cannot be lost; so he cannot say: *I do not know him*.

We should understand, *I would be like you*, as a reverse likeness. For they would not be lying if they said they did not know God; but they would be if they said that they did know him, since they did not know him. But if Christ said that he did not know him, he would be lying, since he did know him. So the meaning of this statement is this: *If I were to say that I do not know him*, then since I really do know him, *I would be like you, a liar*, who say that you know him although you do not.

1064. Could not Christ have said: *I do not know him*? It seems he could, since he could have moved his lips and said the words. And so he could have lied. I reply that Christ did say this and still was not lying. We should explain it this way: If he were to say, *I do not know him*, declaratively, meaning, "I believe in my heart what I profess by my lips," [then he would have been a liar]. Now to say as the truth what is false comes from two defects: from a defect of knowledge in the intellect; and Christ could not have this since he is the wisdom of God (1 Cor 1:30); or it could come from a defect of right will in the affections; and this could not be in Christ either since he is the power of God, according to the same text. Thus he could not say the words *I do not know him*, declaratively. Yet this entire conditional statement is not false although both its parts are impossible.

1065. The reason for this singular and perfect knowledge of Christ is given when he says: *I do know him, because I am from him, and he sent me*. Now all knowledge comes about through some likeness, since nothing is known except insofar as there is a likeness of the known in the knower.[57] But whatever proceeds from something has a likeness to that from which it proceeds; and so, all who truly know have a varied knowledge of God according to the different degrees of their procession from him. The rational soul has a knowledge of God insofar as it participates in a likeness to him in a more imperfect way than other intellectual creatures. An angel, because it has a more explicit likeness to God, being a stamp of resemblance, knows God more clearly.[58] But the Son has the most perfect likeness to the Father, since he has the same essence and power as he does; and so he knows him most perfectly, as was said. And so he says: *But I do know him*, that is, to the extent that he is knowable. And the reason for this is *because I am from him*, hav-

---

56. See *ST* I-II, q. 112, a. 5.
57. See *ST* I, q. 16, aa. 1–2; I, q. 85, aa. 1–2.
58. See *ST* I, q. 54, aa. 1–3; I, q. 75, a. 7; I, q. 88, a. 1; I, q. 117, a. 2.

ing the same essence with him through consubstantiality. Thus, just as he knows himself perfectly through his essence, so *I do know him* perfectly through the same essence. And so that we do not understand these words as referring to his being sent into this world, he at once adds, *and he sent me*. Consequently, the statement, *I am from him*, refers to his eternal generation, through which is he is consubstantial with the Father.[59] But then when he says, *and he sent me*, he is saying that the Father is the author of the Incarnation: "God sent his Son, made from a woman, made under the law" (Gal 4:4).[60] Now just as the Son has a perfect knowledge of the Father because he is from the Father, so because the soul of Christ is united to the Word in a unique way, it has a unique and more excellent knowledge of God than other creatures, although it does not comprehend him. And so Christ can say, according to his human nature: I know him in a more excellent way than other creatures do, but without comprehending him.[61]

1066. Then (v. 30), he considers the effect of his teaching. First on the people; then on the Pharisees (v. 32). He does two things with the first. First, he shows the effect of this teaching on those of the people who were ill-willed; secondly, on those who were favorable (v. 31). He does three things concerning the first. First, he mentions the evil intention of the people; secondly, that they were hindered in carrying out their plan; and thirdly, he mentions the reason why they were hindered.

1067. He presents their evil intention when he says, *They therefore wanted to seize him*. Because our Lord said to them, "whom you do not know," they became angry, feigning that they did know him. And so they formed the evil plan of seizing him, so that they could crucify and kill him: "Go after him, and seize him" (Ps 70:11). Yet there are some who have Christ within themselves, and still seek to seize him in a reverent manner: "I will go up into the palm tree and seize its fruit" (Sg 7:8). And so the Apostle says: "I will go after it to seize it" (Phil 3:12).[62]

1068. He mentions that they were hindered in their plans when he says, *but no one laid a hand on him*: for their rage was invisibly checked and restrained. This shows that a person has the will to inflict injury from himself, while the power to inflict injury is from God.[63] This is clear from the first chapters of Job, where Satan was unable to torment Job except to the extent that he was permitted to do so by God.

1069. The reason they were hindered was *because his hour had not yet come*. Here we should note that "There is a time and fitness for everything" (Ecc 8:6). However, the time for anything is determined

---

59. See *ST* I, q. 27, a. 2; I, q. 39, a. 2; I, q. 42, a. 1.
60. See *ST* I, q. 43, a. 8.   61. See *ST* III, q. 10, a. 1.
62. See *ST* II-II, q. 121.   63. See *ST* I-II, q. 9, a. 6.

by its cause. Therefore, because the heavenly bodies are the cause of physical effects, the time for those things that act in a physical way is determined by the heavenly bodies. The soul, on the other hand, since it is not subject to any heavenly body in its intellect and reason (for in this respect it transcends temporal causes) does not have times determined by the heavenly bodies: rather, its times are determined by its cause, that is, God, who decrees what is to be done and at what time: "Why is one day better than another? . . . They are differentiated by the knowledge of the Lord" (Sir 33:7).[64] Much less, therefore, is Christ's time determined by these bodies. Accordingly, his hour must be regarded as fixed not by fatal necessity, but by the entire Trinity.[65] For as Augustine[66] says: "You should not believe this about yourself; and how much less should you believe it about he who made you? If your hour is his will, that is, God's, what is his hour but his own will? Therefore, he was not speaking here of the hour in which he would be forced to die, but rather of the hour in which he thought it fitting to be killed." "My time has not yet come," as he said before (above 2:4); "Jesus knew that his time had come to leave this world for the Father" (below 13:1).

1070. Then he mentions the effect his teaching had on those who were favorable. First, he shows their faith: **Many of the people however, believed in him.** He does not say, "of the leaders," because the higher their rank, the further away they were from him. So there was no room in them for wisdom: "Where there is humility, there is wisdom" (Pr 11:2). But the people, because they were quick to see their own sickness, immediately recognized our Lord's medicine: "You have hidden these things from the wise and the prudent, and have revealed them to little ones" (Mt 11:25). This is why in the beginning, it was the poor and the humble who were converted to Christ: "God chose what is lowly and despised in the world, and things that are not, to destroy those things that are" (1 Cor 1:28).

Secondly, he gives the motive for their faith when he says, **When the Christ comes, will he work more wonders than this man has done?** For it had been prophesied that when the Christ came, he would work many miracles: "God himself will come, and save us. Then the eyes of the blind will be opened, and the ears of the deaf will hear" (Is 35:4). And so when they saw the miracles Christ was accomplishing, they were led to believe. Yet their faith was weak, because they were led to believe him not by his teaching, but by his miracles; whereas, since they were already believers, and instructed by the law, they should

---

64. See *ST* I, q. 115, aa. 3–4.
65. See *ST* I, q. 116, a. 1.
66. *Tract. in Io.* 31. 5; PL 35, col. 1638; cf. *Catena aurea*, 7:25–30. See also *ST* III, q. 46, a. 9.

have been influenced more by his teaching: "Signs were given to unbelievers; while prophecies were given to believers, not to unbelievers" (1 Cor 14:22).[67]

Secondly, their faith was weak because they seemed to be expecting another Christ; thus they say: **When the Christ comes, will he work more wonders than this man has done?** From this it is obvious that they did not believe in Christ as in God, but as in some just man or prophet. Or, according to Augustine,[68] they were reasoning this way: **When the Christ comes, will he work more wonders than this man has done?** As if to say: We were promised that the Christ would come. But he will not work more signs than this man is doing. Therefore, either he is the Christ, or there will be several Christs.

1071. Then when he says, **The Pharisees heard the people saying these things about him**, we see the effect this had on the Pharisees. And as Chrysostom[69] says, Christ said many things, and yet the Pharisees were not aroused against him. But when they saw that the people were accepting him, they were immediately fired up against him; and in their madness they wanted to kill him. This shows that the real reason why they hated him was not that he broke the sabbath; what provoked them the most was the fact that the people were honoring Christ. And this is clear below: "Do you not see that we can do nothing? Look, the entire world has gone after him!" (12:19). Because they were afraid of the danger they did not dare to seize Christ themselves, but they sent their officers, who were used to such things.

LECTURE 4

33 Jesus then said to them: "For still a short time I am with you; then I am going to him who sent me. 34 You will look for me, and you will not find me; and where I am, you will not be able to come." 35 The Jews therefore said to one another: "Where is he going that we cannot find him? Is he going to those dispersed among the Gentiles, and teach the Gentiles? 36 What does he mean by saying, 'You will look for me, and you will not find me'; and 'where I am, you will not be able to come'?"

1072. After our Lord told the principle of his origin, he then mentions his end, i.e., where he would go by dying. First, the end of Christ's life is given; secondly, we see that the people are puzzled by what he says (v. 35). As to the first he does three things. First, the end of his life

---

67. See *ST* III, q. 43, a. 1.
68. *Tract. in Io.* 31. 7; PL 35, col. 1639; cf. *Catena aurea*, 7:31–36.
69. *Hom. in Io.* 50. 2; PG 59, col. 281.

is mentioned; secondly, he predicts what they will desire in the future (v. 34); and thirdly, he mentions one of their deficiencies (v. 34b). He does two things about the first. First, he predicts the delay of his death until later; and secondly, he states where he will go by dying (v. 33b). And so, in the first, he shows his power; and in the second, his will to suffer.

1073. Our Lord shows his power by the delaying of his death until later; because, although the Jews wanted to seize him, they could not do this until Christ willed. "No one takes it from me. But I lay it down of myself" (below 10:18). And so Jesus said: *For still a short time I am with you*. As if to say: You want to kill me; but this does not depend on your will, but on my will. And I have decided that *For still a short time I am with you*; so wait a while. You will do what you want to do.[70] These words of our Lord first of all satisfied those people who honored him, and made them more eager to listen to him because there was only a short time left to receive his teaching, as Chrysostom[71] says. "While you have the light, believe in the light" (below 12:36). Secondly, he satisfied those who were persecuting him. As if to say: Your desire for my death will not be delayed long; so be patient, because it is *a short time*. For I must accomplish my mission: to preach, to perform miracles, and then to come to my passion. "Go and tell that fox that I will work today and tomorrow, and on the third day I will finish my course" (Lk 13:32).

1074. There are three reasons why Christ wished to preach for only a short time. First, to show his power, by transforming the entire world in such a brief time: "One day in your courts is better than a thousand elsewhere" (Ps 83:11). Secondly, to arouse the desire of his disciples, i.e., to desire him more (him whose physical presence they would have for only a short time): "The days will come when you will desire to see one day of the Son of Man" (Lk 1:22). Thirdly, to accelerate the spiritual progress of his disciples. For since the humanity of Christ is our way to God, as it says below, "I am the way, and the truth, and the life" (14:6), we should not rest in it as a goal, but through it tend to God. And so that the hearts of his disciples, which were moved by the physical presence of Christ, would not rest in him as man, he quickly took his physical presence from them; thus he said: "It is advantageous for you that I go" (below 16:7); "If we knew Christ according to the flesh (i.e., when he was physically present to us) now we no longer know him in this way" (2 Cor 5:16).[72]

1075. He shows his desire for his passion when he says, *I am going to him who sent me*, that is, willingly, by my passion: "He was offered

---

70. See *ST* III, q. 47, a. 1.
71. *Hom. in Io.* 50. 2; PG 59, col. 281; cf. *Catena aurea*, 7:31–36.
72. See *ST* III, q. 55, a. 3.

because it was his own will" (Is 53:7); "He gave himself for us, an offering to God" (Eph 5:2). *I am going*, I say, to the Father, **to him who sent me**. And this is appropriate, for everything naturally returns to its principle: "Rivers return to the place from which they come" (Ecc 1:7); "Jesus ... knowing that he came from God, and was going to God" (below 13:3). And again: "I am going to him who sent me" (below 16:5).

1076. When he says, **You will look for me and you will not find me**, he is predicting what the Jews will desire in the times to come. As if to say: You can enjoy my teaching for a short time; but this brief time, which you are now rejecting, you will look for later, and you will not find it: "Search for the Lord while he can be found" (Is 55:6); and "Seek the Lord (at the present time), and your soul will live" (Ps 68:33).

1077. This statement, **You will look for me, and you will not find me**, can be understood either as a physical search for Christ or as a spiritual search. If we understand it as a physical search, then, according to Chrysostom,[73] this is the way he was sought by the daughters of Jerusalem, i.e., the women who cried for him, as Luke (23:27) mentions; and no doubt many others were affected at the same time. It is not unreasonable to think that when trouble was near, especially when their city was being captured, the Jews remembered Christ and his miracles and wished that he were there to free them. And in this way, **You will look for me**, i.e., for me to be physically present, **and you will not find me**.

If we understand this as a spiritual search for Christ, then we should say, as Augustine[74] does, that although they refused to recognize Christ while he was among them, they later looked for him, after they had seen the people believe and had themselves been stung by the crime of his death; and they said to Peter: "Brothers, what shall we do?" (Acts 2:37). In this way, they were looking for Christ (whom they saw die as a result of their crime) when they believed in him who forgave them.

1078. Then when he says, **and where I am, you will not be able to come**, he points out one of their deficiencies. He does not say, "and where I am going," which would be more in keeping with the earlier thought, "I am going," to the Father, "to him who sent me." He says rather, **where I am**, to show that he is both God and man. He is man insofar as he is going: "I am going to him who sent me" (below 16:5). But insofar as Christ had always been where he was about to return, he shows that he is God: "No one has gone up to heaven except the One who came down from heaven" (above 3:13). And so, as Augus-

---

73. *Hom. in Io.* 50. 3; PG 59, col. 281; cf. *Catena aurea*, 7:31–36.
74. *Tract. in Io.* 31. 9; PL 35, col. 1640–41; cf. *Catena aurea*, 7:31–36.

tine[75] says, just as Christ returned in such a way as not to leave us, so he came down to us, when he assumed visible flesh, but in such a way as still to be in heaven according to his invisible greatness.

He does not say, "You will not find," because some were about to go; but he does say, you will not be able to come, i.e., as long as you keep your present attitude; for no one can obtain the eternal inheritance unless he is God's heir. And one becomes an heir of God by faith in Christ: "he gave them power to become the sons of God, to all who believe in his name" (above 1:12).[76] But the Jews did not yet believe in him; and so he says, **you will not be able to come**. In the Psalm it is asked: "Who will ascend the mountain of the Lord?" And the answer given is: "Those whose hands are innocent and whose hearts are clean" (Ps 23:3). But the hearts of the Jews were not clean, nor were their hands innocent, because they wanted to kill Christ. And so he says: you are not able to ascend the mountain of the Lord.

1079. Then (v. 35), we see that this was bewildering to the Jews, who, although they thought of Christ in a worldly way, still did believe to a certain extent. And three things happen here. First, they are bewildered; secondly, they form an opinion; and thirdly, they argue against their own opinion.

1080. They are perplexed when they say to each other: **Where is he going that we cannot find him?** For, as was said, they understood this in a physical way: "The sensual man does not perceive those things that pertain to the Spirit of God" (1 Cor 2:14).

1081. And so they came to the opinion that Christ was going to go in a physical way, not by dying, to some place where they would not be permitted to go. Thus they say: **Is he going to those dispersed among the Gentiles, and teach the Gentiles?** For the Gentiles were separated from the way of life of the Jews: "separated from Israel's way of life, strangers to the covenants, without hope in the promise, and without God in this world" (Eph 2:12). And so they said, in a way reproaching him, **to those dispersed among the Gentiles**, who had settled in many different places: "These are the families of Noah . . . and they settled among the nations on the earth after the flood" (Gen 10:32). But the Jewish people were united by place, by their worship of the one God, and by the observance of the law: "The Lord builds up Jerusalem, and he will gather the dispersed of Israel" (Ps 146:2).[77]

They did not say that he would go to the Gentiles to become a Gentile himself, but to bring them back; and so they said, **And teach the Gentiles**. They probably took this from Isaiah (49:6): "I have given you to be a light to the Gentiles, to be my salvation to the ends of the

---

75. Ibid.; cf. *Catena aurea*, 7:31–36. See also *ST* III, q. 46, a. 12.
76. See *ST* III, q. 23, a. 1; III, q. 26, a. 2.
77. See *ST* I-II, q. 98, aa. 2, 4.

earth." However, even though they did not understand what they were saying (just as Caiaphas did not understand his own words: "It is expedient for you that one man die for the people, and that the entire nation does not perish"), what they said was true, and they were predicting the salvation of the Gentiles, as Augustine[78] says, for Christ would go to the Gentiles not in his own body, but by his feet, i.e., his apostles. For he sent his own members to us to make us his members. "I have other sheep that are not of this fold, and I must bring them also . . . and there will be one fold and one shepherd" (below 10:16). And so Isaiah says, speaking for the Gentiles: "He will teach us his ways" (Is 2:3).[79]

1082. Finally, they saw an objection to their own opinion when they said: *What does he mean by saying . . . ?* As if to say: If he had said only, *You will look for me, and you will not find me*, we could think that he was going to the Gentiles. But he seems to exclude this when he adds, *where I am, you will not be able to come*, for we can go to the Gentiles.

LECTURE 5

37 On the last and greatest day of the festival Jesus stood up and cried out, saying: "If anyone thirsts, let him come to me and drink. 38 Whoever believes in me, as the Scriptures say, out of his heart shall flow rivers of living water." 39 (He said this concerning the Spirit, whom those who believed in him would receive; for as yet the Spirit had not been given, since Jesus had not yet been glorified.) 40 From that moment some of the people, hearing these words of his, said: "Truly, this is the Prophet." 41 Others said: "This is the Christ." But others said: "Would the Christ come from Galilee? 42 Does not Scripture say that the Christ will come from the seed of David, and from David's town of Bethlehem?" 43 And so there was dissension among the people because of him. 44 Although some of them wanted to apprehend him, no one laid a hand on him. 45 So the officers returned to the chief priests and Pharisees, who said to them: "Why have you not brought him?" 46 The officers replied: "Never has any man spoken like this man." 47 The Pharisees then retorted: "Have you too been seduced? 48 Has any one of the rulers believed in him, or any of the Pharisees? 49 But these people, who do not know the law, they are accursed." 50 Nicodemus (the same one who came to him at night, and was one of them) said: 51 "Does our law judge a man without first hearing from him and knowing what he has done?" 52 They answered and said to him: "Are you too a Galilean? Look at the Scriptures and see that the

---

78. *Tract. in Io.* 31. 10; PL 35, col. 1641; cf. *Catena aurea,* 7:31–36.
79. See *ST* III, q. 42, a. 1.

Prophet will not come from Galilee." 53 Then every man returned to his own house.[80]

1083. After Our Lord told them about the origin of his doctrine and of the teacher, as well as his end, he now invites them to accept his teaching itself. First, we see Christ's invitation; secondly, the dissension among the people (v. 40). He does three things about the first. First, he tells us the manner of this invitation; secondly, we see the invitation itself (v. 37); and thirdly, he explains what it means (v. 39). The manner of the invitation is described in three ways: by its time; by the posture of the one inviting; and by his efforts.

1084. As to the time, we see that it was **the last and greatest day of the festival**. For as we saw before, this feast was celebrated for seven days, and the first and the last day were the more solemn: just as with us, the first day of a feast and its octave are the more solemn. Therefore, what our Lord did here he did not do on the first day, as he had not yet gone to Jerusalem, nor in the intervening days, but on the last day. And he acted then because there are few who celebrate feasts in a spiritual way.[81] Consequently, he did not invite them to his teaching at the beginning of the festival so that the trifles of the following days would not drive it from their hearts; for we read that the word of the Lord is choked by thorns (Lk 8:7). But he did invite them on the last day so that his teaching would be more deeply impressed on their hearts.

1085. As to his posture, **Jesus stood up**. Here we should note that Christ taught both while sitting and standing. He taught his disciples while sitting (Mt 5:1); while he stood when he taught the people, as he is doing here. It is from this that we get the custom in the Church of standing when preaching to the people, but sitting while preaching to religious and clerics. The reason for this is that since the aim in preaching to the people is to convert them, it takes the form of an exhortation; but when preaching is directed to clergy, already living in the house of God, it takes the form of a reminder.

1086. As to his effort we read that he **cried out**, in order to show his own assurance: "Raise up your voice with strength . . . raise it up, and do not be afraid" (Is 40:9); and so that all would be able to hear him: "Cry out, and do not stop; raise your voice like a trumpet" (Is 58:1); and to stress the importance of what he was about to say: "Listen to me, for I will tell you about great things" (Pr 8:6).

1087. Next (v. 37b), we see Christ's invitation: first, those who are invited; secondly, the fruit of this invitation.

---

80. St. Thomas quotes Jn 7:39 in *ST* I, q. 43, a. 6, obj. 1; I-II, q. 106, a. 3; I-II, q. 106, a. 4, ad 2; II-II, q. 37, a. 2, obj. 2; III, q. 72, a. 1, ad 1; and Jn 7:41 in *ST* III, q. 47, a. 5.
81. See *ST* II-II, q. 99, a. 3.

1088. It is the thirsty who are invited. Thus he says: *If anyone thirsts, let him come to me and drink*; "Come to the waters, all you who thirst" (Is 55:1). He calls the thirsty because such people want to serve God. For God does not accept a forced service: "God loves a cheerful giver" (2 Cor 9:7). So we read: "I will sacrifice freely" (Ps 53:8). And such people are described in Matthew this way: "Blessed are they who hunger and thirst for what is right" (Mt 5:6). Now our Lord calls all of these people, not just some; and so he says: *If anyone thirsts*, as if to say: whoever it is. "Come to me, all you who desire me, and be filled with my fruits" (Sir 24:26); "He desires the salvation of all" (1 Tim 2:4).[82]

Jesus invites them to drink; and so he says, *and drink*. For this drink is spiritual refreshment in the knowledge of divine wisdom and truth, and in the realization of their desires: "My servants will drink, and you will be thirsty" (Is 65:13); "Come and eat my bread, and drink the wine I have mixed for you" (Pr 9:5); "She [wisdom] will give him the water of saving wisdom to drink" (Sir 15:3).

1089. The fruit of this invitation is that good things overflow upon others; thus he says: *Whoever believes in me, as the Scriptures say, out of his heart shall flow rivers of living water.* According to Chrysostom,[83] we should read this as follows: *Whoever believes in me, as the Scriptures say.* And then a new sentence begins: *Out of his heart shall flow rivers of living water.* For if we say: *Whoever believes in me,* and follow this with, *as the Scriptures say, out of his heart shall flow rivers of living water,* it does not seem to be correct, for the statement, *out of his heart shall flow rivers of living water,* is not found in any book of the Old Testament. So we should say: *Whoever believes in me, as the Scriptures say*; that is, according to the teaching of the Scriptures. "Search the Scriptures . . . they too bear witness to me" (above 5:39). And then there follows: *Out of his heart shall flow rivers of living water.* He says here, *Whoever believes in me,* while before he said, "He who comes to me," because to believe and to come are the same thing: "Come to him and be enlightened," as we read in the Psalm (33:6).

But Jerome[84] punctuates this in a different way. He says that after *Whoever believes in me,* there follows, *as the Scriptures say, out of his heart shall flow rivers of living water.* And he says that this phrase was taken from Proverbs (5:15): "Drink the water from your own cistern, and from the streams of you own well. Let your fountains flow far and wide."

1090. We should note, with Augustine,[85] that rivers come from

---

82. See *ST* I, q. 19, a. 6; I-II, q. 111, a. 3.
83. *Hom. in Io.* 51. 1; PG 59, col. 283; cf. *Catena aurea,* 7:37–39.
84. *Praef. in Pent.*; PL 28, col. 149.
85. *Tract. in Io.* 32. 4; PL 35, col. 1643; cf. *Catena aurea,* 7:37–39.

fountains as their source. Now one who drinks natural water does not have either a fountain or a river within himself, because he takes only a small portion of water. But one who drinks by believing in Christ draws in a fountain of water; and when he draws it in, his conscience, which is the heart of the inner man, begins to live and it itself becomes a fountain within him" (4:14).[86] This fountain which is taken in is the Holy Spirit, of whom we read: "With you is the fountain of life" (Ps 35:10).[87] Therefore, whoever drinks the gifts of the graces, which are signified by the rivers, in such a way that he alone benefits, will not have living water flowing from his heart. But whoever acts quickly to help others, and to share with them the various gifts of grace he has received from God, will have living water flowing from his heart. This is why Peter says: "According to the grace each has received, let them use it to benefit one another" (1 Pet 4:10).[88]

He says, ***rivers***, to indicate the abundance of the spiritual gifts which were promised to those who believe: "The river of God is full of water" (Ps 64:10); and also their force or onrush: "When they rush to Jacob, Israel will blossom and bud, and they will fill the surface of the earth with fruit" (Is 27:6); and again, "The rush of the rivers gives joy to the city of God" (Ps 45:5). Thus, because the Apostle was governed by the impulsive force and fervor of the Holy Spirit, he said: "The love of Christ spurs us on" (2 Cor 5:14); and "Those who are led by the Spirit of God are the sons of God" (Rom 8:14). The separate distribution of the gifts of the Holy Spirit is also indicated, for we read, "to one the gift of healing . . . to another the gift of tongues" (1 Cor 12:10). These gifts are "rivers of living water because they flow directly from their source, which is the indwelling Holy Spirit.[89]

1091. Then (v. 39), he explains what he said. First we see the explanation; secondly, the reason behind this explanation (v. 39b).

1092. Christ had said: "out of his heart shall flow rivers of living water." The Evangelist tells us that we should understand this ***concerning the Spirit, whom those who believed in him would receive***, because the Spirit is the fountain and river of life. He is the fountain of which we read: "With you is the fountain of life; and in your light we will see light" (Ps 35:10). And the Spirit is a river because he proceeds from the Father and the Son: "The angel then showed me the river of the water of life, clear as crystal, coming from the throne of God and of the Lamb" (Rev 22:1). "He gave the Spirit," that is, to those who obey him (Is 42:1).[90]

---

86. See *ST* I, q. 79, a. 13.
87. See *ST* I, q. 43, aa. 3 and 6.
88. See *ST* II-II, q. 27, a. 1; II-II, qq. 30–33.
89. See *ST* I-II, q. 68.
90. See *ST* I, q. 38.

1093. He gives the reason behind this explanation, saying, *for as yet the Spirit had not been given*. And he says two things: *as yet the Spirit had not been given*, and that *Jesus had not yet been glorified*.

There are two opinions about the first of these. For Chrysostom[91] says that before the resurrection of Christ the Holy Spirit was not given to the apostles with respect to the gifts of prophecy and miracles. And so this grace, which was given to the prophets, was not to be found on earth until Christ came, and after that it was not given to anyone until the above mentioned time. And if anyone objects that the apostles cast out devils before the resurrection, it should be understood that they were cast out by that power which was from Christ, not by the Spirit; for when he sent them out, we do not read that he gave them the Holy Spirit, but rather that "he gave them power over unclean spirits" (Mt 10:1).

However, this seems to conflict with what our Lord says in the Gospel of Luke: "If I cast out devils by Beelzebub by whom do your children cast them out?" (Lk 11:19). But it is certain that our Lord cast out devils by the Holy Spirit, as the children did also, that is, the apostles. Therefore, it is clear that they had received the Holy Spirit. And so we must say, with Augustine,[92] that the apostles had the Holy Spirit before the resurrection, even with respect to the gifts of the prophecy and miracles.[93] And when we read here that *as yet the Spirit had not been given*, we should understand this to refer to a more abundant giving, and one with visible signs, as the Spirit was given to them in tongues of fire after the resurrection and ascension.

1094. But since the Holy Spirit sanctifies the Church and is even now received by those who believe, why does no one speak in the languages of all nations as then? My answer is that it is not necessary, as Augustine says. For now the universal Church speaks the languages of all the nations, because the love of charity is given by the Holy Spirit: "The love of God is poured out into our hearts by the Holy Spirit" (Rom 5:5); and this love, making all things common, makes everyone speak to everyone else. As Augustine[94] says: "If you love unity, then you have everything that anyone else has in it (i.e., in the Church). Give up your envy, and what I have is also yours; ill-will divides, the love of charity unites. If you have this love, you will have everything." But at the beginning, before the Church was spread throughout the world, because it had few members, they had to speak the languages of all so that they could establish the Church among all.

---

91. *Hom. in Io.* 51. 2; PG 59, col. 284–85; cf. *Catena aurea*, 7:37–39.
92. *De Trin.* 4. 20. 29; PL 42, col. 908; cf. *Catena aurea*, 7:37–39. See *ST* III, q. 49, a. 6.
93. See *ST* I, q. 43, a. 6; III, q. 38, a. 6.
94. *Tract. in Io.* 32. 8; PL 35, col. 1646; cf. *Catena aurea*, 7:37–39.

CHAPTER 7

1095. With regard to the second point, we should note that Augustine[95] thinks the statement, ***Jesus had not yet been glorified*** should be understood as the glory of the resurrection. As if to say: Jesus had not yet risen from the dead or ascended into heaven. We read about this below: "Father, glorify me" (17:5). And the reason he willed to be glorified before he gave the Holy Spirit is that the Holy Spirit is given to us so that we might raise our hearts from the love of this world in a spiritual resurrection, and turn completely to God. To those who are afire with the love of the Holy Spirit, Christ promised eternal life, where we will not die, and where we will have no fear. And for this reason he did not wish to give the Holy Spirit until he was glorified, so that he might show in his body the life for which we hope in the resurrection.

1096. For Chrysostom,[96] however, this statement does not refer to the glory of the resurrection, but to the glorification of the passion. When the passion was near, our Lord said: "Now the Son of Man is glorified" (below 13:31). So, according to this view, the Holy Spirit was first given after the Passion, when our Lord said to his apostles: "Receive the Holy Spirit" (below 20:22). The Holy Spirit was not given before the passion because, since it is a gift, it should not be given to enemies, but to friends. But we were enemies. Thus it was necessary that first the victim be offered on the altar of the cross,[97] and enmity be destroyed in his flesh, so that by this we might be reconciled to God by the death of his Son: and then, having been made friends, we could receive the gift of the Holy Spirit.

1097. The Evangelist, having shown us Christ's invitation to a spiritual drink, now presents the disagreement of the people. First, the disagreement among the people themselves; secondly, that of their leaders (v. 45). He does two things about the first. First, he states what those who disagreed said; secondly, he states the fact that there was a disagreement (v. 43).

What the people said varied according to their different opinions about Christ. And he gives three of their opinions: two of these were the opinions of those who were coming for spiritual drink; and the third was held by those who shrank from it.

1098. The first opinion was that Christ was the Prophet. So he says, ***From that moment***, i.e., from the time Christ had spoken on the great day of the feast, ***hearing these words of his, some of the people said***, i.e., those who had now begun to drink that water spiritually, ***Truly, this is the Prophet***. They did not just call him a Prophet, but ***the Proph-***

---

95. Ibid., 32. 9, col. 1646; cf. *Catena aurea*, 7:37–39.
96. *Hom. in Io.* 51. 2; PG 59, col. 284–85; cf. *Catena aurea*, 7:37–39.
97. *Offeri hostiam in ara crucis*. Saint Thomas is quoting here a contemporary hymn of the Easter Season: *Ad cenam Agni providi*, etc. See Philippe (ed.), *Commentaire sur l'évangile de Saint Jean*, 466, n. 4. See also *ST* III, q. 48.

et, thinking that he was the one about whom Moses foretold: "The Lord your God will raise up a prophet for you from your brothers . . . you will listen to him" (Dt 18:15).

1099. Another opinion was of those who said, **This is the Christ**. These people had drawn closer to that [spiritual] drink, and had slaked the thirst of unbelief to a greater extent. This is what Peter himself professed: "You are the Christ, the Son of the living God" (Mt 16:16).

1100. The third opinion conflicts with the other two. First, those who hold this disagree with those who say that Jesus is the Christ; secondly, they support their opinion with an authority. So he says: **But others said**, those remaining in the dryness of unbelief, **Would the Christ come from Galilee?** For they knew that it was not predicted by the prophets that the Christ would come from Galilee. And they said what they did because they thought that Jesus had been born in Nazareth, not knowing that it was really in Bethlehem: for it was well known that he had been brought up in Nazareth, but only a few knew where he was born. Nevertheless, although the Scripture does not say that the Christ would be born in Galilee, it did foretell that he would first start out from there: "The people who walked in darkness saw a great light, and on those who lived in the region of the shadow of death, a light has risen" (Is 9:1). It even foretold that the Christ would come from Nazareth: "A flower will rise up from his roots" (Is 11:1), where the Hebrew version reads: "A Nazarene will rise up from his roots."[98]

1101. They support their objection by the authority of Scripture when they say, **Does not Scripture say that the Christ will come from the seed of David, and from David's town of Bethlehem?** We read in Jeremiah (23:5) that Jesus would come from the seed of David: "I will raise up a just branch for David." And we see that David was "the anointed of God" (2 Sam 23:1). In Micah (5:2) we read that Jesus would come from Bethlehem: "And you, Bethlehem, land of Judah: from you there will come forth, for me, a ruler of Israel."[99]

1102. Then (v. 43), the disagreement among the people is mentioned; secondly, the attempt of some of them to seize Christ; and thirdly, the failure of their attempt.

1103. **And so there was dissension among the people because of him**, that is, Christ. For it often happens that when the truth is made known, it causes dissensions and uneasiness in the hearts of the wick-

---

98. Aquinas is quoting the Latin text of Is 11:1b, "A flower *(flos)* will rise up from his roots" (the Latin text follows the Greek Septuagint). The Hebrew text reads, "A branch shall grow out of his roots." The Hebrew word for "branch" *(nēzer)*, has phonetic similarities to the Greek form of "Nazarene," and it is possible that this is the link that Matthew makes between the name of Jesus' home village and his identity as Messiah (Mt 2:23): "He will be called a Nazarene."

99. See *ST* III, q. 35, a. 7.

ed. So Jeremiah says, representing Christ: "Woe is me, my mother! Why did you give birth to me as a man of strife and dissension for all the earth" (Jer 15:10). And our Lord said: "I have not come to send peace, but the sword" (Mt 10:34).

1104. Some of them attempted to seize Christ; so he says, **some of them**, that is, those who had said, "Would the Christ come from Galilee?" **wanted to apprehend him**, to kill him out of hatred: "Pursue and seize him" (Ps 70:11); "The enemy said: 'I will pursue and seize'" (Ex 15:9). On the other hand, those who are good and those who believe want to seize Christ to enjoy him: "I will go up into the palm tree and seize its fruit" (Sg 7.8).

1105. But they were frustrated by the power of Christ. So he says: **no one laid a hand on him**, that is, because Jesus was not willing that they do so, for this depended on his power: "No one takes my soul from me, but I lay it down of myself" (below 10:18). Accordingly, when Christ did will to suffer, he did not wait for them, but he offered himself to them: "Jesus stepped forward and said to them: 'Whom are you looking for?'" (below 18:4).

1106. Then (v. 45), we see the dissension of the leaders of the people: first, their disagreement with their officers; and secondly, the disagreement among themselves (v. 50). He does three things about the first: first, he shows the leaders rebuking their officers: secondly, the testimony the officers gave about Christ; and thirdly, we see the leaders reprimanding their own officers.

1107. As to the first, let us note the evil of the leaders, that is, the chief priests and Pharisees, when they say to their officers: **Why have you not brought him?** For their evil was so great that their own officers could not please them unless they injured Christ: "They cannot sleep unless they have done something evil" (Pr 4:16).

There is a problem here about the literal meaning of the text. For since it was said before that the officers were sent to apprehend Jesus when the festival was half over (v. 32), that is, on the fourth day, and here we read that they returned on the seventh day, "On the last and greatest day of the festival" (v. 37), it seems that the Evangelist overlooked the days in between. There are two answers to this: either the Evangelist anticipated the disagreement among the people, or the officers had returned before, but it is just mentioned now to show the reason why there was dissension among the leaders.

1108. As to the second point, let us realize how good these officers were in giving this praiseworthy testimony about Christ, saying: **Never has any man spoken like this man**. They deserve our praise for three reasons. First, because of their admiration: for they admired Christ because of his teachings, not his miracles. And this brought them nearer to the truth, and further from the custom of the Jews, who looked for signs, as is said in 1 Corinthians (1:22). Secondly, we should praise them because of the ease with which they were won over: because with just a few words, Christ had captivated them and had drawn their love. Thirdly, because of their confidence: because it was to the Pharisees, who were the enemies of Christ, that they said: ***Never has any man spoken like this man.*** And these things are to be expected, for Jesus was not just a man, but the Word of God; and so his words had power to affect people. "Are not my words like fire, says the Lord, and like a hammer breaking a rock?" (Jer 23:29). And so Matthew says: "He was teaching them as one who had authority" (Mt 7:29). And his words were sweet to contemplate: "Let your voice sound in my ears, for your voice is sweet" (Sg 2:14); "How sweet are your words to my tongue!" (Ps 118:103). And his words were useful to keep in mind, because they promised eternal life: "Lord, to whom shall we go? You have the words of eternal life" (above 6:69); "I am the Lord, who teaches you things that are useful" (Is 48:17).[100]

1109. As to the third point, see the treachery of the Jews in trying to alienate the officers from Christ; ***The Pharisees then retorted***, to the officers, ***Have you too been seduced?*** Here they do three things. First, they attack what they consider a mistake of their officers; secondly, they hold up their leaders as an example; and in the third place, they reject the example of the people.

1110. They attack the officers when they say, ***Have you too been seduced?*** As if to say: We see that what he said was pleasing to you. As a matter of fact, they had been seduced, but in an admirable way, because they left the evil of unbelief and were brought to the truth of the faith. We read about this: "You seduced me, O Lord, and I was seduced" (Jer 20:7).

1111. Then they appeal to their rulers as an example, to turn the officers further from Christ, saying: ***Has any one of the rulers believed in him, or any of the Pharisees?*** There are two reasons why a person should be believed: either because of some authority or because of a religious disposition. And they say that none of these are found with Christ. As if to say: If Christ were worthy to be received, then our rulers, who have authority, would have accepted him; and so would the Pharisees, who have a religious disposition. But none of these believe in him; and so neither should you believe in him. This fulfills the saying (Ps 117:22): "The stone that the builders (that is, the rulers and the Pharisees) rejected has become the cornerstone (that is, in the hearts of the people). The Lord has done this," because his goodness is greater than man's evil.

1112. They reject the statements of the people because they are a rebuke to their own evil. So they say: ***But these people, who do not know the law, they are accursed***; therefore, you should not agree with them.

---

100. See *ST* III, q. 42.

This thought was found in Deuteronomy: "Accursed are they who do not live within the law and do not act according to it" (Dt 27:26). But they did not understand this correctly, because even those who do not have a knowledge of the law but act in harmony with it, live more within the law than those who do have a knowledge of the law yet do not keep it.[101] It is said about such people: "This people honors me with their lips, but their heart is far from me" (Mt 15:8); and in James (1:22): "Be a doer of the word, and not just a hearer."

1113. Next, we see the dissension among the rulers. First, the advice of Nicodemus is given; secondly, the opposition of the rulers; and thirdly, the outcome of the whole affair. The Evangelist does two things about the first: first, he tells us something about Nicodemus; secondly, he gives his advice.

1114. He tells us three things about Nicodemus: the first two show us the attitude of Nicodemus himself; and the second reveals the malice of the rulers. The first concerns the faith of Nicodemus, and he says: **Nicodemus, who came to him**, i.e., who believed, for to come to Christ is the same as to believe in him. The second shows the imperfection of his faith, because he came **at night**. For if he had believed perfectly, he would not have been fearful, for as we read below (12:42): "Many of the rulers believed in him; but they did not admit it because of the Pharisees, so that they would not be expelled from the synagogue." And one of these was Nicodemus.

The third thing the Evangelist tells us shows us that the rulers did not speak the truth: for they said that none of the rulers, or of the Pharisees, believed in Christ. And so the Evangelist says about Nicodemus that he **was one of them**: as if to say: If Nicodemus, who was one of the rulers, believed in Christ, then the rulers and Pharisees are speaking falsely when they say that none of the rulers believed in him. "Truly, a lie was spoken" (Jer 16:19).

1115. The advice of Nicodemus is given when he says: Does our **law judge a man without first hearing from him and knowing what he has done?** For according to the civil laws, a judgment was only to be given after a complete investigation.[102] This is why we read: "It is not the custom of the Romans to condemn any man before he has his accusers face him, and can defend himself from the charges" (Acts 25:16). "I diligently investigated the stranger's cause" (Jb 29:16). And so the law of Moses says: "Do not condemn one who is innocent and just, because I hate the wicked" (Ex 23:7).

Nicodemus said what he did because he believed in Christ and wanted to convert them to Christ; yet because he was afraid, he did not act very candidly. He thought that if they would only listen to

---

101. See *ST* I-II, q. 94.
102. See *ST* II-II, q. 60, aa. 2–3.

Christ, the words of Christ would be so effective that perhaps they would be changed like those whom they sent to Jesus, and who, when they heard Christ, were turned aside from the very act for which they had been sent.

1116. We see the opposition of the rulers to Nicodemus when he says, ***They answered and said to him***. First, they think that he has been seduced; and secondly, that he does not know the law.

As to the first, they say: ***Are you too a Galilean?*** that is, one who has been seduced by this Galilean. For they considered Christ a Galilean because he lived in Galilee. And so anyone who followed Christ they derisively called a Galilean. "The girl servant said to Peter: 'You are a Galilean, are you not?'" (Mt 26:69); "Do you also want to become his disciples?" (below 9:27).

About his ignorance of the law, they say: ***Look at the Scriptures and see that the Prophet will not come from Galilee***. But since Nicodemus was a teacher of the law, he did not have to look again. It is as if they were saying: Although you are a teacher, you do not know this. Something like this was said before: "You are a teacher in Israel and you do not know these things?" (above 3:10). Now even though the Old Testament does not explicitly say that a prophet will come from Galilee, it does say that the Lord of the prophets would come from there, according to: "A flower (i.e., a Nazarene) will arise from his root . . . and the Spirit of the Lord will rest upon him," as we read in Isaiah (11:1).

1117. The outcome of this dissension is seen to be useless. So he says: ***Then every man returned***, leaving the matter unfinished, ***to his own house***, i.e., to what belonged to him, empty of faith and frustrated in his evil desires. "He frustrates the plans of the wicked" (Jb 5:13); "God destroys the plans of rulers, and frustrates the schemes of the people" (Ps 32:10).

Or, each returned ***to his own house***, i.e., to the evil of his unbelief and irreverence. "I know where you live: where the throne of Satan is. You hold to my name, and you have not denied my faith" (Rev 2:13).

CHAPTER 8

LECTURE 1

1 Jesus however proceeded to the Mount of Olives, 2 and early in the morning he came again to the temple. All the people came to him, and sitting down, he taught them. 3 Then the scribes and Pharisees brought in a woman caught in adultery and placed her in their midst. 4 They said to him, "Master, this woman has just now been caught in adultery. 5 In the Law, Moses commanded us to stone such a woman. But what do you say?" 6 (They said this to test him so that they could accuse him.) But Jesus bending down wrote on the ground with his finger. 7 As they persisted in the question, he stood up and said to them: "Whoever among you is without sin, let him be the first to cast a stone at her." 8 And again bending down, he wrote on the ground. 9 On hearing this, one after the other departed, beginning with the oldest, and there remained only Jesus and the woman standing there in the center. 10 Rising up, Jesus asked the woman: "Woman, where are those who accuse you? Has no one condemned you?" 11 To which she replied, "No one, Lord." Then Jesus said: "Nor will I condemn you. Go and do not sin again."[1]

1118. After having treated of the origin of the doctrine of Christ, the Evangelist here considers its power. Now the doctrine of Christ has the power both to enlighten and to give life, because his words are spirit and life. So first, he treats of the power of Christ's doctrine to enlighten; secondly, of its power to give life (10:1). He shows the power of Christ's doctrine to enlighten, first by words; and secondly, by a miracle (9:1). As to the first, he does two things: first, he presents the teaching of Christ; secondly, he shows the power of his teaching (8:12).

There are two things that pertain to the office of a teacher: to instruct the devout or sincere, and to repel opponents. So first, Christ instructs those who are sincere; and secondly, he repels his opponents (v. 3).[2] The Evangelist does three things with respect to the first: first, he mentions the place where this teaching takes place; secondly, he mentions those who listened to it; and thirdly, the teacher. This teach-

---

1. St. Thomas refers to Jn 8:7 in *ST* III, q. 87, a. 4, obj. 1; and to Jn 8:11 in *ST* III, q. 84, a. 5, obj. 3; III, q. 86, a. 2.
2. See *ST* III, q. 42, aa. 1–2.

ing took place in the temple; so he first mentions that Jesus left the temple, and then that he returned.

1119. He mentions that Jesus left the temple when he says, **Jesus however proceeded to the Mount of Olives**. For our Lord made it his practice, when he was at Jerusalem on the festival days, to preach in the temple and to work miracles and signs during the day, and when evening came, he would return to Bethany (which was on the Mount of Olives) as the guest of Lazarus' sisters, Martha and Mary. With this in mind, the Evangelist says that since Jesus had remained in the temple and preached on the last day of the great feast, in the evening, **Jesus proceeded to the Mount of Olives**, where Bethany was located.

And this is appropriate to a mystery: for as Augustine[3] says, where was it appropriate for Christ to teach and show his mercy, if not on the Mount of Olives, the mount of anointing and of grace. The olive (*oliva*) signifies mercy; so also in Greek, *oleos* is the same as mercy. And Luke (10:24) tells us that the Samaritan applied oil and wine, which correspond to mercy and the stringency of judgment. Again, oil is healing: "Wounds and bruises and swelling sores are not bandaged or dressed, or soothed with oil" (Is 1:6). It also signifies the medicine of spiritual grace which has been transmitted to us by Christ: "God, your God, has anointed you with the oil of gladness above your fellows" (Ps 44:8); and again, "like the precious ointment on the head which ran down upon the beard" (Ps 132:2); and in Job we read that "The rock poured out rivers of oil" (Jb 29:6).

1120. Christ's return to the temple is described as being early; thus he says, **and early in the morning he came again to the temple**. This signifies that he was about to impart knowledge and manifest his grace in his temple, that is, in his believers: "We have received your mercy, O God, in the middle of your temple" (Ps 47:10). The fact that he returned early in the morning signifies the rising light of new grace: "His going forth is as sure as the dawn" (Hos 6:3).

1121. Those who listened to his teaching were the sincere among the people; thus he says, **all the people came to him**: "The assembly of the people will surround you" (Ps 7:8).

1122. Their teacher is presented as seated, **and sitting down**, that is, going down to their level, so that his teaching would be more easily understood. His sitting down signifies the humility of his Incarnation: "You knew when I sat down, and when I rose" (Ps 138:1). Because it was through the human nature that our Lord assumed that he became visible, we began to be instructed in the divine matters more easily. So he says, **sitting down, he taught them**, that is, the simple, and those who respected his teaching: "He will teach his ways to the gentle, and

---

3. *Tract. in Io.* 33. 3; PL 35, col. 1648; see also Alcuin, *Comm. in S. Ioannis Evang.* 4. 19; PL 100, col. 853 B–C; cf. *Catena aurea,* 8:1–11.

will guide the mild in judgment" (Ps 24:9); "He will teach us his ways" (Is 2:3).

1123. Then (v. 3), our Lord wards off his opponents. First, we see him tested, so that he can then be accused; and secondly, he checks his accusers (v. 6b). As to the first, the Evangelist does three things: first, he mentions the occasion for the test; secondly, he describes the test itself (v. 4); and thirdly, the purpose of those who were testing our Lord.

1124. The occasion for the test is a woman's adultery. And so first, her accusers detail the crime; and also exhibit the sinner.

As to the first, the Evangelist says, **Then the scribes and Pharisees brought in a woman caught in adultery**. As Augustine[4] says, three things were noteworthy about Christ: his truth, his gentleness, and his justice. Indeed, it was predicted about him: "Go forth and reign, because of truth, gentleness, and justice" (Ps 44:5). For he set forth the truth as a teacher; and the Pharisees and scribes noticed this while he was teaching: "If I speak the truth, why do you not believe me?" (8:46). Since they could find nothing false in his words or his teachings, they had ceased their accusations on that score. He showed his gentleness as a liberator or savior; and they saw this when he could not be provoked against his enemies and persecutors: "When he was reviled, he did not revile" (1 Pet 2:23). Thus Matthew has: "Learn from me, for I am gentle and humble of heart" (11:29). Thus they did not accuse him on this point. And he exercised justice as its advocate; he did this because it was not yet known among the Jews, especially in legal proceedings. It was on this point that they wanted to test him, to see if he would abandon justice for the sake of mercy. So they present him with a known crime, deserving denunciation, adultery: "Every woman who is a harlot will be walked on like dung on the road" (Sir 9:10). Then they present the sinner in person to further influence him: **and placed her in their midst**. "This woman will be brought into the assembly, and among the sons of God" (Sir 23:24).

1125. The Evangelist shows them proceeding with their test. First, they point out the woman's fault; secondly, they state the justice of the case according to the Law; thirdly, they ask him for his verdict.

1126. They point out the woman's fault when they say **this woman has just now been caught in adultery**. They detail her fault in three ways, calculated to deflect Christ from his gentle manner. First, they mention the freshness of her fault, saying *just now*; for an old fault does not affect us so much, because the person might have made amends. Secondly, they note its certainty, saying, *caught*, so that she could not excuse herself. This is characteristic of women, as we see from Proverbs (30:20): "She wipes her mouth and says: 'I have done no evil.'" Thirdly, they point out that her fault is great, *in adultery*, which is a serious

---

4. *Tract. in Io.* 33. 4; PL 35, col. 1648–49; cf. *Catena aurea*, 8:1–11.

crime and the cause of many evils. "Every woman who is an adulteress will sin" (Sir 9:10; Vulgate), and first of all against the law of her God.

1127. They appeal to the justice contained in the Law when they remark, *in the Law*, that is, in Leviticus (20:10) and in Deuteronomy (22:21), *Moses commanded us to stone such a woman.*

1128. They ask Jesus for his verdict when they say, *But what do you say?* Their question is a trap, for they are saying in effect: If he decides that she should be let go, he will not be acting according to justice, yet he cannot condemn her because he came to seek and to save those who are lost: "God did not send his Son into the world to judge the world, but that the world might be saved through him" (3:17). Now the Law could not command anything unjust. Thus, Jesus does not say, "Let her go," lest he seem to be acting in violation of the Law.

1129. The Evangelist reveals the malicious intention behind those who were questioning Jesus when he says, *They said this to test him so that they could accuse him.* For they thought that Christ would say that she should be let go, so as not to be acting contrary to his gentle manner; and then they would accuse him of acting in violation of the Law: "Let us not test Christ as they did," as we read in 1 Corinthians (10:9).

1130. Then, Jesus checks his enemies by his wisdom. The Pharisees were testing him on two points: his justice and his mercy. But Jesus preserved both in his answer. First, the Evangelist shows how Jesus kept to what was just; and secondly, that he did not abandon mercy (v. 7). As to the first, he does two things: first, he mentions the sentence in accordance with justice; secondly the effect of this sentence (v. 9). About the first he does three things: first, we see Jesus writing his sentence; then pronouncing it; and thirdly, continuing again to write it down.

1131. Jesus wrote his sentence on the earth with his finger: *But Jesus bending down wrote on the ground with his finger.* Some say that he wrote the words of Jeremiah: "O earth, earth, listen . . . write down this man as sterile" (Jer 22:29). According to others, and this is the better opinion, Jesus wrote down the very words he spoke, that is, *Whoever among you is without sin, let him be the first to cast a stone at her.* However, neither of these opinions is certain.

Jesus wrote on the earth for three reasons. First, according to Augustine,[5] to show that those who were testing him would be written on the earth: "O Lord, all who leave you will be written on the earth" (Jer 17:13). But those who are just and the disciples who follow him are written in heaven: "Rejoice, because your names are written in heaven" (Lk 10:20). Secondly, he wrote on earth to show that he would perform signs on earth, for he who writes makes signs. Thus, to write on the earth is to make signs. And so he says that Jesus was

---

5. *De cons. Evang.* 4. 10. 17; PL 34, col. 1225–26; cf. *Catena aurea*, 8:1–11.

bending down, by the mystery of the Incarnation, by means of which he performed miracles in the flesh he had assumed. Thirdly, he wrote on the earth because the Old Law was written on tablets of stone (Ex 31; 2 Cor 3), which signify its harshness: "A man who violates the law of Moses dies without mercy" (Heb 10:28). But the earth is soft. And so Jesus wrote on the earth to show the sweetness and the softness of the New Law that he gave to us.[6]

We can see from this that there are three things to be considered in giving sentences. First, there should be kindness in condescending to those to be punished; and so he says, Jesus was *bending down*: "There is judgment without mercy to him who does not have mercy" (Jas 2:13); "If a man is overtaken in any fault, you who are spiritual instruct him in a spirit of mildness" (Gal 6:1). Secondly, there should be discretion in determining the judgment and so he says that *Jesus wrote with his finger*, which because of its flexibility signifies discretion: "The fingers of a man's hand appeared, writing" (Dn 5:5). Thirdly, there should be certitude about the sentence given; and so he says, *Jesus wrote*.

1132. It was at their insistence that Jesus gave his sentence; and so the Evangelist says, *As they persisted in the question, he stood up and said to them: Whoever among you is without sin, let him be the first to cast a stone at her*. The Pharisees were violators of the Law; and yet they tried to accuse Christ of violating the Law and were attempting to make him condemn the woman. So Christ proposes a sentence in accord with justice, saying, *Whoever among you is without sin*. He is saying in effect: Let the sinner be punished, but not by sinners; let the Law be accomplished, but not by those who break it, because "When you judge another you condemn yourself" (Rom 2:1). Therefore, either let this woman go, or suffer the penalty of the Law with her.

1133. Here the question arises as to whether a sinful judge sins by passing sentence against another person who has committed the same sin. It is obvious that if the judge who passes sentence is a public sinner, he sins by giving scandal. Yet, this seems to be true also if his sin is hidden, for we read in Romans (2:1): "When you judge another you condemn yourself." However, it is clear that no one condemns himself except by sinning. And thus it seems that he sins by judging another.

My answer to this is that two distinctions have to be made. For the judge is either continuing in his determination to sin, or he has repented of his sins; and again, he is either punishing as a minister of the law or on his own initiative. Now if he has repented of his sin, he is no longer a sinner, and so he can pass sentence without sinning. But if he continues in his determination to sin, he does not sin in passing sentence if he does this as a minister of the law; although he would be sin-

---

6. See *ST* I-II, q. 106, a. 1.

ning by doing the very things for which he deserves a similar sentence. But if he passes sentence on his own authority, then I say that he sins in justice, but from some evil root; otherwise he would first punish in himself what he notices in someone else, because "A just person is the first to accuse himself" (Pr 18:17).[7]

1134. Jesus continued to write, *and again bending down, he wrote*. He did this, first, to show the firmness of his sentence, "God is not like a man, who may lie, or like a son of man, so that he may change" (Num 23:19). Secondly, he did it to show that they were not worthy to look at him. Because he had disturbed them with his zeal for justice, he did not think it fit to look at them, but turned from their sight. Thirdly, he did this out of consideration for their embarrassment, to give them complete freedom to leave.

1135. The effect of his justice is their embarrassment, for *on hearing this, one after the other departed*, both because they had been involved in more serious sins and their conscience gnawed them more: "Iniquity came out from the elder judges who were seen to rule the people" (Dan 13:5), and because they better realized the fairness of the sentence he gave: "I will go therefore to the great men and speak to them: for they have known the way of the Lord and the judgment of their God" (Jer 5:5).

And there remained only Jesus and the woman standing there, that is, mercy and misery. Jesus alone remained because he alone was without sin; as the Psalm says (Ps 13:1): "There is no one who does what is good not even one," except Christ. So perhaps this woman was afraid, and thought she would be punished by him.

If only Jesus remained, why does it say that the woman was standing there *in the center*? I answer that the woman was standing in the center of the disciples, and so the word *only* excludes outsiders, not the disciples. Or, we could say, in the *center*, that is, in doubt whether she would be forgiven or condemned. And so it is clear that our Lord's answer preserved justice.

1136. Then (v. 10), he shows that Jesus did not abandon mercy, but gave a merciful sentence. First, Jesus questions the woman; then forgives her; and finally, cautions her.

1137. Jesus questioned her about her accusers; thus he says that *Jesus rising up*, that is, turning from the ground on which he was writing and looking at the woman, asked her, **Woman, where are those who accuse you?** He asks about her condemnation saying, **Has no one condemned you?** And she answers, **No one, Lord**.

1138. Jesus forgives her; and so it says, **Then Jesus said: Nor will I condemn you**, I who perhaps you feared would condemn you, because

---

7. See *ST* II-II, q. 60, a. 2.

you saw that I was without sin. This should not surprise us for "God did not send his Son into the world to judge the world, but that the world might be saved through him" (3:17); "I do not desire the death of the sinner" (Ez 18:23). And he forgave her sin without imposing any penance on her because since he made her inwardly just by outwardly forgiving her, he was well able to change her so much within by sufficient sorrow for her sins that she would be made free from any penance. This should not be taken as a precedent for anyone to forgive another without confession and the assigning of a penance on the ground of Christ's example, for Christ has power over the sacraments, and could confer the effect without the sacrament. No mere man can do this.[8]

1139. Finally, Jesus cautions her when he says, **Go, and do not sin again.** There were two things in that woman: her nature and her sin. Our Lord could have condemned both. For example, he could have condemned her nature if he had ordered them to stone her, and he could have condemned her sin if he had not forgiven her. He was also able to absolve each. For example, if he had given her license to sin, saying: "Go, live as you wish, and put your hope in my freeing you. No matter how much you sin, I will free you even from Gehenna and from the tortures of hell." But our Lord does not love sin, and does not favor wrongdoing, and so he condemned her sin but not her nature, saying, **Go, and do not sin again.** We see here how kind our Lord is because of his gentleness, and how just he is because of his truth.

LECTURE 2

12 Again Jesus spoke to them saying: "I am the light of the world. Whoever follows me will not walk in darkness, but he will have the light of life." 13 The Pharisees then said to him, "You are bearing witness to yourself; your testimony is not true." 14 Jesus replied: "Even though I bear witness concerning myself, my testimony is true, because I know where I come from and where I am going. But you do not know where I come from, or where I am going. 15 You judge according to the flesh. I do not judge anyone. 16 And if I do judge, my judgment is true because I am not alone; but there is me and the Father who sent me. 17 And it is written in your Law that the testimony of two men is true. 18 It is I who bear witness to myself, and the Father who sent me who bears witness concerning me." 19 They therefore said to him, "Where is your Father?" Jesus replied, "You know neither me nor my Father. If you did know me, you might also know my Father." 20 Jesus spoke

---

8. See *ST* III, q. 64, a. 3.

these words in the treasury where he was teaching in the temple; and no one arrested him because his hour had not yet come.[9]

1140. The Evangelist has presented Christ as teaching; now he shows, first, the power which this teaching has to give light, and secondly, what Christ himself said about it (v. 13). With respect to the first he does three things: first, he states Christ's prerogative concerning spiritual light; secondly, the effect of this prerogative, **Whoever follows me will not walk in darkness**; and thirdly, its fruit, **but he will have the light of life**.

1141. He says, concerning the prerogative of Christ, who is the light, to the spiritual light, **Again Jesus spoke to them saying: I am the light of the world**. We can relate this statement with what went before in this way. Christ had said, when forgiving the woman's sin, "Nor will I condemn you." And so they would have no doubt that he could forgive and pardon sins, he saw fit to show the power of his divinity more openly by saying that he is the light which drives away the darkness of sin. Or, we could connect this statement with what the Pharisees said before (7:52): "Look at the Scriptures and see that the Prophet will not come from Galilee." For they thought of him as a Galilean and linked to a definite place, and so they rejected his teaching. So our Lord shows them that he is in the universal light of the entire world, saying, **I am the light of the world**, not just of Galilee, or of Palestine, or of Judea.

1142. The Manicheans, as Augustine[10] relates, misunderstood this: for since they judged by their imagination, which does not rise to intellectual and spiritual realities, they believed that nothing but bodies existed. Thus they said that God was a body; and a certain infinite light.[11] Further, they thought that the sun that we see with our physical eyes was Christ the Lord. And that is why, according to them, Christ said, **I am the light of the world**. But this cannot hold up, and the Catholic Church rejects such a fiction. For this physical sun is a light which can be perceived by sense. Consequently, it is not the highest light, which intellect alone grasps, and which is the intelligible light characteristic of the rational creature. Christ says about this light here: **I am the light of the world**. And above we read: "He was the true light, which enlightens every man coming into this world" (1:9). Sense perceptible light, however, is a certain image of spiritual light, for every sensible thing is something particular, whereas intellectual things are a kind of whole. Just as particular light has an effect on the thing seen, inasmuch as it makes colors actually visible, as well as on the one see-

---

9. St. Thomas refers to Jn 8:12 in *ST* II-II, q 8, a. 4, *sed contra*; to Jn 8:16 in *ST* I, q. 43, a. 1 *sed contra* and to Jn 8:17 in *ST* I-II, q. 105, a. 2, ad 8; II-II, q. 70, a. 2.
10. *Tract. in Io.* 34. 2; PL 35, col. 1652; cf. *Catena aurea*, 8:12.
11. See *ST* I, q. 3, a. 1.

ing, because through it the eye is conditioned for seeing, so intellectual light makes the intellect to know because whatever light is in the rational creature is all derived from that supreme light "which enlightens every man coming into the world." Furthermore, it makes all things to be actually intelligible inasmuch as all forms are derived from it, forms which give things the capability of being known, just as all the forms of artifacts are derived from the art and reason on the artisan: "How magnificent are your works, O Lord! You have made all things in wisdom" (Ps 103:24).[12] Thus Christ truly says here: *I am the light of the world*; not the sun which was made, but the one who made the sun. Yet as Augustine[13] says, the Light which made the sun was himself made under the sun and covered with a cloud of flesh, not in order to hide but to be moderated [to our weakness].

1143. This also eliminates the heresy of Nestorius, who said that the Son of God was united to human nature by a mere indwelling.[14] For it is obvious that the one who said, *I am the light of the world*, was a human being. Therefore, unless the one who spoke and appeared as a human being was also the person of the Son of God, he could not have said, *I am the light of the world*, but "The light of the world dwells in me."

1144. The effect of this light is to expel darkness; and so he says, *Whoever follows me will not walk in darkness*. Because this light is universal, it universally expels all darkness. Now there are three kinds of darkness. There is the darkness of ignorance: "They have neither known nor understood; they walk in darkness" (Ps 81:5); and this is the darkness reason has of itself, insofar as it is darkened of itself. There is the darkness of sin: "You were at one time darkness, but now you are light in the Lord" (Eph 5:8). This darkness belongs to human reason not of itself, but from the affections which, by being badly disposed by passion or habit, seek something as good that is not really good.[15] Further, there is the darkness of eternal damnation: "Cast the unprofitable servant into the exterior darkness" (Mt 25:30). The first two kinds of darkness are found in this life; but the third is at the end of life. Thus, *Whoever follows me will not walk in darkness*: the darkness of ignorance, because I am the truth; nor the darkness of sin, because I am the way; nor the darkness of eternal damnation, because I am the life.

1145. He next adds the fruit of his teaching, *but he will have the light of life*, for one who has the light is outside the darkness of damnation. He says, *Whoever follows me*, because just as one who does not want to stumble in the dark has to follow the one who is carrying the

---

12. See *ST* I, q. 84, a. 5.
13. *Tract. in Io.* 34. 4; PL 35, col. 1653–54; cf. *Catena aurea*, 8:12.
14. See *ST* III, q. 2, a. 6.
15. See *ST* I-II, q. 85, a. 3.

light, so one who wants to be saved must, by believing and loving, follow Christ, who is the light.[16] This is the way the apostles followed him (Mt 4). Because physical light can fail because it sets, it happens that one who follows it meets with darkness. But the light we are talking about here does not set and never fails; consequently, one who follows it has an unfailing light, that is, an unfailing light of life. For the light that is visible does not give life, but gives us an external aid because we live insofar as we have understanding, and this is a certain participation in this light. And when this light completely shines upon us we will then have perfect life: "With you is the fountain of life, and in your light we will see the light" (Ps 35:10). This is the same as saying: We will have life perfectly or completely when we see this light as it is.[17] Thus we read further on: "This is eternal life: that they know you, the only true God and Jesus Christ, whom you have sent" (17:3).

Note that the phrase, *whoever follows me*, pertains to our merits; while the statement, *he will have the light of life*, pertains to our reward.

1146. The Evangelist mentions three things that Jesus says about himself. First, *I am the light of the world*; secondly, *I am going away* (v. 21); and thirdly, *if any one keeps my word, he will not see death forever* (v. 51).

The first thing he said was, *I am the light of the world*; and this troubled the Jews. So first, he shows their opposition; secondly, how Jesus proved that they were wrong by showing what he said was true (v. 14).

1147. With respect to the first, it is obvious that what Jesus said in the temple, he said in the presence of the people. But now he is speaking before the Pharisees, and so they said to him: *You are bearing witness to yourself; your testimony is not true*. They were saying in effect: Because you are bearing witness to yourself, your testimony is not true.

Now in human affairs it is neither acceptable nor fitting that a person praise himself: "Let another praise you, and not your own mouth" (Pr 27:2), because self-praise does not make a person commendable, but being commended by God does: "It is not he who commends himself who is approved, but he whom God commends" (2 Cor 10:18), because only God perfectly knows a person.[18] But no one can really sufficiently commend God except God himself; and so it is fitting that he bear witness to himself, and also to men: "My witness is in heaven" (Jb 16:20). Thus the opinion of the Jews was mistaken.

1148. Next (v. 14), our Lord rejects their opposition: first, by the authority of his Father; secondly, by answering their rejection, which

16. See *ST* II-II, q. 2, aa. 3, 7, 8; II-II, q. 4, a. 3.
17. See *ST* I, q. 12, aa. 3, 5.
18. See *ST* II-II, q. 112, a. 2.

arose concerning his Father (v. 19). The opposition of the Jews arose from a certain conclusion which they drew: and so first he shows that their conclusion is not true; secondly, he proves that his own testimony is true (v. 1b). He does two things concerning the first: first, he shows that their conclusion is false; secondly, he adds the reason for their error (v. 14b).

1149. Their conclusion was that the testimony of Christ was not true, because he bore witness to himself. But our Lord says the opposite, namely, that because of this it is true. Jesus replied: *Even though I bear witness concerning myself, my testimony is true*; and it is true because I know where I come from and where *I am going*. It is like saying, according to Chrysostom,[19] my testimony is true because I am from God, and because I am God, and because I am the Son of God: "God is truthful" (Rom 3:4).

He says, *I know where I come from*, that is, my origin, *and where I am going*, that is, to the Father, whom no one but the Son can know perfectly: "No one knows the Father except the Son, and he to whom the Son wishes to reveal him" (Mt 11:27). This does not imply that anyone who knows, by love and understanding, where he comes from and where he is going can speak only the truth, for we all come from God and are going to God. But God is truth: how much more, then, does the Son of God speak the truth, he who knows perfectly where he comes from and where he is going!

1150. Then when he says, *But you do not know where I come from or where I am going*, he shows the reason for their error, which was their ignorance of the divinity of Christ. For it was because they did not know this that they judged him according to his human nature. Thus, there were two reasons for their error. One, because they did not know his divinity; the other, because they judged him only by his human nature. And so he says, with respect to the first, *you do no know where I come from*, that is, my eternal procession from the Father, *or where I am going*, "The one who sent me is truthful. Whatever I have heard from him, this I declare to the world" (8:26); "From where, then, does wisdom come?" (Jb 28:20); "Who will state his origin?" (Is 53:8).

As for the second reason for their error, he says, *you judge according to the flesh*, that is, you judge me thinking that I am merely flesh and not God. Or, we could say, *according to the flesh*, that is, wickedly and unjustly. For just as to live according to the flesh is to live wickedly, so to judge according to the flesh is to judge unjustly.

1151. Then (v. 15b), he shows that his testimony is true, and that it is false to say that he alone is bearing witness to himself. Because mention was now made about judging, he shows, first, that he is not

---

19. *Hom. in Io.* 52. 2; PG 59, col. 289; cf. *Catena aurea*, 8:13–18.

alone in judging; and secondly, that he is not alone in bearing witness (v. 17). He does three things about the first: first, he says that his judgment is deferred; secondly, that his judgment is true; and thirdly, he gives the reason why his judgment is true.

1152. He mentions that his judgment is deferred when he says, *I do not judge anyone*. He is saying in effect: You judge wickedly, *but I do not judge anyone*: "God did not send his Son into the world to judge the world, but that the world might be saved through him" (3:17). Or, we could say, *I do not judge anyone*, according to the flesh, as you judge: "He will not judge by the sight of his eyes, or reprove by what his ears hear" (Is 11:3).

1153. Yet, I will judge at some time, because "The Father has given all judgment to the Son" (5:22). And then, *my judgment is true*, that is, just: "He will judge the people with justice" (Ps 95:10); "We know that the judgment of God is according to the truth" (Rom 2:2).[20] This shows that his judgment is true.

1154. He gives the reason for its truth when he says, *because I am not alone*. What Christ said before, "The Father himself judges no one" (5:22), should be understood to refer to the Father in isolation from the Son. Or, again, he said this because the Father will not appear visibly to all at the judgment.[21] Thus he says, *I am not alone*, because he is not left alone by the Father, but is with him: "I am in the Father, and the Father is in me" (14:10).[22]

This statement rejects the error of Sabellius, who said that the Father and the Son were the same person, the only difference between them being in their names. But if this were true, Christ would not have said: *I am not alone; but there is me and the Father who sent me*. He would rather have said: "I am the Father, and I am the Son." We should, therefore, distinguish between the persons, and realize that the Son is not the Father.

1155. Then (v. 17), he shows that he is not alone in bearing witness. He does not defer bearing witness, as he does his judging. Thus he does not say, "I do not bear witness." First, he mentions the Law; secondly, he gives his conclusion (v. 18).

1156. He says, *And it is written in your Law*, the Law which was given to you—"Moses imposed a law" (Sir 24:33)—*that the testimony of two men is true*; for it is written in Deuteronomy (19:15): "By the mouth of two or three witnesses the issue will be settled."

According to Augustine[23] the statement *that the testimony of two men is true*, involves a great difficulty. For it could happen that both of them would be lying. Indeed, the chaste Susanna was harassed by two

---

20. See *ST* III, q. 59, a. 2. 21. See *ST* III, q. 59, a. 1.
22. See *ST* I, q. 42, a. 5.
23. *Tract. in Io.* 36. 10; PL 35, col. 1669; cf. *Catena aurea*, 8:13–18.

false witnesses (Dan 13), and all the people lied about Christ. I answer that the statement, *the testimony of two men is true*, means that such testimony should be regarded as true when giving a verdict. The reason for this is that true certitude cannot be obtained when human acts are in question, and so in its place one takes what can be considered the more certain, that is, what is said by a number of witnesses: for it is more probable that one person might lie than many: "A threefold cord is not easily broken" (Ecc 4:12).

When we read, "By the mouth of two or three witnesses the issue will be settled" (Dt 19:15), we are led, as Augustine[24] says, to a consideration of the Trinity, in which truth is permanently established, from which all truths are derived. It says, "of two or three," because in Sacred Scripture sometimes three Persons are enumerated and at other times two Persons, in which is implied the Holy Spirit, who is the bond of the other two.

1157. If, therefore, the testimony of two or three is true, my testimony is true, because *It is I who bear witness to myself and the Father who sent me who bears witness concerning me*: "I have testimony that is greater than that of John" (5:36).

But this does not seem to be to the point. First, because the Father of the Son of God is not a man, while Christ says, *the testimony of two men is true*. Secondly, because there are two witnesses to someone when they are testifying about a third person; but if one testifies to one of the two, there are not two witnesses. Thus, since Christ is testifying about himself, and the Father is also testifying about Christ, it does not seem that there are two witnesses. To answer this we must say that Christ is here arguing from the lesser to the greater. For it is clear that the truth of God is greater than the truth of a man. So, therefore, if they believe in the testimony of men, then they should believe the testimony of God much more. "If you receive the testimony of men, the testimony of God is greater" (1 Jn 5:9). In addition, he says this to show that he is consubstantial with the Father, and does not need outside testimony, as Chrysostom[25] says.

1158. Next (v. 19), we see the question arising about Christ's Father. First, the Evangelist mentions the question asked by the Jews; then Christ's answer; and thirdly, he intimates the security of Christ.

1159. The question which the Jews had for Christ was about his Father, where his Father was. They said to him: *Where is your Father?* for they thought that the Father of Christ was a man, just like their own fathers. Because they heard him say, "I am not alone; but there is me and the Father who sent me," and since they saw that he was now alone, they asked him, *Where is your Father?*

---

24. Ibid; cf. *Catena aurea*, 8:13–18.
25. *Hom. in Io.* 52. 3; PG 59, col. 291; cf. *Catena aurea*, 8:13–18.

Or, we could say that they were here speaking with a certain irony and contempt, saying in effect: "Why do you speak to us so often about your Father? Is he so great that his testimony should be believed?" For they were thinking of Joseph, who was an unknown, and a person of low status; and they were ignorant of the Father: "So the Gentiles will not say: 'Where is their God'" (Ps 113:10).

1160. Christ's answer is mysterious: **You know neither me nor my Father.** Christ does not reveal the truth to them because they were questioning him not because they desired to learn, but in order to belittle him. Rather, he first shows them knowledge of the truth. He shows them their ignorance when he says, *you know neither me*. He is saying: You should not be asking about my Father, because you do not know me. For since you regard me as a man, you are asking about my Father as though he were a man. But because you do not know me, neither can you know my Father.

1161. This seems to conflict with what he said above: "You do indeed know me, and you know where I come from" (7:27). The answer to this is that they did know him according to his humanity, but not according to his divinity.

We should note, according to Origen,[26] that some have misunderstood this, and they said that the Father of Christ was not the God of the Old Testament: for the Jews knew the God of the Old Testament, according to "God is known in Judea" (Ps 75:1). There are four answers to this. First, our Lord says that the Jews did not know his Father because insofar as they do not keep his commandments they are acting like those who do not know him. This answer refers to their conduct. Secondly, they are said not to know God because they did not cling to him spiritually by love: for one who knows something adheres to it. Thirdly, because although they did know him through faith, they did not have a full knowledge of him: "No one has ever seen God; it is the Only Begotten Son, who is in the bosom of the Father, who has made him known" (1:18). Fourthly, because in the Old Testament the Father was known under the aspect of God Almighty: "I appeared to Abraham, to Isaac and to Jacob as God Almighty, but my name, Lord, I did not show them" (Ex 6:3), that is, under the aspect of Father. Thus, although they knew him as God Almighty, they did not know him as the Father of a consubstantial Son.[27]

1162. Christ says that he is the way to arrive at a knowledge of the Father, **If you did know me.** He is saying in effect: Because I speak of my Father, who is hidden, it is first necessary that you know me, and then you might also know my Father. For the Son is the way to the knowledge of the Father: "If you had known me, you would have also

---

26. *Comm. in Io.* XIX. 3, no. 12; PG 14, col. 528C; cf. *Catena aurea*, 8:19–20. The four answers of Thomas are inspired by those in Origen.

27. See *ST* I, q. 33, a. 3.

known my Father" (14:7). As Augustine[28] says, what does **If you did know me** mean, except, "I and the Father are one" (10:30). It is customary when you see someone who is like someone else to say: "If you have seen one, you have seen the other"; not that the Son is the Father, but he is like the Father.

He says, **you might**, not to indicate a doubt, but as a rebuke. It would be like being irritated with your servant and saying to him: "Have you no respect for me? Just remember that I might be your master."

1163. The Evangelist shows the security with which Christ answered when he says, **Jesus spoke these words in the treasury**. We see the first from the place where he taught, that is, in the treasury (*gazophylacium*) and in the temple. For *gaza* is the Persian word for "riches," and *philaxe* for "keep." Thus *gazophylacium* is the word used in Sacred Scripture for the chest in which riches are kept. It is used in this sense in 2 Kings (12:9): "And Jehoiada the priest took a chest (*gazophylacium*) and bored a hole in its top, and put it by the altar, to the right of those coming into the house of the Lord. And the priests who kept the doors put into it all the money that was brought to the temple of the Lord." Sometimes, however, it was used to indicate the building where riches were kept; and this is the way it was used here.

We can also see Christ's security from the fact that those who had been sent to arrest him could not do so, because he was not willing. Thus the Evangelist says, **and no one arrested him because his hour had not yet come**, that is, the time for him to suffer, an hour not fixed by fate, but predetermined from all eternity by his own will.[29] Thus Augustine[30] says: "His hour had not yet come, not in which he would be forced to die, but in which he would not refuse being killed."

1164. We may note, according to Origen,[31] that whenever the place where our Lord did something is mentioned, this is done because of some mystery. Thus Christ taught in the treasury, the place where riches were kept, to signify that the coins, that is, the words of his teaching, are impressed with the image of the great King.

Note also that when Christ was teaching, **no one arrested him**, because his words were stronger than those who wanted to seize him; but when he willed to be crucified, then he became silent.

LECTURE 3

21 Again he said to them: "I am going away; and you will seek me, and you will die in your sin. Where I am going, you cannot come."

28. *Tract. in Io.* 37. 7; PL 35, col. 1673; cf. *Catena aurea*, 8:19–20.
29. See *ST* I, q. 116, a. 4; III, q. 24, a. 1; III, q. 46, a. 9.
30. *Tract. in Io.* 37. 9; PL 35, col. 1674; cf. *Catena aurea*, 8:19–20.
31. *Comm. in Io.* XIX. 7, no. 40; PG 14, col. 537A–B; cf. *Catena aurea*, 8:19–20.

22 (So the Jews wondered, "Will he kill himself, since he says, 'Where I am going, you cannot come'?") 23 To them he said: "You are from below; I am from above. You are of this world; I am not of this world. 24 Therefore I said to you that you will die in your sins. For if you do not believe that I AM, you will die in your sin." 25 Then they asked him, "Who are you?" Jesus replied: "The source (beginning) who is also speaking to you. 26 I have much to say about you and much to judge. But the one who sent me is truthful. Whatever I have heard from him, this I declare to the world." 27 (And they did not realize that he was calling God his Father.) 28 So Jesus said to them: "When you have lifted up the Son of Man, then you will understand that I AM, and that I do nothing of myself; but as the Father taught me, so I speak. 29 He who sent me is with me; he has not deserted me, because I always do what is pleasing to him." 30 Because he spoke in this way, many came to believe in him.[32]

1165. After our Lord showed his special position with respect to light, he here reveals the effect of this light, that is, that it frees us from darkness. First, he shows that the Jews are imprisoned in darkness; secondly, he teaches the remedy which can free them (v. 22). He does three things concerning the first: first, our Lord tells them he is going to leave; secondly, he reveals the perverse plans of the Jews, and thirdly, he mentions what they will be deprived of.

1166. Our Lord says that he is going to leave them by his death, *I am going away*. We can see two things from this. First, that he is going to die voluntarily, that is, as going, and not as one led by someone else: "I am going to him who sent me" (16:5); "No one takes my life from me, but I lay it down of myself" (10:18). And so this appropriately follows what went before: for he had said, "and no one arrested him" (8:20). Why? Because he is going willingly, on his own.[33]

Secondly, we can see that the death of Christ was a journey to that place from which he had come, and which he had not left, for just as one who walks heads toward what is ahead, so Christ, by his death, reached the glory of exaltation: "He became obedient unto death, even the death of the cross. Because of this God exalted him" (Phil 2:8); "Jesus... knowing that he came from God, and is going to God" (13:3).[34]

1167. We see their sinful plans by their deceitful search for Christ; he says, *you will seek me*. Some look for Christ in a devout way through charity, and such a search results in life: "Seek the Lord, and your soul will live" (Ps 68:33). But they wickedly searched for him out of hatred, to persecute him: "Those who sought my soul used vio-

---

32. St. Thomas quotes Jn 8:29 in *ST* III, q. 20, a. 1.
33. See *ST* III, q. 47, a. 1.
34. See *ST* III, q. 47, a. 2.

lence" (Ps 37:13). He says, **you will seek me**, by attacking me after my death with your accusations: "We remembered that while still living the seducer said: 'After three days I will rise'" (Mt. 27:63). And they will also seek out my members: "Saul, Saul, why are you persecuting me" (Acts 9:4).

1168. This will be followed by their death, and so he adds what they will be deprived of, foretelling to them, **and you will die in your sin**. First, he foretells that deprivation which consists in the condemnation of death; secondly, that deprivation which consists in their exclusion from glory, **Where I am going, you cannot come**.³⁵

1169. He is saying: Because you will wickedly search for me, **you will die** while continuing **in your sin**. We can understand this in one way as applying to physical death: and then one dies in his sins who keeps on sinning up to the time of his death. And so in saying, **you will die in your sin**, he emphasizes their obstinacy: "There is no one who does penance for his sin, saying: 'What have I done?'" (Jer 8:6); "They went down to the lower regions with their weapons" as we read in Ezekiel (32:2).

In another way, we can understand this as applying to the death of sin, about which the Psalm says, "The death of sinners is the worst" (Ps 33:22). And just as a physical weakness precedes physical death, so a certain weakness precedes this kind of death. For as long as sin can be remedied, it is a kind of weakness which precedes death: "Have mercy on me, O Lord, for I am weak" (Ps 6:3). But when sin can no longer be remedied, either absolutely, as after this life, or because of the very nature of the sin, as a sin against the Holy Spirit, it then causes death: "There is a sin that leads to death; I do not say that one should pray for that" (1 Jn 5:16). And according to this, our Lord is foretelling them that the weakness of their sins results in death.³⁶

1170. He shows the deprivation which consists in their exclusion from glory when he says, **Where I am going, you cannot come**. Our Lord goes by death, and so also do they. But our Lord goes without sin, while they go with their sins, because they are dying in their sin, and so do not come to the glory of the vision of the Father. So he says, **Where I am going**, willingly, by my passion, to the Father and to his glory, **you cannot come**, because you do not want to. For if they had wanted to and had not been able to do so, it could not have reasonably been said to them, "You will die in your sin."

1171. Note that one can be hindered from going where Christ goes in two ways. One way is by reason of some contrary factor, and this is the way that sinners are hindered. This is what he is speaking of here;

---

35. See *ST* II-II, q. 10, a. 3.
36. See *ST* I, q. 19, a. 9; I, q. 49, a. 2; I, q. 97, a. 1; I-II, q. 87, a. 3; II-II, q. 14; II-II, q. 164, a. 1.

and so to those who are absolutely continuing in their sin he says, **Where I am going, you cannot come.** "He who is proud will not live in my house" (Ps 100:7); "It will be called a holy way, and the unclean will not pass over it" (Is 35:8); "Who will dwell in your tent?... He who walks without blame" (Ps 14:1–2).[37]

One is hindered another way by reason of some imperfection or indisposition. This is the way the just are hindered as long as they live in the body: "While we are in the body, we are absent from the Lord" (2 Cor 5:6). To persons such as these our Lord does not say absolutely, **Where I am going, you cannot come**, but he adds a qualification as to the time: "Where I am going, you cannot follow me now" (13:36).

1172. Then (v. 22), he treats of the remedy which can set them free from the darkness. First, he gives the remedy for escaping the darkness; secondly, he shows the efficacy of the remedy (v. 31). Concerning the first, he does three things: first, he indicates what is the unique remedy for escaping the darkness; secondly, he states the reasons why they should ask for this remedy (v. 25); and thirdly, we see Christ foretelling the means of obtaining it (v. 28). As for the first, he does two things: first, he gives the circumstances for Christ's words; and secondly, the reason why Christ can propose the remedy (v. 23).

1173. The circumstances surrounding Christ's words was the perverse understanding of the Jews. For since they were carnal, they understood what Christ said, "Where I am going, you cannot come," in a carnal way: "The sensual man does not perceive those things that pertain to the Spirit of God" (1 Cor 2:14). Thus the Jews said, **Will he kill himself?** As Augustine[38] says, this is indeed a foolish notion. For if Christ was going to kill himself, couldn't they go where he was going? For they could kill themselves also. Thus, death was not the term of Christ's going: it was the way he was going to the Father. Accordingly, he did not say that they could not go to death but that they could not go through death to the place where Christ, through his death, would be exalted, that is, at the right hand of God.[39]

According to Origen,[40] however, perhaps the Jews did have a reason why they said this. For they had learned from their traditions that Christ would die willingly, as he himself said: "No one takes my life from me, but I lay it down of myself'" (10:18). They seem to have especially gathered this from Isaiah (53:12): "I will give him many things, and he will divide the spoils of the strong, because he delivered himself to death." And so because they suspected that Jesus was

---

37. See *ST* II-II, q. 162, a. 6; II-II, q. 163, aa. 1–2.
38. *Tract. in Io.* 38. 3; PL 35, col. 1676; cf. *Catena aurea*, 8:21–24.
39. See *ST* III, q. 47, a. 1; III, q. 58, a. 1.
40. *Comm. in Io.* XIX. 17, no. 104; PG 14, col. 556D–57A; cf. *Catena aurea*, 8:21–24.

the Christ, when he said, "Where I am going you cannot come," they understood it according to this opinion that he would willingly deliver himself to death. But they interpreted this in an insulting way, saying, **Will he kill himself?** Otherwise [if they were not speaking contemptuously] they would have said: "Is his soul going to depart, leaving his body when he wishes? We are unable to do this, and this is the reason for his saying, 'Where I am going, you cannot come.'"

1174. Then (v. 23), he proposes the remedy for escaping from the darkness. First, he mentions his own origin, and then theirs; secondly, he concludes to his point (v. 24).

1175. With respect to the first, he distinguishes his own origin from theirs in two ways. First, because he is from above, and they are from below. Secondly, because they are of this world, and Christ is not. As Origen[41] says, to be from below is not the same as to be of this world, for "above" and "below" refer to differences in place. Thus, so that they do not understand the statement that he is from above as meaning that he is from a part of the world which is above, he excludes this by saying that he is not of this world. He is saying in effect: I am from above, but in such a way that I am entirely above the entire world.

1176. It is clear that they are of this world and from below. But we have to understand correctly how Christ is from above and not of this world. For some who thought that all visible created realities were from the devil, as the Manicheans taught, said that Christ was not of this world even with respect to his body, but from some other created world, an invisible world. Valentinus also incorrectly interpreted this statement, and said that Christ assumed a heavenly body. But it is obvious that this is not the true interpretation, since our Lord said to his apostles: "You are not of this world" (15:19).

We must say, therefore, that this passage can be understood of Christ as the Son of God, and of Christ as human. Christ, as Son of God, is from above: "I came forth from the Father, and have come into the world" (16:28).[42] Likewise, he is not of this sensible world, that is, this world which is made up of sense perceptible things, but he is of the intelligible world, because he is the very Word of God, being the supreme Wisdom. For all things were made in wisdom. Thus we read of him: "Through him the world was made" (1:10).[43]

Christ, as human, is from above, because he did not have any affection for worldly and weak things, but rather for higher realities, in which the soul of Christ was at home, as in "our home is in heaven" (Phil 3:20); "Where your treasure is, there is your heart also" (Mt 6:21). On the other hand, those who are from below have their origin

---

41. Ibid. XIX. 20, nos. 131–34; PG 14, col. 564C–D; cf. *Catena aurea*, 8:21–24.
42. See *ST* I, q. 34, a. 2; III, q. 1, a. 2.
43. See *ST* I, q. 45, aa. 6–7.

from below, and are of this world because their affections are turned to earthy things: "The first man was of the earth, earthly" (1 Cor 15:47).[44]

1177. Then (v. 24), he concludes his point. First, he explains what he said about their deprivation; secondly, he points out its remedy (v. 24b).

1178. We should note with respect to the first, that everything in its development follows the condition of its origin. Thus, a thing whose origin is from below naturally tends below if left to itself. And nothing tends above unless its origin is from above: "No one has gone up to heaven except the One who has come down from heaven" (3:13). Thus our Lord is saying: This is the reason why you cannot come where I am going, because since you are from below, then so far as you yourself are concerned, you can only go down. And so what I said is true, *that you will die in your sins*, unless you adhere to me.

1179. Then, in order not to entirely exclude all hope for their salvation, he proposes the remedy, saying, *For if you do not believe that I am, you will die in your sin*. He is saying in effect: You were born in original sin, from which you cannot be absolved except by my faith: because, *if you do not believe that I am, you will die in your sin*.

He says, *I am*, and not "what I am," to recall to them what was said to Moses: "I am who am" (Ex 3:14), for existence itself (*ipsum esse*) is proper to God. For in any other nature but the divine nature, existence (*esse*) and what exists are not the same: because any created nature participates its existence (*esse*) from that which is being by its essence (*ens per essentiam*), that is, from God, who is his own existence (*ipsum suum esse*), so that his existence (*suum esse*) is his essence (*qua essentia*).[45] Thus, this designates only God. And so he says, *For if you do not believe that I am*, that is, that I am truly God, who has existence by his essence, *you will die in your sin*.

He says, *that I am*, to show his eternity. For in all things that begin, there is a certain mutability, and a potency to nonexistence; thus we can discern in them a past and a future, and so they do not have true existence of themselves. But in God there is no potency to nonexistence, nor has he begun to be. And thus he is existence itself (*ipsum esse*), which is appropriately indicated by the present tense.[46]

1180. Next we are given the reasons that can lead them to believe. First, we see the question asked by the Jews; secondly, the answer of Christ (v. 25b); and thirdly, the blindness of their understanding (v. 27).

1181. Since our Lord had said, "If you do not believe that I am," it was left to them to ask who he was. And so they said to him, *Who are you?* So that we may believe: "The poor man spoke" (Sir 13:29).

1182. When he says, *the source, who is also speaking to you*, he

---

44. See *ST* III, q. 61, aa. 1–2. 45. See *ST* I, q. 3, a. 4; I, q. 13, a. 11.
46. See *ST* I, qq. 9–10.

CHAPTER 8

gives an answer which can lead them to believe: first, because of the sublimity of his nature; secondly, because of the power he has to judge (v. 26); and thirdly, because of the truthfulness of his Father (v. 26b).

1183. Indeed, the sublimity of Christ's nature can lead them to believe in him, because he is the source (*principium:* source, beginning, origin). In Latin the word for source, *principium*, is neuter in gender, and so there is a question whether it is used here in the nominative or accusative case. (In Greek, it is feminine in gender and is used here in the accusative case.) Thus, according to Augustine,[47] we should not read this as "I am the source," but rather as "Believe that I am the source," lest you die in your sins.

The Father is also called the source or beginning. In one sense the word "source" is common to the Father and the Son, insofar as they are the one source of the Holy Spirit through a common spiration. Again, the three Persons together are the source of creatures through creation. In another way, the word "source" is proper to the Father, insofar as the Father is the source of the Son through an eternal generation.[48] Yet, we do not speak of many sources, just as we do not speak of many gods: "The source is with you in the day of your power" (Ps 109:3). Here, however, our Lord is saying that he is the source or beginning with regard to all creatures: for whatever is such by essence is the source and the cause of those things which are by participation. But, as was said, his existence is an existence by his very essence.

Yet because Christ possesses not only the divine nature but a human nature as well, he adds, **who is also speaking to you**. Man cannot hear the voice of God directly, because as Augustine[49] says: "Weak hearts cannot hear the intelligible word without a sensible voice." "What is man that he may hear the voice of the Lord his God" (Ex 20). So, in order for us to hear the divine Word directly, the Word assumed flesh, and spoke to us with a mouth of flesh. Thus he says, **who is also speaking to you**, that is, I, who was humbled for your sakes, have come down to speak these words: "In many and various ways God spoke to our fathers through the prophets; in these days he has spoken to us in his Son" (Heb 1:1); "It is the Only Begotten Son, who is in the bosom of the Father, who has made him known" (1:18).

1184. Chrysostom[50] explains this a little differently, so that in saying, **the beginning, who is also speaking to you**, our Lord is reproving the Jews for their slowness to understand. For in spite of the many signs which they had seen our Lord perform, they were still impenetrable, and asked our Lord, "Who are you?" Our Lord then answers: I

---

47. *Tract. in Io.* 38. 11; PL 35, col. 1681; cf. *Catena aurea*, 8:25–27.
48. See *ST* I, q. 33, aa. 1, 4; I, q. 36, a. 4; I, q. 45, a. 6.
49. *Tract. in Io.* 38. 11; PL 35, col. 1681; cf. *Catena aurea*, 8:25–27.
50. *Hom. in Io.* 53. 1; PG 59, col. 293; cf. *Catena aurea*, 8:25–27.

am *the beginning*, that is, the one who has spoken to you from the beginning. It is the same as saying: You should not have to ask who I am, because it should be clear to you by now: "For although you should be masters by this time, you have to be taught again the first rudiments of the word of God" (Heb 5:12).

1185. Secondly, they can be led to believe in Christ by his judicial authority; and so he says, *I have much to say about you and much to judge*, which means in effect: I have authority to judge you. Let us note that it is one thing to speak to us, and another to speak about us. Christ speaks to us for our benefit, that is, to draw us to himself; and he speaks to us this way while we are living, by means of preaching, by inspiring us, and by things like that. But Christ speaks about us, not for our benefit, but for showing his justice, and he will speak about us this way at the future judgment.[51] And this is what is meant by, *I have much to say about you*.

1186. This seems to conflict with what was said above: "God did not send his Son into the world to judge the world, but that the world might be saved through him" (3:17). I answer by saying that it is one thing to judge, and another to have judgment. For to judge implies the act of judging, and this does not belong to the first coming of our Lord, as he said above: "I do not judge anyone" (8:15), that is, at present. But to have judgment implies the power to judge; and Christ does have this: "The Father has given all judgment to the Son" (5:22); "It is he who was appointed by God to be the judge of the living and of the dead" (Acts 10:42). And so he says, explicitly, *I have much to say about you and much to judge*, but at a future judgment.[52]

1187. The truthfulness of the Father can also lead them to believe in Christ, and as to this he says, *but the one who sent me is truthful*. He is saying in effect: The Father is truthful; but what I say is in agreement with him; therefore, you should believe me. Thus he says, *the one who sent me*, that is, the Father, *is truthful*, not by participation, but he is the very essence of truth; otherwise, since the Son is truth itself, he would be greater than the Father: "God is truthful" (Rom 3:4).[53] *Whatever I have heard from him*, what I have received, not by my human sense of hearing, but by my eternal generation, *this I declare*: "What I have heard from the Lord of hosts, the God of Israel, I have announced to you" (Is 21:10); "The Son cannot do anything of himself" (5:19).

1188. The statement, *the one who sent me is truthful*, can be connected in two ways with what went before. One way is this: I say that *I have much to judge about you*; but my judgment will be true, because *the one who sent me is truthful*: "The judgment of God is according to

---

51. See *ST* III, q. 59, a. 4.
52. See *ST* III, q. 59, a. 3.
53. See *ST* I, q. 16, a. 5.

the truth" (Rom 2:2). The other way of relating this to what went before is from Chrysostom,[54] and is this: I say that *I have much to judge about you*; but I am not doing so now, not because I lack the power, but out of obedience to the will of the Father. For *the one who sent me is truthful*: thus, since he promised a Savior and a Defender, he sent me this time as Savior. And since I only say what I have heard from him, I speak to you about life-giving things.

1189. When he says, *And they did not realize that he was calling God his Father*, he reproves their slowness to understand: for they had not yet opened the eyes of their hearts by which they could understand the equality of the Father and the Son. The reason for this was because they were carnal: "The sensual man does not perceive those things that pertain to the Spirit of God" (1 Cor 2:14).

1190. Here, for the first time, Christ foretells how they are to come to the faith, which is the remedy for death. He does two things: first: he shows what will lead them to the faith; and secondly, he teaches what must be believed about himself (v. 28).

1191. He says, first, that they ought to come to the faith by means of his passion: *So Jesus said to them: When you have lifted up the Son of Man, then you will understand*. He is saying in effect: You do not know now that God is my Father, but *when you have lifted up the Son of Man*, that is, when you have nailed me to the wood of the cross, *then you will understand*, that is, some of you will understand by faith. "And I, if I am lifted up from the earth, will draw all things to myself" (12:32). And so, as Augustine[55] says, he recalls the sufferings of his cross to give hope to sinners, so that no one will despair, no matter what his crime, or think that he is too evil, since the very people who crucified Christ are freed from their sins by Christ's blood. For there is no sinner so great that he cannot be freed by the blood of Christ.

Chrysostom's[56] explanation is this: *When you have lifted up the Son of Man*, on the cross, *then you will understand*, that is, you will be able to understand what I am, not only by the glory of my resurrection, but also by the punishment of your captivity and destruction.

1192. With respect to the second, he teaches three things that must be believed about himself: first, the greatness or grandeur of his divinity; secondly, his origin from the Father; thirdly, his inseparability from the Father.

He mentions the greatness of his divinity when he says, *that I am*, that is, that I have in me the nature of God, and that it is I who spoke

---

54. *Hom. in Io.* 53. 1; PG 59, col. 293; cf. *Catena aurea*, 8:25–27.
55. *Tract. in Io.* 40. 2; PL 35, col. 1686; cf. *Catena aurea*, 8:28–30. See also *ST* III, q. 47, a. 5; III, q. 48, a. 4.
56. *Hom. in Io.* 53. 2; PG 59, col. 294; cf. *Catena aurea*, 8:28–30.

to Moses, saying: "I am who am" (Ex 3:14). But because the entire Trinity pertains to existence itself, and so that we do not overlook the distinction between the Persons, he teaches that his origin from the Father must be believed, saying, I do **nothing of myself; but as the Father taught me**, so I speak.[57] Because Jesus began both to do and to teach, he indicates his origin from the Father in these two respects. As regards those things he does, he says, *I do nothing of myself*: "The Son cannot do anything of himself" (5:19). And as regards what he teaches, he says, **as the Father taught me**, that is to say, he gave me knowledge by generating me as one who knows. Since he is the simple nature of truth, for the Son to exist is for him to know. And so, just as the Father, by generating, gave existence to the Son, so he also, by generating, gave him knowledge: "My doctrine is not mine" (7:16).

So that we do not think that the Son was sent by the Father in such a way as to be separated from the Father, he teaches, thirdly, that they must believe that he is inseparable from the Father when he says, **he who sent me**, the Father, **is with me**, by a unity of essence: "I am in the Father, and the Father is in me" (14:10). And the Father is also with me by a union of love, "The Father loves the Son, and shows him everything that he does" (5:20). And so the Father sent the Son in such a way that the Father did not separate himself from the Son; and so the text continues, **he has not deserted me**, because I am the object of his love. For although both are together, one sends and the other is sent: for the sending is the Incarnation, and this pertains only to the Son, and not to the Father.[58] That he has not deserted me is clear from this sign: **because I always do what is pleasing to him**. We should not understand this to indicate a meritorious cause, but a sign; it is the same as saying: The fact that *I always do*, without beginning and without end, **what is pleasing to him**, is a sign that he is always with me and **has not deserted me**, "I was with him forming all things" (Pr 8:30).

Another interpretation would be this: **he has not deserted me**, that is, as man, protecting me, **because I always do what is pleasing to him**. In this interpretation it does indicate a meritorious cause.

1193. Then when he says, **Because he spoke in this way, many came to believe in him**, he shows the effect of his teaching, which is the conversion of many of them to the faith because they had heard Christ's teaching: "Faith comes by hearing, and what is heard by the word of Christ" (Rom 10:17).[59]

---

57. See *ST* I, q. 3, a. 4; I, q. 34, a. 2; I, q. 39, aa. 1–2.
58. See *ST* I, q. 42, a. 5; I, q. 43, aa. 1, 4.
59. See *ST* II-II, q. 1, a. 2.

LECTURE 4

31 Jesus then said to those Jews who believed in him: "If you remain in my word, you will truly be my disciples. 32 You will know the truth, and the truth will make you free." 33 They replied, "We are of the seed of Abraham, and we have never been the slaves of anyone. How is it that you say, 'You will be free?'" 34 Jesus replied: "Amen, amen, I say to you: everyone who commits sin is a slave to sin. 35 A slave does not remain in the household forever; but the Son remains forever. 36 If therefore the Son frees you, you will be truly free. 37 I know that you are sons of Abraham. Yet you want to kill me, because my message is not grasped by you. 38 I speak of what I have seen with my Father. And what you have seen with your father, that you do."[60]

1194. After he had shown the remedy for escaping from the darkness, he now shows the effectiveness of this remedy. First, he shows the effectiveness of this remedy; then their need for remedy (v. 33). He does two things about the first. First, he shows what is required from those to whom the remedy is granted, and this concerns merit; secondly, he shows what is given for this, and this concerns their reward (v. 31).

1195. He says first: It was said that many believed in him, and so he told them, the Jews who believed in him, what they had to do, which was to remain in his word. So he says, *If you remain in my word, you will truly be my disciples*. He is saying in effect: You will not be my disciples if you just believe superficially, but you must *remain in my word*.

We need three things with respect to the word of God. A concern to hear it: "Let every man be quick to hear" (Jas 1:19). Then we need faith to believe it: "Faith comes by hearing" (Rom 10:17). And also perseverance in continuing with it: "How exceedingly bitter is wisdom to the unlearned. The foolish will not continue with her" (Sir 6:21). And so he says, *If you remain*, that is, by a firm faith, through continual meditation: "He will meditate on his law day and night" (Ps 1:2); and by your ardent love: "His will is the law of the Lord" (Ps 1:2).[61] Thus Augustine[62] says that those who remain in the word of our Lord are those who do not give in to temptations.

1196. He mentions what will be given to those who do remain when he says, *you will truly be my disciples*, and with three charac-

---

60. St. Thomas refers to Jn 8:34 in *ST* I-II, q. 80, a. 4, obj. 2; III, q. 48, a. 4; III, q. 71, a. 2, obj. 2.
61. See *ST* II-II, q. 4, aa. 3–4; II-II, q. 137, a. 4.
62. *Serm. de Scrip.* 134. 2. 2; PL 38, col. 743; cf. *Catena aurea*, 8:31–36. See also *ST* I-II, q. 109, a. 10.

teristics. First, they will have the excellence of being disciples of Christ; secondly, they will have a knowledge of the truth; and then, they will be free.

1197. Indeed, it is a great privilege to be a disciple of Christ: "Children of Zion, rejoice and delight in the Lord your God, because he has given you a teacher of justice" (Jl 2:23). Concerning this he says, *you will truly be my disciples*; for the greater the master, the more honorable or excellent it is to be his disciple. But Christ is the greatest and most excellent of teachers; therefore, his disciples will be of the highest dignity.[63]

Three things are required to be a disciple. The first is understanding, to grasp the words of the teacher: "Are you also still without understanding?" (Mt 15:16). But it is only Christ who can open the ears of the understanding: "Then he opened their minds so that they could understand the Scriptures" (Lk 24:45); "The Lord opened my ears" (Is 50:5).

Secondly, a disciple needs to assent, so as to believe the doctrine of his teacher, for "The disciple is not above his teacher" (Lk 6:40), and thus he should not contradict him: "Do not speak against the truth in any way" (Sir 4:30). And Isaiah continues in the same verse, "I do not resist."[64]

Thirdly, a disciple needs to be stable, in order to persevere. As we read above: "From this time on, many of his disciples turned back, and no longer walked with him" (6:67); and Isaiah adds: "I did not turn back" (Is 50:5).

1198. But it is a greater thing to know the truth, since this is the end of a disciple. And our Lord also gives this to those who believe; thus he says, *you will know the truth*, the truth, that is, of the doctrine that I am teaching: "I was born for this, and I came for this, to give testimony to the truth" (18:37); and they will know the truth of the grace that I produce: "Grace and truth came through Jesus Christ" (1:17)—in contrast to the figures of the Old Law—and they will know the truth of the eternity in which I remain: "O Lord, your word remains forever, your truth endures from generation to generation" (Ps 118:89).

1199. Yet the greatest thing is the acquisition of freedom, which the knowledge of the truth produces in those who believe. Thus he says, *and the truth will make you free*. In this context, to free does not mean a release from some confinement, as the Latin language suggests, but rather a being made free; and this is from three things. The truth of this doctrine will free us from the error of falsity: "My mouth will speak the truth; my lips will hate wickedness" (Pr 8:7). The truth

---

63. See *ST* III, q. 42, a. 4.
64. See *ST* II-II, q. 2, a. 1.

of grace will free us from the slavery to sin: "The law of the Spirit of life in Christ Jesus has freed me from the law of sin and of death" (Rom 8:2). And the truth of eternity, in Christ Jesus, will free us from corruption: "The creature will be freed from its slavery to corruption" (Rom 8:21).[65]

1200. Next (v. 33), he shows that the Jews need this remedy. First, he amplifies on their presumption in denying that they need any such remedy; secondly, he shows in what respect they need this remedy (v. 34).

1201. The presumption of the Jews is shown by their disdainful question: **They replied: We are of the seed of Abraham, and we have never been the slaves of anyone. How is it that you say, You will be free?** First, they affirm one thing; then deny another; and thirdly, pose their question.

They assert that they are the descendants of Abraham: **We are of the seed of Abraham.** This shows their vainglory, because they glory only in the origin of their flesh: "Do not think of saying: 'We have Abraham as our father'" (Mt 2:9). Those who seek to be praised for their noble birth act in the same way: "Their glory is from their birth, from the womb and from their conception" (Hos 9:11).

Further, they deny their slavery; thus they say, **and we have never been the slaves of anyone.** This reveals them as dull in mind and as liars. It shows them as dull because while our Lord is speaking of spiritual freedom, they are thinking of physical freedom: "The sensual person does not perceive what pertains to the Spirit of God" (1 Cor 2:14). It shows them as liars because if they mean their statement as, we **have never been the slaves of anyone**, to apply to physical slavery, then they are either speaking generally of the entire Jewish people, or in particular of themselves. If they are speaking generally, they are obviously lying: for Joseph was sold into slavery and their ancestors were slaves in Egypt, as is clear from Genesis (chap. 40) and from Exodus (chap. 3). Thus Augustine[66] says: "Ungrateful! Why does the Lord so often remind you that he freed you from the house of bondage, if you have never been slaves to anyone?" For we read in Deuteronomy (13:10): "I have called you out of Egypt, from the house of your slavery." But even if they are speaking of themselves, they are still guilty of lying, because they were at that time paying taxes to the Romans. Thus they asked: "Is it lawful to pay taxes to Caesar or not?" (Mt 22:17).

They ask him about the kind of freedom he is talking about when they say, **How is it that you say, You will be free?** Our Lord had promised them two things: freedom and knowledge of the truth, when he said, "you will know the truth, and the truth will make you free." The

---

65. See *ST* I-II, q. 5, a. 4.
66. *Tract. in Io.* 41. 2; PL 35, col. 1693; cf. *Catena aurea*, 8:31–36.

Jews took this to mean that our Lord regarded them as ignorant slaves. And although it is more harmful to lack knowledge than freedom, yet because they were carnal they pass over the truth part and ask about the kind of freedom: "They have set their eyes, lowering themselves to the earth" (Ps 16:11).

1202. Our Lord ignores their presumption and shows them that they do need the remedy he mentioned. First, he mentions their slavery; secondly, he treats of their freedom (v. 35); and thirdly, of their origin (v. 37).

1203. He shows that they are slaves, not in the physical sense they thought he meant, but spiritually, that is, slaves of sin. And in order to make this clear he starts with two things. The first is a solemn affirmation that he repeats, saying, **Amen, amen, I say to you**. *Amen* is a Hebrew word which means "truly," or "May it be this way." According to Augustine,[67] neither the Greeks nor the Latins translated it so that it might be honored and veiled as something sacred. This was not done to hide it, but to prevent it from becoming commonplace if its meaning were stated. It was done especially out of reverence from our Lord who frequently used it. Our Lord makes use of it here as a kind of oath, and he repeats it to reinforce his statement: "He interposed an oath, so that by two immutable things, in which it is impossible for God to lie, we might have the strongest comfort" (Heb 6:17).

Secondly, he makes a general statement when he says, **everyone**, whether Jew or Greek, rich or poor, emperor or beggar: "There is no difference between Jews and Greeks: all have sinned" (Rom 3:22). He mentions slavery when he says, **who commits sin is a slave to sin**.[68]

1204. But one might argue against this in the following way: A slave does not act by his own judgment, but by that of his master; but one who commits sin is acting by his own judgment; therefore, he is not a slave. I answer by saying that a thing is whatever is appropriate to it according to its nature, it acts of itself; but when it is moved by something exterior, it does not act of itself, but by the influence of that other: and this is a kind of slavery. Now according to his nature, man is rational. And thus when he acts according to reason, he is acting by his own proper motion and is acting of himself; and this is a characteristic of freedom. But when he sins, he is acting outside reason; and then he is moved by another, being held back by the limitations imposed by that other. Therefore, **everyone who commits sin is a slave of sin**: "Whatever overcomes a person, is that to which he is a slave" (2 Pet 2:19). And to the extent that someone is moved by something exterior, to that extent he is brought into slavery; and the more one is overcome by sin, the less he acts by his own proper motion, that is, by rea-

---

67. Ibid., 41. 3, col. 1694; cf. *Catena aurea*, 8:31–36.
68. See *ST* I-II, q. 109, a. 2.

son, and the more he is made a slave. Thus, the more freely one does the perverse things he wills, and the less the difficulty he has in doing them, the more he is subjected to the slavery of sin, as Gregory[69] says.

This kind of slavery is the worst, because it cannot be escaped from: for wherever a person goes, he carries his sin with him, even though its act and pleasure may pass: "God will give you rest from your harsh slavery (that is, to sin) to which you were subjected before" (Is 14:3). Physical slavery, on the other hand, can be escaped, at least by running away. Thus Augustine[70] says: "What a wretched slavery (that is, slavery to sin)! A slave of man, when worn out by the harsh commands of his master, can find relief in flight; but a slave of sin drags his sin with him, wherever he flees: for the sin he did is within him. The pleasure passes, the sin (the act of sin) passes; what gave pleasure has gone, what wounds has remained."

1205. Then (v. 35) he considers their liberation from slavery; for since all have sinned, all were slaves to sin. Now the hope of liberation is held out by the one who is free of sin, and this is the Son.[71] Thus he does three things with respect to this. First, he mentions the status of a slave as distinguished from that one who is free; secondly, he shows that the status of the Son is different from that of a slave; and thirdly, he concludes that the Son has the power to set us free.

1206. The status of a slave is transient and unstable; so he says, *A slave does not remain in the household forever.* This house is the Church: "So you may know how to act in the house of God, which is the Church of the living God" (1 Tim 3:15). In this house some who are spiritually slaves remain only for a time, just as in a household those who are physically slaves remain only for a while. But the former will not remain forever, for although those who are evil are not now separated from the faithful in a separate group, but only by merit, in the future they will be separated in both ways: "Cast out the slave and her son: for the son of the slave woman will not inherit with the son of the free woman" (Gal 4:30).

1207. On the other hand, the status of the Son is everlasting and stable; so he says, *but the Son*, that is, Christ, *remains forever*, namely, in the Church, as in his own house. In Hebrews (3:6) Christ is described as a son in his own house. And indeed, it is of himself that Christ remains in his house forever, because he is immune from sin. As for us, just as we are freed from sin through him, so it is through him that we remain in his house.[72]

1208. The Son has the power to free us; so he adds, *If therefore the*

---

69. *Mor.* 25. 16; PL 76, col. 343; cf. *Catena aurea*, 8:31–36.
70. *Tract. in Io.* 41. 4; PL 35, col. 1694; cf. *Catena aurea*, 8:31–36.
71. See *ST* III, q. 15, aa. 1–2; III, q. 20, a. 1; III, q. 48, a. 4; III, q. 49, aa. 1–2.
72. See *ST* III, q. 22, a. 5.

Son frees you, you will be truly free: "We are not the children of the slave woman, but of the free, by whose freedom Christ has freed us" (Gal 4:31). For as the Apostle says, he paid a price not in gold, but of his own blood, for he came in the likeness of sinful flesh although he had no sin; and so he became a true sacrifice for sin. Thus, through him, we are freed, not from barbarians, but from the devil.[73]

1209. Note that there are several kinds of freedom. There is a perverted freedom, when one abuses his freedom in order to sin; there is a freedom from justice, a freedom that no one is compelled to keep: "Be free, and do not make your freedom a cloak for evil," as we read in 1 Peter (2:16). Then there is a vain freedom, which is temporal or bodily: "A slave, free from his master" (Jb 3:19). Then we have true and spiritual freedom, which is the freedom of grace, and consists in the absence of sin. This freedom is imperfect because the flesh lusts against the spirit, and we do what we do not want to do (Gal 5:17).[74] Then there is the freedom of glory; this is a perfect and full freedom, which we will have in our homeland: "The creature will be delivered from its slavery" (Rom 8:21), and this will be so because there will be nothing there to incline us to evil, nothing to oppress us, for then there will be freedom from sin and punishment.

1210. Chrysostom[75] explains this in another way: since he had said, *everyone who commits sin is a slave to sin*, then lest the Jews anticipate him and say, "Even though we are slaves to sin, we can be freed by the sacrifices and ceremonies of the Law," our Lord shows that they cannot be freed by these, but only by the Son. Hence he says, *a slave*, i.e., Moses and the priests of the Old Testament, *does not remain in the household forever*: "Moses was faithful in all God's house as a servant" (Heb 3:5). Furthermore, the ceremonies are not eternal; therefore they cannot confer a freedom which will continue forever.[76]

1211. Then he considers their origin (v. 37). First, he gives their origin according to the flesh; secondly, he inquires into their origin according to the spirit (v. 37b).

1212. He traces their origin in the flesh to Abraham. *I know that you are sons of Abraham*, by carnal origin only, and not by resembling him in faith: "Look to Abraham your father and to Sarah who bore you" (Is 51:2).

1213. He inquires into their spiritual origin when he says, *yet you want to kill me*. First he shows that they have a spiritual origin; secondly, he rejects what they presume to be their origin (v. 34); thirdly, he shows them their true origin (v. 44). As to the first he does two

---

73. See *ST* III, q. 48, aa. 3–4.
74. See *ST* III, q. 69, a. 3.
75. *Hom. in Io.* 54. 1; PG 59, col. 297–98; cf. *Catena aurea*, 8:31–36.
76. See *ST* I-II, q. 103, a. 3.

things: first, he points out their guilt; secondly, he infers their spiritual origin (v. 38). As to the first he does three things: first, he lays on them the guilt of murder; secondly, the sin of unbelief; and thirdly, he anticipates an excuse they might give.

1214. Our Lord shows that they have their spiritual origins from an evil root. Hence he expressly accuses them of sin and passing over all the other crimes in which the Jews were implicated, he mentions only the one which they continued to nurture in their minds, the sin of murder, because, as was said, they wished to kill him. This is why he says, **you want to kill me**, which is against your Law: "You shall not kill" (Ex 20:13); "So from that day on they took counsel how to put him to death" (11:53).[77]

1215. Because they might say that to kill someone for his crime is not a sin, our Lord says that the cause of this murder is not any crime committed by Christ or their own righteousness, but rather their unbelief.[78] As if to say: you seek to kill me not because of your own righteousness but because of your unbelief: **because my message is not grasped by you**: "Not all men can receive this message, but only those to whom it is given" (Mt 19:11). Our Lord uses this way of speaking, first of all, to show the excellence of his message. As if to say: my message transcends your ability, for it is concerned with spiritual things, whereas you have a sensual understanding, that is why you do not grasp it: "The sensual man does not perceive the things that are of the Spirit of God" (1 Cor 2:14). He speaks this way also to recall a certain similarity: for as Augustine[79] says, the Lord's message to unbelievers is what a hook is to a fish, it does not grasp unless it is grasped.[80] And so he says his message does not grasp them in their hearts, because it is not grasped by them, as Peter was grasped: "Lord, to whom shall we go? You have the words of eternal life" (6:68). Yet it does not harm those who are grasped, for they are grasped to salvation, and left uninjured.

1216. In Deuteronomy (chap. 18) we read that a prophet who speaks, as coming from the mouth of the Lord, things that the Lord did not say, should be killed. So, lest the Jews say that he should be killed for speaking from himself, and not from the mouth of the Lord, he adds, **I speak of what I have seen with my Father**. As if to say: I cannot be accused of speaking things that I have not heard, for I speak not only what I have heard, but what is more, I speak of what I have seen. Other prophets spoke the things they heard, whereas I speak the things I have seen: "No one has ever seen God; the only Son, who is in

---

77. See *ST* II-II, q. 64.
78. See *ST* II-II, q. 10, a. 1.
79. *Tract. in Io.* 42. 1; PL 35, col. 1700; cf. *Catena aurea*, 8:37–41.
80. See *ST* II-II, q. 10, a. 1.

the bosom of the Father, he has made him known" (1:18); "That which we have seen and heard we proclaim also to you" (1 Jn 1:3). This must be understood of a vision which gives the most certain knowledge, because the Son knows the Father as he knows himself: "No one knows the Father except the Son" (Mt 11:27).[81]

1217. He then infers their spiritual origin when he says, **and what you have seen with your father, that you do.** As if to say: I speak things that are in accord with my origin; but you do the things that are done by your father, namely, the devil, whose children they were, according to Augustine,[82] not insofar as they were men, but insofar as they were evil. You do those things, I say, which you see, at the devil's suggestion: "Through the devil's envy death entered the world" (Wis 2:24).

Chrysostom[83] uses another text: **What you see with your father, do it.** As if to say: just as I reveal my Father in truth by my words, so you reveal the father of our origin, namely, Abraham, by your deeds. Thus he says: Do what you see your father doing, you who are taught by the law and the prophets.

LECTURE 5

39 They answered him, "Abraham is our father." Jesus said to them, "If you were Abraham's children, you would do what Abraham did [If you are Abraham's children, do what Abraham did], 40 but now you seek to kill me, a man who has told you the truth which I heard from God; this is not what Abraham did. 41 You do what your father did." They said to him, "We were not born of fornication, we have one Father, even God." 42 Jesus said to them, "If God were your Father, you would love me, for I proceeded and came forth from God; I came not of my own accord, but he sent me. 43 Why do you not understand what I say? It is because you cannot bear to hear my word."[84]

1218. After showing that the Jews had a certain spiritual origin, our Lord here rejects certain origins which they had presumptuously attributed to themselves. First, he rejects the origin they claimed to have from Abraham; secondly, the origin they thought they had from God (v. 41). As to the first he does two things: first, he gives the opinion of the Jews about their origin; secondly, he rejects it (v. 39b).

1219. It should be noted with respect to the first, that our Lord had said to them, **what you have seen with your father, that you do,** and so,

---

81. See *ST* III, q. 10, a. 4.
82. *Tract. in Io.* 42. 2; PL 35, col. 1700–1701.
83. *Hom. in Io.* 54. 2; PG 59, col. 299; cf. *Catena aurea,* 8:37–41.
84. St. Thomas quotes Jn 8:42 in *ST* I, q. 27, a. 1, *sed contra.*

CHAPTER 8   131

glorying in their carnal descent, they aligned themselves with Abraham. Thus they said, **Abraham is our father**. This is like saying: If we have a spiritual origin we are good, because our father Abraham is good: "O offspring of Abraham his servant" (Ps 104:6). And as Augustine[85] says, they tried to provoke him to say something against Abraham and so give them an excuse for doing what they had planned, namely, to kill Christ.

1220. Our Lord rejects this opinion of theirs as false (v. 39). First, he gives the true sign of being a child of Abraham; secondly, he shows that this sign is not verified in the Jews (v. 40); thirdly, he draws his conclusion, *you do what your father did*.

1221. The sign of anyone being a child is that he is like the one whose child he is; for just as children according to the flesh resemble their parents according to the flesh, so spiritual children (if they are truly children) should imitate their spiritual parents: "Be imitators of God, as beloved children" (Eph 5:1). And as to this he says, *If you are Abraham's children, do what Abraham did*. This is like saying: if you imitated Abraham, that would be a sign that you are his children: "Look to Abraham your father and to Sarah who bore you" (Is 51:2).

1222. Here a question arises, for when he says, *if you are Abraham's children*, he seems to be denying that they are the children of Abraham, whereas just previously he had said, "I know that you are children of Abraham" (v. 37). There are two ways of answering this. The first, according to Augustine,[86] is that before he said that they were children of Abraham according to the flesh, but here he is denying that they are children in the sense of imitating his works, especially his faith. Therefore, they took their flesh from him, but not their life: "It is men of faith who are the sons of Abraham" (Gal 3:7).

For Origen,[87] who has another explanation, both statements refer to their spiritual origin. Where our text reads, "I know that you are children of Abraham," the Greek has, "I know that you are the seed of Abraham." But Christ says here, *if you are Abraham's children, do what Abraham did*, because the Jews, spiritually speaking, were the seed of Abraham, but were not his children. There is a difference between a seed and a child: for a seed is unformed, although it has in it the characteristics of that of which it is a seed. A child, however, has a likeness to the parent after the seed has been modified by the informing power infused by the agent acting upon the matter which has been furnished by the female. In the same way, the Jews were indeed the seed of Abraham, insofar as they had some of the characteristics which God had infused into Abraham; but because they had not reached the

---

85. *Tract. in Io.* 42. 3; PL 35, col. 1701; cf. *Catena aurea*, 8:37–41.
86. Ibid., 42. 4, col. 1701; cf. *Catena aurea*, 8:37–41.
87. *Comm. in Io.* XX. 2, nos. 3–5; PG 14, col. 573B–C; cf. *Catena aurea*, 8:37–41.

perfection of Abraham, they were not his children. This is why he said to them, *if you are Abraham's children, do what Abraham did*, i.e., strive for a perfect imitation of his works.

1223. Again, because he said, *do what Abraham did*, it would seem that whatever he did, we should do. Consequently, we should have a number of wives and approach a maidservant, as Abraham did. I answer that the chief work of Abraham was faith, by which he was justified before God: "He believed the Lord; and he reckoned it to him as righteousness" (Gen 15:6). Thus, the meaning is, *do what Abraham did*, i.e., believe according to the example of Abraham.

1224. One might say against this interpretation that faith should not be called a work, since it is distinguished from works: "Faith apart from works is dead" (Jas 2:26) ["Do what Abraham did" if translated literally gives "Do the works of Abraham."] I answer that faith can be called a work according to what was said above: "This is the work of God, that you believe in him whom he has sent" (6:29). An interior work is not obvious to man, but only to God, according to, "The Lord sees not as man sees; man looks on the outward appearance, but the Lord looks on the heart" (1 Sam 16:7). This is the reason we are more accustomed to call exterior action works. Thus, faith is not distinguished from all works, but only from external works.[88]

1225. But should we do all the works of Abraham? I answer that works can be considered in two ways. Either according to the kind of works they are, in which sense we should not imitate all his works; or, according to their root, and in this sense we should imitate the works of Abraham, because whatever he did, he did out of charity. Thus Augustine[89] says that the celibacy of John was not esteemed above the marriage of Abraham, since the root of each was the same. Or, it might be said that all of Abraham's works should be imitated as to their symbolism, because "all these things happen to them in figure" (1 Cor 10:11).

1226. Then (v. 40) he shows that they do not have the above mentioned sign of being children. First, the conduct of the Jews is given; secondly, he shows that it does not resemble the conduct of Abraham (v. 40b).

1227. The conduct of the Jews is shown to be wicked and perverse, because they were murderers; so he says, *now you seek to kill me*: "How the faithful city has become a harlot, she that was full of justice! Righteousness lodged in her, but now murderers" (Is 1:21). This murder was an unfathomable sin against the person of the Son of God. But because it is said, "If they had understood, they would not have crucified the Lord of glory" (1 Cor 2:8), our Lord does not say that they

---

88. See *ST* II-II, q. 2, a. 2; II-II, q. 3.
89. *De bono conj.* 21. 26; PL 40, col. 391; also 18. 21, col. 387–88.

sought to kill the Son of God, but a man. For although the Son of God is said to have suffered and died by reason of the oneness of his person, this suffering and death was not insofar as he was the Son of God, but because of his human weakness, as it says: "For he was crucified in weakness, but lives by the power of God" (2 Cor 13:4).

1228. In order to further elucidate this murder, he shows that they have no reason to put him to death; thus he adds, *a man who has told you the truth which I heard from God*. This truth is that he said that he is equal to God: "This is why the Jews sought all the more to kill him, because he not only broke the Sabbath, but also called God his Father, making himself equal with God" (5:18). He heard this truth from God inasmuch as from eternity he received from the Father, through an eternal generation, the same nature that the Father has: "For as the Father has life in himself, so has he granted the Son also to have life in himself" (5:26).

Furthermore, he excludes the two reasons for which the Law commanded that prophets were to be killed.[90] First of all, for lying, for Deuteronomy (chap. 13) commands that a prophet should be killed for speaking a lie or feigning dreams. Our Lord excludes this from himself, saying, *a man who has told you the truth*: "My mouth will utter truth" (Pr 8:7). Secondly, a prophet ought to be killed if he speaks in the name of false gods, or says in the name of God things that God did not command (Deut 13). Our Lord excludes this from himself when he says, *which I heard from God*.

1229. Then when he says, *this is not what Abraham did*, he shows that their works are not like those of Abraham. He is saying in effect: Because you act contrary to Abraham, you show that you are not his children, for it is written about him: "He kept the law of the Most High, and was taken into covenant with him" (Sir 44:20).

Some frivolously object that Christ did not exist before Abraham and therefore that Abraham did not do this [kill Christ], since one who did not exist could not be killed. I answer that Abraham is not commended for something he did not do to Christ, but for what he did not do to anyone in like circumstances, i.e., to those who spoke the truth in his day. Or, it might be answered that although Christ had not come in the flesh during the time of Abraham, he nevertheless had come into his mind, according to Wisdom (7:27): "in every generation she [Wisdom] passes into souls." And Abraham did not kill Wisdom by sinning mortally. Concerning this we read: "They crucify the Son of God" (Heb 6:6).

1230. Then when he says, *you do what your father did*, he draws his conclusion. It was like saying: from the fact that you do not do the works of Abraham, it follows that you have some other father whose

---

90. See *ST* II-II, q. 64, a. 2.

works you are doing. A similar statement is made in Matthew (23:32): "Fill up, then, the measure of your fathers."

1231. Then when he says, **they said to him, we were not born of fornication**, he shows that they do not take their origin from God, for since they knew from our Lord's words that he was not speaking of carnal descent, they turn to spiritual descent, saying, **we were not born of fornication**. First, they give their own opinion; secondly, our Lord rejects it (v. 42).

1232. According to some, the Jews are denying one thing and affirming another. They are denying that they were born of fornication. According to Origen,[91] they said this tauntingly to Christ, with the unspoken suggestion that he was the product of adultery. It was like saying: **we were not born of fornication** as you were.

But it is better to say that the spiritual spouse of the soul is God: "I will betroth you to me forever" (Hos 2:19), and just as a bride is guilty of fornication when she admits a man other than her husband, so in Scripture Judea was said to be fornicating when she abandoned the true God and turned to idols: "For the land commits great harlotry by forsaking the Lord" (Hos 1:2). And so the Jews said: **we were not born of fornication**. It was like saying: although our mother, the synagogue, may now and then have departed from God and fornicated with idols, yet we have not departed or fornicated with idols: "We have not forgotten thee, or been false to thy covenant. Our heart has not turned back" (Ps 43:18–19); "But you, draw near hither, sons of the sorceress, offspring of the adulterer and the harlot" (Is 57:3).

Further, they affirm that they are children of God; and this seems to follow from the fact that they did not believe that they were born of fornication. Thus they say, **we have one Father, even God**: "Have we not all one father?" (Mal 2:10); "And I thought you would call me, My Father" (Jer 3:19).[92]

1233. Next (v. 42), our Lord refutes their opinion: first we see the sign of being a child of God; secondly, the reason for this sign is given (v. 42); and thirdly, we see that the Jews lack this sign (v. 43).

1234. With respect to the first it should be noted that above he had said that the sign of being a child according to the flesh was in the exterior actions that a person performs; but here he places the sign of being a child of God in one's interior affections. For we become children of God by sharing in the Holy Spirit: "you did not receive the spirit of slavery to fall back into fear, but you have received the spirit of sonship" (Rom 8:15). Now the Holy Spirit is the cause of our loving God, because "God's love has been poured into our hearts through the Holy Spirit which has been given to us" (Rom 5:5). Therefore, the special

---

91. *Comm. in Io.* XX. 16, no. 128; PG 14, col. 608B; cf. *Catena aurea*, 8:41–43.
92. See *ST* I, q. 33, a. 3.

sign of being a child of God is love: "Be imitators of God, as beloved children. And walk in love" (Eph 5:1).[93] Therefore he says, *If God were your Father, you would love me*: "The innocent and the right in heart," who are the children of God, "have clung to me" (Ps 24:21).

1235. Then (v. 42) he gives the reason for this sign. First, he states the truth; secondly, he rejects an error (v. 42b).

1236. The truth he asserts is that he *proceeded and came forth from God*. It should be noted that all friendship is based on union, and so brothers love one another inasmuch as they take their origin from the same parents. Thus our Lord says: you say that you are the children of God; but if this were so, *you would love me, for I proceeded and came forth from God*. Therefore, any one who does not love me is not a child of God.

I say *I proceeded from God* from eternity as the Only Begotten, of the substance of the Father: "From the womb before the daystar I begot you" (Ps 109:3); "In the beginning was the Word" (1:1). And *I came forth* as the Word made flesh, sent by God [into the world] through Incarnation. "I came [proceeded] from the Father," from eternity, as the Word, "and have come into the world" when I was made flesh in time (16:28).[94]

1237. He rejects an error when he says, *I came not of my own accord* [*a meipso*]. And first, he rejects the error of Sabellius, who said that Christ did not have his origin from another, for he said that the Father and the Son were the same in person. In regard to this he says, *I came not of my own accord*, i.e., according to Hilary, I came, not existing of myself, but in a way as sent by another, that is, the Father. Thus he adds, *but he sent me*: "God sent forth his Son, born of woman, born under the law" (Gal 4:4).

Secondly, he rejects an error of the Jews who said that Christ was not sent by God, but was a false prophet, of whom we read in Jeremiah (23:21): "I did not send the prophets, yet they ran." And in regard to this he says, according to Origen,[95] *I came not of my own accord*, but he sent me. Indeed, this is what Moses prayed for: "O, my Lord, send, I pray, whom you will send" (Ex 4:13).

1238. He shows that they lack this sign when he says, *Why do you not understand what I say?* For as was stated above, to love Christ is the sign of being a child of God; but they did not love Christ; therefore it is obvious that they did not have this sign. That they do not love Christ is shown by the effect of love: for the effect of loving someone is that the lover joyfully hears the words of the beloved; thus we read:

---

93. See *ST* I-II, q. 26, a. 3.
94. See *ST* I, q. 34, a. 2; III, q. 1, a. 2.
95. *Comm. in Io.* XX. 19, no. 160; PG 14, col. 616A; cf. *Catena aurea*, 8:41–43. See also *ST* I, q. 43, aa. 1–2.

"Let me hear your voice, for your voice is sweet" (Sg 2:14). And again, "My companions are listening for your voice; let me hear it" (Sg 8:13). Therefore, because they did not love Christ, it seemed tedious to them even to hear his voice: "This is a hard saying, who can listen to it?" (6:60); "The very sight of him is a burden to us" (Wis 2:15).

It sometimes happens that a person is not glad to hear the words of another because he cannot weigh them and for that reason does not understand them, and so he contradicts them: "Answer, I beseech you, without contention ... and you shall not find iniquity on my tongue" (Job 6:29). Therefore he says, **Why do you not understand what I say?** You question what I mean, as "Where I am going, you cannot come" (8:21). I say that you do not **understand because you cannot bear to hear my word**, i.e., your heart is so hardened against me that you do not even want to hear me.

LECTURE 6

44 *"You are of your father the devil, and your will is to do your father's desires. He was a murderer from the beginning, and has nothing to do with the truth [and did not stand in the truth] because there is no truth in him. When he lies, he speaks according to his own nature, for he is a liar and the father of lies."*[96]

1239. After showing that the Jews had a certain spiritual origin, and after rejecting the origin they presumed they had, our Lord here gives their true origin, ascribing their fatherhood to the devil. First, he makes his statement; secondly, he gives its reason; and thirdly, he explains this reason.

1240. He says: You do the works of the devil; therefore, **you are of your father the devil**, that is, by imitating him: "Your father was an Amorite, and your mother a Hittite" (Ez 16:3).

Here one must guard against the heresy of the Manicheans who claim that there is a definite nature called "evil," and a certain race of darkness with its own princes, from which all corruptible things derive their origin.[97] According to this opinion, all men, as to their flesh, have come from the devil. Further, they say that certain souls belong to that creation which is good, and others to that which is evil. Thus they said that our Lord said, **you are of your father, the devil**, because they came from the devil according to the flesh, and their souls were

---

96. St. Thomas quotes Jn 8:44 in *ST* I, q. 63, a. 5, obj. 2 and 4; I, q. 114, a. 3, obj. 2; II-II, q. 172, a. 6, obj. 3.
97. See *ST* I, q. 49, a. 3.

CHAPTER 8

part of that creation which was evil. But as Origen[98] says, to suppose that there are two natures because of the difference between good and evil seems to be like saying that the substance of an eye which sees is different from that of an eye that is clouded or crossed. For just as a healthy and bleary eye do not differ in substance, but the bleariness is from some deficient cause, so the substance and nature of a thing is the same whether it is good or has a defect in itself, which is a sin of the will. And so the Jews, as evil, are not called the children of the devil by nature, but by reason of their imitating him.

1241. Then when he says, *and your will is to do your father's desires*, he gives the reason for this, for their being of the devil. It is like saying: you are not the children of the devil as though created and brought into existence by him, but because by imitating him *your will is to do your father's desires*. And these desires are evil, for as he envied and killed man—"through the devil's envy death entered the world" (Wis 2:24)—so you too envy me and "you seek to kill me, a man who has told you the truth" (8:40).

1242. Then when he says, *he was a murderer from the beginning*, he explains the reason he gave. First, he mentions the characteristic of the devil that they imitate; secondly, he shows that they are truly imitators of that (8:45).

With respect to the first it should be noted that two sins stand out in the devil: the sin of pride towards God, and of envy towards man, whom he destroys.[99] And from the sin of envy towards man, because of which he injures him, we can know his sin of pride. And so first, he mentions the devil's sin against man; secondly, his sin against God, *he did not stand in the truth*.

1243. His sin of envy against man lies in the fact that he kills him. So he says, *he*, that is, the devil, *was a murderer from the beginning*. Here it should be noted that the devil kills man not with the sword, but by persuading him to do evil. "Through the devil's envy death entered the world" (Wis 2:24). First, the death of sin entered: "The death of the wicked is very evil" (Ps 33:22); then came bodily death: "Sin came into the world through one man and death through sin" (Rom 5:12). As Augustine[100] says: "Do not think that you are not a murderer when you lead your brother into evil." However, it should be noted with Origen,[101] that the devil is not called a murderer with respect to only some particular person, but with respect to the whole race, which

---

98. *Comm. in Io.* XX. 23, nos. 199–200; PG 14, col. 625B; cf. *Catena aurea*, 8:44–47.
99. See *ST* I, q. 63, aa. 2–3.
100. *Tract. in Io.* 42. 11; PL 35, col. 1704; cf. *Catena aurea*, 8:44–47.
101. *Comm. in Io.* XX. 25, nos. 224–25; PG 14, col. 632B–C; cf. *Catena aurea*, 8:44–47.

he destroyed in Adam, in whom all die, as we read in 1 Corinthians (chap. 15). Thus he is called a murderer because that is a chief characteristic, and he is so indeed *from the beginning*, that is, from the time that a man existed who could be killed, who could be murdered; for one cannot be murdered unless he first exists.

1244. Then when he says, *he did not stand in the truth*, he mentions the devil's sin against God, which consists in the fact that he turned away from the truth, which is God. First, he shows that he is turned from the truth; secondly, he shows that he is contrary to *the truth: when he lies, he speaks according to his own nature*. As to the first he does two things: first, he shows that the devil is turned from the truth; secondly, he explains what he has said, *because there is no truth in him*.

1245. He says, *he did not stand in the truth*. Here it should be noted that truth is of two kinds, namely, the truth of word and the truth of deed. The truth of word consists in a person saying what he feels in his heart and what is in reality: "Therefore, putting away falsehood, let every one speak the truth with his neighbor" (Eph 4:25); "He who speaks truth from his heart, who does not slander with his tongue" (Ps 14:3). The truth of deed, on the other hand, is the truth of righteousness, i.e., when a person does what befits him according to the order of his nature. Concerning this it says above: "He who does what is true comes to the light, that it may be clearly seen that his deeds have been wrought in God" (3:21). Speaking of this truth our Lord says, in *the truth*, namely, the truth of righteousness, *he did not stand*, because he abandoned the order of his nature, which was that he be subject to God, and through him acquire his happiness and the fulfillment of his natural desire. And so, because he wanted to obtain this through himself, he fell from the truth.

1246. The statement, *he did not stand in the truth*, can be understood in two ways. Either he never had anything to do with the truth, or that he once did, but did not continue in it. Now never to have anything to do with the truth of righteousness has two meanings. One is according to the Manicheans, who say that the devil is evil by nature. From this it follows that he was always evil, because whatever is present by nature is always present. But this is heretical, for we read: "God made heaven and earth, the sea, and all that is in them" (Ps 145:6). Therefore, every being is from God; but everything which is from God, insofar as it is, is good.[102]

Consequently, others have said that the devil was created good in his nature by God, but became evil in the first instant by his own free choice. And this opinion differs from that of the Manicheans who say

---

102. See *ST* I, q. 44, a. 1; I, q. 63, a. 4.

that the devils were always and by nature evil, whereas this opinion claims that they were always evil by free choice.

Someone might suppose that since an angel is not evil by nature but by a sin of his own will—and sin is an act—it is possible that at the beginning of the act the angel was good, and at the end of the evil act he became evil. For it is plain that the act of sin in the devil is subsequent to his creation, and that the terminus of creation is the existence of an angel; but the terminus of the act of sin is that he is evil. Consequently, according to this explanation, they conclude that it is impossible that an angel be evil in the first instant in which the angel came to exist.

But this explanation does not seem to be sufficient, because it is true only in motions that occur in time and that are accomplished in a successive manner, not in instantaneous motions. For in every successive motion the instant in which an act begins is not the one in which the action is terminated; thus, if a local motion follows upon an alteration, the local motion cannot be terminated in the same instant as the alteration. But in changes that are instantaneous, the terminus of a first and of a second change can occur together and in the same instant. Thus, in the same instant that the moon is illumined by the sun, the air is illumined by the moon. Now it is clear that creation is instantaneous, and likewise the act of free choice in the angels, since they do not go through the weighings and discoursings of reason. Thus, in the case of an angel there is nothing to prevent the same instant from being the terminus of creation (in which he was good), and the terminus of a free decision (in which he was evil). Some admit this, although they do not say that it so happened, but that it could have so happened. And they base themselves on the authority of Scripture, for under the figure of the king of Babylon it is said of the devil: "How have you fallen from heaven, O Lucifer, who did rise in the morning?" (Is 14:12); and under the person of the king of Tyre it says: "You were in the pleasures of the paradise of God" (Ez 28:13). Accordingly, they say that he was not evil at the first instant of his creation, but that he was once good, and fell through his free choice.

But it must be said that he could not be evil at the first instant of his creation.[103] The reason for this is that no act is sinful except insofar as it is outside the nature of the voluntary agent. But in order of acts, the natural act is first: thus in understanding, first principles are understood first, and through them other things are understood; and in willing, we likewise first will the ultimate perfection and ultimate end, the desire for which is naturally in us, and on account of this we seek other things. Now that which is done according to nature is not sin.

---

103. See *ST* I, q. 63, a. 5.

Therefore, it is impossible that the first act of the devil was evil; consequently, at some instant the devil was good. But **he did not stand in the truth**, i.e., he did not remain in it. Concerning the statement from 1 John (3:8): "The devil has sinned from the beginning," one may say that he did indeed sin from the beginning in the sense that once he began to sin he never stopped.

1247. Then when he says, **because there is no truth in him**, he explains what he has said. And this explanation can be understood in two ways. In one way, according to Origen,[104] so that it is an explanation of the general by the particular, as when I explain that Socrates is an animal by the fact that he is a man. It is then like saying: **he did not stand in the truth**, but fell from it, and this **because there is not truth in him**. Now there are two classes of those that do not stand in the truth: some do not stand in the truth because they are not convinced, but waiver: "My feet had almost stumbled, my steps had well nigh slipped" (Ps 72:2); others, on the other hand, because they have entirely recoiled from the truth. And this was the way the devil did not stand in the truth, but turned away from it in aversion.

But is there no truth at all in him? For if there is no truth in him, he would not understand himself or anything else, since understanding is concerned only with things that are true. I answer that there is some truth in the evil spirits, just as there is something true [a nature]. For no evil utterly destroys a good thing, since at least the subject in which evil is found is good. Thus Dionysius says that the natural goods remain intact in evil spirits. Thus there is some truth in them, but not the fulfilling truth from which they have turned, namely, God, who is fulfilling truth and wisdom.[105]

1248. In a second way, this explanation is understood as a sign, as Augustine[106] says. For it seems that he should rather have said the converse, namely, "there is not truth in him, because he did not stand in the truth." But just as a cause is sometimes shown by its effect, so our Lord wished to show that the truth was not in him because he did not stand in the truth; for truth would have been in him had he stood in the truth. A similar pattern of speech is found in "I cried because you heard" (Ps 16:6): as if to say that it is evident that I cried because you heard me.

1249. Then he shows that the devil is contrary to the truth, **when he lies, he speaks according to his own nature** (on his own). First, he makes this point; secondly, he explains it.

1250. The contrary of truth is falsity and a lie.[107] The devil is con-

---

104. *Comm. in Io.* XX. 27, no. 239; PG 14, col. 636B.
105. See *ST* I, q. 64, a. 1.
106. *De civ. Dei* 11. 14; PL 41, col. 330; cf. *Catena aurea*, 8:44–47.
107. See *ST* II-II, q. 110, a. 1.

trary to the truth because he speaks a lie. Thus he says, **he lies**. Here we should note that, God excepted, whoever speaks on his own speaks a lie; although not everyone who speaks a lie speaks on his own. God alone, when speaking on his own, speaks the truth, for truth is an enlightenment of the intellect, and God is light itself and all are enlightened by him: "the true light that enlightens every man" (1:9). Thus he is truth itself, and no one speaks the truth except insofar as he is enlightened by him.[108] So Ambrose[109] says: "Every truth, by whomsoever spoken, is from the Holy Spirit." Thus the devil, when he speaks on his own, speaks a lie; man, too, when he speaks on his own, speaks a lie; but when he speaks from God, he speaks the truth: "Let God be true though every man be false" (Rom 3:4). But not every man who tells a lie speaks on his own, for sometimes he gets this from someone else, not indeed from God, who is truthful, but from him who did not stand in the truth and who first invented lying. So in a unique way when the devil tells a lie, he is speaking on his own: "I will go forth and will be a lying spirit in the mouth of all prophets" (1 Kgs 22:22); "The Lord mingled" (that is, allowed to mingle) "a spirit of error in their midst" (Is 19:14).

1251. He explains this statement when he says, **for he is a liar and the father of lies**. The Manicheans did not understand this, and placed some kind of procreation in the evil spirits, with the devil as their father. They said that the devil "is a liar and his father." It should not be understood this way, as our Lord said that the devil is a liar and its father, the father of lies. Not everyone who lies is the father of his lie. As Augustine[110] says, "If you have learned a lie from someone else and you repeat it, you have indeed lied, but you are not the father of that lie." But the devil, because he did not learn from someone else the lie by which he destroyed humankind as with poison, is the father of the lie, just as God is the father of truth. The devil was the first to invent the lie, namely, when he lied to the woman: "You will not die" (Gen 3:4). Just how true this statement was, was proved by the outcome.

1252. Here we should note that the book *Questions of the New and Old Testament*[111] takes the words **you are of your father the devil**, and applies them to Cain, in the sense that one is called a devil who performs the works of the devil, and you are imitating him; hence you are of your father the devil, that is, of Cain, who did the work of the devil, and you are imitating him. Cain "was a murderer from the begin-

---

108. See *ST* I, q. 16, a. 5.
109. *Comm. in ep. ad Cor. primam* 12. 3; PL 17, col. 245 B.
110. *Tract. in Io.* 42. 14; PL 35, col. 1705; cf. *Catena aurea*, 8:44–47.
111. Augustine, *Quaest. vet. et novi Test.* 90; PL 35, col. 2282; cf. *Catena aurea*, 8:44–47.

ning," because he killed his brother Abel. And he "did not stand in the truth, because there is not truth in him." This is obvious because when the Lord asked him, "Where is Abel your brother?" he said, "I do not know; am I my brother's keeper?" (Gen 4:9). Thus he is a liar. But the first explanation is better.

LECTURE 7

45 *"But because [If] I tell the truth, you do not believe me. 46 Which of you convicts me of sin? If I tell the truth, why do you not believe me? 47 He who is of God hears the words of God; the reason why you do not hear them is that you are not of God." 48 The Jews answered him, "Are we not right in saying that you are a Samaritan and have a demon?" 49 Jesus answered, "I have not a demon; but I honor my Father, and you dishonor me. 50 Yet I do not seek my own glory; there is One who seeks it and he will be the judge."*[112]

1253. After mentioning some characteristics of the devil, he then shows that the Jews are imitating these. Our Lord ascribed two kinds of evil to the devil, murder and lying. He reproved them before for their imitation of one of these, namely, murder: "Now you seek to kill me, a man who has told you the truth" (8:40). Then passing from this, he reproves them for turning away from the truth: first, he shows that they are turned away from the truth; secondly, he rejects a certain reason they might give for this (v. 46); thirdly, he concludes to the true reason for their being turned away from the truth (v. 46b).

1254. He says first: It was said that the devil is a liar and the father of lies, and you are imitating him because you do not wish to adhere to the truth. Thus he says, ***If I tell the truth*** to you ***you do not believe me***; "If I tell you, you will not believe" (Lk 22:67); "If I have told you earthly things and you do not believe me, etc." (3:12). And Isaiah complains: "Who has believed what we have heard?" (Is 53:1).

1255. The reason which the Jews might allege for their unbelief is that Christ is a sinner, for it is not easy to believe a sinner even when he is telling the truth. Thus we read: "But to the wicked God says: 'What right have you to recite my statutes?'" (Ps 49:16). So they might have said: We do not believe you since you are a sinner.

Accordingly, he excludes this reason when he says, ***Which of you convicts me of sin?*** As if to say: You have no good reason for not believing me when I speak the truth, since you can find no sin in me: "He committed no sin; no guile was found on his lips" (1 Pt 2:22). Ac-

---

112. St. Thomas refers to Jn 8:46 in *ST* III, q. 15, a. 1, *sed contra*; III, q. 83, a. 4; and to Jn 8:50 in *ST* III, q. 13, a. 4, ad 2.

cording to Gregory,[113] we are invited to consider the mildness of God, who did not consider it beneath himself to show by rational grounds that he who can justify sinners by the power of his divinity is not a sinner: "If I have rejected the cause of my manservant or my maidservant, when they brought a complaint against me; what then shall I do when God rises up?" (Jb 31:13). We should also honor the unique greatness of Christ's purity, for as Chrysostom says, no mere man could have confidently said, **Which of you convicts me of sin?** Only God, who had no sin, could say this: "Who can say, 'I have made my heart clean; I am pure from my sin?'" (Pr 20:9)—this is like saying: No one but God alone. "They have all gone astray, they are all alike corrupt; there is none that does good, no, not one" (Ps 13:3), except Christ.[114]

1256. Next, he concludes to the real reason they have turned away from the truth. First, he mentions the reason; secondly, he rejects their rejoinder (v. 48). As to the first he does three things: first, he asks a question; secondly, he begins with a reasonable starting point; thirdly, he draws from his conclusion.

1257. First, he says: Since you cannot say that you do not believe me because I am a sinner, one can ask why **if I tell the truth, you do not believe me**, since I am not a sinner? This is like saying: If you cannot convict me, whom you hate, of sin, it is obvious that you hate me because of the truth, that is, because I say that I am the Son of God: "A fool takes no pleasure in understanding, but only in expressing his opinion" (Pr 18:2).

1258. He then begins with a reasonable and true starting point, saying, **he who is of God hears the words of God**. For we read in Sirach (13:15): "Every creature loves its like." Therefore, whoever is of God, to that extent possesses a likeness to the things of God and clings to them.[115] Thus, **he who is of God** gladly **hears the words of God**: "Every one who is of the truth hears my voice" (18:37). The word of God ought to be heard gladly by those, above all, who are of God, since it is the seed by which we are made the children of God: "He called them gods to whom the word of God came" (10:35).

1259. He draws his conclusion from this saying, **the reason why you do not hear them is that you are not of God**. This is like saying: The reason for your unbelief is not my sin, but your own wickedness; as Sirach (6:20) says: "She [Wisdom] seems very harsh to the uninstructed."

Augustine[116] says about them that as to their nature, they are of God, indeed; but by reason of their vice and evil affection they are not of God. For this statement was made to those who were not just sinful, for this was common to all; it was made to those of whom it was

---

113. *XL hom. in Evang.* I, *Hom.* 18. 1; PL 76, col. 1150; cf. *Catena aurea,* 8:44–47.
114. See *ST* III, q. 15, a. 1.
115. See *ST* I, q. 82, aa. 1–2; also *III Sent.*, d. 27, q. 1, a. 1, c.
116. *Tract. in Io.* 42. 15–16; PL 35, col. 1705–6; cf. *Catena aurea,* 8:44–47.

foreknown that they would not believe with that faith by which they could have been set free from the chains of their sins.

1260. It should be noted, as Gregory[117] says, that there are three degrees of being badly disposed in one's affections. Some refuse to physically hear God's precepts. Of these we read: "Like the deaf adder that stops its ear" (Ps 57:5). Others hear them physically, but they do not embrace them with the desire of their heart, since they do not have the will to obey them: "They hear what you say, but they will not do it" (Ez 33:32). Finally, there are those who joyfully receive the words of God and even weep with tears of sorrow; but after the time of crying is past and they are oppressed with troubles or allured by pleasures, they return to their sins. An example of this is given in Matthew (chap. 13) and Luke (chap. 8), where we read of the word being choked by cares and anxieties. "But the house of Israel will not listen to you; for they are not willing to listen to me" (Ez 3:7). Consequently, a sign that a person is of God is that he is glad to hear the words of God, while those who refuse to hear, either in affection or physically, are not of God.[118]

1261. Next he rejects the rejoinder made by the Jews. First, the Evangelist mentions this rejoinder; and secondly, our Lord's rejection of it (v. 49).

1262. In their response the Jews charge Christ with two things: first, that he is a Samaritan, when they say, **Are we not right in saying that you are a Samaritan?** Secondly, that he has a demon, when they add, **and have a demon?**

In saying, **Are we not right?** we can infer that they often reproached Christ this way. In fact, concerning the second, that he has a demon, we read in Matthew, "It is only by Beelzebul, the prince of demons, that he casts out demons" (12:24). But this is the only place where it is recorded that they called him a Samaritan, although they probably said it often: for many of the things that were said and done about Christ and by Christ were not written in the Gospels, as it says below (21:25).

Two reasons can be given why the Jews said this about Christ. First, because the Samaritans were hateful to the people of Israel, for when the ten tribes were led into captivity, they took their land: "For Jews have no dealings with Samaritans" (4:9). Thus, because Christ reproved the Jews, they believed that he did it out of hatred, so that they regarded him as a Samaritan, an adversary, as it were. Another reason was that the Samaritans observed the Jewish rites in some things and not in others. Therefore, the Jews, seeing that Christ observed the law in some matters and broke it in others, for example, the law of the Sabbath, called him a Samaritan.

---

117. *XL hom. in Evang.* I, *Hom.* 18. 1; PL 76, col. 1150; cf. *Catena aurea*, 8:44–47.
118. See *ST* I-II, q. 112, a. 2.

Again, there are two reasons why they said he had a demon. First, because they did not attribute the miracles he worked, and the thoughts he revealed, to a divine power in Christ; rather, they suspected that he did these things by some demonic art. Thus they said: "It is only by Beelzebul, the prince of demons, that he casts out demons" (Mt 12:24). The other reason was based on the fact that his words exceeded human understanding, such as his statements that God was his Father, and that he had come down from heaven. And when uneducated people hear such things they usually regard them as diabolical. Accordingly, they believed that Christ spoke as one possessed by a demon: "Many of them said, 'he has a demon, and he is mad; why listen to him?'" (10:20). Furthermore, they said these things in an attempt to accuse him of sin, to dispute what he had said: "Which of you convicts me of sin?"

1263. Then when he says, **Jesus answered: I have not a demon**, our Lord rejects the response of the Jews. Now they had taxed Christ with two things, that he was a Samaritan and that he had a demon. Concerning the first, our Lord makes no apology, and this for two reasons. First, according to Origen,[119] because the Jews always wanted to keep themselves apart from the Gentiles. But the time had now come when the distinction between Jews and Gentiles was to be removed, and everyone was to be called to the way of salvation. Accordingly, our Lord, in order to show that he had come for the salvation of all, made himself all things to all men, more so than Paul, so that he might win all (cf. 1 Cor 9:22); and so he did not deny that he was a Samaritan. The other reason was that "Samaritan" means "keeper," and because he especially is our keeper, as we read, "He who keeps Israel will neither slumber nor sleep" (Ps 121:4), so he did not deny that he was a Samaritan.

But he did deny that he had a demon, saying, **I have not a demon**. First, he rejects the insult; secondly, he reproves the insulters for the obstinacy (v. 49b). As to the first he does two things: first, he rejects the insult; secondly, he shows that the opposite is true, **I honor my Father**.

1264. It should be noted with respect to the first that when correcting the Jews our Lord often spoke harshly to them: "Woe to you, Scribes and Pharisees" (Mt 23:14), and many other instances are recorded in Matthew. But there is no record that our Lord spoke harsh or injurious words in answer to their harsh words or deeds against himself.[120] Rather, as Gregory[121] said, God accepted their insults, and did not answer with insulting words, but simply said, **I have not a de-**

---

119. *Comm. in Io.* XX. 35, nos. 316–19; PG 14, col. 653D–56B; cf. *Catena aurea*, 8:48–51.
120. See *ST* III, q. 42, a. 2.
121. *XL hom. in Evang.* I, *Hom.* 18. 2; PL 76, col. 1151; cf. *Catena aurea*, 8:48–51.

mon. And what does this suggests to us if not that when we are falsely attacked by our neighbor with railing words, we should keep silence, even about his abusive words, so as not to pervert our ministry of correcting in a just manner into a weapon of our anger. However, while we should not value our own goods, we should vindicate the things that are of God. As Origen[122] says, Christ alone is capable of claiming, *I have not a demon*, for he has nothing, either slight or serious, of the devil in him; thus he says: "The ruler of this world is coming. He has no power over me" (14:30). "What accord has Christ with Belial?" (2 Cor 6:15).

1265. He supports his stand by saying the opposite: but *I honor my Father*. Now the devil hinders honor being given to God; therefore, any person who seeks God's honor is a stranger to the devil. Thus, Christ, who honors his Father, that is, God, has not a demon. Furthermore, it is a proper and singular mark of Christ that he honor his Father, as we read: "A son honors his father" (Mal 1:6). And Christ is most singularly the Son of God.

1266. Next he reproves the impudence of those insulting him. First, he reproves them; secondly, he rejects the supposed reason for their reproof; and thirdly, he foretells their deserved condemnation.

1267. He says first, *I honor my Father, and you dishonor me*. This is like saying: I do what I ought, but you do not do what you ought. Indeed, by dishonoring me you dishonor my Father: "He who does not honor the Son does not honor the Father who sent him" (5:23).

1268. But they could say: You are too severe, you are too concerned for your own glory, and so you reprove us. He rejects this, and speaking as man, says, *I do not seek my own glory*. For it is God alone who can seek his own glory without fault; others must seek it in God: "Let him who glories, glory in the Lord" (2 Cor 10:17); "If I glorify myself, my glory is nothing."

But does not Christ as man have glory? He does indeed, and it is great in every respect, because, although he does not seek it, nevertheless, *there is One who seeks it*, that is, the Father; for we read: "Thou dost crown him with glory and honor" (Ps 8:5), referring to Christ in his human nature.[123]

1269. Not only will he seek my glory in those who accomplish works of great virtue, but he will punish and condemn those who speak against my glory; thus he adds: *and he will be the judge*.[124] This, however, seems to conflict with the statement above (5:22): "The Father judges no one, but has given all judgment to the Son." I answer that the Father does not judge anyone apart from the Son, because even

---

122. *Comm. in Io.* XX. 36, no. 335; PG 14, col. 660A–B; cf. *Catena aurea*, 8:48–51.
123. See *ST* III, q. 49, a. 6.
124. See *ST* I-II, q. 62, a. 4; II-II, q. 23, a. 8.

that judgment which he will make concerning the fact that you insult me, he will make through the Son. Or, one might say that judgment is sometimes taken for condemnation, and this judgment the Father has given to the Son, who alone will appear in visible form in judgment, as has been said. Sometimes, however, it is understood as meaning to distinguish one from another; and this is the way it is used here. Thus we read: "Judge me, O God, and distinguish my cause" (Ps 42:1). It is like saying: It is the Father who will distinguish my glory from yours, for he discerns that you glory in the world; and he sees the glory of his Son, whom he has anointed above his fellows and who is without sin. But you are men with sin.

LECTURE 8

51 "Truly, truly, I say to you, if any one keeps my word, he will never see death." 52 The Jews said to him, "Now we know that you have a demon. Abraham died, as did the prophets; and you say, 'If any one keeps my word, he will never taste death.' 53 Are you greater than our father Abraham, who died? And the prophets died! Who do you claim to be?" 54 Jesus answered, "If I glorify myself, my glory is nothing; it is my Father who glorifies me, of whom you say that he is your God. 55 But you have not known him; I know him. If I said, I do not know him, I should be a liar like you; but I do know him and I keep his word. 56 Your father Abraham rejoiced that he was to see my day; he saw it and was glad." 57 The Jews then said to him, "You are not yet fifty years old, and have you seen Abraham?" 58 Jesus said to them, "Truly, truly, I say to you, before Abraham was [came to be], I am." 59 So they took up stones to throw at him; but Jesus hid himself, and went out of the temple.[125]

1270. Above, our Lord had promised two things to his followers: liberation from darkness and the attainment of life, saying, "He who follows me does not walk in darkness, but will have the light of life" (8:12). The first of these has been treated above; so we are now concerned with the second, the obtaining of life through Christ. First, he states the truth; secondly he counters its denial by the Jews (v. 52).

1271. It should be noted that although Christ had been loaded down with insults and criticisms, he did not stop his teaching; indeed, after being accused of having a demon, he offers the benefits of his teachings more generously, saying: **Truly, truly, I say to you, if any one keeps my word, he will never see death.** He is here giving us an exam-

---

125. St. Thomas refers to Jn 8:55 in *ST* III, q. 9, a. 2, *sed contra*; to Jn 8:56 in *ST* II-II, q. 1, a. 3, obj. 2; III, q. 52, a. 5, ad 1; and to Jn 8:59 in *ST* III, q. 44, a. 3, ad 1.

ple that when the malice of wicked men increases, and those that are converted are abused with insults, preaching, so far from being curtailed, should be increased: "And you, son of man, be not afraid of them, nor be afraid of their words" (Ez 2:6); ". . . the gospel for which I am suffering and wearing fetters like a criminal. But the word of God is not fettered" (2 Tim 2:9).

In this statement our Lord does two things: he requires something, and he promises something. What he requires is that his words be kept, *if any one keeps my word*—for the word of Christ is the truth. Therefore, we should keep it, first of all, by faith and continual meditation: "Do not forsake her, and she will keep you" (Pr 4:6); secondly, by fulfilling it in action: "He who has my commandments and keeps them, he it is who loves me" (14:21).

What he promises is freedom from death; thus he says, *he will never see death*, that is, experience it: "They who act by me (i.e., by divine wisdom) shall not sin; they who explain me shall have life everlasting" (Sir 24:30). Such a reward suits such merit, for life everlasting consists especially in the divine vision: "This is eternal life, that they know thee the only true God, and Jesus Christ whom thou has sent" (17:3). Now the seedbed and source of this vision comes into us by the word of Christ; "The seed is the word of God" (Lk 8:11). Therefore, just as a person who keeps the seed of some plant or tree from being destroyed succeeds in obtaining its fruit, so the person who keeps the word of God attains to life everlasting: "Keep my statutes and my ordinances by doing which a man shall live" (Lev 18:5).[126]

1272. Next we see the opposition of the Jews being repelled. They oppose Christ in three ways: first, by accusing him of making a false statement; secondly, by their derision (v. 57); and thirdly, by assaulting him (v. 59). As to the first, there are two things: first, they try to accuse him of presumption; secondly, Christ answers some of their retorts (v. 54). As to the first they do three things: first, they insult Christ; secondly, they state a certain fact (v. 52); and thirdly, they ask a question (v. 53).

1273. They reproached him for lying when they said, *now we know that you have a demon*. They said this because the Jews knew that the inventor of sin, and especially of lying, was the devil: "I will go forth and will be a lying spirit in the mouth of his prophets" (1 Kgs 22:22). It seemed to them that our Lord's statement, "If any one keeps my word, he will never see death," was an obvious lie—for since they were carnal minded, they understood of physical death what he said about spiritual and eternal death; and especially also because it was contrary to the authority of Sacred Scripture, which says, "What man can live and never see death? Who can deliver his soul from the power of Sheol?"

---

126. See *ST* I-II, q. 114, a. 3.

(Ps 89:48). For these reasons they said to him: *you have a demon*. It was like saying: You are lying because prompted by the devil.

1274. Further, they do two things to convict him of lying: first, they mention the death of the ancients; secondly, they quote Christ's own words (v. 52b). So they say: What you say, if *any one keeps my word, he will never see death*, is obviously false, for *Abraham died*, as is clear from Genesis (chap. 25); and *the prophets died*: "We must all die, we are like water spilt on the ground, which cannot be gathered up again" (2 Sam 14:14). But although they are dead in the bodily sense, they are not dead spiritually, for in Matthew (22:32) our Lord says: "I am the God of Abraham and the God of Isaac and the God of Jacob," and then he adds, "He is not God of the dead, but of the living." Thus, they were dead as to the body, but they were living in the spirit, because they kept the word of God and lived by faith. This was the death the Lord was speaking of, and not bodily death. Then, when they continue they quote Christ's own words: And you say, *If any one keeps my word, he will never taste death*. But they were careless and evil listeners and so garbled our Lord's words and did not repeat them exactly. For our Lord had said, "he will never see death," but they quote it as "he will never taste death." However, as far as their understanding was concerned, it was all the same, because in both cases they understood that they would never experience a bodily death. But as Origen[127] tells us, there is a real difference between seeing death and tasting death: for to see death is to experience it completely; while to taste it is to have some taste or share in death.

Now, just as it is a greater punishment to see death than to taste it, so not to taste death is more of a glory than not to see death. For the ones who do not taste death are those who are on high with Christ, i.e., who remain in an intellectual order: "There are some standing here who will not taste death before they see the Son of man coming in his kingdom" (Mt 16:28). And there are others who, if they do not see death by sinning mortally, nevertheless taste it, because they have a slight affection for earthly things. Consequently, our Lord, as it is written in the Greek, and as Origen[128] explains it, said, *he will never see death*, because the person who has accepted and kept the words of Christ will not see death, even though he might taste something of it.

1275. Then they ask their question, saying, *Are you greater than our father Abraham, who died?* They are asking, first of all, about a comparison between him and their fathers of old. But as Chrysostom[129] says, in their carnal understanding they could have asked something higher, that is, "Are you greater than God?" For Abraham

---

127. *Comm. in Io.* XX. 43, no. 402; PG 14, col. 676A; cf. *Catena aurea*, 8:52–56.
128. Ibid., nos. 402–4; col. 676A; cf. *Catena aurea*, 8:52–56.
129. *Hom. in Io.* 55. 1; PG 59, col. 302; cf. *Catena aurea*, 8:52–56.

and the prophets kept God's commands, yet they died in the bodily sense. Therefore, if any one who keeps your word will never die, it seems that you are greater than God. Yet they were satisfied with their retort, because they considered him less than Abraham, in spite of the fact that we read: "There is none like thee among the gods, O Lord" (Ps 86:8); and "Who is like thee, O Lord, among the gods?" (Ex 15:11); as if to say: No one.

Secondly, they ask about his estimate of himself, i.e., who does he take himself to be? As if to say: If you are greater than them, namely, Abraham and the prophets, it seems to imply that you are of a higher nature, say an angel or God. But we do not think you are. So they do not ask, "Who are you?" but *Who do you claim to be?* For whatever you say in this matter, we who know will regard it as a fiction. They spoke in a similar fashion below (10:33): "We stone you for no good work but for blasphemy; because you being a man, make yourself God."

1276. Then (v. 54), our Lord's answer is given. First, he answers the second question; secondly, the first question (v. 56). As to the first, the Lord does three things: first, he rejects their error; secondly, he teaches them a truth which they did not know (v. 54); and thirdly, he clarifies both of these things (v. 55).

1277. He says: You ask me, **Who do you claim to be?** As if I am usurping a glory that I do not have. But this is a false assumption on your part, because I do not make myself what I am, but I have received it from the Father: for *if I glorify myself, my glory is nothing*. Now this could be understood of Christ according as he is the Son of God, as though saying in precise language; if I, namely, myself, *glorify myself*, that is, ascribe to myself a glory which the Father does not give me, *my glory is nothing*. For the glory of Christ according as he is God is the glory of the Word and the Son of God. But the Son has nothing except being begotten, i.e., what he has received from another [the Father] by being begotten. Therefore, assuming the impossible, if his glory were not from another, it would not be the glory of the Son.

However, it seems better to suppose that this is said of Christ according as he is man, because anyone who ascribes to himself a glory he does not have from God, has a false glory. For whatever is true is from God, and whatever is contrary to the truth is false, and consequently, nothing. Therefore, a glory which is not from God is nothing. We read of Christ: "Christ did not exalt himself to be made a high priest" (Heb 5:5); and "It is not the man who commends himself that is accepted, but the man whom the Lord commends" (2 Cor 10:18). Thus the error of the Jews is obvious.

1278. He sets down the truth he intends to teach and says: *it is my Father who glorifies me*. It is like saying: I do not glorify myself, as you think; but it is another who glorifies me, namely, *my Father*, whom he describes by his proper characteristic and by his nature. He describes him by his proper characteristic of fatherhood; thus he says that *it is my Father* and not I. As Augustine[130] says, the Arians use this statement to injure our faith, and they claim the Father is greater than the Son, for one who glorifies is greater than the one glorified by him. If, therefore, the Father glorifies the Son, the Father is greater than the Son. Now this argument would be valid unless it were found that, conversely, the Son glorifies the Father. But the Son says: "Father, the hour has come: glorify thy Son that thy Son may glorify thee" (17:1); and "I glorified thee on earth" (17:4).

It is my Father who glorifies me, can be applied to Christ both according as he is the Son of God, and also as the Son of man. As the Son of God, the Father glorifies him with the glory of the divinity, generating him from eternity as equal to himself: as we read, "He reflects the glory of God and bears the very stamp of his nature . . . he sat down at the right hand of the Majesty on high" (Heb 1:3); "And every tongue confess that Jesus Christ is Lord, to the glory of God the Father" (Phil 2:11). But as man, he had glory through an overflowing into him of the divinity, an overflowing of unique grace and glory: "We have seen his glory, the glory as of the only Begotten of the Father, full of grace and truth" (1:14).

1279. He describes the Father by his nature, that is, by his divinity, when he says, *of whom you say that he is your God*. But lest anyone suppose that his Father is other than God, he says that he is glorified by God: "Now is the Son of man glorified, and in him God is glorified; if God is glorified in him, God will also glorify him in himself" (13:31). According to Augustine,[131] these words are against the Manicheans, who say that the Father of Christ was not proclaimed in the Old Testament, but rather it was one of the princes of the evil angels. However, it is plain that the Jews do not say that their God is any other than the God of the Old Testament. Therefore, the God of the Old Testament is the Father of Christ and the One who glorifies him.[132]

1280. Then he shows both these things, that is, the error of the Jews, and his own truth, when he says, *but you have not known him*. He shows these in two ways: first, by pointing out the ignorance of the Jews; secondly, his own knowledge (v. 55).

1281. With respect to the first it should be noted that the Jews could say: You say that you are glorified by God; but his judgments are known by us, according to "He has not dealt thus with any other nation; they do not know his ordinances" (Ps 147:20). Therefore, if what

---

130. *Tract. in Io.* 43. 14; PL 35, col. 1711; cf. *Catena aurea*, 8:52–56. See also *ST* I, q. 42, a. 4.
131. Ibid., 43. 15, col. 1711; cf. *Catena aurea*, 8:52–56.
132. See *ST* I, q. 33, a. 3.

you say is true, we would certainly know it; but since we do not know of it, it is obviously not true. Christ concludes saying, **but you have not known him**. This is like saying: It is not strange if you do not know about the glory with which my Father, who you say is your God, glorifies me, for you do not know God.

1282. This seems to conflict with the Psalm (75:1): "In Judah God is known." I answer that he was known by them as God, but not as the Father; thus he said above: "It is my Father who glorifies me" (v. 54). Or, one might answer that **you have not known him** with affection, because you adore him in a bodily way, whereas he should be adored spiritually: "God is spirit, and those who worship him must worship in spirit and truth" (4:24). And there is no affection because you are reluctant to keep his commandments: "They profess to know God; but they deny him by their deeds" (Ti 1:16).

1283. But they might say: "Granted that we do not know about your glory, how do you know that you have glory from God the Father?" For this reason Christ speaks of his own knowledge, saying, **I know him**. First, he mentions his own knowledge; secondly, he shows the need for mentioning it; and thirdly, he explains what he said (v. 55b).

1284. He says: I know that I have glory from God the Father, because **I know him**, namely, with that knowledge with which he knows himself; and no one else except the Son knows him: "No one knows the Father except the Son" (Mt 11:27), i.e., with a perfect and comprehensive knowledge.[133] And because every imperfect thing derives from the perfect, all our knowledge is derived from the Word; thus Christ continues, "and any one to whom the Son chooses to reveal him."

1285. Now because some who judge in a carnal manner might attribute arrogance to Christ for saying that he knows God, he mentions why his statement is necessary. For, according to Augustine,[134] arrogance should not be so guarded against that the truth is neglected and a lie committed. Thus Christ says: **If I said, I do not know him, I should be a liar like you**. This is like saying: Just as you are lying when you say that you know him, so **if I said I do not know him**, whereas I do, **I should be a liar like you**. There is a similarity here in the fact of lying: as they lie in saying that they know him whom they do not know, so Christ would be a liar were he to say that he does not know him whom he knows. But there is a lack of similarity because they do not know him, whereas Christ does.

But could Christ say these things ["I do not know him" and "I should be a liar"]? He could, indeed, have spoken the words materially, but not so as to intend expressing a falsehood, because this could

---

133. See *ST* III, q. 10, a. 1.
134. *Tract. in Io.* 43. 15, col. 1712; cf. *Catena aurea*, 8:52–56.

be done only by Christ's will inclining to falsehood, which was impossible, just as it was impossible for him to sin.

However, the conditional statement is true, although both antecedent and consequent are impossible.

1286. When he continues he shows that he knows the Father, **But I do know him**, i.e., I know the Father intellectually, with speculative knowledge. And I also know him with affective knowledge, by consenting to him with my will: thus he says, **and I keep his word**: "For I have come down from heaven, not to do my own will, but the will of him who sent me" (6:3).[135]

1287. Then when he says, **your father Abraham rejoiced that he was to see my day**, he gives his answer to the first question asked by the Jews: "Are you greater than our father Abraham?" He shows that he is greater for the following reason: Whoever waits for someone as for his good and perfection is less than the one he waits for; but Abraham placed the entire hope of his perfection and good in me; therefore, he is less than I. In regard to this he says, **your father Abraham**, in whom you glory, **rejoiced that he was to see my day; he saw it and was glad**. He is stating two visions and two joys, but the second vision and its joy is mentioned first. In the first part of the statement, he first mentions the joy of exultation when he says, **Abraham rejoiced**, and then adds the vision, saying that he was to see my day. Then in the second part he first mentions the vision, saying, **he saw** my day, and adds the joy, **and was glad**. Thus [taking the statement in reverse order] a joy lies between two visions, proceeding from the one and tending to the other. He is saying in effect: "He saw my day, and rejoiced that he was to see my day."

First of all, let us examine what that day is which he saw, and also what that day is which he rejoiced that he was to see. Now the day of Christ is twofold: the day of eternity, "Today I have begotten you" (Ps 2:7); and the day of his Incarnation and humanity, "I must work the works of him who sent me, while it is day" (9:4). We say that Abraham saw, by faith, each day of Christ: the day of eternity and the day of the Incarnation: "He believed the Lord; and he reckoned it to him as righteousness" (Gen 15:6). It is clear that he saw the day of eternity, for otherwise he would not have been justified by God, because as it says in Hebrews (11:6): "Whoever would draw near to God must believe that he exists and that he rewards those who seek him."[136] That he saw the day of the Incarnation is clear from three things. First, from the oath he exacted from his servant. For he said to his servant: "Put your hand under my thigh, and I will make you swear by the Lord" (Gen 24:2). This signified, as Augustine[137] says, that the God of heav-

---

135. See *ST* III, q. 20, a. 1.
136. See *ST* II-II, q. 2, a. 7.
137. *Tract. in Io.* 43. 16; PL 35, col. 1712; cf. *Catena aurea*, 8:52–56.

en was to come out of his thigh. Secondly, as Gregory[138] says, when he showed hospitality to the three angels, a symbol of the Most High Trinity. Thirdly, when he knew the passion of Christ as prefigured in the offering of the ram and of Isaac (Gen 22). So he was glad over this vision [of faith], but he did not rest in it. Indeed, from it he rejoiced in another vision, namely, the direct face-to-face vision [of God], as though placing all his joy in this. Thus he says, **Abraham rejoiced that he was to see my day**—the day of my divinity and of my human nature—that is, that he was to see it by direct face-to-face vision.

1288. Then (v. 57), he shows how the Jews ridiculed Christ's words: first, we have their ridicule, in an attempt to belittle what Christ said; secondly, Christ clarifies what he said in order to counteract this ridicule (v. 58).

1289. Because Christ had said that Abraham rejoiced that he was to see his day, the Jews, having a carnal mind and considering only his physical age, ridiculed him and said, **you are not yet fifty years old**. Indeed, he was not yet fifty years old, or even forty, but closer to thirty: "And Jesus, when he began his ministry, was about thirty years of age" (Lk 3:23). The Jews said, **you are not yet fifty years old**, probably because they held the year of Jubilee in the greatest reverence and computed everything in terms of it—it was a time for freeing captives and giving up certain possessions. They were saying in effect: You have not yet lived beyond the span of a Jubilee, **and have you seen Abraham?** However, our Lord did not say that he saw Abraham, but that Abraham saw his day.

1290. To counteract their ridicule, our Lord answers the Jews by explaining his words, saying, **Truly, truly, I say to you, before Abraham came to be, I am**. These words of our Lord mention two things about himself that are noteworthy and efficacious against the Arians. One is that, as Gregory[139] says, he combines words of present and past time, because **before** signifies the past, and **am** signifies the present. Therefore, in order to show that he is eternal, and to indicate that his existence is an eternal existence, he does not say, "before Abraham, I was," but **before Abraham, I am**. For eternal existence knows neither past nor future time, but embraces all time in one indivisible [instant]. Thus it could be said: "He who is, sent me to you," and "I am who am" (Ex 3:14). Jesus had being both before Abraham and after him, and he could approach him by showing himself in the present and be after him in the course of time.

The other point, according to Augustine,[140] is that when speaking

---

138. *XL hom. in Evang.* I, Hom. 18. 3; PL 76, col. 1152; cf. *Catena aurea*, 8:52–56. See also *ST* II-II, q. 2, a. 8.

139. *XL hom. in Evang.* I, Hom. 18. 3; PL 76, col. 1152; cf. *Catena aurea*, 8:57–59. See also *ST* I, q. 2, a. 3; I, q. 3, a. 4.

140. *Tract. in Io.* 43. 17; PL 35, col. 1713; cf. *Catena aurea*, 8:57–59.

of Abraham, a creature, he did not say, "before Abraham was," but *before Abraham came to be*. Yet when speaking of himself, in order to show that he was not made as a creature is, but was eternally begotten from the essence of the Father, he does not say, "I came to be," but I am he who "in the beginning was the Word" (1:1); "Before the hills, I was brought forth" (Pr 8:25).

1291. Then (v. 59), we see the attitude of the Jews towards Christ: first, their harassment of him; secondly, Christ's escape. The harassment of the Jews came from their unbelief: for the minds of unbelievers, being unable to tolerate words of eternity, or understand them, regard them as blasphemy. Therefore, according to the command of the Law, they decided to stone Christ *as a blasphemer: they took up stones to throw at him*. As Augustine remarks: What hardness of heart! To what could it resort except the hardness of stones? And they act in the same way who from the hardness of their own hearts, failing to understand the clearly stated truth, blaspheme the one who speaks it; for we read: "These men revile whatever they do not understand" (Jude 10).

1292. Jesus escapes from them by his own power; he continues, *but Jesus hid himself*—he, who, if he had wished to exercise his divine power, could have bound and delivered them to the punishment of a sudden death. Jesus hid himself for two main reasons. First, as an example to his followers to avoid those who persecute them: "When they persecute you in one town, flee to the next" (Mt 10:23).[141] Secondly, because he had not chosen this form of death, but rather wanted to be sacrificed on the altar of the cross. He also fled because his time had not yet come. Thus, as man, he avoids their stoning. But he did not conceal himself under a rock or in a corner, but made himself invisible by his divine power and left the temple. He acted in a similar way when they wanted to throw him from the top of a hill (Lk 4:29). As Gregory[142] says, this leads us to understand that the truth is hidden from those who disdain to follow his words. Indeed, the truth shuns a mind that it does not find to be humble: "The Lord is hiding his face from the house of Jacob" (Is 8:17). Finally, he hid himself because it was fitting that he leave them because they refused to accept correction and the truth, and that he go to the Gentiles: "Behold your house is forsaken and desolate" (Mt 23:38).

141. See *ST* II-II, q. 185, a. 5.
142. *XL hom. in Evang.* I, *Hom.* 18. 5; PL 76, col. 1153; cf. *Catena aurea*, 8:57–59.

CHAPTER 9

LECTURE 1

1 As he passed by, he saw a man blind from his birth. 2 And his disciples asked him, "Rabbi, who sinned, this man or his parents, that he was born blind?" 3 Jesus answered, "It was not that this man sinned, or his parents, but that the works of God might be made manifest in him. 4 We must work the works of him who sent me, while it is day; night comes, when no one can work. 5 As long as I am in the world, I am the light of the world." 6 As he said this, he spat on the ground and made clay of the spittle and anointed the man's eyes with the clay, 7 saying to him, "Go, wash in the pool of Siloam" (which means Sent). So he went and washed and came back seeing.[1]

1293. After showing the enlightening power of his teaching by his own words [cf. 1118], our Lord confirms this by his action, when he gives sight to one physically blind. In regard to this three things are presented: first, the man's infirmity; secondly, his healing (v. 6); thirdly, a discussion among the Jews about this health (v. 8). In regard to the first he does two things: first, the man's infirmity is mentioned; secondly, we see an inquiry about its cause (v. 2).

1294. It should be noted in regard to the first that Jesus hid himself and left the temple, and while passing by he saw this blind man, *as he passed by, he saw a man blind from his birth*. Three things are considered here. First, he passed by to avoid the anger of the Jews: "Do not kindle the coals of a sinner lest you be burned in his flaming fire" (Sir 8:10). Secondly, he wanted to try and soften their hardness of heart by working a miracle: "If I had not done among them the works which no one else did, they would not have sin" (15:24). Thirdly, he went on his way in order to confirm his words by working a sign; for our Lord's works produce faith in the things that he says: "He confirmed the message by the sign that attended it" (Mk 16:20).[2]

In the mystical sense, according to Augustine,[3] this blind man is the human race. Sin is a spiritual blindness: "Their wickedness blinded them" (Wis 2:21). The human race is blind from birth, because it con-

---

1. St. Thomas refers to Jn 9:3 in *ST* I-II, q. 87, a. 7, obj. 1; III, q. 44, a. 3, obj. 3; Jn 9:4: *ST* III, q. 35, a. 8, obj. 3; q. 83, a. 2, ad 4; Jn 5: *ST* III, q. 46, a. 9, obj. 4; q. 83, a. 2, ad 4; Jn 9:6: *ST* III, q. 44, a. 3, ad 2.
2. See *ST* III, q. 43, a. 1.
3. *Tract. in Io.* 44. 1; PL 35, col. 1713; cf. *Catena aurea*, 9:1–7.

tracted sin from its origin, for the blindness occurs through sin in the first man, from whom all of us draw our origin. We read, "We were by nature," by natural origin, "children of wrath" (Eph 2:3).

1295. Then (v. 2), the cause of this man's infirmity is discussed: first, the disciples ask about its cause; secondly, Christ explains it.

1296. In regard to the first, three things are to be considered. The first is the reason for the disciples questioning Christ. According to Chrysostom,[4] this was because Jesus, leaving the temple and seeing this blind man, looked at him intently, as though seeing in him an opportunity to manifest his power. And so the disciples seeing him look so intently at the blind man were impelled to question him.

Secondly, we see the seriousness of the disciples, because they say, **Rabbi**, calling him Teacher, to indicate that they are questioning him in order to learn. Thirdly, we see why they asked, **who sinned?** when they inquire into the reason for the man's blindness.

It must be said, according to Chrysostom,[5] that because the Lord said to the paralytic, when he healed him, "See, you are well! Sin no more, that nothing worse befall you," the disciples thought that his infirmity was due to sin. They also thought that every human illness arose from sin, as Eliphaz said: "Think now, who that was innocent ever perished?" (Jb 4:7). Therefore, they asked whether he had been born blind on account of his own sin or that of his parents. It does not seem to have been on account of his own sin, because no one sins before he is born, since souls do not exist before their bodies, nor do they sin, as some mistakenly think: "Though they were not yet born and had done nothing, either good or bad ... not because of works but because of his call, she was told 'The elder will serve the younger'" (Rom 9:11). Nor does it seem that he suffered on account of a sin of his parents, for we read: "The fathers shall not be put to death for their children, nor shall the children be put to death for the fathers" (Deut 24:16).

Note that people are punished with two kinds of punishment. One is spiritual and concerns the soul; the other is bodily and concerns the body. A child is never punished on account of his father with a spiritual punishment, because the soul of a child is not from his father but from God: "All souls are mine," that is, by creation, "the soul of the father as well as the soul of the child is mine: the soul that sins shall be punished" (Ez 18:4). Augustine[6] also says this in one of his letters. But a child is punished on account of his father with a bodily punishment, since he is of his father as far as his body is concerned.[7] This is expressly shown in Genesis (chap. 19) where when Sodom was destroyed the

---

4. *Hom. in Io.* 56. 1; PG 59, col. 305; cf. *Catena aurea*, 9:1–7.
5. Ibid.; cf. *Catena aurea*, 9:1–7.
6. *Ep.* 44. 5. 12; PL 33, col. 179.
7. See *ST* I-II, q. 87, a. 8.

children of the inhabitants of Sodom were killed on account of the sins of their parents. Again, the Lord very often threatened to destroy the children of the Jews on account of the sins of their parents.

1297. To understand why one person is punished on account of the sins of another, we must realize that a punishment has two aspects: it is an injury and a remedy. Sometimes a part of the body is cut off to save the entire body. And a punishment of this kind causes an injury insofar as a part is cut off, but it is a remedy insofar as it saves the body itself. Still, a doctor never cuts off a superior member to save one which is inferior, but the other way around. Now in human matters, the soul is superior to the body, and the body is superior to external possessions. And so it never happens that someone is punished in his soul for the sake of his body, but rather he is punished in his body as a curing remedy for his soul. Therefore, God sometimes imposes physical punishments, or difficulties in external concerns, as a beneficial remedy for the soul. And then punishments of this kind are not given just as injuries, but as healing remedies. Thus, the killing of the children of Sodom was for the good of their souls: not because they deserved it, but so they would not be punished more severely for increasing their sins in a life spent in imitating their parents. And in this way some are often punished for the sins of their parents.[8]

1298. Then when he says, **Jesus answered**, our Lord reveals the reason for the man's infirmity: first, he excludes the reason they assumed; secondly, he mentions the real reason; and thirdly, he explains it.

1299. He excludes the reason they assumed when he says, **it was not that this man sinned, or his parents**: for the disciples had assumed that this was the reason for his infirmity, as was said. But a contrary statement is found in Romans (3:23): "All have sinned and are in need of God's glory." And again we read that sin has passed into all men from Adam. I answer to this that both the blind man and his parents did contract original sin and even added other actual sins during their lives, for we read: "If we say we have no sin, we deceive ourselves and the truth is not in us" (1 Jn 1:8). But when the Lord says, **it was not that this man sinned, or his parents**, he means that his blindness did not come as a result of their sins.[9]

1300. He mentions the real reason when he says, **but that the works of God might be made manifest in him**, for through the works of God we are led to a knowledge of him: "his invisible nature has been clearly perceived in the things that have been made" (Rom 1:20); "The very works which my Father has given me to perform . . . they bear witness to me" (5:36).[10] But the knowledge of God is man's greatest good,

---

8. See *ST* I-II, q. 87, a. 8, especially ad 1, 3.
9. See *ST* I-II, q. 87, a. 7.
10. See *ST* I, q. 2, a. 3; III, q. 1, a. 1.

since his happiness consists in this: "This is eternal life, that they know thee the only true God, and Jesus Christ whom thou hast sent" (17:3); "Let him who glories glory in this, that he understands and knows me" (Jer 9:24).[11] If, therefore, an infirmity occurs in order that God's works be manifested, and God is made known through this manifestation, it is clear that such bodily infirmities occur for a good purpose.[12]

1301. It might seem that the manifestation of God's works is not a sufficient reason for such an infirmity, especially since neither he nor his parents sinned. Therefore, some say that the words **but that** do not indicate the reason but merely the sequence of events. The sense then being: the man was blind, and the works of God were manifested in his cure. But this does not seem to be reasonable; and so it is better to say that the reason is being given. For evil is twofold: the evil of fault and the evil of punishment. Now God does not cause the evil of fault, but permits it; yet he would not permit it unless he intended some good from it.[13] So Augustine[14] says in his *Enchiridion:* "God is so good that he would never permit any evil to occur, unless he was so powerful as to draw some good from every evil." Therefore, he allows certain sins to be committed because he intends some good; in this way, he allows the rage of tyrants so that martyrs may be crowned.[15] Much more, therefore, should it be said that the evil of punishment, which he causes—as Amos (3:6) says: "Does evil befall a city, unless the Lord has done it?"—is never applied except for the good he intends. And among these goods the best is that the works of God be manifested, and from them that God be known. Therefore, it is not unfitting if he sends afflictions or allows sins to be committed in order that some good come from them.

1302. It should be noted, as Gregory[16] says in *Moralia* book I, that God sends afflictions to men in five ways. Sometimes they are the beginning of damnation, according to Jeremiah: "Strike them with a double punishment." A sinner is struck with this kind of punishment in this life so that without interruption or end he might be punished in the other life. For example, Herod, who killed James, was punished in this life and also in hell (Acts 12:23). Sometimes afflictions are sent as a correction, as we read: "Your discipline will teach me" (Ps 17:36). And sometimes a person is afflicted not to correct past wrongs, but to preserve him from future ones, as we read of Paul: "And to keep me from being too elated by the abundance of revelations, a thorn was given me in the flesh, a messenger of Satan, to harass me, to keep me

---

11. See *ST* I-II, q. 3, a. 8.
12. See *ST* I-II, q. 87, a. 7, ad 1.
13. See *ST* I, q. 19, a. 9.
14. *Enchir.* 11, PL 40, col. 236; cf. *Ep.* 155. 1. 3; PL 33, col. 668.
15. See *ST* I, q. 19, a. 9, ad 1.
16. *Mor.,* Praef. 5. 12; PL 75, col. 523 A–B; cf. *Catena aurea,* 9:1–7.

from being too elated" (2 Cor 12:7). Again, sometimes it is done to encourage virtue: as when a person's past sins are not being corrected, nor future ones hindered, but he is led to a stronger love by knowing the power of the one who unexpectedly delivered him from some difficulty: "Virtue is made perfect in infirmity" (2 Cor 12:9); "Patience has a perfect work" (Jas 1:4). And finally, sometimes afflictions are sent to manifest the divine glory; thus we read here, **that the works of God might be made manifest in him.**[17]

1303. Next he explains the true reason. And because he had mentioned God's works, first he states the opportunity for manifesting God's works; secondly, the reason for this opportunity or need, **night comes**; and thirdly, he explains this (v. 5).

1304. He says, therefore, this man was born blind **that the works of God might be made manifest in him.** And it was necessary that they be manifested, for **we must work the works of him who sent me**, that is, the works entrusted to me by my Father: "I have come to do the will of him who sent me" (6:38). And below he says: "Father, I have accomplished the work you gave me to do" (17:4). Or, these words can refer to Christ insofar as he is God; and then they indicate the equality of his power with that of the Father. Then the meaning is, **we must work the works of him who sent me**, that is, the works which I have from the Father. For everything that the Son does, even according to his divine nature, he has from his Father: "The Son can do nothing of his own accord, but only what he sees the Father doing" (5:19).[18]

1305 I say we must work **while it is day**. Our natural day is produced by the presence of the sun to the earth. But the Sun of Justice or Righteousness is Christ, our God: "But for you who fear my name the sun of righteousness shall rise" (Mal 4:2). Therefore, as long as this Sun is present to us, the works of God can be done in us, for us, and by us. At one time this Sun was physically present to us; and then it was day: "This is the day which the Lord has made; let us rejoice and be glad in it" (Ps 117:24). Therefore, it was fitting to do the works of God. He is also present to us by grace; and then it is the day of grace, when it is fitting to do the works of God, **while it is day**; "The night is far gone, the day is at hand. Let us then cast off the works of darkness and put on the armor of light" (Rom 13:12); "Those who sleep, sleep at night" (1 Thes 5:7).[19]

1306. If the presence of the sun produces day, and its absence night, then, since the sun is always present to itself, it is always day for the sun; and so for the sun, it is always the time for acting and illuminating. But with regard to ourselves, to whom it is sometimes present and

---

17. See *ST* I-II, q. 87, aa. 7–8.
18. See *ST* I, q. 41, a. 5; I, q. 42, a. 1.
19. See *ST* I, q. 43, a. 5.

CHAPTER 9

at other times absent, it is not always acting and illuminating. In the same way for Christ, the Sun of Justice, it is always day and the time for acting; but not with respect to us, because we are not always able to receive his grace due to some obstacle on our part.[20]

1307. He mentions why this is our opportunity when he says, **night comes, when no one can work**. Just as there are two kinds of day, so there are two kinds of night. One is by the physical departure of the Sun of Justice, which is what the apostles experienced when they were demoralized at the time of the passion, when Christ was physically taken from them: "You will all fall away because of me this night" (Mt 26:31). Then it was not the time for acting, but for suffering.

But it is better to say that even when Christ was physically absent because of his ascension, it was still day for the apostles insofar as the Sun of Justice shone on them, and it was a time for working.[21] And so night in this passage refers to that night which comes from the spiritual separation from the Sun of Justice, that is, by the separation from grace. This night is of two kinds. One is by the loss of actual grace through mortal sin: "Those who sleep, sleep at night" (1 Thess 5:7). When this night comes, no one can perform works that merit eternal life.[22] The other night is total, when one is deprived not only of actual grace by mortal sin, but even of the ability of obtaining grace because of an eternal damnation in hell. Here there is a vast night for those to whom it will be said: "Depart from me, you cursed, into the eternal fire" (Mt 24:41). During this night no one can work, because it is not the time for meriting, but for receiving according to one's merits.[23] Therefore, while you are living, do now what you will want to have done then: "Whatever your hand finds to do, do it with your might; for there is no work or thought of knowledge or wisdom in Sheol, to which you are going" (Ecc 9:10).

1308. He gives the reason for what he has just said, saying, **as long as I am in the world, I am the light of the world**. This is like saying: If you want to know what is that day and what is that night of which I speak, I say that *I am the light of the world*, for my presence makes day, and my absence night; "I am the light of the world" (8:12). **As long as I am in the world** by my bodily presence—"I came forth from the Father and have come into the world; again, I am leaving the world and going to the Father" (16:28)—*I am the light of the world*. And thus this day lasted until the ascension of Christ. Or again, **as long as I am in the world** spiritually by grace—"I am with you until the consummation of the world" (Mt 28:20)—*I am the light of the world*. And this day will last until the consummation of the world.

---

20. See *ST* I-II, q. 79, a. 3.
21. See *ST* I, q. 43, a. 5; III, q. 57, a. 1, ad 3; III, q. 57, a. 6.
22. See *ST* I-II, q. 88, a. 1; I-II, q. 109, aa. 4–5; I-II, q. 114, a. 2.
23. See *ST* I-II, q. 87, a. 3.

1309. Next, when the Evangelist says, *as he said this, he spat on the ground*, he describes the healing of the blind man. Here five things were done by Christ. First, he moistens the earth, *he spat on the ground*. Secondly, he made the clay, as we read, he *made clay of the spittle*. Thirdly, Christ smeared the man's eyes *and anointed the man's eyes*. Fourthly, he commands the man to wash, with *go, wash in the pool of Siloam*. And fifthly, the man's sight is restored, *and he came back seeing*. Each of these has both a literal and a mystical explanation.

1310. The literal meaning is explained by Chrysostom[24] in this way. Christ restored the man's sight by spittle in order to show that he accomplished this by a power coming from himself, and that the miracle should not be attributed to anything else: "Power came forth from him" (Lk 6:19). Although our Lord could have performed all his miracles by his mere word, because "he commanded and they were created" (Ps 148:5), he frequently used his body in them to show that as an instrument of his divinity it held a definite healing power. He made clay from his spittle to show that he who had formed the entire first man can reshape the deficient members of a man. Thus, just as he formed the first man from clay, so he made clay to re-form the eyes of the one born blind.[25]

He rubbed the clay on the eyes of the one born blind to show, by healing what is most important in bodies, that he was the creator of bodies. For man is more excellent than all other bodily substances; and among his members, the head is the more excellent; and among the organs of the head, the eye is more excellent than the others: "The eye is the lamp of the body" (Mt 6:22).[26] Therefore, by repairing the eye, which is more excellent than the other bodily members, he showed that he was the creator of the entire man and of all corporeal nature. He said, *go, wash in the pool of Siloam*, so that it would not seem that the clay he rubbed on the eyes had the power to heal them. Thus, as long as he had the clay on his eyes, the man did not see, but saw only after he washed.

He sent him some distance to wash, to the pool of Siloam, first, to overcome the obstinacy of the Jews. For he had to cross the city, and so all would see the blind man going with the clay on his eyes, and then returning with his sight restored. Secondly, he did this to acclaim the obedience and faith of the blind man; for perhaps he had frequently had clay put on his face, and had often washed in the pool of Siloam, and yet had not seen. So he could have said: "Clay usually makes me worse, and I have often washed in the pool but was never helped," as we read of Naaman in 2 Kings (5:10). Yet he did not argue, but sim-

---

24. *Hom. in Io.* 57. 1; PG 59, col. 311; cf. *Catena aurea*, 9:1–7.
25. See *ST* III, q. 44, a. 3, ad 2.
26. See *ST* I, q. 91, a. 3, ad 3.

ply obeyed. Thus it follows, *so he went and washed*. The reason why he sent him to the pool of Siloam was because the Jewish people were signified by that water: "Because this people have refused the waters of Shiloah that flow gently" (Is 8:6). Therefore, he sent him to Siloam to show that he still loved the Jewish people.

The effect follows, because *he came back seeing*. This was predicted in Isaiah (35:5): "Then the eyes of the blind shall be opened."

1311. Augustine[27] gives the mystical and allegorical explanation. He says that the spittle, which is saliva that descends from the head, signifies the Word of God, who proceeds from the Father, the head of all things: "I came forth from the mouth of the Most High" (Sir 24:3). Therefore, the Lord made clay from spittle and the earth when the Word was made flesh. He anointed the eyes of the blind man, that is, of the human race. And the eyes are the eyes of the heart, anointed by faith in the Incarnation of Christ. But the blind man did not yet see, because the anointing produced a catechumen, who has faith but has not yet been baptized. So he sends him to the pool of Siloam to wash and receive his sight, i.e., to be baptized, and in baptism to receive full enlightenment. Thus, according to Dionysius,[28] baptism is an enlightenment: "I will sprinkle clean water upon you, and you shall be clean from all your uncleanness" (Ez 36:25). And so this Gospel is appropriately read in Lent, on Holy Saturday, when those about to be baptized are examined. Nor is it without reason that the Evangelist adds the meaning of the pool, saying, *which means Sent*, because whoever is baptized must be baptized in Christ, who was sent by the Father: "As many of you as were baptized in Christ have put on Christ" (Gal 3:27). For if Christ had not been sent, none of us would have been freed from sin.[29]

According to Gregory,[30] however, the spittle signifies the savor of intimate contemplation, which flows from the head into the mouth, because due to the love of our Creator we have been touched even in this life with the savor of revelation. Thus the Lord mixed spittle with earth and restored sight to the man born blind because heavenly grace illuminates our carnal thoughts with his contemplation, and heals our understanding from its original blindness.[31]

---

27. *Tract. in Io.* 44. 2; PL 35, col. 1714; cf. *Catena aurea*, 9:1–7.
28. *De ecc. hier.* 2. 1; PG 3, col. 392.
29. See *ST* III, q. 1, a. 3; III, q. 49, a. 1; III, q. 66, a. 2, ad 1.
30. *Mor.* 8. 30. 49; PL 75, col. 832 C; cf. *Catena aurea*, 9:1–7.
31. See *ST* I, q. 94, a. 1; II-II, q. 180, a. 1.

LECTURE 2

8 The neighbors and those who had seen him before as a beggar, said, "Is not this the man who used to sit and beg?" 9 Some said, "It is he"; others said, "No, but he is like him." He said, "I am the man." 10 They said to him, "Then how were your eyes opened?" 11 He answered, "The man called Jesus made clay and anointed my eyes an said to me, 'Go to Siloam and wash'; so I went and washed and received my sight." 12 They said to him, "Where is he?" He said, "I do not know." 13 They brought to the Pharisees the man who had formerly been blind. 14 Now it was a Sabbath day when Jesus made the clay and opened his eyes. 15 The Pharisees again asked him how he had received his sight. And he said to them, "He put clay on my eyes, and I washed, and I see." 16 Some of the Pharisees said, "This man is not from God, for he does not keep the Sabbath." But others said, "How can a man who is a sinner do such signs?" There was a division among them. 17 So they again said to the blind man, "What do you say about him, since he has opened your eyes?" He said, "He is a prophet." 18 The Jews did not believe that he had been blind and had received his sight, until they called the parents of the man who had received his sight, 19 and asked them, "Is this your son, who you say was born blind? How then does he now see?" 20 His parents answered, "We know that this is our son, and that he was born blind; 21 but how he now sees we do not know, nor do we know who opened his eyes. Ask him; he is of age, he will speak for himself." 22 His parents said this because they feared the Jews, for the Jews had already agreed that if any one should confess him to be Christ, he was to be put out of the synagogue. 23 Therefore his parents said, "He is of age, ask him."[32]

1312. After the description of the miraculous healing of the blind man, the Evangelist tells of the miracle being examined. First, the miracle is examined by the people; secondly, by the Pharisees (v. 13); and thirdly, on account of his confession the blind man is instructed and commended by Christ (v. 35). In regard to the first, the Evangelist mentions three things: first, we see an inquiry about the person who received his sight; secondly, about the restoration itself (v. 10); and thirdly about the one who restored his sight (v. 1). In regard to the first he does three things: first, we have a question about the one who received his sight; secondly, the different opinions about this are given; thirdly, the question is settled.

1313. The question is asked by the people. He says, **the neighbors**

---

32. St. Thomas refers to Jn 9:16 in *ST* I-II, q. 107, a. 2, obj. 3; III, q. 40, a. 4, ad 1.

CHAPTER 9   165

and those who had seen him before as a beggar said: Is not this the man who used to sit and beg? Here two things are to be considered. One is that due to the greatness of the miracle, it was considered incredible. So we read below: "Never since the world began has it been heard that any one opened the eyes of a man born blind" (9:32). This fulfills for them what is said in Habakkuk (1:5), "I am doing a work in your days that you would not believe if told." Secondly, we should note the wonderful compassion of God, because our Lord performs miracles not only for the powerful, but also for outcasts, since he healed, with great pity, those who begged. This shows that he who came for our salvation rejected no one because of their poverty: "Has not God chosen those who are poor in the world to be rich in faith and heirs of the kingdom?" (Jas 2:5). Thus they explicitly say, *Is not this the man who used to sit and beg?* This is like saying: He is an outcast and does not deserve to be cured. But Baruch says the opposite: "The giants who were born there ... God did not choose them" (3:26).

1314. The opinions of the people are presented when he says, *Some said*: It is he, the beggar, because they had often seen him begging, and later hurrying through the town when he went to the pool with the clay on his eyes. Thus they could not deny that it was he. But others were on the contrary opinion, so they said, *No, but it is like him*. The reason for this, as Augustine[33] says, is that the man's appearance changed when he regained his sight, for nothing is so characteristic as the expression a person gets from his eyes: "A sensible man is known by his face" (Sir 19:29).

1315. The question is settled by the blind man because *he said*, the blind man, *I am the man*, the one who used to beg. His voice was grateful. For since he could not be ungrateful for such a great favor and was unable to show any other sign of gratitude than to constantly declare that he had been cured by Christ, he said, *I am the man*, the one who was blind and begged; and now I see: "Praise God and give thanks to him . . . for what he has done for you" (Tb 12:6).

1316. Then (v. 10), we see the investigation of the act, which was the restoration of the man's sight. First, we have the question asked by the Jews; secondly, the answer of the blind man (v. 11).

1317. They continue: If you are the blind man who used to beg, then tell us, *how were your eyes opened?* This question came from their vain curiosity because neither the one who was cured nor we ourselves know how it was done: "Do not meddle in what is beyond your tasks" (Sir 3:23).

1318. The blind man's answer was remarkable; he says, *the man called Jesus made clay and anointed my eyes*. In his answer he first points out the person who gave him his sight, saying *the man called*

---

33. *Tract. in Io.* 44. 8; PL 35, col. 1716; cf. *Catena aurea*, 9:8–17.

Jesus. He was right in calling him a man; he knew that he was a man, and he was a true man: "Born in the likeness of man" (Phil 2:7). For although he had not seen Jesus, because he had left while still blind to go to Siloam, he knew him from his voice and from the conversations of others about him.

Secondly, he tells what was done, saying, *he made clay and anointed my eyes*. Here he shows that he is truthful, not asserting what is not certain. For our Lord had made clay from spittle, but he did not know this; yet through his sense of touch he recognized the clay which was made and placed over his eyes. So he did not say, "He made clay from spittle," but only, he *made clay and anointed my eyes*: "That which we have heard, which we have seen with our eyes, which we have looked upon and touched with our hands . . . we proclaim also to you" (1 Jn 1:1).

Thirdly, he mentions the command, saying, *and he said to me, Go to Siloam and wash*. This was also necessary for us, for if we wish to be cleansed from our blindness of heart, it is necessary that we be spiritually washed; "Wash yourselves; make yourselves clean" (Is 1:16).

Fourthly, he shows his obedience, saying, *so I went and washed*. He is saying in effect: Because I heard this command and desired to see, I obeyed. And it is no wonder, because we read: "For the commandment," that is, when obeyed, "is a lamp and the teaching a light" (Pr 6:23).

Fifthly, he mentions the good effect, saying, *and I received my sight*. It was fitting that he be enlightened after obeying, because as it says in Acts (5:32): "It is the Holy Spirit whom God has given to those who obey him." Notice the perseverance of the blind man. As Augustine[34] says: "Look at him! He became a preacher of grace. See him! He preaches and testifies to the Jews. This blind man testified, and the hearts of the wicked were vexed, because they did not have the light in their hearts which he had in his face."

1319. Next, we have the inquiry about the person who restored his sight (v. 12). First, there is the question asked by the Jews, *Where is he?* They asked this maliciously, as they were thinking of killing him; for they had already formed a conspiracy against Christ: "But now you seek to kill me" (8:40).

Secondly, we have the answer of the blind man, *I do not know*. As Augustine[35] says, from these words it is clear that what was accomplished in him physically represents what is accomplished spiritually at different stages. For at first, the blind man is anointed, and then sees after his washing. The anointing represents the beginning of his physical health, and the washing leads to complete health. In particular, an

---

34. Ibid.; cf. *Catena aurea*, 9:8–17.
35. Ibid., col. 1716–17.

anointing produces a catechumen; and the washing, that is, baptism, perfects and enlightens him. Thus we have a representation of the difference in faith found at different stages.[36] For when he says, *I do not know*, this represents the imperfect faith of catechumens: "You worship what you do not know" (4:22). This can also signify our faith: "For our knowledge is imperfect and our prophesying is imperfect" (1 Cor 13:9).

1320. Then when he says, **they brought to the Pharisees the man who had formerly been blind**, we see his examination by the Pharisees. First, they question the man born blind; secondly, his parents (v. 18). He does three things with the first. First, we see the person to be examined; secondly, he mentions the intention of the examiners; and thirdly we have the interrogation itself.

1321. The one to be examined, the blind man, is led to the Pharisees by the people. **They brought**, that is, the crowd, **to the Pharisees the man who had formerly been blind**. They did this because the crowd was trying to find out from him where Jesus was, so that if they found him they could bring him to the Pharisees and accuse him of breaking the Sabbath. So because they did not have Christ they took the blind man, so that by questioning him more roughly they might force him by fear to make up something false about Christ: "I will go to the great, and will speak to them; for they know the way of the Lord, the law of their God. But they all alike had broken the yoke, they had burst the bonds" (Jer 5:5).

1322. The Evangelist shows that their intention was perverse, saying, **it was a Sabbath day when Jesus made the clay**. He says this to show their evil intention and the reason why they sought Jesus, that is, to find a charge against him and detract from his miracle by his supposed violation of the law. Nevertheless, it should be said that "The Son of man is Lord of the Sabbath" (Mt 12:8).

1323. His examination is conducted by the Pharisees, since it is said, **The Pharisees again asked him**. First, they question him about what was done; secondly, about the person who did it (v. 16).

1324. The Evangelist does two things about the first: first, he presents their interrogation; secondly, the blind man's answer. They ask him about the sign he received, **the Pharisees again asked him**, not in order to learn, but to find a reason to accuse him of lying. The blind man answers them, not contradicting what he said before, nor deviating from the truth. **He**, that is, the blind man, **said to them, he put clay on my eyes**. We must, first, admire the perseverance of this blind man, for although it may not seem such a great thing to have spoken the truth when he, without danger, was questioned by the crowd, he showed remarkable perseverance when in greater danger before the

---

36. See *ST* II-II, q. 5, a. 4.

Pharisees he neither denied what he had said before nor changed his account: "I will also speak of thy testimonies before kings, and shall not be put to shame" (Ps 118:46). Secondly, we should admire his skill, for it is good practice to first relate an event in detail and with all its circumstances, and then if it has to be repeated, to speak more concisely. So here, he does not repeat the name of the one who spoke to him, nor that he was told to go and wash. But without hesitation he relays only the essential, and says, **He put clay on my eyes.**

1325. Next (v. 16), an inquiry is made about the one who restored the man's sight. First, the different opinions of the Pharisees concerning Christ are given; secondly, the opinion of the blind man is sought (v. 17). In regard to the first he does three things: first, he presents the opinion of those who were blaspheming Christ; then, the opinion of those who were commending him; thirdly, he concludes with the fact that they were arguing and disagreeing among themselves.

1326. We should note, concerning the first, that those who act maliciously against someone keep silent if they see anything good in his work, and they reveal the evil, if any is seen, even turning what is good into evil, according to "Beware of a scoundrel, for he devises evil, lest he give you a lasting blemish" (Sir 11:33). This is what they are doing here: for they do not mention what seemed good, that is, the restoration of the blind man's sight, but stress what they can against Christ, that is, his breaking of the Sabbath. Thus **some of the Pharisees said,** that is, those who were malicious and corrupt, **this man is not from God, for he does not keep the Sabbath.** But Christ did keep the Sabbath, for when the Lord forbade work on the Sabbath he had in mind servile work, which is a sin: "Every one who commits sin is a slave to sin" (8:34). Therefore, one who does sinful works on the Sabbath breaks the Sabbath. So Christ, who was without sin, rather than they, kept the Sabbath.[37]

1327. The opinion of those commending him is presented when he reports them as saying, **How can a man who is a sinner do such signs?** These others had some faith due to the signs that Christ worked, but were still weak and imperfect; it was out of fear of the Pharisees and the elders that they asked with hesitation, **How can a man who is a sinner do such signs?** We read below that "Many even of the authorities believed in him, but for fear of the Pharisees they did not confess it" (12:42). They should have shown how our Lord had not broken the Sabbath, and have appropriately replied in defense of Jesus.

1328. The difference of opinion among them is mentioned when he says, **there was a division among them;** and this division was also found in the people. This was a sign of their destruction: "Their heart is

---

37. See *ST* I-II, q. 100, a. 5; III, q. 40, a. 4.

false; now they must bear their guilt" (Hos 10:2); "Every kingdom divided against itself is laid waste" (Mt 12:25).

1329. Next (v. 17), they ask the blind man for his opinion. And first we have the question the Pharisees asked; secondly, the blind man's answer.

They question him, saying, **what do you say about him?** According to Chrysostom,[38] this question was not asked by those who were blaspheming Christ, but by those favorably disposed. This is clear from the way they questioned him; for they call his attention to the gift he received, saying, **since he has opened your eyes**. If the others had been doing the questioning, they would not have said this, but would rather recall that Christ broke the Sabbath. But these remind him of the benefit that he received to make him grateful and lead him to testify to Christ.

But according to Augustine,[39] this question was asked by Christ's enemies, who wanted to deprecate this man who constantly professed the truth; or they were trying to get him to change his opinion out of fear; or at least were attempting to exclude him from the synagogue.

The answer of the blind man remained the same, **he said, he is a prophet**. Although up to this time, as though unanointed in heart, he did not yet profess that Christ was the Son of God, he firmly expressed what he thought and did not lie. For our Lord said of himself: "A prophet is not without honor except in his own country" (Mt 13:57); "The Lord your God will raise up for you a prophet ... him shall you heed" (Dt 18:15).[40]

1330. Next (v. 18), we see his parents questioned. First, we have the reason why they were questioned; secondly, the question itself (v. 19); thirdly their answer (v. 20); and fourthly, the reason for this answer (v. 22).

1331. The reason for this second questioning was the unbelief of the Pharisees. He says, **the Jews**, that is, the Pharisees, **did not believe that he had been blind and had received his sight, until they called the parents of the man**. They did this in an attempt to nullify the miracle of Christ and to preserve their own glory: "How can you believe, who receive glory from one another?" (Jn 5:44).

1332. The Pharisees now question his parents. Here they ask about three things. First, about their son, saying **Is this your son?** Secondly, about his blindness; and so they add, **who you say was born blind**. They did not say, "who at one time was blind," but **who you say**, implying that they made this up. What father would lie in such a way about his son? Yet they were trying to make him say he did.

---

38. *Hom. in Io.* 58. 1; PG 59, col. 315–16; cf. *Catena aurea*, 9:8–17.
39. *Tract. in Io.* 44. 9; PL 35, col. 1717; cf. *Catena aurea*, 9:8–17.
40. See *ST* III, q. 7, a. 8.

Thirdly, they ask how he had obtained his sight, **How then does he now see?** This was like saying: Either it is false that he now sees, or that he was once blind; but obviously the truth is that he sees; therefore it was false to say that he had been blind: "The powerful man will test you through much talking, and while he smiles he will be examining you" (Sir 13:11).

1333. Then, the answer of his parents is given (v. 20). The Pharisees had asked about three things; they answer firmly about two and in regard to the third they refer them to their son. First, they admit the first, namely, that he is their son; so they say, **we know that this is our son**. They also admit the second when they add, **and that he was born blind**. This shows that the truth always conquers what is false, as we read in the apocryphal 3 Esdras (3:12): "Truth conquers all." Yet as to the third question, how their son sees, they answer, **but how he now sees we do not know**.

They reply, secondly, about the person who gave him his sight, **nor do we know who opened his eyes**. They answer this way because the question was directed against the one who gave sight to their son, and so they refer this to their son, saying, **Ask him, he is of age**. This was like saying: He was born blind, not mute; thus he can speak for himself in this matter. The testimony about this miracle was from several sources so as to make it more believable: the parents told what they knew, and their blind son confirmed that he had been cured.

1334. The reason for their answer is given when he says, **his parents said this because they feared the Jews**; for they were still imperfect and did not dare do what our Lord says: "Do not fear those who kill the body" (Mt 10:28). The reason for their fear was **that the Jews had already agreed that if any one should confess him to be Christ, he was to be put out of the synagogue**. "I have said all this to you to keep you from falling away. They will put you out of the synagogues" (Jn 16:11). As Augustine[41] says, it was no longer an evil to be cast out of the synagogue, for the ones they rejected Christ welcomed.

LECTURE 3

24 So for the second time they called the man who had been blind, and said to him, "Give God the praise; we know that this man is a sinner." 25 He answered, "Whether he is a sinner, I do not know; one thing I know, that though I was blind, I now see." 26 They said to him, "What did he do to you? How did he open your eyes?" 27 He answered them, "I have told you already, and you would not listen. Why do

---

41. *Tract. in Io.* 44. 10; PL 35, col. 1717; cf. *Catena aurea*, 9:18–23.

CHAPTER 9   171

you want to hear it again? Do you too want to become his disciples?"
28 And they reviled him, saying, "You are his disciple, but we are disciples of Moses. 29 We know that God has spoken to Moses, but as for this man, we do not know where he comes from." 30 The man answered, "Why, this is a marvel! You do not know where he comes from, and yet he opened my eyes. 31 We know that God does not listen to sinners, but if any one is a worshiper of God and does his will, God listens to him. 32 Never since the world began has it been heard that any one opened the eyes of a man born blind. 33 If this man were not from God, he could do nothing." 34 They answered him, "You were born in utter sin, and would you teach us?" And they cast him out.[42]

1335. After the questioning of the blind man and his parents, an attempt is made to make him deny the truth and affirm what is false. First, they attempt to make him deny the truth; secondly, they revile him (v. 28); and thirdly, they condemn him (v. 34). The Evangelist does two things about the first. First, he shows how they tried to get the man born blind to deny the truth; secondly, how they continued to question him in order to malign him (v. 26). In regard to the first he does two things: first, he shows their malice; and secondly, the steadfastness of the man born blind (v. 25). The malice of the Pharisees is shown by their attempt to have him deny the truth, while the steadfastness of the blind man appears by his resolute profession of the truth.

1336. In regard to the first he says, **for the second time they called the man who had been blind,** for his parents had referred them to the blind man, **and said to him: Give God the praise.** They say one thing but mean another. For they wish to force him to say that his sight was not restored by Christ, or if they are unable to do this, to force him to admit that he was cured by him through sorcery. They do not say this openly, but implicitly, with an appearance of devotion. They attempt this by saying, **Give God the praise.** As if to say: Your sight has been given to you. But only God can do this. Therefore, you should not attribute this to anyone but God, and not to this man, that is, Christ, because if you do this you are indicating that you have not received the gift of your healing from God, for the reason that God does not perform miracles through sinners.[43] Thus they add, **we know that this man is a sinner.** But, as Augustine[44] says, if he had done this, he would not be giving glory to God but rather, being ungrateful, would be blaspheming. But in truth, the Pharisees were lying when they said, **we know that this man is a sinner;** for above (8:46), they could not convict him of sin, and he said: "which of you convicts me of sin?"

---

42. St. Thomas refers to Jn 9:31 in *ST* II-II, q. 83, a. 16, obj. 1; q. 178, a. 2, obj. 1; III, q. 64, a. 1, obj. 2; Jn 9:32: *ST* III, q. 43, a. 4.
43. See *ST* II-II, q. 178, a. 2.
44. *Tract. in Io.* 44. 11; PL 35, col. 1718; cf. *Catena aurea*, 9:24–34.

And no wonder, because "He committed no sin; no guile was found on his lips" (1 Pet 2:22).

1337. Here we see the steadfastness of the blind man. For amazed at the hardness of the Pharisees, and impatient with what they were saying, he says, in all truth, **Whether he is a sinner, I do not know.**

Yet because he had said before that "He is a prophet," is he not now saying, **Whether he is a sinner I do not know**, out of fear, as if he were doubtful? Not at all! Rather, he is angry and mocking the Pharisees. He is saying in effect: You say that he is a sinner; but I do not know that he is a sinner, and I am amazed that you say this, because he accomplished a work which does not seem to be the work of a sinner, because **though I was blind, now I see**, by his kindness. According to Augustine,[45] he said this in order not to be maligned nor to conceal the truth. For perhaps if he had said, "I know that he is a just man," which was true, they would have maligned him. But according to Chrysostom,[46] he said this to give them a more impressive testimony to the miracle, and to make his answer believable by calling attention to the gift itself he received.

1338. They again question the man born blind in order to malign him. First, we have the cunning interrogation of the Pharisees; and secondly, the contemptuous reply of the blind man (v. 27).

1339. He says, with respect to the first, **They said to him: What did he do to you?** The blind man had said that he had received his sight from Christ, which the Pharisees had not asked about. It was their intention to malign Christ, so they now ask rather how he did it. So they did not ask "How is it that you see?" but **How did he open your eyes?** It was like saying: "He did this by some trick or sorcery, didn't he?" "Those who seek my hurt speak of ruin, and meditate treachery all the day long" (Ps 37:13).

1340. Now the man's answer is given. The man born blind, because he really had received his sight, answers them further, not timidly, but with boldness. He first belittles the repeated questioning of the Pharisees, saying, **I have told you already and you would not listen. Why do you want to hear it again?** This was like saying: I told you once. Why do you want to hear it again? That's foolish! It looks like you are not paying attention to what I am saying. So, I have nothing further to say to you because your questioning is useless, and you want to cavil rather than learn. "He who tells a story to a fool tells it to a drowsy man; and at the end he will say: 'What is it'" (Sir 22:8).

Secondly, he mocks the presumptuous intention of the Pharisees, saying, **Do you too want to become his disciples?** When someone care-

---

45. In the *Catena aurea*, 9:24–34, this comment is attributed to Alcuin. See Alcuin, *Comm. in S. Ioannis Evang.* 9:25–26; PL 100, col. 880.

46. *Hom. in Io.* 58. 2; PG 59, col. 317; cf. *Catena aurea*, 9:24–34.

fully investigates a matter, he does so either with a good intention, to accept it, or with an evil intention, to condemn it. Now because the Pharisees were carefully investigating this, and because the man born blind did not dare impute an evil intention to them, he takes the alternative, saying, *Do you too want to become his disciples?* He means by this: If you are not investigating this maliciously, you therefore wish to join him: "Can the Ethiopian change his skin or the leopard his spots? Then also you can do good who are accustomed to do evil" (Jer 13:23). As Augustine[47] says: The one who had received his sight gladly desired to give them light. Thus, he significantly says, *you too*, implying that he himself was a disciple. He is saying in effect: *Do you want to become his disciples* as I am? I already see, and do not envy your coming to the light. And as Chrysostom[48] says, from the steadfastness of the blind man we can see how strong truth really is, for when it convinces the lowly, it makes them noble and strong. And we can see how weak is a lie, which even if it is maintained by the powerful, shows and makes them weak.[49]

1341. Next, the Pharisees revile the man born blind. First, we see them revile him; then, secondly, the defense of the blind man (v. 30). He does two things concerning the first: first, he presents the revilement of the Pharisees; secondly, the reason behind it (v. 28b).

1342. With respect to the first he says, *and they reviled him, saying, You are his disciple*. This is, indeed, scornful, if you consider their vicious hearts. But if you consider their words, it is the greatest blessing. May we and our children be treated with such scorn! "If you continue in my word, you are truly my disciples" (Jn 8:31). Still, the Evangelist stated that they reviled him by saying this because what they said came from their evil hearts: "Like the glaze covering an earthen vessel are smooth lips with an evil heart" (Prov 26:23). We read about this revilement in the Psalm (108:28): "Let them curse, but do thou bless"; and in Matthew (5:11): "Blessed are you when men revile you."[50]

1343. He next adds the reason for their reviling when he says, *we are disciples of Moses*. They were thinking of how they were ridiculed by the man born blind when he asked if they wanted to become Christ's disciples; for they took pride in being disciples of Moses, whom they thought was greater. First, they set forth their own situation, saying, *we are disciples of Moses*. But this pride of theirs is false, because they neither followed Moses nor fulfilled his commands: "If you believed Moses, you would believe me" (5:46); this was like saying: You do not follow the servant [Moses], and later go against his Lord.

---

47. *Tract. in Io.* 44. 11; PL 35, col. 1718.
48. *Hom. in Io.* 58. 2; PG 59, col. 318; cf. *Catena aurea*, 9:24–34.
49. See *ST* II-II, q. 110, aa. 1, 3.
50. See *ST* II-II, q. 72, a. 3.

Secondly, they praise the dignity of Moses when they say, *we know that God has spoken to Moses*. Here they are telling the truth, for as we read: "The Lord used to speak to Moses face to face, as a man speaks to his friend" (Ex 33:11); and "If there is a prophet among you, I, the Lord, make myself known to him in a vision, I speak with him in a dream. Not so with my servant Moses; he is entrusted with all my house. With him I speak mouth to mouth" (Num 12:6). Thus God spoke to Moses in a more excellent way than to the other prophets.[51] And it is about this that they are speaking. However, it is clear that since God spoke his Word to Moses, the dignity of Moses came from the Word of God. And so the Word of God is of greater dignity than Moses: "Yet Jesus has been counted worthy of as much more glory than Moses as the builder of a house has more honor than the house" (Heb 3:3).[52]

Thirdly, they hint at the dignity of Christ in a veiled manner when they say, *as for this man*, Christ, *we do not know where he comes from*. This is true, but not the way they understood it: for they did not know the Father, and Christ was from the Father: "You know neither me nor my Father" (8:19). But their statement is false as they understood it, for when they said, we do *not know where he comes from*, they meant he had no authority and was unverified, so that is was not clear whether or not he came from God. They seem to be applying to him the words of Jeremiah: "I did not send you prophets, yet they ran" (23:21).

1344. Now, the blind man's argument against the Pharisees is presented. First, he is amazed at their hardness of heart; secondly, he refutes their false opinion (v. 31).

1345. Concerning the first, we must recall that we are not amazed at what happens frequently, and in the usual way; but we are amazed at what is unusual and great, whether this be good or evil. We are struck by unusual and great good: "You are wonderful, my Lord, and your countenance is full of grace," as we read in Esther (15:17). We are also amazed at great evil: "Be appalled, O heavens, at this ... for my people have committed two evils" (Jer 2:12). In line with this, the blind man says in answer, *Why this is a marvel! You do not know where he comes from*. He is saying in effect: It would not be remarkable if you regarded someone insignificant and like me as having no authority. But it is extremely amazing that you can see an explicit and evident sign of divine power in Christ and say that you do not know where he comes from, especially because he did open my eyes.[53]

1346. The man born blind refutes their false opinion by saying, *we know that God does not listen to sinners*. He is reasoning this way:

---

51. See *ST* II-II, q. 174, a. 4.　　52. See *ST* I-II, q. 98, aa. 2–3.
53. See *ST* III, q. 43, a. 4.

Whomever God hears is from God; but God heard Christ; therefore, Christ is from God. He first states his main premise; then the minor premise (v. 32); and thirdly, he draws his conclusion (v. 33). He does two things about the first: first, he mentions those whom God does not hear; secondly, those he does hear (v. 31b).

1347. God does not hear sinners. In regard to this he says, **we know that God does not hear sinners**. He is saying: Both you and I agree that sinners are not heard by God. Thus a Psalm (17:42) says, "They cried to the Lord and he did not hear them"; and again, "Then they will call upon me, but I will not answer" (Pr 1:28). But there are statements which contradict this: "If they sin against thee—for there is no man who does not sin—but later repent with all their heart, then hear thou from heaven and forgive thy people" (2 Chr 6:36-39); and in Luke (18:14) we read that the tax collector "went down to his house justified."

Because of this Augustine[54] says that this blind man is speaking as one who has not been anointed, as one who does not yet have complete knowledge. For God does hear sinners, otherwise it would have been futile for the tax collector to have prayed: "God, be merciful to me a sinner." Accordingly, if we wish to save the statement of the blind man we must say that God does not hear those sinners who persist in their sinning; but he does hear those sinners who are sorry for their sins, and who should be regarded more as repentant than as sinners.[55]

1348. Yet there is a difficulty here. It is clear that miracles are not accomplished by us due to our own power, but through prayer. But sinners often perform miracles: "Lord, Lord, did we not prophesy in your name ... and do many mighty works in your name?" (Mt 7:22); and yet God did not know them. Thus, what the blind man said does not seem to be true, namely, **we know that God does not listen to sinners**.

There are two answers to this. The first is general. Prayer has two characteristics, that is, it can obtain [what it asks for] and it can merit.[56] Thus, sometimes it obtains what it asks, and does not merit; at other times, it merits and does not obtain. And so nothing prevents the prayer of a sinner from obtaining what it asks although it does not merit. This is the way that God hears sinners; not as a matter of merit, but they obtain what they ask from the divine power, which they acknowledge. The other answer is special and applies to this particular case, when the miracle that was done makes known the person of Christ.

1349. It should be mentioned that every miracle is a sort of testimony. Sometimes, a miracle is accomplished as a testimony to the truth

---

54. *Tract. in Io.* 44. 13; PL 35, col. 1718; cf. *Catena aurea*, 9:24–34.
55. See *ST* III, q. 84, a. 7, ad 1.
56. See *ST* III, q. 21, a. 1.

that is being preached; at other times, it is a testimony to the person performing it. We must also realize that no true miracle happens except by the divine power, and that God is never a witness to a lie. I say, therefore, that whenever a miracle is performed in testimony to a doctrine that is being preached, that doctrine must be true, even if the person who is preaching it is not good. And when it is performed in testimony to the person, it is also necessary that the person be good. Now it is evident that the miracles of Christ were performed in testimony to his person: "The works which the Father has granted me to accomplish . . . bear me witness that the Father has sent me" (5:36).[57] It was with this meaning that the blind man said that *God does not listen to sinners*, that is, so that they could perform miracles as a testimony to their supposed holiness.

1350. Then when he says, *but if any one is a worshiper of God*, he shows that God hears the just through merit. We must realize that the performing of miracles is attributed to faith: "If you say to this mountain, 'Be taken up and cast into the sea,' it will be done" (Mt 21:21). The reason for this is that miracles are accomplished by the omnipotence of God, on which faith relies. Therefore, whoever wishes to obtain something from God has to have faith: "Let him ask in faith" (Jas 1:6). However, if he wishes to obtain it through merit, he must do God's will.[58] And these two conditions are mentioned here. As to the first, he says, *If any one is a worshiper of God* by sacrifices and offerings: "They will worship him with sacrifice and burnt offering" (Is 19:21). These belong to the worship of *latria*, which attests to one's faith. As to the second he says, *and does his will* by obeying his commandments, *God listens to him*.[59]

1351. Here he takes the minor premise of his argument. He is saying: Because of what Christ did, which no man has ever done, it is obvious that he did this by the action of God, and that he has been heard by God: "If I had not done among them the works which no one else did, they would not have sin" (Jn 15:24).

1352. Next, he draws his conclusion. He is saying, in effect: From the kind of works that Christ does, it is obvious that he is from God. For *if this man were not from God, he could do nothing*, that is, freely, often and truly, because "apart from me you can do nothing" (15:5).

1353. Here the Pharisees condemn the blind man. In this condemnation they fall into three defects or sins, namely, untruth, pride, and injustice. They fall into untruth in reviling the blind man, *saying, you were born in utter sin*. Here it should be noted that the Jews were of the opinion that all infirmities and temporal adversities beset us on

---

57. See *ST* III, q. 43, aa. 1–2.
58. See *ST* I-II, q. 114, a. 1.
59. See *ST* I-II, q. 109, a. 4; II-II, q. 81, aa. 5, 7; III, q. 25, aa. 1–2.

account of our previous sins. This was the opinion given by Eliphaz: "Think now, who that was innocent ever perished? Or where were the upright cut off? As I have seen those who plow iniquity and sow trouble reap the same. By the breath of God they perish" (Job 4:7). The reason for this opinion is that in the Old Law temporal goods were promised to the good, and temporal punishment to the evil: "If you are willing and obedient, you shall eat the good of the land" (Is 1:19). Therefore, seeing that this man had been born blind, they believed that this happened on account of his sins, and so they say, *you were born in utter sin*. But they were wrong, because the Lord said: "It was not that this man sinned, or his parents."

They say *in utter sin* to show that he is defiled by sins not only in his soul, insofar as all of us are born sinners, but even as regards the traces of sin which appear in his body, as blindness. Or according to Chrysostom,[60] *in utter sin* means that he was in sin all his life, from his earliest years.

They are guilty of pride by rejecting what the man born blind was teaching, when they say, **Would you teach us?** This was like saying: You are not worthy. This makes their pride clear: for no person, no matter however wise, ought to reject being taught by any inferior. Thus the Apostle teaches (1 Cor 14:30) that if something is revealed to one who is inferior, those who are greater should keep silent and listen. In Daniel we read that all the people, and the elders, listened to the judgment of a young boy, Daniel, whose spirit had been raised up by God.[61]

They are guilty of injustice by unjustly casting him out. Thus we read, **and they cast him out**, that is, because he spoke the truth. However, in this man born blind there is already fulfilled what our Lord had said: "Blessed are you when men hate you, and when they exclude you and revile you, and cast out your name as evil, on account of the Son of man!" (Lk 6:22).

LECTURE 4

35 Jesus heard that they had cast him out, and having found him he said, "Do you believe in the Son of God?" 36 He answered, "And who is he, sir, that I may believe in him?" 37 Jesus said to him, "You have seen him, and it is he who speaks to you." 38 He said, "Lord, I believe"; and he worshiped him. 39 Jesus said, "For judgment I came into this world, that those who do not see may see, and that those who

---

60. *Hom. in Io.* 58. 3; PG 59, col. 319; cf. *Catena aurea*, 9:24–34.
61. See *ST* II-II, q. 161, a. 3; II-II, q. 162, a. 4.

see may become blind." 40 Some of the Pharisees near him heard this, and they said to him, "Are we also blind?" 41 Jesus said to them, "If you were blind, you would have no guilt; but now that you say, 'we see', your guilt remains."[62]

1354. After the Evangelist showed how the Jews cast out the man born blind because he persisted in the truth, he here shows how Jesus received him and taught him. First, we see Christ teaching him; secondly, the devotion of the man born blind (v. 38); thirdly, the approval of his devotion (v. 39). He does three things about the first. First, he shows the eagerness of Christ to teach him; secondly, we see the desire of the man born blind to believe (v. 36); and thirdly, the teaching of the faith is given to perfect him (v. 37).

1355. Christ's eagerness to teach is described in three ways. First, by his attentive consideration to what was done to the man born blind. For just as a trainer carefully considers what his athlete undergoes for his sake, so Christ attentively considered what the man born blind underwent for the sake of the truth and because of his assertions. And so he says that **Jesus heard**, attentively considered, that the Pharisees **had cast him out**, of the temple: "Give heed to me, O Lord, and to the voices of my adversaries" (Jer 18:19).

Secondly, we see Christ's eagerness from his efforts in searching for him, for the Evangelist says, **and having found him**; for we are said to find what we diligently seek: "She seeks diligently, until she finds it" (Lk 15:8). It is clear from this that Christ was looking for him alone, because he found more faith in him alone than in all the others. And we can see from this that God loves one just person more than ten thousand sinners: "I will make men more rare than fine gold, and mankind than the gold of Ophir" (Is 13:12). And in Genesis we read that God was willing to spare Sodom for the sake of ten just men.

Thirdly, our Lord's eagerness is seen from the seriousness of his question; he said, **Do you believe in the Son of God?** The blind man was an image of those to be baptized. Thus the custom arose in the Church of questioning those to be baptized about their faith: "Baptism ... now saves you, not as a removal of dirt from the body, but as an appeal to God for a clean conscience" (1 Pet 3:21). When asked about his faith he does not say, "Do you believe in Christ?" but **Do you believe in the Son of God?** He does this, as Hilary[63] says, because it would develop that some would profess Christ, and yet deny that he was the Son of God and God, as Arius erred. These words clearly exclude this error: for if Christ were not God, we would not have to believe in him, since God alone is the object of faith, which rests on the first truth. Thus he

---

62. St. Thomas refers to Jn 9:41 in *ST* II-II, q. 15, a. 1, obj. 1.
63. *De Trin.* 6. 48; PL 10, col. 196B; cf. *Catena aurea*, 9:35–41.

significantly says, ***in the Son*** (*in Filium*); for I am certainly able to believe some creature, such as Peter and Paul (*credere Petro et Paulo*), yet I do not believe in Peter (*credere in Petrum*), but in God (*in Deum*) alone as the object of faith [cf. no. 901].[64] Thus it is clear that the Son of God is not a creature: "You believe in God, believe also in me" (Jn 14:1).

1356. Next he mentions the desire of the man born blind to believe. We have to recall that this man had not yet physically seen Christ: for he had not seen him when Christ anointed his eyes and sent him to the pool of Siloam, and when he wanted to go back to him he was detained by the Pharisees and the Jews. However, although he had not physically seen Jesus, he believed that the one who opened his eyes was the Son of God. And so he breaks out in words of desire and intense longing, and says, ***And who is he, sir***, namely, the Son of God, who opened my eyes, ***that I may believe in him?*** It is clear from this that he knew something about Jesus, and did not know other things about him. For if he had not known him, he would not have argued so firmly on his behalf; and if he had not been ignorant of other things, he certainly would not have said, ***Who is he, sir?*** "My soul yearns for you in the night," that is, the night of ignorance (Is 26:9).

1357. Because, as we read in Wisdom (6:16), "She," that is, Wisdom, "goes about seeking those worthy of her," Christ reveals himself to the man born blind, who desired her, when he says, ***You have seen him, and it is he who speaks to you***. Here Christ is giving him a teaching of faith. First, he mentions the gift he received, saying ***you have seen him***, that is, you, who did not see before, have now seen him. He is saying in effect that the man born blind received the ability to see from him: "Blessed are the eyes which see what you see" (Lk 10:23); "Lord, now let your servant depart in peace . . . for my eyes have seen your salvation" (Lk 2:29). Secondly, the teaching itself is given when he says, ***It is he who speaks to you***: "In these last days he has spoken to us by a Son" (Heb 1:2).[65]

These words refute the error of Nestorius, who said that in Christ the *suppositum* [or person] of the Son of God is different from the *suppositum* of the Son of man. They refute it because the one who spoke these words was born from Mary and was the son of man, and the very same one is the Son of God, as our Lord says. Therefore, there are not two *supposita* [persons] in Christ, although the natures [the divine and the human] are not the same.[66]

1358. Then when the Evangelist says, ***he said, Lord, I believe***, we see the devout faith of the man born blind. And first, he professes with his lips the faith in his heart, saying, ***Lord, I believe***: "Man believes

---

64. See *ST* II-II, q. 1, a. 1; II-II, q. 2, a. 2.
65. See *ST* II-II, q. 2, a. 7; II-II, q. 6, a. 1.
66. See *ST* III, q. 2, a. 3.

with his heart and so is justified, and he confesses with his lips and so is saved" (Rom 10:10). Secondly, he shows it in his conduct, *and he worshiped him*. This shows that he believes in the divine nature of Christ, because those whose consciences have been cleansed know Christ not only as the son of man, which was externally obvious, but as the Son of God, who had taken flesh: for adoration is due to God alone: "You will adore the Lord, your God" (Dt 6:13).[67]

1359. Next (v. 39), the devotion of the man born blind is commended: first, his devotion is commended; secondly, we see the grumbling of the Jews (v. 40); and then they are answered (v. 41).

1360. The man born blind is commended for his faith. We read, *for judgment I came into this world*. But on the other hand, we also read: "God sent the Son into the world, not to judge the world" (Jn 3:17). My answer is this: In the second statement (3:17) he is speaking of the judgment of condemnation, about which we read: "Those who have done evil [will rise] to the resurrection of judgment" (Jn 5:29), that is, to a judgment of condemnation. And God did not send his Son for this purpose at his first coming; he was sent to save us. But here in the present statement (9:39), he is speaking of the judgment of distinction, about which we read: "Vindicate me, O Lord, and distinguish my cause" (Ps 42:1). For Jesus came to distinguish the good from the evil. The words which follow show this: *that those who do not see may see, and that those who see may become blind.*[68]

According to Augustine,[69] those who think they see do not see, and those who do not think they see, see. Now, we are said to be blind, spiritually, insofar as we sin: "Their wickedness blinded them" (Wis 2:21).[70] Thus, the one who does not recognize his own sins regards himself as seeing; while one who recognizes himself as a sinner regards himself as not seeing. The first is characteristic of the proud; the second, of the humble. So the meaning is this: I have come to distinguish the humble from the proud, so that the humble, *who do not see*, that is, who regard themselves as sinners, *may see*, having been illuminated by faith, *and that those who see*, that is, the proud, *may become blind*, that is, may remain in the darkness.[71]

1361. Chrysostom[72] understands this passage in terms of the judgment of condemnation, so that the statement, *for judgment I came into this world* is not understood in a causal sense, but it indicates the sequence of events. It is like saying: After my coming into the world,

---

67. See *ST* II-II, q. 3, a. 1, ad 1.
68. See *ST* III, q. 59, a. 2.
69. *Tract. in Io.* 44. 17; PL 35, col. 1719; cf. *Catena aurea*, 9:35–41.
70. See *ST* II-II, q. 15, a. 1.
71. See *ST* II-II, q. 161, a. 2.
72. *Hom. in Io.* 59. 1; PG 59, col. 323; cf. *Catena aurea*, 9:35–41.

there follows for some the judgment of condemnation insofar as the reason for their condemnation increases in them. In Luke (2:23) we find something similar: "This child is sent for the falling and rising of many in Israel," not because Christ is the cause of their fall, but because this follows his coming. He adds, *that those who do not see*, that is, the Gentiles, who lacked the light of divine knowledge, *may see*, i.e., be admitted to the knowledge of God: "The people who walked in darkness have seen a great light" (Is 9:2); *and that those who see*, the Jews, who did have a knowledge of God—"In Judah God is known" (Ps 75:2)—*may become blind*, fall away from the knowledge of God. The Apostle explicitly mentions this: "The Gentiles who did not pursue righteousness have attained it" (Rom 9:30).

1362. Now we see the grumbling of the Jews. They had understood our Lord's words in a bodily sense because they had seen the man born blind physically restored to sight, and had thought that our Lord was concerned only with the light in his eyes rather than in his mind. And so they believed that he was warning and threatening them with physical blindness when he said *may become blind*. Therefore, the Evangelist says, *some of the Pharisees near him heard this*, the above words. He says who were *near him*, to show their vacillation: for sometimes they were with him because of some miracles which they saw, and then would leave when the truth was made known to them: "They believe for a while, and in time of tribulation fall away" (Lk 8:13). *And they said to him, Are we also blind*, i.e., physically? Yet they were spiritually blind: "Let them alone; they are blind guides" (Mt 15:14).

1363. Next, we see the Jews silenced. According to Augustine,[73] this shows the meaning of the previous passage, that is, that our Lord was referring to spiritual blindness. He says, *If you were blind, you would have no guilt*, because you would be running to the remedy. For sin is taken away by grace, which is given only to the humble: "God gives grace to the humble" (Jas 4:6). *But now that you say, We see*, i.e., proudly thinking that you do see, you do not recognize that you are sinners, *your guilt remains*, i.e., is not taken away: "God opposes the proud" (Jas 4:6).[74]

Chrysostom[75] understands this passage as referring to physical blindness. The meaning is then: *If you were blind*, physically, you would have no guilt, because since blindness is a physical defect, it does not have the nature of sin. *But now that you say, We see*, your sin is clear, because while seeing the miracles that I do, you do not believe me: "Blind the heart of this people" (Is 6:10).

Here is another explanation. *If you were blind*, i.e., ignorant of the

---

73. *Tract. in Io.* 44. 17; PL 35, col. 1719; cf. *Catena aurea*, 9:35–41.
74. See *ST* II-II, q. 162, a. 6.
75. *Hom. in Io.* 59. 1; PG 59, col. 323; cf. *Catena aurea*, 9:35–41.

judgments of God and of the sacraments of the law; *you would have no guilt*, i.e., so much. As if to say: If you were sinning out of ignorance, your sin would not be so serious. ***But now that you say, We see***, i.e., arrogate to yourselves an understanding of the law and a knowledge of God, and still sin, then *your guilt remains*, i.e., becomes greater: "That servant who knew his master's will, but did not make ready or act according to his will, shall receive a severe beating" (Lk 12:47).

CHAPTER 10

LECTURE 1

1 *"Truly, truly, I say to you, he who does not enter the sheepfold by the door but climbs in by another way, that man is a thief and a robber; 2 but he who enters by the door is the shepherd of the sheep. 3 To him the gatekeeper opens; the sheep hear his voice, and he calls his own sheep by name and leads them out. 4 When he has brought out all his own, he goes before them, and the sheep follow him, for they know his voice. 5 A stranger they will not follow, but they will flee from him, for they do not know the voice of strangers.*

1364. After our Lord showed that his teaching had power to enlighten, he here shows that he has power to give life. First, he shows this by word; secondly, by a miracle (chap 11). Concerning the first he does three things. First, he shows that he has life-giving power; secondly, his manner of giving life (v. 11); thirdly, he explains his power to give life (v. 19). The first part is divided into three parts. First, our Lord relates a parable; secondly, the Evangelist mentions the necessity for explaining it (v. 6); thirdly, our Lord explains the parable (v. 7).

He relates the parable to them, saying, **Truly, truly, I say to you.** It concerns two things, a thief and the shepherd of the sheep. Thus he does three things. First, he mentions the mark of a thief and robber; secondly, a characteristic of the shepherd (v. 2); thirdly, the effect each of these has (v. 4).

1365. To understand this parable we must consider who the sheep are, namely, that they are the faithful of Christ and those in the grace of God: "We are the people of his pasture, and the sheep of his hand" (Ps 94:7); "You, the people, are the sheep of my pasture" (Ez 34:31). And so the sheepfold is the multitude of the faithful: "I will surely gather all of you, O Jacob, I will gather the remnant of Israel; I will set them together like sheep in a fold" (Mic 2:12). The door of the sheepfold is explained in different ways by Chrysostom and by Augustine.

1366. According to Chrysostom,[1] Christ calls Sacred Scripture the door, according to "Pray for us also that God may open to us a door for the word" (Col 4:3). Sacred Scripture is called a door, as Chrysostom says, first of all, because through it we have access to the knowledge of God: "which he promised beforehand through his prophets in the

---

1. *Hom. in Io.* 59. 2; PG 59, col. 324; cf. *Catena aurea*, 10:1–5.

holy scriptures" (Rom 1:2). Secondly, for just as the door guards the sheep, so Sacred Scripture preserves the life of the faithful: "You search the scriptures, because you think that in them you have eternal life" (5:39). Thirdly, because the door keeps the wolf from entering; so Sacred Scripture keeps heretics from harming the faithful: "Every scripture inspired by God is also profitable for teaching, for reproof, for correction" (2 Tim 3:16). So, the one who does not enter by the door is the one who does not enter by Sacred Scripture to teach the people.[2] Our Lord says of such: "In vain do they worship me, teaching as doctrines the precepts of men" (Mt 15:9); "You have made void the word of God" (Matt 15:6). This, then, is the mark of the thief: he does not enter by the door, but in some other way.

He adds that the thief *climbs*, and this is appropriate to this parable because thieves climb the walls, instead of entering by the door, and drop into the sheepfold. It also corresponds to the truth, because the reason why some teach what conflicts with Sacred Scripture is due to pride: "If any one teaches otherwise and does not agree with the sound words of our Lord Jesus Christ and the teaching which accords with godliness, he is puffed up with conceit, he knows nothing" (1 Tim 6:3). Referring to this he says that such a person *climbs*, that is, through pride. The one who *climbs in by another way, that man is a thief*, because he snatches what is not his, *and a robber*, because he kills what he snatches: "If thieves came to you, if plunderers by night—how you have been destroyed" (Ob 1:5).

According to this explanation, the relation with what preceded is made in this way: Since our Lord had said, "If you were blind, you would have no guilt," the Jews might have answered: "We do not believe you, but this is not due to our blindness. It is because of your own error that we have turned away from you." And so our Lord rejects this, and wishes to show that he is not in error because he enters by the door, by Sacred Scripture, that is, he teaches what is contained in Sacred Scripture.

1367. Against this interpretation is the fact that when our Lord explains this further on, he says, *I am the door*. So it seems that we should understand the door to be Christ. In answer to this, Chrysostom[3] says that in this parable our Lord refers to himself both as the door and the shepherd; but this is from different points of view, because a door and a shepherd are different. Now aside from Christ nothing is more fittingly called a door than Sacred Scripture, for the reasons given above. Therefore, Sacred Scripture is fittingly called a door.

1368. According to Augustine,[4] the door is Christ, because one en-

---

2. See *ST* I, q. 1, a. 10.
3. *Hom. in Io.* 59. 3; PG 59, col. 324–25; cf. *Catena aurea*, 10:1–5.
4. *Tract. in Io.* 45. 2; PL 35, col. 1720; cf. *Catena aurea*, 10:1–5.

ters through him: "After this I looked, and lo, in heaven an open door!" (Rev 4:1). Therefore, any one who enters the sheepfold should enter by the door, that is, by Christ, and not by another way.

Note that both the sheep and their shepherd enter into the sheepfold: the sheep in order to be secure there, and the shepherd in order to guard the sheep. And so, if you wish to enter as a sheep to be kept safe there, or as a shepherd to keep the people safe, you must enter the sheepfold through Christ. You must not enter by any other way, as did the philosophers who treated the principle virtues, and the Pharisees who established the ceremonial traditions. These are neither sheep nor shepherds because, as our Lord says, **he who does not enter the sheepfold by the door**, i.e., does not enter by Christ, **but climbs in by another way, that man is a thief and a robber**, because he destroys both himself and others. For Christ and no one else is the door into the sheepfold, that is, the multitude of the faithful: "We have peace with God through our Lord Jesus Christ" (Rom 5:1); "There is no other name under heaven given among men by which we must be saved" (Acts 4:12).[5]

According to this exposition, the connection with what went before is made in this way: Because they said that they could see without Christ—"now that you say, 'We see'"—our Lord shows that this is not true, because they do not enter by the door. Thus he says, **Truly, truly, I say to you** .

It should be noted that just as one who does not enter by the door as a sheep cannot be kept safe, so one who enters as a shepherd cannot guard the sheep unless he enters by the door, namely, by Christ. This is the door through which the true shepherds have entered: "And one does not take the honor upon himself, but he is called by God, just as Aaron was" (Heb 5:4). Evil shepherds do not enter by the door, but by ambition and secular power and simony; and these are thieves and robbers: "They set up princes, but without my knowledge," that is, without my approval (Hos 8:5). Further, he says such a person **climbs in by another way**, because the door, namely, Christ, since it is small through humility—"Learn from me; for I am gentle and lowly in heart" (Matt 11:29)—can be entered only by those who imitate the humility of Christ.[6] Therefore, those who do not enter by the door but climb in by another way are the proud. They do not imitate him who, although he was God, became man; and they do not recognize his lowering of himself.

1369. Now he considers the shepherd. First, he mentions the mark of the shepherd; secondly, he shows through signs that he is the shepherd (v. 3).

1370. The mark of the true shepherd is to enter by the door, that

---

5. See *ST* I-II, q. 103, aa. 3–4; II-II, q. 4, a. 7; II-II, q. 10, a. 4; II-II, q. 23, a. 7.
6. See *ST* II-II, q. 161, a. 5.

is, by the testimony of Sacred Scripture. Thus Christ said: "Everything written about me in the Law of Moses and the prophets and the Psalms must be fulfilled" (Lk 24:44).[7] He is called a shepherd: "I am not troubled when I follow you as my shepherd" (Jer 17:16); "He rebukes and trains and teaches them, and turns them back, as a shepherd his flock" (Sir 18:13).

But if the door is Christ, as Augustine[8] explains it, then in entering by the door, he enters by himself. And this is special to Christ: for no one can enter the door, i.e., to beatitude, except by the truth, because beatitude is nothing else than joy in the truth.[9] But Christ, as God, is the truth; therefore, as man, he enters by himself, that is, by the truth, which he is as God. We, however, are not the truth, but children of the light, by participating in the true and uncreated light. Consequently, we have to enter by the truth which is Christ: "Sanctify them in the truth" (17:17); "If any one enters by me, he will be saved" (10:9).[10] If one wishes to enter even as a shepherd, he must enter by the door, that is, Christ, according to his truth, will, and consent. Thus we read in Ezekiel (24:23): "And I will set up over them one shepherd, my servant David, and he shall feed them." This is like saying: they must be given by me, and not by others or themselves.

1371. Now he mentions the signs of a good shepherd; and there are three. The first relates to the gatekeeper, and is that the good shepherd is let in by him. As to this he says, **to him the gatekeeper opens**. This gatekeeper, according to Chrysostom,[11] is the one who opens the way to a knowledge of Sacred Scripture. The first one to do this was Moses, who first received and established Sacred Scripture. And Moses opened to Christ, because as was said above: "If you believed Moses, you would believe me, for he wrote of me" (5:46).

Or, according to Augustine,[12] the gatekeeper is Christ himself, because he brings us himself. He says, "He opens himself who reveals himself, and we enter only by his grace." "For by grace you have been saved" (Eph 2:8). It does not matter if Christ, who is the door, is also the gatekeeper; for certain things are compatible in spiritual matters that cannot occur in physical reality. Now there seems to be a greater difference between a shepherd and a door than between a door and a gatekeeper. Therefore, since Christ can be called both a shepherd and a door, as was said, much more so can he be called a door and a gatekeeper. But if you prefer that someone other than Moses or Christ be the gatekeeper, then consider the Holy Spirit the gatekeeper, as Augus-

7. See *ST* I-II, q. 107, a. 2; III, q. 46, a. 1.
8. *Tract. in Io.* 47. 1; PL 35, col. 1733; cf. *Catena aurea*, 10:11–13.
9. See *ST* I-II, q. 3, a. 8.
10. See *ST* I, q. 26, aa. 2–3.
11. *Hom. in Io.* 59. 3; PG 59, col. 325; cf. *Catena aurea*, 10:1–5.
12. *Tract. in Io.* 46. 2–3; PL 35, col. 1728–29; cf. *Catena aurea*, 10:1–5.

tine[13] says. For it is the office of a gatekeeper to open the door, and it says below of the Holy Spirit that "He will guide you into all the truth" (16:13). And Christ is the door insofar as he is the Truth.[14]

1372. The second sign relates to the sheep, and it is that they obey the shepherd. This is what he says, **the sheep hear his voice**. This is reasonable if the resemblance to a natural shepherd is considered: because just as sheep recognize the voice of their shepherd due to familiar experience, so righteous believers hear the voice of Christ: "O that today you would hearken to his voice" (Ps 94:8).

1373. But what of the fact that many who are Christ's sheep did not hear his voice, as Paul; or that some who were not his sheep did hear it, as Judas? One might reply that Judas was Christ's sheep for that time as to his present righteousness. And Paul, when he did not hear the voice of Christ, was not a sheep but a wolf; but when the voice of Christ came it changed the wolf into a sheep. This reply could be accepted if it were not contrary to a statement in Ezekiel (34:4): "The crippled you have not bound up, the strayed you have not brought back." It seems from this that even when they were crippled and strayed they were sheep. Therefore, one must say that here our Lord is speaking of his sheep not only according to their present righteousness but even according to their eternal predestination. For there is a certain voice of Christ that only the predestined can hear, i.e., "He who endures to the end" (Mt 10:22).[15]

Again, he says, **the sheep hear his voice**, because they might offer as an excuse for their unbelief the fact that not only they, but none of the leaders believed in him. So he says in answer to this, **the sheep hear his voice**, as if saying: They do not believe because they are not my sheep.

1374. The third sign is taken from the actions of the shepherd. Here he mentions four actions of a good shepherd: the first being that he knows his sheep. He says, **he calls his own sheep by name**, which shows his knowledge of and familiarity with his sheep, for we call by name those whom we know familiarly: "I know you by name" (Ex 33:17). This is part of the office of a shepherd according to: "Be diligent to know the countenance of your flock" (Pr 27:23). This applies to Christ according to his present knowledge, but even more so considering eternal predestination, by which he knew them by name from eternity: "He determined the number of the stars, he gives to all of them their names" (Ps 147:4); "The Lord knows those who are his" (2 Tim 2:19).[16]

The second action of a good shepherd is that he **leads them out**, i.e.,

---

13. Ibid. 46. 4, col. 1729; cf. *Catena aurea*, 10:1–5.
14. See *ST* I-II, q. 106, a. 1.
15. See *ST* III, q. 8, a. 3; III, q. 24, aa. 3–4.
16. See *ST* I, q. 23, a. 4.

he separates them from the society of those who are evil: "He brought them out of darkness and gloom" (Ps 106:13).

The third is that having separated them from evil and having brought them into the sheepfold, *he has brought out all his own*, from the sheepfold. He does this, first, for the salvation of others: "I will send survivors to the nations" (Is 66:19); "Behold, I send you as sheep in the midst of wolves" (Matt 10:16), so that they can make sheep out of the wolves. Secondly, they are to show the direction and way to eternal life: "To guide our feet into the way of peace" (Lk 1:79).

Fourthly, the good shepherd goes before his sheep by the example of a good life; so he says, *he goes before them*, although this is not what the literal shepherd does, for he follows, as in "I took him from following the ewes" (Ps 77:70). But the good shepherd goes before them by example, "not as domineering over those in your charge but being examples to the flock" (1 Pet 5:3). And Christ does go before them: for he was the first to die for the teaching of the truth—"If any man would come after me, let him deny himself and take up his cross and follow me" (Matt 16:24); and he went before all into everlasting life—"He who opens the breach will go up before them" (Mic 2:13).[17]

1375. Now he considers the effect that both the thief and the shepherd have upon the sheep. First, he mentions the effect of the good shepherd; secondly, the effect of the wolf and the thief (v. 5).

1376. He says, first, that *the sheep follow him* who goes before them. This is easy to see, because subjects follow in the steps of their leaders, as is stated: "Christ also suffered for you, leaving you an example, that you should follow in his steps" (1 Pet 2:21); "My foot has held fast to his steps" (Job 23:11). The sheep follow *for they know his voice*, i.e., they know it and take delight in it: "Let me hear your voice, for your voice is sweet" (Sg 2:14).

1377. The effect that the thief has is that the sheep do not follow him for very long, but only for a time; so he says, *a stranger they will not follow*, i.e., they do not follow a false and heretical teacher: "The children who are strangers have lied to me" (Ps 17:46). Thus Paul did not follow false teachers for long. But *they will flee from him*, because "Bad company ruins good morals" (1 Cor 15:33). They flee *for they do not know*, that is, do not approve of, *the voice of strangers*, meaning their teaching, which spreads stealthily like a cancer.[18]

---

17. See *ST* III, q. 46, a. 3; III, q. 53, a. 1.
18. See *ST* II-II, q. 11, a. 2.

LECTURE 2

6 This figure Jesus used with them, but they did not understand what he was saying to them. 7 So Jesus again said to them, "Truly, truly, I say to you, I am the door of the sheep. 8 All who came before me are thieves and robbers; but the sheep did not heed them. 9 I am the door; if any one enters by me, he will be saved, and will go in and out and find pasture. 10 The thief comes only to steal and kill and destroy; I came that they may have life, and have it abundantly."[19]

1378. Here the Evangelist tells why it was necessary to explain the above similitude; and this necessity was caused by the failure of his listeners to understand. First, he mentions the reason why they failed to understand; secondly, he says they failed to understand.

1379. The cause of their failure to understand was that Christ was speaking in figures. The Evangelist says, **This figure** [*proverbium*] **Jesus used with them.** A figure [*proverbium*], properly speaking, is the use of one word in place of another, when it is intended that one word be understood from its likeness to the other. This is also called a parable [*parabola*]. Our Lord spoke in figures, first of all, because of the wicked, in order to conceal from them the mysteries of the kingdom of heaven: "To you it has been given to know the secrets of the kingdom of God; but for others they are in parables" (Lk 8:10). Secondly, because of the good, so that his figures might stir them up to make further inquiry. So, after our Lord spoke his figures or parables to the crowds, his disciples questioned him in private, as mentioned in Matthew (13:10) and Mark (4:10). This is the reason why Augustine[20] says: "Our Lord feeds" the believing crowds "with clear words, and stirs up" his disciples "with things that are obscure."[21]

1380. The Evangelist discloses their failure to understand when he says, **but they did not understand what he was saying to them.** The ignorance which resulted from Christ's figures was both useful and harmful. For the good and the just [who tried to understand them] it was useful for giving praise to God; for although they did not understand, they believed and praised the Lord and his wisdom which was so far above them: "It is the glory of God to conceal the word" (Pr 25:2). But for the wicked, it was a source of harm, because, failing to understand, they blasphemed: "But these men revile whatever they do not understand" (Jude 10). As Augustine[22] observes, when both the good and the wicked hear the words of the Gospel, and neither of

---

19. St. Thomas refers to Jn 10:10 in *ST* III, q. 50, a. 1, obj. 3; q. 55, a. 5, obj. 3.
20. *Tract. in Io.* 45. 6; PL 35, col. 1721; cf. *Catena aurea*, 10:6.
21. See *ST* III, q. 42, a. 3.
22. *Tract. in Io.* 45. 7; PL 35, col. 1722.

them understands, the good person says that what was said was true and good, but that he does not understand it. Such a person is knocking and deserves to have the door opened, provided he perseveres. But the wicked person says that what was said had no meaning or was evil.

1381. Now our Lord explains the similitude. If the above similitude is examined correctly, it contains two principal clauses, followed by others. The first is: "He who does not enter the sheepfold by the door . . . is a thief and a robber." The second is: "He who enters by the door is the shepherd of the sheep." Accordingly, this section is divided into two parts. First, he explains the first clause; then the second clause (v. 11). Concerning the first he does two things: first, he explains the first clause; secondly, he proves it (v. 7). The first clause mentions a door, a thief and a robber; so first he explains the door, then the thief and then the robber (v. 8).

1382. Concerning the first he says, **So Jesus again said to them**, to gain their attention and have them understand the similitude: "The man of understanding may acquire skill to understand a proverb and a figure" (Pr 1:6). Jesus said, **Truly, truly, I say to you, I am the door**. Now the purpose of a door is to conduct one into the inner rooms of a house; and this is fitting to Christ, for one must enter into the secrets of God through him: "This is the gate of the Lord," that is, Christ, "the righteous shall enter through it" (Ps 117:20). He says, **I am the door of the sheep**, because through Christ not only the shepherds are brought into the present Church or enter into everlasting happiness, but the sheep also. Thus he says below: "My sheep hear my voice . . . and they follow me; and I give them eternal life" (10:27).

1383. Then when he says, **All who came before me are thieves and robbers**, he explains what he had said about thieves and robbers. First, he shows who the thieves and robbers are; secondly, their sign.

1384. In regard to the first, we should avoid the error of the Manicheans, who rejected the Old Testament on the ground that it says here **that all who came before me are thieves**. They maintained that the fathers of the Old Testament, who came before Christ, were evil and have been damned.

The falsity of this view is clear from three things. First, from what this parable says. For the statement, **all who came before me**, is intended as a description of the previous statement, which mentioned those who do not enter by the door. Therefore, **all who came before me**, but not through me, that is, not entering by the door, **are thieves and robbers**. It is clear that all the patriarchs and prophets, whom the Christ-to-come had sent as forerunners, entered by the door, i.e., Christ.[23] For although he took flesh and became man in time, he was the Word of God from all eternity: "Jesus Christ is the same yesterday and today

---

23. See *ST* II-II, q. 2, a. 7; III, q. 49, a. 5, ad 1.

and for ever" (Heb 13:8). Indeed, the prophets were sent by the Word and Wisdom of God: "In every generation she," the Wisdom of God, "passes into holy souls and makes them friends of God, and prophets" (Wis 7:27). Accordingly, we expressly read in the prophets that the word of God came to this or that prophet, who prophesied by participating in the Word of God.

Secondly, the falsity of the teaching of the Manicheans is seen when our Lord says, **all who came before me**, implying that they were thrusting themselves forward on their own authority and were not sent by God: "I did not send the prophets, yet they ran" (Jer 23:21). Indeed, such prophets have not come from the Word of God: "Woe to the foolish prophets who follow their own spirit, and have seen nothing" (Ez 13:3).[24] But the fathers of the Old Testament were not of this type, as has been said.

Thirdly, this falsity is seen from the fact that he shows what effect their words had, for we read, **but the sheep did not heed them**. Therefore, those whom the sheep did heed were not thieves and robbers. Now the people of Israel did listen to the prophets, and those who did not heed them were rebuked in Sacred Scripture: "Which of the prophets did not your fathers persecute?" (Acts 7:52); "O Jerusalem, Jerusalem, killing the prophets and stoning those who are sent to you!" (Mt 23:37).

1385. Having excluded this error, it must be said that **all who came before me**, that is, independently of me, without divine inspiration and authority, and not with the intention of seeking the glory of God but acquiring their own, **are thieves**, insofar as they take for themselves what is not theirs, that is, the authority to teach—"Your princes are rebels and companions of thieves" (Is 1:23)—**and robbers**, because they kill with their corrupt doctrine—"You make it a den of robbers" (Matt 21:13); "As robbers lie in wait for a man . . . they murder on the way" (Hos 6:9). **But the sheep**, that is, the predestined, **did not heed them**, the thieves and robbers, otherwise they would not have been Christ's sheep, because, as was said before, "A stranger they will not follow, but they will flee from him." Furthermore, this is commanded in Deuteronomy: "You shall not listen to the words of that prophet or to that dreamer of dreams" (13:3).

1386. *I am the door*. Here he clarifies his explanation: first, of the door; secondly, of the thief (v. 10). Concerning the first, he does two things: first, he repeats what he intends to explain; and secondly, he gives the explanation (v. 9).

1387. He repeats what he had already said, namely, *I am the door*: "If she is a door, we will enclose her with boards of cedar" (Sg 8:9), that is, let us grant her an incorruptible power.

---

24. See *ST* II-II, q. 172, a. 5.

1388. He explains this when he says, *if any one enters by me, he will be saved*. First, he shows that the purpose of a door, which is to keep the sheep safe, applies to himself; secondly, he mentions the manner in which they are kept safe (v. 9b).

1389. The door safeguards the sheep by keeping those within from going out, and by protecting them from strangers who want to come in. And this applies to Christ, for he is our safeguard and protection. And this is what he says: *if any one*, not with insincerity, *enters*, into the fellowship of the Church and of the faithful, *by me, the door, he will be saved*, i.e., if he perseveres: "For there is no other name under heaven given among men by which we must be saved" (Acts 4:12); "We shall be saved by his life" (Rom 5:10).

1390. The way the sheep are safeguarded is set forth when he says that *he will go in and out and find pasture*. This statement can be explained in four ways. First of all, according to Chrysostom,[25] it simply affirms the security and freedom of those who cling to Christ. For one who enters some other way than by the door does not have free entry and exit; but one who does enter by the door has free exit, because he can leave freely. Therefore, when he says, *he will go in and out*, the meaning is that the apostles adhering to Christ enter with security by living with the faithful, who are within the Church, and with unbelievers who are outside, when they became masters of the whole world and no one wished to cast them out: "Let the Lord, the God of the spirits of all flesh appoint a man over the congregation, who shall go out before them and come in before them ... that the congregation of the Lord may not be as sheep which have no shepherd" (Num 27:16). *And find pasture*, find delight in converting others, and find joy even when persecuted by unbelievers for the name of Christ: "Then they left the presence of the council, rejoicing that they were counted worthy to suffer dishonor for the name," as we read in Acts (5:41).

1391. Secondly, this can be explained as Augustine[26] does in his *Commentary on John*. Two things are incumbent upon anyone who acts well, namely to be well-ordered to the things that are within him, and to those that are without. Within a person is the spirit, and without is the body: "Though our outer nature is wasting away, our inner nature is being renewed every day" (2 Cor 4:16). Therefore, a person who clings to Christ *will go in* through contemplation, to protect his conscience—"When I enter my house," i.e., my conscience, "I shall find rest with her," i.e., with wisdom (Wis 8:16)—*and out*, namely, by good actions, to tame the body—"Man goes forth to his work and to his labor until the evening" (Ps 103:23)—*and find pasture*, in a clean and

---

25. *Hom. in Io.* 59. 3; PG 59, col. 325.
26. *Tract. in Io.* 45. 15; PL 35, col. 1726–27; cf. *Catena aurea*, 10:7–10.

sincere conscience—"I will appear before your sight: I will be satisfied when your glory appears" (Ps 16:15). Again, by his actions he will *find pasture*, i.e., fruit—"He shall come home with shouts of joy, bringing his sheaves with him" (Ps 125:6).[27]

1392. The third explanation is also Augustine's[28] as well as that given by Gregory[29] in his *Commentary on Ezekiel*. The meaning, then, is this. Such a one *will go in*, i.e., into the Church, by believing—"I shall go over into the place of the wonderful tabernacle" (Ps 41:5), and this is to enter the Church Militant; *and out*, from the Church Militant into the Church Triumphant—"Go forth, O daughters of Zion, and behold King Solomon, with the crown with which his mother crowned him on the day of the wedding" (Sg 3:11); *and find pasture*, that is, the pastures of doctrine and grace in the Church Militant—"He makes me lie down in green pastures"; and the pastures of glory in the Church Triumphant: "I will feed them with good pasture" (Ez 34:14).[30]

1393. Fourthly, there is an explanation found in the work, *On the Spirit and the Soul*,[31] which has been incorrectly attributed to Augustine. Here it is said that such a one *will go in*, that is, the saints will go in to contemplate the divinity of Christ, *and out*, to consider his humanity; and they will *find pasture* in both, because in both they will taste the joys of contemplation: "Your eyes shall see the king in his beauty" (Is 33:17).

1394. Now he considers the thief. First, he mentions the mark of the thief; secondly, he says that he himself has the opposite characteristic, *I came that they may have life*.

1395. He says that those who do not enter by the door, i.e., those who have come independently of me, are thieves and robbers; and they are evil. For in the first place, *the thief comes only to steal*, i.e., to usurp what is not his; these are the agitators and heretics, who fasten on to those who belong to Christ: "He lies in ambush to catch the ones who are poor" (Ps 9:30). Secondly, the thief comes to kill, and he kills by bringing in perverse teachings and evil practices: "As robbers lie in wait for a man . . . they murder on the way" (Hos 6:9). Thirdly, the thief comes to *destroy*, by casting into everlasting destruction: "My people have been lost sheep" (Jer 50:6). But these traits are not in me.

1396. *I came that they may have life.* This is like saying: The above have not come in by me, otherwise they would do as I do. But they do the contrary, because they steal, and kill and destroy. *I came that they*

---

27. See *ST* II-II, q. 182, a. 3.
28. *Tract. in Io.* 45. 15; PL 35, col. 1727; cf. *Catena aurea*, 10:7–10.
29. *Hom. in Ezech.*, II, *Hom.* 1; PL 76, col. 946B–47B; cf. *Catena aurea*, 10:7–10.
30. See *ST* III, q. 66, a. 4, ad 1.
31. *De Spiritu et Anima*, 9; PL 40, col. 785. The authorship of the *Liber de Spiritu et Anima* is now commonly ascribed to a twelfth-century Cistercian monk, Alcher of Clairvaux.

may have life, that is, the life of righteousness, by entering into the Church Militant through faith: "My righteous one shall live by faith" (Heb 10:38). We read of this life in 1 John (3:14) that "We know that we have passed out of death into life, because we love the brethren." *And have it abundantly*, that is, have eternal life, when they leave the body. We read below of this life: "This is eternal life, that they know thee the only true God" (17:3).[32]

LECTURE 3

11 "I am the good shepherd. The good shepherd lays down his life for the sheep. 12 He who is a hireling and not a shepherd, whose own the sheep are not, sees the wolf coming and leaves the sheep and flees; and the wolf snatches them and scatters them. 13 He flees because he is a hireling and cares nothing for the sheep."[33]

1397. Here he explains the second clause of the parable, "he who enters by the door is the shepherd of the sheep" (10:2). First, he gives the explanation; secondly, he makes it clear (v. 14). First, he explains that he is the good shepherd; secondly, he states the office of a good shepherd (v. 11b); thirdly, he shows that the opposite is found in an evil shepherd (v. 12).

1398. He says, in regard to the first, *I am the good shepherd*. That Christ is a shepherd is clear enough, for as a flock is led and fed by the shepherd, so the faithful are nourished by Christ with spiritual food, and even with his own body and blood: "For you were straying like sheep, but now have returned to the Shepherd and Guardian of your souls" (1 Pet 2:25); "He will feed his flock like a shepherd" (Is 40:11).[34] To distinguish himself from an evil shepherd and thief, he adds, *good*. Good, I say, because he fulfills the office of a shepherd, just as a soldier is called good who fulfills the office of a soldier. But since Christ had said above that the shepherd enters by the door, and here he says that he is the shepherd, and before he said he was the door (v. 9), then he must enter through himself. And he does enter through himself, because he manifests himself and through himself knows the Father. We, however, enter through him, because it is by him that we are led to happiness.

Note that only he is the door, because no one else is the true light, but only shares in the light: "He," John the Baptizer, "was not the light,

---

32. See *ST* III, q. 49, a. 5.
33. St. Thomas refers to Jn 10:11 in *ST* II-II, q. 184, a. 5; q. 185, a. 4; Jn 10:12: *ST* II-II, q. 185, a. 5, obj. 1.
34. See *ST* III, q. 73, a. 5, ad 1.

but came to bear witness to the light" (1:8). But we read of Christ that "He was the true light, which enlightens every man" (1:9). Therefore, no one else refers to himself as a door; Christ reserved this for himself. But being a shepherd he did share with others, and conferred it on his members: for Peter was a shepherd, and the other apostles were shepherds, as well as all good bishops: "I will give you shepherds after my own heart" (Jer 3:15). Now, although the Church's rulers, who are her children, are all shepherds, as Augustine[35] says, yet he expressly says, *I am the good shepherd*, in order to emphasize the virtue of charity. For no one is a good shepherd unless he has become one with Christ by love, and has become a member of the true shepherd.[36]

1399. The office of a good shepherd is charity; thus he says, **the good shepherd lays down his life for the sheep**. It should be noted that there is a difference between a good shepherd and an evil one: the good shepherd is intent upon the welfare of the flock, but the evil one is intent upon his own. This difference is touched upon by Ezekiel (34:2): "Ho, shepherds of Israel who have been feeding yourselves! Should not shepherds feed the sheep?" Therefore, one who uses the flock only to feed himself is not a good shepherd. From this it follows that an evil shepherd, even over animals, is not willing to sustain any loss for the flock, since he does not intend the welfare of the flock, but his own. But a good shepherd, even over animals, endures many things for the flock whose welfare he has at heart. Thus Jacob said in Genesis (31:40): "By day the heat consumed me, and the cold by night." However, when dealing with mere animals it is not necessary that a good shepherd expose himself to death for the safety of the flock. But because the spiritual safety of the human flock outweighs the bodily life of the shepherd, when danger threatens the safety of the flock the spiritual shepherd ought to suffer the loss of his bodily life for the safety of the flock. This is what our Lord says, **the good shepherd lays down his life**, i.e., his bodily life, **for the sheep**, the sheep who are his by authority and charity. Both are required, for they must belong to him and he must love them; the first without the second is not enough. Furthermore, Christ has given us an example of this teaching: "He laid down his life for us; and we ought to lay down our lives for the brethren" (1 Jn 3:16).

1400. Now he considers the evil shepherd, showing that he possesses characteristics contrary to those of the good shepherd. First, he mentions the marks of an evil shepherd; secondly, he shows how these marks follow one another (v. 12). Concerning the first he does two things: first, he gives the marks of an evil shepherd; secondly, he mentions the danger which threatens the flock because of an evil shepherd: **the wolf snatches them and scatters them.**

---

35. *Tract. in Io.* 47. 3; PL 35, col. 1734; cf. *Catena aurea*, 10:11–13.
36. See *ST* III, q. 8, aa. 3, 6.

1401. Note that from what has been said about the good and evil shepherd, there are three differences in their traits: first in their intentions; secondly, in their solicitude; and thirdly in their affections.

1402. First, they differ in their intentions, and this is implied by their very names. For the first is called a good shepherd, and this implies that he intends to feed the flock: "Should not shepherds feed the sheep?" (Ez 34:2). But the other one, the evil shepherd, is called a hireling, as though he were intent on his wages. Thus they differ in this: the good shepherd looks to the benefit of the flock, while the hireling seeks mainly his own advantage. This is also the difference between a king and a tyrant, as the Philosopher[37] says, because when a king rules he intends to benefit his subjects, while a tyrant seeks his own interest. So a tyrant is like a hireling: "If it seems right to you, give me my wages" (Zec 11:12).

1403. But may not even good shepherds seek a wage? It seems so, for "Reward those who wait for thee" (Sir 36:16); "The Lord God comes ... his reward is with him" (Is 40:10); "How many of my father's hired servants have bread enough and to spare!" (Lk 15:17).

I answer that wages can be taken in a general sense and in a proper sense. In a general sense, a wage is anything conferred by reason of merits. And because everlasting life, which is God—"This is true God and eternal life" (1 Jn 5:20)—is conferred by reason of merits, everlasting life is said to be a wage. And this is a wage that every good shepherd can and should seek.[38] In the strict sense, however, a wage is different from an inheritance, and a wage is not sought after by a true child, who is entitled to the inheritance. A wage is sought after by servants and hirelings. Thus, since everlasting life is our inheritance, any one who works with an eye towards it is working as a child; but any one who aims at something different (for example, one who longs for worldly gain, or takes delight in the honor of being a prelate) is a hireling.[39]

1404. Secondly, they differ in their solicitude. We read of the good shepherd that the sheep are his own, not only as a trust, but also by love and solicitude: "I hold you in my heart" (Phil 1:7). On the other hand, it is said of the hireling, **whose own the sheep are not**, i.e., the hireling has no care for them: "My shepherds have not searched for my sheep, but the shepherds have fed themselves" (Ez 34:8).

1405. Thirdly, they differ in their affections. For the good shepherd, who loves his flock, **lays down his life** for it, i.e., he exposes himself to dangers that affect his bodily life. But the evil shepherd, because he has no love for the flock, flees when he sees the wolf.[40] Thus he says,

---

37. Aristotle, *Nicomachean Ethics*, VIII. 10. 1–3.
38. See *ST* I-II, q. 114, a. 3.   39. See *ST* II-II, q. 185, a. 1.
40. See *ST* II-II, q. 185, a. 5.

he sees the wolf coming and leaves the sheep and flees. Here, the wolf is understood in three ways. First, for the devil as tempting: "What fellowship has a wolf with a lamb? No more has a sinner with a godly man" (Sir 13:17). Secondly, it stands for the heretic who destroys: "Beware of false prophets, who come to you in sheep's clothing, but inwardly are ravenous wolves" (Matt 7:15); "I know that after my departure fierce wolves will come in among you, not sparing the flock" (Acts 20:29). Thirdly, it stands for the raging tyrant: "Her princes in the midst of her are like wolves" (Ez 22:27). Therefore, the good shepherd must guard the flock against these three wolves, so that when he sees the wolf, i.e., the devil tempting, the deceiving heretic, and the raging tyrant, he can oppose him. Against those who do not, we read, "You have not gone up into the breaches, or built up a wall for the house of Israel" (Ez 13:5).

Accordingly, we read of the evil shepherd that he **leaves the sheep and flees**: "Woe to my worthless shepherd, who deserts the flock" (Zech 11:17). As if to say: You are not a shepherd, but only appear to be one: "Even her hired soldiers in her midst are like fatted calves; yea, they have turned and fled together, they do not stand" (Jer 46:21).

1406. But in Matthew (10:23) we find the contrary: "When they persecute you in one town, flee to the next." Therefore, it seems to be lawful for a shepherd to flee. I reply that there are two answers to this. One is that given by Augustine[41] in his *Commentary on John*. There are two kinds of flight: that of the soul and that of the body. When we read here, he **leaves the sheep and flees**, we can understand it to mean the flight of the soul: for when an evil shepherd fears personal danger from a wolf, he does not dare to resist his injustices but flees, not by running away, but by withdrawing his encouragement, refusing to care for his flock.

This should be the explanation when considering the first kind of wolf [the tempting devil], because it is not necessary to physically flee from the devil.

But since sometimes a shepherd does flee physically because of certain wolves, such as powerful heretics and tyrants, another answer must be given, as found in Augustine's *Letter to Honoratus*.[42] As he says, it seems lawful to flee, even physically, from the wolves, not only because of the authority of our Lord, as cited above, but because of the example of certain saints, as Athanasius and others, who fled from their persecutors. For what is censured is not the flight itself, but the neglect of the flock; so, if the shepherd could flee without abandoning his flock, it would not be blameworthy. Sometimes it is the prelate himself who is the one sought, and at other times, it is the entire flock.

---

41. *Tract. in Io.* 46. 8; PL 35, col. 1732; cf. *Catena aurea*, 10:11–13.
42. *Ep.* 228. 2–6; PL 33, col. 1014–16; cf. *Catena aurea*, 10:11–13.

It is obvious that if the prelate alone is sought, others can be assigned to guard the flock in his territory, and console and govern the flock in his place. So if he flees under these circumstances, he is not said to leave the sheep. In this way, it is lawful to flee in certain cases. But if the whole flock is sought, then either all the shepherds should be with the people, or some should remain while the others leave. But if all desert the flock, then these words apply, *he sees the wolf coming and leaves the sheep and flees*.[43]

1407. Here he mentions the twofold danger that threatens. One is the ravaging of the sheep; so he says, *and the wolf snatches them*, i.e., takes for himself what belongs to another, for the faithful are Christ's sheep. Therefore, leaders of sects and wolves snatch the sheep when they entice Christ's faithful to their own teachings: "My sheep have become food for all the wild beasts" (Ez 34:8). The other danger is that the sheep be scattered; so he says, *and scatters them*, insofar as some are led astray and others persevere: "My sheep were scattered over all the face of the earth, with none to search or seek for them" (Ez 34:6).

1408. Now he shows how the above-mentioned marks are related, for the third follows from the first two. Since the evil shepherd seeks his own advantage and has no love or solicitude for the flock, it follows that he is not willing to endure any inconvenience for them. Thus he says of the hireling, *he flees*, for this reason, *because he is a hireling*, that is, he seeks his own advantage, which is the first mark; *and cares nothing for the sheep*, i.e., he does not love them, and is not solicitous for them, which is the second mark. So we read in Job (39:16) about the evil shepherd: "She deals cruelly with her young, as if they were not hers." The opposite is true of the good shepherd, for he seeks the welfare of his flock, and not his own: "Not that I seek the gift; but I seek the fruit which increases to your credit" (Phil 4:17). Furthermore, he is concerned for his sheep, that is, he loves them and is solicitous for them: "I hold you in my heart" (Phil 1:7).

LECTURE 4

14 "I am the good shepherd; I know my own and my own know me, 15 as the Father knows me and I know the Father; and I lay down my life for the sheep. 16 And I have other sheep, that are not of this fold; I must bring them also, and they will heed my voice. So there shall be one flock, one shepherd. 17 For this reason the Father loves me, because I lay down my life, that I may take it again. 18 No one takes it from me, but I lay it down of my own accord. I have power to lay it

---

43. See *ST* II-II, q. 185, a. 5.

down, and I have power to take it again; this charge I have received from my Father."[44]

1409. Here our Lord proves his explanation. First, he restates what he intends to prove; secondly, he gives the proof, *I know my own . . .* (v. 14b); and thirdly, he amplifies on it (v. 17).

1410. He says, *I am the good shepherd*, which has been explained above: "As a shepherd seeks out his flock . . . so will I seek out my sheep" (Ez 34:12).

1411. Then when he says, *I know my own*, he proves what he says. Now he says two things about himself, that he is a shepherd, and that he is good. First, he proves that he is a shepherd; secondly, that he is a good shepherd.

1412. He proves he is a shepherd by the two signs of a shepherd already mentioned. The first of these is that he calls his own sheep by name. Concerning this he says, *I know my own*: "The Lord knows those who are his" (2 Tim 2:19). *I know*, I say, not just with mere knowledge only, but with a knowledge joined with approval and love: "To him who loves us and has freed us from our sins" (Rev 1:5). The second sign is that the sheep hear his voice and know him. And concerning this he says, *and my own know me. My own*, I say, by predestination, by vocation, and by grace. This is like saying: They love me and obey me. Thus, we must understand that they have a loving knowledge about which we read: "They shall all know me, from the least of them to the greatest" (Jer 31:34).[45]

1413. He shows that he is a good shepherd by mentioning that he has the office of a good shepherd, which is to lay down his life for his sheep. First, he shows the reason for this; secondly, he gives a sign of it; and thirdly, he shows the fruit of his sign.

1414. The reason for this sign, that is, of his laying down his life for his sheep, is the knowledge he has of the Father. Concerning this he says, *as the Father knows me and I know the Father, and I lay down my life for the sheep*. This statement can be explained in two ways. In one way, so that "as" indicates just a similarity in knowledge; and taken this way, such knowledge can be given to a creature: "I shall know even as I am known" (1 Cor 13:12), i.e., *as* I am known without obscurity, so I will know without obscurity. In another way, the "as" implies an equality of knowledge. And then to know the Father as he is known by him is proper to the Son alone, because only the Son knows the Father comprehensively, just as the Father knows the Son comprehensively: "No one knows the Son except the Father, and no one

---

44. St. Thomas refers to Jn 10:16 in *ST* III, q. 35, a. 8, ad 1; Jn 10:17: *ST* III, q. 5, a. 4, s. c.; Jn 10:18: *ST* III, q. 5, a. 3; q. 47, a. 1, obj. 1; q. 47, a. 2, ad 1; q. 50, a. 3, obj. 1; q. 53, a. 4, s. c.
45. See *ST* I, q. 23, a. 4.

knows the Father except the Son" (Matt 11:27), that is, with a comprehensive knowledge.[46] Our Lord says this because in knowing the Father, he knows the will of the Father that the Son should die for the salvation of the human race. He is also saying here that he is the mediator between God and man. For as he is related to the sheep as known by them and as knowing them, so also he is related to the Father, because as the Father knows him, so he knows the Father.

1415. Then when he says, *and I lay down my life for the sheep*, he gives the sign: "By this we know love, that he laid down his life for us" (1 Jn 3:16). But since there are three substances in Christ, namely the substance of the Word, of the soul, and of the body, one might ask who is speaking when he says, *I lay down my life* ["my life" can also be literally translated as "my soul"]. If you say that the Word is speaking here, it is not true, because the Word never laid down his soul, since He was never separated from his soul. If you say that the soul is speaking, this too seems impossible, because nothing is separated from itself. And if you say that Christ says this referring to his body, it does not seem to be so, because his body does not have the power to take up its soul. Therefore, one must say that when Christ died, his soul was separated from his flesh, otherwise Christ would not have been truly dead. But in Christ, his divinity was never separated from his soul or his flesh; but was united to his soul, as it descended to the lower world, and to his body, as it lay in the tomb. And therefore, his body, by the power of his divinity, laid down his soul [or life] by the power of his divinity, and took it up again.[47]

1416. Then when he says, *and I have other sheep*, he sets down the fruit of Christ's death, which is the salvation not only of the Jews but of the Gentiles as well. For since he had said, "I lay down my life for the sheep," the Jews, who regarded themselves as God's sheep—"We thy people, the flock of thy pasture" (Ps 78:13)—could have said that he laid down his life for them alone. But our Lord adds that it is not only for them, but for others too: "He prophesied that Jesus should die for the nation, and not for the nation only, but to gather into one the children of God who are scattered abroad" (11:51).

1417. In regard to this fruit our Lord does three things. First, he mentions the predestination of the Gentiles; secondly, their vocation through grace; and thirdly their justification.

As to the first he says, *and I have other sheep*, that is, the Gentiles, *that are not of this fold*, i.e., of the family of the flesh of Israel, which was in a way a flock: "I will surely gather all of you, O Jacob" (Mic 2:12). For as sheep are enclosed in a fold, so the Jews were kept enclosed within the precepts of the Law, as we read in Galatians (chap.

---

46. See *ST* I, q. 12, a. 7; I, q. 34, a. 1; III, q. 10, a. 1.
47. See *ST* III, q. 50, a. 2.

3). These other sheep, I say, that is, the Gentiles, I have from my Father through an eternal predestination: "Ask of me, and I will make the nations your heritage" (Ps 2:8); "I will give you as a light to the nations, that my salvation may reach to the end of the earth" (Is 49:6).[48]

1418. As to the second he says, *I must bring them also*, i.e., according to the plans of divine predestination it is time to call them to grace.

This seems to conflict with what our Lord says in Matthew (15:24): "I was sent only to the lost sheep of the house of Israel." I answer that Jesus was sent only to the sheep of the house of Israel in the sense of preaching to them personally, as we read in Romans (15:8): "Christ became a servant to the circumcised to show God's truthfulness, in order to confirm the promises given to the patriarchs."[49] It was through the apostles that he brought in the Gentiles: "From them I will send survivors to the nations" (Is 66:19).

1419. In regard to the third he says, *and they will heed my voice*. Here he mentions three things necessary for righteousness in the Christian religion. The first is obedience to the commandments of God. Concerning this he says, *and they will heed my voice*, i.e., they will observe my commandments: "Teaching them to observe all that I have commanded you" (Matt 28:20); "People whom I had not known," i.e., whom I did not approve, served me. As soon as they heard of me they obeyed me" (Ps 17:45).[50]

The second is the unity of charity, and concerning this he says, *so there shall be one flock*, i.e., one Church of the faithful from the two peoples, the Jews and the Gentiles: "One faith" (Eph 4:5); "For he is our peace, who has made us both one" (Eph 2:14).

The third is the unity of faith, and in regard to this he says, *one shepherd*: "They shall all have one shepherd," that is, the Jews and the Gentiles (Ez 37:24).

1420. Now our Lord explains his proof: first, he amplifies on the reason for the sign [his death for his sheep]; secondly, he explains the sign, or the effect (v. 18); thirdly, he shows that the reason is appropriate (v. 18b).

1421. Our Lord says that the reason for his death is the knowledge he has of the Father, saying, "as the Father knows me and I know the Father, and I lay down my life for the sheep." In explaining this he says, *for this reason the Father loves me*. From this it is clear that the Father knows him with a knowledge joined with approval, *for this reason*, I say, *because I lay down my life, that I may take it again*.

1422. But is it true that his death is the cause of the Father's love? It seems not, because something temporal is not the cause of something

---

48. See *ST* III, q. 24, a. 4.
49. See *ST* III, q. 42, a. 1.
50. See *ST* I-II, q. 106, a. 1; II-II, q. 44, a. 3.

eternal. But Christ's death is in the temporal order, while the love of God for Christ is eternal. I answer that Christ is speaking here of the Father's love for him as having a human nature. Accordingly, this passage can be understood in three ways. In one way, so that *because* indicates a cause, while in the other way it indicates the term or sign of love.

If it is taken casually, then the meaning is: *because I lay down my life*, i.e., endure death, *for this reason the Father loves me*, that is, he grants me the effect of his love, which is the glory and exaltation of my body: "He humbled himself and became obedient unto death, even death on a cross. Therefore God has highly exalted him and bestowed on him a name which is above every name" (Phil 2:8).[51]

But one might object to this that good works cannot merit the divine love. For since our works are meritorious to the extent that they are given life by charity—"If I give away all I have ... but have not love, I gain nothing" (1 Cor 13:3)—and since God is the first to love—"In this is love, not that we love God but that he first loved us" (1 Jn 4:10)—it is clear that his love precedes all our merit.[52] This can be answered by saying that no one can merit God's love; nevertheless, we can merit by our good works the effect of God's love, that is, an increase of grace and the reception of the good of glory, both of which God bestows on us because of his love.[53] Thus we can say that for this reason God loves this or that person, that is, bestows on him the effect of his love, because he obeys his commandments. And so we can say about Christ as man, that for this reason the Father loves him, that is, has exalted him and given him the brightness of glory, because he laid down his life in death.[54]

But if *because* indicates a sign of love, then the meaning is this: *for this reason the Father loves me, because I lay down my life*, as if to say: This is a sign that the Father loves me, *because I lay down my life, that I may take it again*, that is, I fulfill his commands and will and endure death. For an obvious sign of love is that a person, out of charity, fulfills the commands of God.

1423. Now he explains the effect of the sign. And since the sign was "I lay down my life for the sheep," he explains how he lays it down. First, he excludes violence; secondly, he speaks of his power.

1424. The violence he excludes is that which could be employed in taking a life: such violence was not accomplished in Christ. Concerning this he says, *no one takes it from me*, that is, my life, by violence, *but I lay it down*, by my own power, that is, *of my own accord*: "Can the prey be taken from the mighty?" (Is 49:24).[55]

---

51. See *ST* III, q. 47, a. 3.
53. See *ST* I-II, q. 114, aa. 3, 8–9.
55. See *ST* III, q. 47, a. 1.

52. See *ST* I, q. 20, a. 3.
54. See *ST* III, q. 49, a. 6.

But did not the Jews use violence against Christ? They did insofar as it was in them; but this violence was not in Christ because he laid down his life voluntarily, when he willed. Thus we read above (7:30) that the Jews wanted to arrest him but were unable "because his hour had not yet come." It was voluntary "not as though he was forced to die, but he condescended to be killed," as Augustine[56] says.

1425. He adds something about his power when he says, *I have power to lay it down*. Apropos of this it should be noted that since the union of the soul and body is natural, their separation is natural. And although the cause of this separation and death can be voluntary, yet among human beings death is always natural. Now nature is not subject to the will of any mere human, since nature, as well as the will, are from God. Therefore, the death of any mere human person must be natural. But in Christ, his own nature and every other nature are subject to his will, just like artifacts are subject to the will of the artisan. Thus, according to the pleasure of his will, he could lay down his life when he willed, and he could take it up again; no mere human being can do this, although he could voluntarily use some instrument to kill himself.[57] This explains why the centurion, seeing that Christ did not die by a natural necessity, but by his own [will]—since "Jesus cried again with a loud voice and yielded up his spirit" (Matt 27:50)—recognized a divine power in him, and said: "Truly, this was the Son of God" (Matt 27:54). Again, the Apostle says in 1 Corinthians (1:18): "For the word of the cross is folly to those who are perishing, but to us who are being saved it is the power of God," that is, his great power was revealed in the very death of Christ.

1426. Here he shows that the above-mentioned reason is appropriate, for to fulfill a command shows love for the one commanding. Thus he says, *this charge I have received from my Father*, that is, to lay down my life and take it up again: "If a man loves me, he will keep my word, and my Father will love him" (14:23).

LECTURE 5

19 There was again a division among the Jews because of these words. 20 Many of them said, "He has a demon, and he is mad; why listen to him?" 21 Others said, "These are not the sayings of one who has a demon. Can a demon open the eyes of the blind?" 22 It was the feast of the Dedication at Jerusalem; 23 it was winter, and Jesus was walking in the temple, in the portico of Solomon. 24 So the Jews gathered round

---

56. *Tract. in Io.* 31. 5; PL 35, col. 1638.
57. See *ST* I, q. 97, a. 1; III, q. 14, a. 2; III, q. 47, a. 1.

204   COMMENTARY ON THE GOSPEL OF JOHN

him and said to him, "How long will you keep us in suspense? If you are the Christ, tell us plainly." 25 Jesus answered them, "I told you, and you do not believe. The works that I do in my Father's name, they bear witness to me; 26 but you do not believe, because you do not belong to my sheep. 27 My sheep hear my voice, and I know them, and they follow me; 28 and I give them eternal life, and they shall never perish, and no one shall snatch them out of my hand. 29 What my Father has given to me is greater than all, and no one is able to snatch them out of the Father's hand. 30 I and the Father are one."[58]

1427. After showing that he has power to give life and showing his manner of doing so, our Lord here shows how this power to give life belongs to him. First, the Evangelist mentions the dispute which arose among the crowd on his point; secondly, he gives the discussion between the Jewish leaders and Christ (v. 22). Concerning the first he does three things. First, he mentions the dispute within the crowd; secondly, he gives the opinion of one side; and then states the reasonable position of the other side.

1428. The dispute arose within the crowd which was listening to Christ because of what he said. The Evangelist says, **There was again a division among the Jews because of these words**. Since some of them understood his words correctly, and others did not, they argued among themselves: "I have not come to bring peace, but a sword," that is, the sword of gospel teaching, which some believed and others deny (Matt 10:34). "He pours contempt upon princes" (Ps 106:40).

1429. The opinion of one party to the argument was false. About this he says, **Many of them said**. He says, **Many**, because as we read in Ecclesiastes (1:15): "The number of fools is infinite." They said, **He has a demon, and he is mad**, for it is the habit of the foolish to always give an evil interpretation to matters about which they are in doubt; whereas the opposite should be done. Thus they revile whatever they do not know, as we read in the letter of Jude. And so because they were incapable of understanding our Lord's words—for "the light shines in the darkness, and the darkness did not comprehend it" (1:5)—they blasphemed, saying, **he has a demon, and he is mad**. And they try to turn others away from him, saying **Why listen to him?**

These blasphemers accuse Christ of two things. First, that he has a demon. As if to say: He is not speaking due to the Holy Spirit, but from a wicked spirit. Something similar is found in Acts about Paul: "He seems to be a preacher of foreign divinities [demons]" (17:18). Now the fact is that a person who has his own and familiar demon is always spiritually mad, but not always mad in a bodily way. But some can be

---

58. St. Thomas refers to Jn 10:27 in *ST* I-II, q. 108, a. 4, ad 3; Jn 10:30: *ST* III, q. 17, a. 1, obj. 5.

possessed by a demon, and these are always mad even in a bodily way. Thus it was said of Christ "He has become mad" (Mk 3:21). Secondly, to show that Christ has a demon in this way, they say, **and he is mad.** "Your great learning is turning you mad" (Acts 26:24). Yet their blasphemy is not surprising, because they are sensual and, as we read in 1 Corinthians (2:14): "The sensual person does not perceive those things that pertain to the Spirit of God."[59]

1430. This opinion is refuted by the statements of the other side, and this is in two ways. First, by the profundity of Christ's words. Thus he says, **Others,** that is, those who rightly understood, **said, These are not the sayings of one who has a demon.** This was like saying: It is clear from what he is saying that he is not mad, because his words are orderly and profound: "Lord, to whom shall we go? You have the words of eternal life" (6:69). And Paul says, "I am not mad, most excellent Festus, but I am speaking the sober truth" (Acts 26:25). Secondly, this opinion is refuted by the greatness of the miracle worked by Christ. Thus they say, **Can a demon open the eyes of the blind?** This means: Was not this one of the greatest of miracles? They were correct in believing that it could be performed only by the power of God: "If this man were not from God, he could do nothing" (9:33).

1431. It should be noted that there are certain "miracles" which can be performed by the power of demons and angels, and there are others which in no way can be accomplished by their power. Those things which are above the order of nature no creature whatever can perform by its own power, since the creature itself is subject to the laws of nature. God alone, who is above nature, can act above the order of nature. Therefore, whatever any creature performs must remain within the order of nature, an angel, either good or wicked, is able to do, when it is permitted. Thus, by using the seeds which in natural things are ordered to the generation of certain animals, they are able to effect the generation of these animals, as Pharaoh's magicians did (Ex 7:11). Again, they can produce changes affecting the nature of a thing; thus, they can heal the sick who could be helped by the power of nature.

But things that absolutely transcend the order of nature can be performed by God alone, or by good angels and saintly men through God's power, which they obtain through prayer. Such would be the conferring of sight on the blind and the raising of the dead; for the power of nature cannot extend to the restoring of sight or to the raising of the dead. Consequently, a demon cannot open the eyes of a blind man or raise the dead, because this is done by God alone, and by the saints through the power of God.[60]

1432. Here we see the dispute which the Jewish leaders initiated

---

59. See *ST* II-II, q. 13, a. 2; II-II, q. 15, a. 1.
60. See *ST* II-II, q. 178, aa. 1–2.

with Christ. First, the Evangelist gives the question asked by the Jews; secondly, Christ's answer (v. 25); and thirdly, the effect of this answer (v. 31). Concerning the first he does two things: first, he describes the circumstances of the questioning; secondly, he gives the question itself (v. 24). The circumstances of the questioning are described with respect to three things: the time, the place, and the persons who ask the question.

1433. He mentions the specific time first, saying, **it was the feast of the Dedication** (*encaenia*) **at Jerusalem**. To understand this we have to know, as Augustine[61] says, that an "encaenia" was the feast of the dedication of a church. The Greek word, *kainos*, is the same as the Latin word for "new." Thus an *encaenia* is the same as a renewal; and even in everyday speech, when something is dedicated to some use, it is said to be "encaeniated," which is the same thing as being renewed. Thus the *encaenia*, the feast of the Dedication, was the feast and commemoration of the dedication of the temple, for when we newly dedicate some church to the divine worship, we celebrate its being set aside for a sacred purpose; and in memory of this we celebrate it every year on the same day. Thus every year the Jews celebrated the *encaenia*, the remembrance of the dedication of the temple.

1434. To understand why there is a feast for the consecration of a church, we should note that all the feasts in the Church are celebrated in remembrance of God's blessings: "I will recount the steadfast love of the Lord" (Is 63:7). Again in Psalm 117 (v. 1), after David called to mind God's many blessings, saying, "Give praise to the Lord, for he is good," he adds, "Solemnize this day, with shady boughs, even to the horn of the altar" (v. 26).

We recall God's benefits to us as being of three kinds. Sometimes, as they are found in our head, the Lord Jesus Christ. Thus we celebrate the feast of his birth, and of his resurrection, and so on. Sometimes we recall them as found in our fellow members, that is, in the saints, who are members of the Church. This is fitting, for as the Apostle says: "If one member is honored, all rejoice together" (1 Cor 12:26). Thus we celebrate the feasts of Saints Peter and Paul, and the other saints. But at times we recall God's benefits as found in the entire Church: for example, the benefits of the sacraments and other things granted to the Church in general. Now a material church building is like a sign of the gathering of the faithful of the Church, and in this building all the sacraments of grace are dispensed. So it is in memory of these benefits that we celebrate the feast of the dedication of a church. Indeed, such a feast is greater than the feast of any saint, just as the benefits conferred upon the whole Church, which benefits we celebrate, exceed the benefits conferred on some saint and recalled during his feast.[62]

---

61. *Tract. in Io.* 48. 2; PL 35, col. 1741; cf. *Catena aurea*, 10:22–30.
62. See *ST* III, q. 83, a. 3, ad 4.

1435. Recall that the temple at Jerusalem had been consecrated three times: first by Solomon (1 Kgs chap. 8); secondly, during the time of Ezra by Zerubbabel and Joshua, the high priest (Ezra chap. 6); thirdly, by the Maccabees, for it says in 1 Maccabees (chap. 4) that they went up to Jerusalem to cleanse the holy places. Now this feast was not celebrated in memory of the dedication by Solomon, because that took place in the fall, i.e., in the seventh month; nor was it in memory of the dedication made at the time of Ezra, for this took place during the spring, i.e., the ninth day of March. But it was in memory of the dedication made by the Maccabees, which took place during the winter. And so to show this he mentions the specific time, saying, *it was winter.*

There is also a mystical reason for mentioning the time. As Gregory[63] says (*Morals* 2), the Evangelist took care to mention the season as winter in order to indicate the chill of evil in the hearts of those listening, that is, the Jews: "As a well keeps its water cold, so she keeps cold her wickedness" (Jer 6:7); and we read of this winter: "The winter is past, the rain is over and gone" (Sg 2:11).

1436. Then he describes the place, *and Jesus was walking in the temple, in the portico of Solomon.* He describes it first in a general way, *in the temple*: "The Lord is in his holy temple" (Ps 10:5); secondly, in more detail, saying, *in the portico of Solomon.* We have to know that the temple included not just its main building, but the surrounding porticos as well; it was on these porticos that the people stood and prayed, for only the priests prayed in the temple. It was called the portico of Solomon because it was the place where Solomon stood and prayed when the temple was being dedicated: "Then Solomon stood before the altar of the Lord in the presence of all the assembly of Israel" (1 Kgs 8:22).

1437. One might object that the temple which Solomon built was destroyed, and so was his portico. I answer that the temple was rebuilt according to the specifications of the previous one; and so just as that portico was called the portico of Solomon in the first instance, it was called the same later out of respect for him.

1438. The persons who question Christ are described as to their malice; thus he says, *so the Jews gathered round him,* unwarmed by loving charity, but burning with the desire to harm him. They came to attack him, surrounding and pressing him in on all sides: "Many bulls encompass me" (Ps 21:13); "Ephraim has encompassed me" (Hos 11:12).

1439. Then when he says, *and said to him,* we see the Jews questioning him. First, he mentions the pretended reason for their questions when he says, *How long will you keep us in suspense?* Their manner is flattering because they want it to appear that they desire to

---

63. *Mor.* 2. 2. 2; PL 75, col. 555C; cf. *Catena aurea,* 10:22–30.

know the truth about him. It is like they were saying: We are hanging in anticipation. How long will you keep us unsatisfied? "Hope deferred makes the heart sick" (Pr 13:12).

Secondly, they state their question, *If you are the Christ, tell us plainly*. Note their perversity; for since they resent Christ's calling himself the Son of God (5:18), they do not ask him if he is the Son of God, but *If you are the Christ, tell us plainly*. They hoped by this to obtain grounds for accusing him before Pilate for inciting sedition and making himself king—which was in opposition to Caesar and offensive to the Romans. Thus it was that when the Jews accused Christ of making himself the Son of God, Pilate was not very impressed; but when they said: "Every one who makes himself a king sets himself against Caesar" (19:12), he was swayed against Christ. This is why they say, *If you are the Christ*, or a king, or anointed, *tell us plainly*.

Secondly, notice their wickedness, because they say, *plainly*. It was like saying: Up to now you have not taught in public, but more or less in secret; but in reality, Christ said everything openly and was present for the festival days, and said nothing in secret: "I have spoken openly to the world . . . I have said nothing secretly" (18:20).[64]

1440. Now we have the answer of Christ, where he shows their unbelief, proving they were deceitful in saying they wished to know the truth when they said, "How long will you keep us in suspense?" He shows this in two ways. First, because they did not believe his words; and about this he says, *I told you, and you do not believe*. As if to say: You say to me, "If you are the Christ," the king, "tell us." But *I told you*, that is, I told you the truth, *and you do not believe*. "If I tell you, you will not believe" (Lk 22:67).

He shows this in a second way because they do not believe his works. And about this he says: *the works that I do in my Father's name, they bear witness to me*. He first shows their unbelief in his works; secondly, the reason for their unbelief (v. 26).

1441. As to the first he says, *the works that I do*. This was like saying: You cannot be persuaded and satisfied by my words, nor even by those great works which I do *in my Father's name*, i.e., for his glory. *They bear witness to me*, because they can be performed by God alone. Thus they clearly show that I have come from God: "The tree is known by its fruit" (Matt 12:33); "These very works which I am doing, bear witness" (5:36). *But you do not believe*: "Though he had done so many signs before them, yet they did not believe in him" (12:37). For this reason they are inexcusable: "If I had not done among them the works which no one else did, they would not have sin; but now they have seen and hated both me and my Father" (15:24).[65]

---

64. See *ST* III, q. 42, a. 3.
65. See *ST* III, q. 43, a. 4.

1442. The reason for their unbelief is that they are separated from Christ's sheep. So he says, **but you do not believe, because you do not belong to my sheep**. He does three things concerning this. First, he says that they are excluded from membership in the sheep of Christ; secondly, he shows the dignity of his sheep (v. 27); thirdly, he proves that no one will snatch his sheep out of his hands (v. 29).

1443. He mentions that they are not among his sheep when he says, **you do not belong to my sheep**, i.e., you are not predestined to believe, but foreknown to eternal destruction. For the very fact that we believe is due to God: "For it has been granted to you that for the sake of Christ you should not only believe in him but also suffer for his sake" (Phil 1:29); "For by grace you have been saved thorough faith; and this is not your own doing, it is the gift of God" (Eph 2:8). And this is given only to those for whom it was prepared from eternity; thus, only those believe in him who have been ordained to this by God through an eternal predestination: "As many as were ordained to eternal life believed" (Acts 13:48); "We believe that we shall be saved through the grace of the Lord Jesus" (Acts 15:11).[66]

1444. But should anyone be told that he is not predestined? It seems that he should not be told: for since no one can be saved unless he is predestined, if one is told that he is not predestined, he would be driven to despair. And so our Lord was driving the Jews to despair when he said to them, **you do not believe, because you do not belong to my sheep**. My answer to this is that in this group there was something common to all, that is, they were not preordained by God to believe at that time; and there was also something special, that is, some of them were preordained to believe later. Thus, some of them did believe later, for we read in Acts (chap. 2) that three thousand of them believed in one day. But some were not preordained to do this. Therefore, it did not militate against hope to say to a group, some of whom were preordained to believe later, that they did not belong to his sheep, because no one of them could apply this definitely to himself.[67] But it would militate against hope if Christ had said this to some definite person.

1445. Now he reveals the dignity of his sheep when he says, **my sheep hear my voice**. He here mentions four things: two of them are what we do in reference to Christ; the other two, which correspond to the first two are what Christ does in us.

1446. The first thing we do is to obey Christ. Concerning this he says, **my sheep**, through predestination, **hear my voice**, by believing and obeying my precepts: "O that today you would hearken to his voice! Harden not your hearts" (Ps 94:8).

1447. The second thing, corresponding to this, is what Christ does,

---

66. See *ST* I, q. 23, a. 1; I-II, q. 106, a. 1; II-II, q. 6, a. 1.
67. See *ST* I, q. 23, a. 2, ad 4; I-II, q. 109, a. 10; I-II, q. 112, a. 5.

which is to give his love and approval. Concerning this he says, *and I know them*, that is, I love and approve of them: "The Lord knows those who are his" (2 Tim 2:19). This is like saying: The very fact that they hear me is due to the fact that *I know them* by an eternal election.

But if a person cannot believe unless God gives this to him, it seems that unbelief should not be imputed to anyone. I answer that it is imputed to them because they are the cause why it is not given to them. Thus, I cannot see the light unless I am enlightened by the sun. Yet if I were to close my eyes, I would not see the light; but this is not due to the sun but to me, because by closing my eyes I am the cause of my not being enlightened. Now sin, for example, original sin, and in some persons actual sin, is the cause why we are not enlightened by God through faith. This cause is in everyone. Thus, all who are left by God are left by reason of the just judgment of God, and those who are chosen are lifted up by God's mercy.[68]

1448. The third thing, which is what we do, concerns our imitation of Christ. So he says, *and they follow me*: "My foot has held fast his steps" (Job 23:11); "Christ also suffered for you, leaving you an example, that you should follow in his steps" (1 Pet 2:21).

1449. The corresponding fourth part, which is what Christ does, is the bestowing of a reward. Concerning this he says, *and I give them eternal life*. This is like saying: They follow me by walking the path of gentleness and innocence in this life, and I will see that afterwards they will follow me by entering into the joys of eternal life.

Our Lord shows in three ways that this reward will never end. Something can end in three ways. First of all, by its very nature, for example, if it is corruptible. But this reward is incorruptible of its very nature. Thus He says, *I give them eternal life*, which is incorruptible and ever-living enjoyment of God: "This is eternal life, that they know thee the only true God, and Jesus Christ whom thou hast sent" (17:3). As Augustine[69] says, this is the pasture which he spoke of before (v. 9). Indeed, eternal life is called a good pasture because it is entirely verdant and nothing withers away. Secondly, a thing can end because the one receiving it ends, or does not guard it well. But this will not happen to that reward; so he says, *and they shall never perish*, that is, the sheep will never perish. This conflicts with Origen,[70] for he said that the saints in glory are able to sin. Yet our Lord says, *they shall never perish*, because they will be preserved forever: "He who conquers I will make him a pillar in the temple of my God; never shall he go out of it" (Rev 3:12). Thirdly, a thing can end by being snatched by force:

68. See *ST* I, q. 21, a. 4; I, q. 23, a. 5, ad 3; I-II, q. 79, aa. 3–4.
69. *Tract. in Io.* 48. 5; PL 35, col. 1742; cf. *Catena aurea*, 10:22–30.
70. *De Prin.* 2. 3. 3; PG 11, col. 190–92. Origen appears to propose this position only tentatively, in response to those who deny a bodily reality in the age to come.

for perhaps Adam would not have been cast out if the Deceiver had not been there. But this will not happen in eternal life, and so he says, *and no one shall snatch them*, that is, the sheep, *out of my hand*, that is, from my protection and loyalty: "The souls of the righteous are in the hand of God" (Wis 3:1). As Augustine[71] says: "There the wolf does not snatch, nor the thief steal, nor the robber kill."[72]

1450. He now proves what he had said above about the dignity of his sheep, namely, that no one can snatch them from his hand. His reason is this: No one can snatch what is in the hand of my Father; but the Father's hand and mine are the same; therefore, no one can snatch what is in my hand. Concerning this he does three things: first, he gives the minor premise by showing that the Father had communicated divinity to him, saying, *what my Father has given to me*, through an eternal generation, *is greater than all*. "For as the Father has life in himself, so he has granted the Son also to have life in himself" (5:26). It is *greater* than any power: "He has given him authority to execute judgment, because he is the Son of man" (5:27); it is *greater* than any reverence and honor: "God had bestowed on him the name which is above every name, that at the name of Jesus every knee should bow" (Phil 2:9). Therefore, *what my Father has given to me*, that is, that I am his Word, his only begotten, and the splendor of his light, *is greater than all*.[73]

Secondly, he mentions the greatness of the Father's power, which concerns the major premise, when he says, *and no one is able to snatch*, take by violence or secretly pilfer, *out of my Father's hand*, from the power of my Father, or from me, who am the might of the Father—although as Augustine[74] says, it is better to say "from the power of the Father" than "from me." Now *no one is able to snatch out of my Father's hand*, because he is the almighty One who is not subject to violence, and he is all-wise from whom nothing is hidden: "He is wise in heart, and mighty in strength" (Job 9:4).[75]

Thirdly, he affirms his unity with the Father, and from this the conclusion follows. Thus he says, *I and the Father are one*. As if to say: *no one shall snatch them out of my hand*, because *I and the Father are one*, by a unity of essence, for the Father and the Son are the same in nature.[76]

1451. This statement rejects two errors: that of Arius, who distinguished the essence [of the Father from that of the Son], and that of Sabellius, who did not distinguish the person [of the Father from the

71. *Tract. in Io.* 48. 6; PL 35, col. 1743; cf. *Catena aurea*, 10:22–30.
72. See *ST* I-II, q. 3, a. 8; I-II, q. 4, a. 4.
73. See *ST* I, q. 34, a. 2, ad 3.
74. *Tract. in Io.* 48. 6; PL 35, col. 1743; cf. *Catena aurea*, 10:22–30.
75. See *ST* I, q. 42, a. 4.
76. See *ST* I, q. 39, aa. 1–2.

person of the Son]. We escape both Charybdis and Scylla, for by the fact that Christ says, *one*, he saves us from Arius, because if one, then they are not different [in nature]. And by the fact that he says, *we are*, he saves us from Sabellius, for if we are, then the Father and the Son are not the same [person].[77]

Yet the Arians, deceived by their wickedness, try to deny this, and say that a creature can in some sense be one with God, and in this sense the Son can be one with the Father. The falsity of this can be shown in three ways. First, from our very manner of speaking. For it is clear that "one" is asserted as "being"; thus, just as something is not said to be a being absolutely except according to its substance, so it is not said to be one except according to its substance or nature. Now something is asserted absolutely when it is asserted with no added qualification. Therefore, because *I and the Father are one*, is asserted absolutely, without any qualifications added, it is plain that they are one according to substance and nature. But we never find that God and a creature are one without some added qualification, as in 1 Corinthians (6:17): "He who is united to the Lord becomes one spirit with him." Therefore, it is clear that the Son of God is not one with the Father as a creature can be.[78]

Secondly, we can see this from his previous statement, *what my Father has given me is greater than all*. He draws the conclusion from this: *I and the Father are one*. This is like saying: We are one to the extent that the Father has given me that which is greater than all.

Thirdly, it is clear from his intention. For our Lord proves that no one will snatch the sheep from his hand precisely because no one can snatch from the hand of his Father. But this would not follow if his power were less than the power of the Father. Therefore, the Father and Son are one in nature, honor and power.

LECTURE 6

31 The Jews took up stones again to stone him. 32 Jesus answered them, "I have shown you many good works from the Father; for which of these do you stone me?" 33 The Jews answered him, "We stone you for no good work but for blasphemy; because you, being a man, make yourself God." 34 Jesus answered them, "Is it not written in your law, 'I said, you are gods'? 35 If he called them gods to whom the word of God came (and scripture cannot be broken), 36 do you say of him whom the Father consecrated [sanctified] and sent into the world, 'You are blaspheming,' because I said, 'I am the Son of God'? 37 If I am not

77. See *ST* I, q. 27, a. 1.
78. See *ST* I, q. 4, a. 3.

doing the works of my Father, then do not believe me; 38 but if I do them, even though you do not believe me, believe the works, that you may know and understand [believe] that the Father is in me and I am in the Father." 39 Again they tried to arrest him, but he escaped from their hands. 40 He went away again across the Jordan to the place where John at first baptized, and there he remained. 41 And many came to him; and they said, "John did no sign, but everything that John said about this man was true." 42 And many believed in him there.[79]

1452. We have seen the teaching of Christ; and now we see the effect this teaching has on the Jews. First, Jesus reproves their fierceness; secondly, he defends himself against the charge of blasphemy; and thirdly, he escapes from their violence (v. 39).

1453. Concerning the first, two things are done. First, we see the violence of the Jews inciting them to stone Christ. The Evangelist says, **The Jews took up stones again to stone him**. They were hard of heart and unable to understand his profound message; and so, being like stones, they resort to stones: "When I spoke to them they fought against me without cause" (Ps 119:7).

1454. Secondly, we see our Lord reprove their violence, saying, *I have shown you many good works*. First, he reminds them of the benefits given to them; secondly, he reproves their violence. He recalls the benefits he granted in healing the sick, in teaching them and performing his miracles. So he answered them saying, *I have shown you many good works*, by healing, teaching and working miracles—"He has done all things well" (Mk 7:37)—*from the Father*, whose glory I have sought in all these things—"Yet I do not seek my own glory" (8:50). And he reproves their violence when he says, *for which of these do you stone me?* This was like saying: You should honor one who does good to you, not stone him: "Is evil a recompense for good?" (Jer 18:20).

1455. Now our Lord defends himself from the charge of blasphemy. First, we see him accused of blasphemy by the Jews; and secondly, Christ proves his innocence (v. 34).

1456. With respect to the first, the Evangelist says, *The Jews answered him, We stone you for no good work but for blasphemy*. There are five things to be considered here. First, what seems to be the motive for their stoning him, namely, his blasphemy. For Leviticus commands that blasphemers be stoned: "Bring out of the camp him who has blasphemed; and let all who heard him lay their hands upon his head, and let the congregation stone him" (24:14). Mentioning this motive, they say, *We stone you for no good work but for blasphemy*.

Secondly, they specify his blasphemy. It is blasphemy not only to

---

79. St. Thomas refers to Jn 10:36 in *ST* III, q. 34, a. 1, s. c.; Jn 10:38: *ST* III, q. 43, a. 1; Jn 10:41: *ST* III, q. 27, a. 5, ad 3; q. 38, a. 2, obj. 2.

attribute to God what is not appropriate to him, but also to attribute to another what belongs to God alone. So, it is blasphemy not only to say that God is a body, but also to say that a creature can create: "It is blasphemy! Who can forgive sins but God alone?" (Mk 2:7). Thus the Jews were saying that our Lord was a blasphemer not in the first way, but for usurping for himself what is proper to God: *because you, being a man, make yourself God.*[80]

The third thing to be considered is that the Jews understood the words of Christ, *I and the Father are one*, better than the Arians did. Thus they were incensed because they understood that *I and the Father are one* could only be said if the Father and Son are equal. This is what they say, *you make yourself God*, claiming by your words that you are God, which is not true, you, *being a man*.

The fourth point to consider is that the distance between God and man is so great that it was unbelievable to them that someone with a human nature could be God.[81] So they significantly say, *because you, being a man, make yourself God*. Yet this unbelief could have been dispelled by what is read in the Psalm, "What is man that you are mindful of him? Or the son of man that you visit him?" (Ps 8:5); and in Habakkuk (1:5): "For I am doing a work in your days that you would not believe if told," this is, the work of the Incarnation, which surpasses every mind.

The fifth thing to consider is that they do not agree with themselves: for on the one hand, they say that Christ does good works, saying, *we stone you for no good work*; and on the other hand, they accuse him of blasphemy, usurping for himself the honor of God. Now these conflict with each other, for he could not accomplish miracles from God if he blasphemed God, because "A sound tree cannot bear evil fruit, nor can a bad tree bear good fruit" (Mt 7:18). And this applied especially to Christ.

1457. Here our Lord defends himself against the charge of blasphemy. First, he gives his defense; secondly, he shows them the truth (v. 37). He defends himself by divine authority, and so first, he mentions the authority of Scripture; secondly, he explains its meaning; and thirdly, he draws his conclusion.

1458. The Evangelist says, *Jesus answered them: Is it not written in your law* (in Psalm 81:6): *I said, you are gods?* Here we should note that "law" is understood in three ways in Scripture. Sometimes it is taken in a general sense for the entire Old Testament, containing the five books of Moses, the prophets and the hagiographies. This is the way *in your law* is understood here, meaning in the Old Testament. For this quotation is from the Psalms which are referred to as the law

---

80. See *ST* I, q. 3, a. 1; I, q. 45, a. 5; II-II, q. 13, a. 1.
81. See *ST* I, q. 4, a. 3; I, q. 93, aa. 1, 9.

because the entire Old Testament is considered to have the authority of law. Sometimes "law" is understood as distinct from the prophets, psalms, and the hagiographies; this is the way Luke uses it in "Everything written about me in the law of Moses and the prophets and the Psalms must be fulfilled" (Lk 24:44). Again, at other times it is distinguished from the prophets. In this sense the Psalms and the other books of the Old Testament, other than the Pentateuch, are included within the prophets, on the ground that the Old Testament was produced by a prophetic spirit.[82] This is the way it is understood in Matthew: "On these two commandments depend all the law and the prophets" (Mt 23:40).

1459. The word "God" is also used in three senses. Sometimes it signifies the divine nature itself, and then it is used only in the singular: "Hear, O Israel: The Lord our God is one Lord" (Deut 6:4). At other times it is taken in a denominative sense: in this way idols are called gods: "All the gods of the peoples are idols" (Ps 95:5). And sometimes someone is called a god because of a certain participation in divinity, or in some sublime power divinely infused. In this way, even judges are called gods in Scripture: "If the thief is not known, the owner of the house shall be brought to the gods," that is, to the judges (Ex 22:8); "You shall not speak ill of the gods," that is, of the rulers (Ex 22:28). This is the way the word "god" is taken here, when he says, *I said, you are gods*, i.e., you share in some divine power superior to the human.[83]

1460. Then when he says, *If he called them gods to whom the word of God came*, he shows the meaning of the authority he cited. This was like saying: He called them gods because they participated in something divine insofar as they participated in God's word, which was spoken to them. For due to God's word a person obtains some participation in the divine power and purity: "You are already made clean by the word which I have spoken to you" (15:3); and in Exodus (chap. 34) we read that the face of Moses shone when he heard the words of the Lord.

From what has been said above, one might argue in this way: It is clear that a person by participating in the word of God becomes god by participation. But a thing does not become this or that by participation unless it participates in what is this or that by its essence: for example, a thing does not become fire by participation unless it participates in what is fire by its essence. Therefore, one does not become god by participation unless he participates in what is God by essence. Therefore, the Word of God, that is the Son, by participation in whom we become gods, is God by essence.[84] But our Lord, rather than argue

---

82. See *ST* I-II, q. 98, aa. 2–3; II-II, q. 171, a. 3; II-II, q. 172, a. 3.
83. See *ST* I, q. 13, a. 9.
84. See *ST* I, q. 13, a. 9; I, q. 34, a. 3; I-II, q. 110, aa. 1–2.

so profoundly against the Jews, preferred to argue in a more human way. He says, *and scripture cannot be broken*, in order to show the irrefutable truth of Scripture: "O Lord, your word endures forever" (Ps 118:89).

1461. Then when he says, *Do you say of him whom the Father sanctified and sent into the world, You are blaspheming*, he draws his conclusion. If, with Hilary,[85] we refer this to Christ insofar as he has a human nature, the meaning is this: Some people are called gods only because they participate in God's word. How then can you say, *you are blaspheming*, that is, how can you consider it blasphemy, if that man who is united in person to the Word of God is called God? This is why he says, *whom the Father sanctified*. For although God sanctifies all who are sanctified—"Sanctify them in truth" (17:17)—he sanctified Christ in a special way. He sanctifies others to be adopted children—"You have received the spirit of adoption" (Rom 8:15)—but he sanctified Christ to be the Son of God by nature, united in person to the Word of God. These words, *whom the Father sanctified*, show this in two ways. For if God sanctifies as Father, it is clear that he sanctifies Christ as his Son: "He was predestined to be the Son of God by the Spirit of sanctification" (Rom 1:4). We can also see this by his saying, *and sent into the world*. For it is not fitting for a thing to be sent some place unless it existed before it was sent there. Therefore, he whom the Father sent into the world in a visible way, is the Son of God, who existed before he was visible: for as we saw above, "He was in the world, and the world was made through him" (1:10); and "God sent the Son into the world" (3:17). *Do you say of him whom the Father sent into the world, you are blaspheming, because I said, I am the Son of God?* This was like saying: I, who am united in person to the Word, have much more reason to say this than those *to whom the word of God came*.[86]

1462. But how did the Jews realize that he was claiming to be the Son of God? Our Lord did not say this expressly. I answer that although our Lord did not say this expressly, yet from what he did say—*I and the Father are one and what my Father has given to me is greater than all*—they understood that he received his nature from the Father and was one in nature with him. But to receive the same nature from another, and to be it, is to be a son.[87]

1463. But if, with Augustine,[88] we refer *him whom the Father sanctified* to Christ as God, then the meaning is this: *him whom the Father sanctified* is he whom he has begotten holy, or sanctified, from eter-

---

85. *De Trin.* 7. 24; PL 10, col. 219C–21A; cf. *Catena aurea*, 10:31–38.
86. See *ST* I, q. 43, aa. 1–2; III, q. 23, a. 4.
87. See *ST* I, q. 27, a. 2.
88. *Tract. in Io.* 48. 9; PL 35, col. 1745; cf. *Catena aurea*, 10:31–38.

nity. The other things which follow should be explained in the same way as Hilary does. Yet the better explanation is to refer everything to Christ as man.

1464. Then when he says, *If I am not doing the works of my Father, then do not believe me*, he proves the truth of the foregoing. This is like saying: Although in your opinion I am only human, yet I am not blaspheming when I say that I am truly God, because I truly am. He does two things concerning this: first, he presents the argument of his works; secondly, he draws his conclusion (v. 38b).

1465. He does two things concerning the first. In the first place he says that in the absence of his works they would have an excuse. He says, *If I am not doing the works of my Father*, i.e., the same ones that he does, and with the same might and power, *then do not believe me*. "Whatever he [the Father] does, that the Son does likewise" (5:19).

Secondly, he says that they are convicted by his very works: *but if I do them*, the same works the Father does, then *even though you do not believe me*, who appears as a son of man, *believe the works*, i.e., these works show that I am the Son of God: "If I had not done among them the works which no one else did, they would not have sin" (15:24).

1466. Now he draws his conclusion, saying, *that you may know and believe that the Father is in me and I am in the Father*. For the clearest indication of the nature of a thing is taken from its works. Therefore, from the fact that he does the works of God it can be clearly known and believed that Christ is God.[89] Accordingly he says: I will argue from my works themselves, *that you may know and believe* what you cannot see with your own eyes, that is, *that the Father is in me and I am in the Father*: "I am in the Father and the Father in me," by a unity of essence (14:10). *The Father is in me and I am in the Father* and "I and the Father are one," have the same meaning.

Hilary[90] explains this well by saying that there is this difference between God and man: man being a composite, is not his own nature; but God, being entirely simple, is his own existence and his own nature.[91] Therefore, in whomever the nature of God is, there is God. And so, since the Father is God and the Son is God, where the nature of the Father is, there is the Father, and where the nature of the Son is, there is the Son. Therefore, since the nature of the Father is in the Son, and conversely, the Father is in the Son, and conversely. But as Augustine[92] remarks, although God is in man and man is in God—"He who abides in love abides in God, and God abides in him" (1 Jn 4:16)—this does not mean that they are one in essence. Rather, man is in God,

---

89. See *ST* III, q. 43, a. 4.
90. *De Trin.* 9. 61; PL 10, col. 330B.
91. See *ST* I, q. 3, aa. 4, 7–8.
92. *Tract. in Io.* 48. 10; PL 35, col. 1745; cf. *Catena aurea*, 10:31–38.

that is, under the divine care and protection, and God is in man, by the likeness of his grace. However, the only Son is in the Father and the Father is in him as equals.[93]

1467. Now our Lord turns away from the obstinacy of the Jews. First, the Evangelist shows they were obstinate; secondly, we see that Christ turns away from this; thirdly, we see what effect this had.

1468. The Evangelist shows their inflexibility by the fact that after so many confirmations of the truth, after the evidence of so many miracles and wonders, they still persist in their evil. So *again they tried to arrest him*, to apprehend him, not in order to believe and understand, but in their rage to do him harm; they were even the more enraged because he had more clearly expressed his equality with the Father: "They hold fast to deceit, they refuse to return" (Jer 8:5).

1469. But our Lord turns away from their rage, and so the Evangelist says, *but he escaped from their hands*. Here we see, first, that he left them by escaping from their hands. He did this for two reasons. To show that he could not be restrained unless he willed: "Passing through the midst of them he went away" (Lk 4:30); "No one takes it from me, but I lay it down of my own accord" (10:18). Secondly, to give us the example of turning away from persecution when this can be done without endangering the faith: "Do not make your stand against one who can injure you" (Sir 8:14).[94]

We see, secondly, where he went when the Evangelist says, *he went away again across the Jordan to the place where John at first baptized*. The mystical reason for this is that at some time, through the apostles, Jesus would go to convert the Gentiles. The literal reason is twofold. First, this place was near Jerusalem, and since his passion was near, he did not wish to be too far away. Secondly, he wanted to recall the witness which John had given there, when he said, "Behold, the Lamb of God, who takes away the sin of the world" (1:29), as well as the Father's testimony to his Son, Christ, at the time of his baptism.[95]

1470. The effect of this turning away was that many were converted to the faith. Three points are made about this conversion. First, many imitated his works; so he says, *and many came to him*, namely, by imitating his works: "Come to me, all who labor and are heavy laden, and I will give you rest" (Matt 11:28). Secondly, many professed him in word, *and they said, John did no sign*. By this they profess Christ's superiority to John. The reason for this was that John was sent as a witness to Christ; thus he should show that he was worthy to be believed and his testimony would be shown to be true. Now this is fittingly done by holiness of life. On the other hand, Christ came as God; consequently, it was fitting that he show the signs of divine power.

---

93. See *ST* I, q. 42, aa. 1, 5–6.
95. See *ST* III, q. 39, aa. 4, 8.
94. See *ST* II-II, q. 124, a. 5.

And so John stood out by the sanctity of his life; Christ, however, in addition to this, performed works which manifested his divine power.[96] This was in accord with the practice of the rulers of antiquity that when in the presence of a higher power a lesser power did not display the insignia of its power. Thus, in the presence of the Dictator, the Consuls took down their insignia. So it was not fitting that John, who possessed less power, because he was a precursor and witness, should employ the insignia of divine power; only Christ should have done this. They profess the truth of John's witness to Christ, saying, *but everything that John said about this man*, Christ, **was true**. They were saying: Although John did no sign, he nevertheless said all things truthfully about Christ. Thirdly, he reveals the faith in their hearts, saying, *and many believed in him there*. As Augustine[97] remarks, they grasped Christ remaining, whom the Jews wanted to seize waning, because through the lamp they had come to the day. For John was that lamp and gave testimony to the day.

96. See *ST* III, q. 43, a. 1.
97. *Tract. in Io.* 48. 12; PL 35, col. 1746; cf. *Catena aurea*, 10:39–42.

CHAPTER 11

LECTURE 1

1 Now a certain man was ill, Lazarus of Bethany, the village of Mary and her sister Martha. 2 It was Mary who anointed the Lord with ointment and wiped his feet with her hair, whose brother Lazarus was ill. 3 So the sisters sent to him, saying, "Lord, he whom you love is ill." 4 But when Jesus heard it he said, "This illness is not unto death; it is for the glory of God, so that the Son of God may be glorified by means of it." 5 Now Jesus loved Martha and her sister and Lazarus.[1]

1471. Above, our Lord shows his life-giving power by word; here he confirms it with a miracle, by raising Lazarus from the dead. First, we see the illness of Lazarus; secondly, his being raised from the dead (v. 6); and thirdly, the effect this produced (v. 45). The Evangelist does three things concerning the first: first, the illness of Lazarus is mentioned; secondly, his illness is made known (v. 3); thirdly, we see the reason for his illness (v. 4). Concerning the first he does three things: first, he describes the person who was ill; secondly, where he was living; and thirdly, he mentions one of his relatives.

1472. The one who was ill was Lazarus; *Now a certain man was ill, Lazarus.* This presents to us a believer who hopes in God, but still suffers the weakness introduced by sin, of whom we read: "Be gracious to me, O Lord, for I am languishing" (Ps 6:3). For Lazarus means "one who is helped by the Lord"; and so this name signifies one who has confidence in divine help: "My help comes from the Lord" (Ps 120:2).

1473. Lazarus was at Bethany, *of Bethany, the village of Mary and her sister Martha.* The village of Bethany was near Jerusalem, and our Lord was often a guest there, as has been said above many times. It means "a house of obedience," and leads us to understand that if one who is ill obeys God, he can easily be cured by him, just as one who is sick and obeys his doctor gains his health. In 2 Kings (5:13) the servants of Naaman said to him: "My father, if the prophet had commanded you to do some great thing, would you not have done it?"

Bethany was the home of Mary and Martha, the sisters of Lazarus. Martha and Mary represent two ways of life, the active and the contemplative. And we can understand from the above that it is by obedience that one becomes perfect, both in the active and in the contemplative life.

---

1. St. Thomas refers to Jn 11:3 in *ST* II-II, q. 83, a. 17.

1474. His relative was Mary, *it was Mary who anointed the Lord with ointment and wiped his feet with her hair*. The Evangelist describes this Mary by her most famous action so we can distinguish her from the many other women with the same name. Still, there is some disagreement among the saints about this Mary. Some, like Jerome[2] and Origen,[3] say that this Mary, the sister of Lazarus, is not the same as the sinner mentioned in Luke (7:37): "A woman of the city, who was a sinner ... brought an alabaster flask of ointment, and standing behind him at his feet, weeping, she began to wet his feet with her tears, and wiped them with the hair of her head." So, as Chrysostom[4] says, she was not the prostitute mentioned in Luke. The Mary mentioned by John was an honorable woman, eager to receive Christ, while the name of the woman who was the sinner was kept secret. Furthermore, the Mary mentioned here by John could have done for Christ at the time of his passion because of her special devotion and love something similar to what was done for him by the sinner out of remorse and love. John, in order to praise her, is mentioning here, in anticipation, the action she would perform later (Jn 12:1–8).

Others, such as Augustine[5] and Gregory,[6] say that this Mary, mentioned by John, is the same as the sinner mentioned by Luke. Augustine bases his reason on this text. For the Evangelist is speaking here of the time before Mary anointed our Lord [for the second time] at the time of the passion; as John says further on: "Mary took a pound of costly ointment of pure nard and anointed the feet of Jesus." So he says that what the Evangelist has mentioned here is the same event mentioned by Luke (7:37). [Ambrose[7] maintains both sides.] So, according to the opinion of Augustine, it is clear that the sinner mentioned by Luke is this Mary *whose brother Lazarus was ill*. [Augustine says] a consuming fever was wasting his wretched body with its furnace-like flames.

1475. The sisters of Lazarus, who were taking care of him, inform Jesus of his illness. Grief-stricken at the misfortune of the ailing youth, *the sisters sent to him*, Jesus, *saying, Lord, he whom you love is ill*. This message brings to mind three things for consideration. First, we see that the friends of God are sometimes afflicted with bodily illness; thus, if someone has a bodily illness, this is not a sign that the person is not a friend of God. Eliphaz mistakenly argued against Job that it was: "Think now, who that was innocent ever perished? Or where were the upright cut off?" (Job 4:7). Accordingly, they say, *Lord, he whom you*

---

2. *Comm. in Matt.* 4. 26. 7; PL 26, col. 191.
3. *Comm. in Matt.* 77; PG 13, col. 1721–22.
4. *Hom. in Io.* 62. 1; PG 59, col. 342; cf. *Catena aurea*, 11:1–5.
5. *De cons. Evang.* 2. 79; PL 34, col. 1154–55; cf. *Catena aurea*, 11:1–5.
6. *XL hom. in Evang.* 25; PL 76; col. 1189.
7. *Expos. Evang. sec. Luc.* 1. 9; PL 15, col. 1537.

love is ill: "For the Lord reproves him whom he loves, as a father the son in whom he delights" (Pr 3:12).

The second thing to note is that his sisters do not say, "Lord, come and heal him," but simply to mention his sickness, he ***is ill***. This indicates that it is enough merely to state one's need to a friend, without adding a request. For a friend, since he wills the good of his friend as his own good, is just as interested in warding off harm from his friends as he is in warding it off from himself. And this is especially true of the one who most truly loves: "The Lord preserves all who love him" (Ps 144:21).

The third thing to consider is that these two sisters, who wanted the cure of their sick brother, did not come in person to Christ, as did the paralytic (Lk 5:18), and the centurion (Matt 8:5). This was because of the confidence they had in Christ due to the special love and friendship which he had shown for them; or, perhaps it was their grief that kept them away: "A friend, if he is steadfast, will be to you as yourself" (Sir 6:11).

1476. Now we have the reasons for the foregoing: first, the illness of Lazarus; secondly, the reason why, according to Augustine,[8] his sisters did not come in person to Christ (v. 5).

1477. The reason for the illness of Lazarus is the glorification of the Son of God; thus the Evangelist says, **when Jesus heard it he said, This illness is not unto death; it is for the glory of God**. Here we should note that some physical illness is unto death and some is not. Those are unto death which are not ordained to something else. Further, every evil of punishment is inflicted by divine providence: "Does evil befall a city, unless the Lord has done it?" (Am 3:6). But as for the evil of fault, God is not the author, but the punisher.[9] Now all things that are from God are ordered. Consequently, every evil of punishment is ordered to something: some to death, and some to something else. This illness was not ordered to death, but to the glory of God.

1478. But Lazarus did die! Yes, otherwise he would not have had the odor of one four days in the tomb, nor would his raising have been a miracle. I answer that his illness was not ordained to death as a final end, but to something else, as has been said, that is, that he who was raised, chastened as it were, might live a holy life for the glory of God, and that the Jewish people who saw this miracle might be converted to the faith: "The Lord has chastened me sorely but he has not given me over to death" (Ps 117:18). Thus he adds, ***it is for the glory of God, so that the Son of God may be glorified by means of it***.

In this passage, according to Chrysostom,[10] the words "for" and

---

8. *Tract. in Io.* 49. 5; PL 35, col. 1749; cf. *Catena aurea*, 11:1–5.
9. See *ST* I, q. 19, a. 9; I-II, q. 79, a. 2.
10. *Hom. in Io.* 62. 1; PG 59, col. 343; cf. *Catena aurea*, 11:1–5.

"that" do not indicate the reason for the events, but their sequence. For Lazarus was not made ill so that from it God might be glorified; rather, his illness came from some other cause, and from it the fact followed that the Son of God would be glorified insofar as Christ used it for the glory of God by raising Lazarus.

This is true in one way, but not in another. It is possible to consider two reasons for Lazarus' illness. One is the natural cause, and from this point of view the statement of Chrysostom is true, because Lazarus' illness, considering its natural causes, was not ordained to his rising from the dead. But we can consider another reason, and this is divine providence; and then Chrysostom's statement is not true. For under divine providence an illness of this kind was ordained to the glory of God.[11] And so according to this, the "for" and the "that" do indicate the reason. It is the same as saying: *it is for the glory of God*, because although it was not ordained to this from the intent of its natural cause, yet from the intent of divine providence it was ordained to the glory of God, insofar as, once the miracle had been performed, people would believe in Christ and escape real death. So he says, *so that the Son of God may be glorified by means of it*.

Here our Lord clearly calls himself the Son of God: for he was to be glorified in the resurrection of Lazarus because he is true God: "that we may be in his true Son" (1 Jn 5:20); "It was not that this man sinned, or his parents, but that the works of God might be manifest in him" (9:3).

1479. Here, according to Augustine,[12] the Evangelist gives the reason why Lazarus' two sisters did not come to Christ, and it was due to their confidence in him because of the special love he had for them; so the Evangelist remarks, *now Jesus loved Martha and her sister and Lazarus*. Indeed, he who is the Consoler of the sorrowful loved the sorrowing sisters, and he who was the Savior of the weary loved the weary and dead Lazarus: "Yea, he loved his people; all those consecrated to him were in his hand" (Deut 33:3).

LECTURE 2

6 So when he heard that he was ill, he stayed two days longer in the place where he was. 7 Then after this he said to the disciples, "Let us go into Judea again." 8 The disciples said to him, "Rabbi, the Jews were but now seeking to stone you, and are you going there again?" 9 Jesus answered, "Are there not twelve hours in the day? If any one walks in the day, he does not stumble, because he sees the light of this world.

---

11. See *ST* I, q. 22, a. 2, ad 2.
12. *Tract. in Io.* 49. 5; PL 35, col. 1749; cf. *Catena aurea*, 11:1–5.

10 But if any one walks in the night, he stumbles, because the light is not in him."

1480. Here the Evangelist presents the raising of the dead Lazarus. First, we see that Christ desired to do this; and secondly, the sequence of events surrounding the raising are given (v. 17). We see three things related to the first. First, our Lord allows the death; secondly, he states his intention to go to the place where Lazarus died (v. 7); and thirdly, he reveals his intention to raise him (v. 11).

1481. Christ allowed this death by prolonging his stay beyond the Jordan: *so when he heard that he was ill, he stayed two days longer in the place where he was.* One may infer from this that Lazarus died on the very day that Jesus received the message from his sisters: for when Christ went to the place where he died, it was already the fourth day. After receiving the message, Christ then remained two days in the same place, and on the day after these two days, he went to Judea. He delayed these few days for two reasons. First, so that the death of Lazarus would not be prevented by his presence; for where life is present, death has no entry. In the second place, in order to make the miracle more credible, and so that people would not say that Christ revived Lazarus, not from death, but only from a coma.

1482. Here (v. 7) our Lord declares his intention to go to the place where Lazarus died. First, we see our Lord's plan; secondly, we see the fear in the disciples (v. 8); and thirdly, we have our Lord dispelling their fear (v. 9).

1483. With respect to the first the Evangelist says, **Then after this**, the prolonged delay, **he said**, Jesus did, **to the disciples, Let us go into Judea again.** One might ask here why Christ made a point of mentioning to the apostles that he was about to go into Judea again, since he had not done this on other occasions. The reason for this was that the Jews had just recently persecuted Christ in Judea and had almost stoned him; indeed, that is why he had left. So it was to be expected that when Christ wanted to go there again, the disciples would become fearful. And because "Darts that are foreseen do not strike and foreseen evils are more easily borne," as Gregory[13] says, our Lord mentioned his planned journey to them to calm their fears. As to the mystical sense, we can understand by the fact that Christ is returning once again to Judea, that he will return again at the end of the world to the Jews, who will be converted to Christ: "A hardening has come upon part of Israel, until the full number of the Gentiles come in" (Rom 11:25).

1484. The fear of the disciples is mentioned when the Evangelist says, **the disciples said to him, Rabbi, the Jews were but now seeking**

---

13. See *Mor.* 7. 28. 34; PL 75, col. 784C.

to stone you, and you are going there again? This was like saying: It seems that you are deliberately going to your death. Yet their fear was unreasonable, because the disciples had God with them as their protector, and one who is with God should not fear: "Let us stand up together. Who is my adversary?" (Is 50:8); "The Lord is my light and my salvation: whom shall I fear?" (Ps 26:1).[14]

1485. Our Lord dispels this fear by strengthening them. The Evangelist says, ***Jesus answered***, his disciples, ***Are there not twelve hours in the day?*** First, we see something about the time; secondly, what time is suited for walking; thirdly, what time is not.

1486. To understand this passage we should note that it has been explained in three ways. The first way is that of Chrysostom,[15] and is this. ***Are there not twelve hours in the day?*** is like saying: You hesitate to go up to Judea because the Jews recently wanted to stone me; but the day has twelve hours, and what happens at one hour does not happen in another. So, although they would have stoned me before, they would not want to do this at another hour: "For everything there is a season" (Ecc 3:1); "Every matter has its time and way" (Ecc 8:6).

1487. A literal question arises because he is speaking here either of the natural or of the artificial day. If he is speaking of the natural day, then what he says is false: because the natural day does not have twelve but twenty-four hours. Again, if he is speaking of the artificial day, his statement is false: because it is true only at the equinox, for not all artificial days have twelve hours. I answer that we should understand this to refer to the artificial day, because all artificial days have twelve hours. For the hours of such days are distinguished in two ways. Some are equal in length and some are not. Those equal in length are distinguished according to the circle of the equator: and according to this not all days have twelve hours, but some have more and some less, except at the equator. The hours not equal in length are more distinguished according to the ascensions of the zodiac on account of its obliquity: because the zodiac does not ascend equally in all its parts, but at the equator equally. Now each artificial day has twelve of these unequal hours, because every day has six signs which ascend during the day, and six at night; but those which ascend in summer have a slower motion than those which ascend in winter, and of course the ascent of each sign makes up two hours.

1488. ***If any one walks in the day***, that is, honorably, and without consciousness of any evil—"Let us conduct ourselves becomingly as in that day" (Rom 13:13)—***he does not stumble***, that is, he does not come upon anything that might harm him. And this is ***because he sees the light of this world***, i.e., the light of righteousness is in him: "Light

---

14. See *ST* II-II, q. 125, a. 1.
15. *Hom. in Io.* 62. 1; PG 59, col. 343.

dawns for the righteous, and joy for the upright in heart" (Ps 96:11). It is like our Lord were saying: We can go securely because we are walking during the day.

1489. *But if any one walks in the night*, that is, in the night of iniquities, he will easily find dangers. Concerning this night we read: "Those who sleep at night" (1 Thes 5:7). But such a one, *he stumbles*, that is, strikes against something, *because the light*, of righteousness, *is not in him*.

1490. A certain Greek, Theophylact,[16] explains this another way. Beginning at *If any one walks in the day*, he says that the "day" is the presence of Christ in the world, and the "night" is the time after Christ's passion. So the meaning is this: The Jews are not to be feared because as long as I am in the world it is not you, but I, who am in danger. Thus, when the Jews wanted to arrest Christ, he said to the crowd: "If you seek me, let these men go. This was to fulfill the word which he had spoken, 'Of those whom you gave me I lost not one'" (18:8). *But if any one walks in the night*, that is, in the time after the passion, you should be afraid to go into Judea, because you will suffer persecution from the Jews: "Strike the shepherd and the sheep will be scattered."

1491. Augustine[17] explains it another way, so that the "day" indicates Christ: "We must work the works of him who sent me, while it is day" (9:4), and "As long as I am in the world, I am the light of the world" (9:5). The twelve hours of this day are the twelve apostles: "Did I not choose you, the twelve?" (6:71). But what should we say of what follows: "And one of you is a devil?" Judas, therefore, was not an hour of this day because he gave no light. We should say that our Lord spoke these words [about the twelve] not in reference to Judas, but to his successor, who was Matthias. Thus, the sense of *Are there not twelve hours in the day?* is as though he were saying: You are the hours, I am the day. Just as the hours follow the day, so you must follow me. So, if I wish to go to Judea you ought not to precede me or change my will, but you should follow me. He said something similar to Peter: "Get behind me, Satan!" (Matt 16:23), i.e., do not go ahead of me, but follow me by imitating my will. *If any one walks in the day* is the same as saying: You should not fear any danger, because you are going with me who am the day. So just as one who walks in the day does not run into anything, that is, *does not stumble*, so also you who walk with me: "If God is for us, who is against us?" (Rom 8:31). And this is *because he sees the light of this world* in me. *But if any one walks in the night*, in the darkness of ignorance and sin, then *he stum-*

---

16. *Enar. in Evang. S. Ioannis*, 11. 9; PG 124, col. 90; cf. *Catena aurea*, 11:6–10. Theophylact (c. 1055–1107), archbishop of Achrida in Bulgaria, was a scholar and biblical commentator, renowned especially for his commentaries on the Gospels and the Pauline letters.

17. *Tract. in Io.* 49. 8; PL 35, col. 1750; cf. *Catena aurea*, 11:6–10.

bles; and this is *because the* spiritual *light is not in him*, not because of a defect in the light, but because of his own rebellion: "There are those who rebel against the light" (Job 24:13).[18]

LECTURE 3

11 Thus he spoke, and then he said to them, "Our friend Lazarus has fallen asleep, but I go to awake him out of sleep." 12 The disciples said to him, "Lord, if he has fallen asleep, he will recover." 13 Now Jesus had spoken of his death, but they thought that he meant taking rest in sleep. 14 Then Jesus told them plainly, "Lazarus is dead; 15 and for your sake I am glad that I was not there, so that you may believe. But let us go to him." 16 Thomas, called the Twin, said to his fellow disciples, "Let us also go, that we may die with him."

1492. Above, our Lord mentioned his intention of going to the place where Lazarus had died; now he reveals his intention to raise him. The Evangelist first mentions this intention; secondly, the attitude of the disciples (v. 16). First, we see our Lord stating his intention implicitly and rather obscurely; secondly, the Evangelist mentions how slow the disciples were to understand this (v. 12); and thirdly, we see our Lord stating his intention plainly (v. 14).

1493. The Evangelist says, *Thus he spoke, and then he said to them*, that is, having said those things already mentioned, Jesus now says to his disciples, *Our friend Lazarus has fallen asleep*. According to Chrysostom,[19] this seems to be a second reason for the disciples not to fear: the first was based on their innocence, because he who walks in the day does not stumble; but this reason is based on current necessity, it being necessary to go there.

1494. We see three things about this. First, he recalls his previous friendship with the dead man, saying, *Our friend Lazarus*. This was to say: He was a friend because of the many things and favors he did for us; so we should not neglect him in his needs: "He who overlooks his own advantage for the sake of a friend is just" (Pr 12:26).

1495. Secondly, he mentions that help is needed now, saying, *has fallen asleep*, and so should be helped: "A brother is born for adversity" (Pr 17:17). *Lazarus has fallen asleep*, with respect to the Lord, as Augustine[20] says; but with respect to men he was dead, as they were unable to revive him. We should note that the word "sleep" can be understood in several ways. Sometimes it refers to a natural sleep: "So

---

18. See *ST* II-II, q. 15, a. 1.
19. *Hom. in Io.* 62. 1; PG 59, col. 343; cf. *Catena aurea*, 11:11–16.
20. *Tract. in Io.* 49. 9; PL 35, col. 1751; cf. *Catena aurea*, 11:11–16.

Samuel went and lay down [slept] in his place" (1 Sam 3:9); and "You shall sleep securely" (Job 11:18). Sometimes it indicates the sleep of death: "We would not have you ignorant, brethren, concerning those who are asleep, that you may not grieve as others do who have no hope" (1 Th 4:13). Sometimes it is understood as some kind of negligence: "Behold, he who keeps Israel will neither slumber nor sleep" (Ps 120:4). And sometimes it means the sleep of sin: "Awake, O sleeper, and arise from the dead" (Eph 5:14). Again, it can mean the repose of contemplation: "I slept, but my heart was awake" (Sg 5:2). It can also signify the rest of future glory: "In peace I will both lie down and sleep" (Ps 4:8).

Death is called a sleep because of the hope we have of a resurrection; so death has come to be called a sleep from the time that Christ died and arose: "I lie down and sleep" (Ps 3:6).

1496. Thirdly, he shows his power to raise one from death when he says, **but I go to awake him out of sleep.** By this he tells us that he woke him from the grave with as little effort as you wake a person who is sleeping in bed. This is not surprising because he is the one who raises the dead and gives life; so it was said above (5:28): "The hour is coming, and now is, when the dead will hear the voice of the Son of God."[21]

1497. The Evangelist now mentions that the disciples were slow to understand this (v. 12). First, he gives a sign of their slowness, and this is that they did not answer our Lord in accord with his meaning. Secondly, their slowness is clearly shown (v. 13).

1498. Concerning the first note that although our Lord was speaking of the sleep of death, they understood him to mean a natural sleep. And because it is a sign of health when the sick sleep, the disciples said, **if he has fallen asleep, he will recover.** They were saying: This is clearly a sign of health; and since he is sleeping, it does not seem to be helpful to go and awake him.

1499. The Evangelist mentions their slowness to understand, saying, **now Jesus had spoken of his death**, since they did not realize this. Our Lord said to them, according to Matthew, "Are you also still without understanding?" And we read of the wise: "The wise man may also hear ... and understand a proverb and a figure, the words of the wise and their riddles" (Pr 1:5–6)

1500. Then our Lord explicitly states his intention to raise him (v. 14). First, he tells them that Lazarus has died, which shows his knowledge; secondly, he mentions his attitude towards his death, which shows his providence; and thirdly, he makes known his intention to go to the place where he died, which shows his compassion or mercy.

1501. He states that Lazarus has died when he says plainly, **Lazarus**

---

21. See *ST* III, q. 53, a. 4; III, q. 56, a. 1, ad 3.

is dead, i.e., he has submitted to the common law of death which no one can escape: "What man can live and never see death?" (Ps 88:49).

1502. He shows his own attitude towards this death, saying, **and for your sake I am glad that I was not there, so that you may believe**. This can be explained in two ways.

The first way is this. We have heard that Lazarus was sick. And although I was not there I have told you that he has died **and for your sake I am glad**, i.e., because it is for your benefit, so that you may experience my divinity, because even though I was not there I saw all this: "All are open and laid bare to the eyes of him with whom we have to do" (Heb 4:13). This is not surprising, because the divinity is present to all things: "Do I not fill heaven and earth?" (Jer 23:24). So that you may believe not as though they were to believe for the first time, but in order that they might believe more firmly and more strongly, in the sense of "I believe; help my unbelief" (Mk 9:23).

The other explanation is this: *I am glad* that he is dead and this is *for your sake*, for our benefit, *so that you may believe*. Accordingly, *I am glad that I was not there*, for if I had been there, he would not have died. But because he is now dead, it will be a greater miracle when I raise one already decomposing. As a result, your faith will get stronger, for it is greater to raise one who is dead than to keep him from dying.

We can learn from this that evils are sometimes a reason for joy, insofar as they are directed to some good: "We know that everything works for good with those who love him" (Rom 8:28).

1503. He mentions his plan to go when he says, **but let us go to him**. Here we see God's mercy, for in his mercy he takes the initiative and draws to himself those living in sin, who are dead and unable of themselves to come to him: "I have loved you with an everlasting love; therefore have I drawn you, taking pity on you" (Jer 31:3).

1504. Now the attitude of the disciples is given, and this can be interpreted in two ways; in one way as indicating a lack of confidence; and in the other as indicating love. Chrysostom[22] interprets it in the first way. As was mentioned above, all the disciples feared the Jews, but especially Thomas. Indeed, before the passion he was weaker than the others and had less faith, but after he became stronger and was beyond reproach, traveling the whole world alone. So, because of this lack of confidence he says to his fellow disciples, **Let us also go, that we may die with him**. This was like saying: He does not fear death; he fully wants to go, willing to deliver both himself and us over to death.

Augustine[23] interprets it in the second way. For Thomas and the other disciples loved Christ so much that they wanted either to live

---

22. *Hom. in Io.* 62. 2; PG 59, col. 344; cf. *Catena aurea*, 11:11–16.
23. For Augustine's commentary on v. 16, see *Tract. in Io.* 49. 12; PL 35, col. 1752.

with him while he was here, or die with him, so that they would not find themselves again without consolation if he left them alone by dying. It was with this feeling that Thomas said to his fellow disciples, *Let us also go, that we may die with him*. He was saying: He wants to go, and is in danger of death. Shall we stay here to live? No. *Let us also go, that we may die with him*: "If we suffer with him, we shall reign with him" (Rom 8:17); "One has died for all; therefore all have died" (2 Cor 5:14).

LECTURE 4

17 Now when Jesus came, he found that Lazarus had already been in the tomb for four days. 18 Bethany was near Jerusalem, about two miles off, 19 and many of the Jews had come to Martha and Mary to console them concerning their brother. 20 When Martha heard that Jesus was coming, she went and met him, while Mary sat in the house. 21 Martha said to Jesus, "Lord, if you had been here, my brother would not have died. 22 And even now I know that whatever you ask from God, God will give you." 23 Jesus said to her, "Your brother will rise again." 24 Martha said to him, "I know that he will rise again in the resurrection at the last day." 25 Jesus said to her, "I am the resurrection and the life; he who believes in me, though he die, yet shall he live, 26 and whoever lives and believes in me shall never die. Do you believe this?" 27 She said to him, "Yes, Lord; I believe that you are the Christ, the Son of [the living] God, he who is coming into the world."

1505. The Evangelist, after telling us that Lazarus was to be raised, now describes the events surrounding it. First, he mentions some others; secondly, he reveals Christ's feelings (v. 33); thirdly, he describes the actual raising of Lazarus (v. 38). As for the others, he first mentions the condition of Lazarus; secondly, the consolation the Jews were giving to his sisters (v. 19); and thirdly, the devotion of these sisters (v. 20).

1506. The condition of Lazarus is described as to the time of his death and to his location; *Now when Jesus came, he found that Lazarus had already been in the tomb for four days*. This makes it clear, as we said above, that Lazarus had died the very day Christ was told about his illness.

1507. According to Augustine,[24] these four days signify four deaths. The first day indicates the death of original sin, which we humans contract as offspring: "Sin came in to the world through one man and death through sin" (Rom 5:12). The other three days refer to death by actual sin: for every mortal sin is called a death: "Evil shall slay the

---

24. Ibid., col. 1752–53; cf. *Catena aurea*, 11:17–27.

wicked" (Ps 33:22). These days are differentiated according to which law is transgressed.

Thus the second day indicates the transgression of the law of nature: "They have transgressed the laws ... broken the everlasting covenant," that is, the law of nature (Is 24:5). The third day signifies the transgression of the written law: "Did not Moses give you the law? Yet none of you keeps the law" (7:19). The fourth day represents the transgression of the Law of the Gospel and of grace; and this is more serious than the others: "A man who has violated the law of Moses dies without mercy at the testimony of two or three witnesses. How much worse punishment do you think will be deserved by the man who has spurned the Son of God, and profaned the blood of the covenant by which he was sanctified, and outraged the Spirit of grace?" (Heb 10:28–29).

Another interpretation would be this: The first day is the sin of the heart: "Remove the evil of your thoughts from before my eyes" (Is 1:16). The second day is the sin of speech: "Let no evil talk come out of your mouths" (Eph 4:29). The third day is the sin of deed: "Cease to do evil" (Is 1:16). The fourth day is customary sin arising from evil habit: "You can do good who are accustomed to do evil" (Jer 13:23).

But no matter how it is interpreted, our Lord sometimes heals those who have been dead four days, that is, those who have transgressed the law of the Gospel, and those who are held fast by habits of sin.[25]

1508. Next we are told what favored the presence of the visitors and how many there were. Their presence was facilitated due to the fact that the deceased was near Jerusalem; the Evangelist says, **Bethany was near Jerusalem, about two miles [fifteen stadia] off.** This was almost two miles, because a mile contains eight stadia. Thus it was easy for many of the Jews to go there from Jerusalem.

The mystical interpretation is this: Bethany means "the house of obedience," and Jerusalem means "the vision of peace." Thus we may understand that those who are in the state of obedience are near the peace of eternal life: "My sheep hear my voice ... and I give them eternal life" (10:27). He says *fifteen stadia*, because anyone who wishes to go from Bethany, i.e., the state of obedience, to the heavenly Jerusalem, must pass through fifteen stadia. The first seven belong to the observance of the Old Law, for the number seven pertains to the Old Law, which keeps the seventh day holy. The other eight belong to the fulfilling of the New Testament, for the number eight refers to the New Testament because of the octave of the resurrection.

Their number is mentioned as being many; **and many of the Jews had come to Martha and Mary to console them.** This was an act of piety: "Rejoice with those who rejoice, weep with those who weep"

---

25. See *ST* I-II, q. 113, a. 3.

(Rom 12:15); "Do not fail those who weep, but mourn with those who mourn" (Sir 7:34).

1509. Now the Evangelist describes the sisters: first, Martha; then Mary. He describes Martha in three ways: as going to meet Christ; the devotion she showed to Christ (v. 21); and thirdly, the degree of enlightenment to which Christ raised her.

1510. We are told that Martha immediately went to meet Jesus, **when Martha heard that Jesus was coming, she went and met him** without delay. The Evangelist says, **was coming**, perhaps because when Christ was drawing near someone went ahead and told Martha that Jesus was on his way; and when she heard this, she at once ran to meet him. The reason why Martha was the first to hear about this and hurry out alone was due to her anxiety; thus our Lord says in Luke (10:41), "Martha, Martha, you are anxious and troubled about many things." And so, since she was occupied with every detail, she was constantly coming and going and was more likely to meet the messengers. But Mary sat with those who had come from Jerusalem, and the news would not have reached her as soon. Chrysostom[26] thinks that Martha did not tell Mary about this at once because Mary was with the Jews, and Martha knew that they were persecuting Christ and had already planned his death. So, she was afraid that if she told her, and Mary also came to meet Christ, they too would have come with her. For this reason she preferred not to tell her.

But if the Jews were conspiring against Christ, why were they there with Lazarus and his sisters, who were intimate friends of Christ, and like his disciples? Chrysostom[27] answers that they were there in spite of the orders of their leaders, to comfort them, because they were good women and in great need. Or again, they were there because they were not evil men, but were well-disposed toward Christ; for a great number of the people were believers.

Mystically, these events signify the active life, which is signified by Martha, who went to meet Christ in order to serve his members; and the contemplative life, which is signified by Mary, who sat at home dedicating herself to the repose of contemplation and to purity of conscience: "When I enter my house, I shall find rest with her" (Wis 8:16).[28]

1511. Martha is shown to have an extraordinary devotion; **Martha said to Jesus, Lord, if you had been here, my brother would not have died**. Here she reverently mentions two things to Christ: one of these

26. Chrysostom does not appear to say what Aquinas attributes to him. In his commentary on vv. 16–17, Chrysostom proposes that Mary did not tell her sister Martha at once because she wanted to speak first with Christ alone. See *Hom. in Io.* 62. 3; PG 59, col. 345.
27. *Hom. in Io.* 62. 2; PG 59, col. 344; cf. *Catena aurea*, 11:17–27.
28. See *ST* I, q. 79, a. 13; II-II, q. 182, a. 1.

look to the past, and the other to the future. She looks to the past when she says, **Lord, if you had been here, my brother would not have died**: for she believed that there would be no place for death when the Lord was present, since she had seen the woman healed by merely touching the fringe of Jesus' garment (Matt 9:20). This was reasonable, for life is contrary to death; but Christ is life and the tree of life: "She [wisdom] is a tree of life to those who lay hold of her" (Pr 3:18). So if the tree of life could preserve one from death, much more could Christ. However, her faith was as yet imperfect, for she thought that Christ had less power when he was absent than when he was present.[29] Thus she said, **Lord, if you had been here, my brother would not have died**. Of course, this can be said of a limited and created power, but it should not be said of the infinite and uncreated power which is God, because God is equally related to things both present and absent; indeed, all things are present to him: "Am I a God at hand, says the Lord, and not a God afar off?" (Jer 23:23).[30]

She looks to the future when she adds, **and even now I know that whatever you ask from God, God will give you**. In saying this she spoke the partial truth—for it belonged to Christ as having a human nature to petition God; thus we read that he often prayed, and above it is said, "If any one is a worshipper of God and does his will, God listens to him" (9:31).[31] Yet it was less than the whole truth; for by saying this she seemed to be thinking of Christ as a saintly man who could by his prayer revive one already dead, just as Elisha by his prayer raised one who was dead.

1512. We see how she advanced when the Evangelist adds, **Jesus said to her, Your brother will rise again**. Because she was still imperfect in her understanding, our Lord raised her to higher things by his teaching. First, he foretells the resurrection of her brother; secondly, he shows that he has the power to resurrect (v. 25). Concerning the first, he does two things. First, he foretells the coming miracle; secondly, we see Martha's understanding of the resurrection (v. 24).

1513. The miracle our Lord foretold is the raising of Lazarus; thus he says, **Your brother will rise again**: "Thy dead shall live, their bodies shall rise" (Is 26:19). We should note here that Christ raised three persons from death: the daughter of the ruler of the synagogue (Matt 9:25); the widow's son, who was being carried outside the gate of the city (Lk 7:12); and Lazarus, who had been four days in the tomb. The girl was still in her home, the youth was outside the gate, and Lazarus was in the tomb.[32] He raised the girl in the presence of only a few

---

29. See *ST* II-II, q. 5, a. 4.
30. See *ST* I, q. 8, aa. 3–4.
31. See *ST* III, q. 21, a. 1; III, q. 43, a. 2, ad 2.
32. See *ST* III, q. 53, a. 3.

witnesses: the girl's father and mother, and the three disciples, Peter, James, and John. He raised the young man in the presence of a large group. And Lazarus was raised with a number of people standing by, and when Christ was deeply affected. These three persons represent three kinds or genera of sins. Some sin by consenting in their hearts to mortal sin; and these are signified by the girl who was dead in her own home. Others sin by outside signs and acts, and these are signified by the dead youth who was being carried outside the city gate. Finally, those who are firmly habituated to sin are buried in the tomb. Yet, our Lord raises all of them. But those who sin only by consent, and die by sinning mortally, are more easily raised. And because their sin is private, it is healed with a private corrective. When sin advances without, it needs public remedy.

1514. Martha's understanding of the promised resurrection is given when the Evangelist says, **Martha said to him, I know that he will rise again in the resurrection at the last day**. It had never been heard that anyone had raised a person who had been four days in the tomb, so it would not have entered Martha's heart that Jesus would raise Lazarus from the dead then and there. But she did believe that this would happen at the general resurrection. Therefore, she says, *I know*, that is, I hold it with the greatest certainty, **that he will rise again at the last day**: "I will raise him up at the last day" (6:40).

1515. When the Evangelist says, **Jesus said to her, I am the resurrection and the life**, our Lord raises Martha to higher things. First, Jesus shows his own might and power; secondly, he mentions the effect of his power, **he who believes in me, though he die, yet shall he live**; and thirdly, he demands faith, **Do you believe this?**

1516. His power is life-giving; thus he says, *I am the resurrection and the life*. It is as though he were saying to Martha: Do you believe that your brother will rise on the last day? But this general event, that all will rise, will be caused by my power. Consequently, I, by whose power all will rise at that time, am also able to raise your brother now.[33]

He is saying two things, namely, that he is **the resurrection and the life**. We should note that some need to share in the effect of life: some, indeed, because they have lost life; and others, not because they have lost it, but in order that the life they have may be preserved. In regard to the first he says, *I am the resurrection*, because those who have lost their life by death are restored. In regard to the second he says, *and the life*, by which the living are preserved.

We should note further that the statement, *I am the resurrection*, is a causal one. It is the same as saying: I am the cause of the resurrection, for this manner of speaking is usually applied only to those who

---

33. See *ST* III, q. 59, a. 5.

are the cause of something. Now Christ is the total cause of our resurrection, both of bodies and souls; and so the statement, *I am the resurrection*, indicates the cause. He is saying: The entire fact that everyone will rise in their souls and in their bodies will be due to me: "For as by a man came death, by a man has come also the resurrection of the dead" (1 Cor 15:21).[34]

Furthermore, the fact that *I am the resurrection* is due to the fact that *I am the life*: for it is because of life that they are restored to life, just as it is because of fire that something aflame which has been extinguished is rekindled: "In him was life, and the life was the light of men" (1:4).

1517. However, the effect corresponds to the power; thus he says, *he who believes in me, though he die, yet shall he live, and whoever lives and believes in me shall never die*. First, he treats of the effect which corresponds to the first power [the power to resurrect]; secondly, the effect which corresponds to the second power [the power to give life].

The first thing he said about his power is that he is the resurrection. The effect which corresponds to this is that the dead are brought to life by him. Referring to this he says, *he who believes in me, though he die, yet shall he live*. The reason for this is that I am the cause of the resurrection, and the effect of this cause is obtained by believing in me. He says, *he who believes in me, though he die, yet shall he live*, because by believing he has me within himself—"that Christ may dwell in your hearts through faith" (Eph 3:17). And one who has me, has the cause of the resurrection. *Therefore, he who believes in me shall live.* We saw before (5:25) that some will rise through faith: "The hour is coming, and now is, when the dead will hear the voice of the Son of God, and those who hear will live," with a spiritual life, by rising from the death of sin, and they will also live with a natural life by rising from the penalty of [physical] death.

The second thing he says of his power is that he is life. The effect which corresponds to this is the preservation of life. Thus he says, *and whoever lives and believes in me*, whoever lives a life of righteousness, "the righteous shall live by his faith" (Hab 2:4), *shall never die*, that is, with an eternal death. But they will have eternal life: "For this is the will of my Father, that every one who sees the Son and believes in him should have eternal life" (6:40). This should not be understood to mean that one will not physically die; he will die, but he will be raised up in a soul to a never-ending life, and his flesh will rise and he will never die again.[35] Thus John continued, "and I will raise him up at the last day" (6:40).

1518. Jesus requires faith so he can bring her to perfection: thus he

---

34. See *ST* III, q. 56, aa. 1–2.
35. See *ST* III, q. 54, aa. 2–3.

says, ***Do you believe this?*** First, our Lord's question is given. Our Lord does not ask this out of ignorance, because he knew her faith. Indeed, it was he who had infused the faith into her: for the act of faith is from God. But he asks this question in order that she might profess outwardly the faith she had in her heart: as we read, "For man believes with his heart and so is justified, and he confesses with his lips and so is saved" (Rom 10:10).[36]

1519. Secondly, we are given the woman's answer, ***Yes, Lord; I believe that you are the Christ, the Son of the living God***. Yet this answer seems to be unrelated to what our Lord had said. For he had said, ***I am the resurrection and the life***, and then he asked her whether she believed this. She did not answer: "I believe that you are the resurrection and the life," but ***I believe that you are the Christ, the Son of the living God***.

There are two explanations for this. Chrysostom[37] thinks that Martha did not understand the profound words of Christ and answered as one bewildered: Lord, I do not understand what you are saying, namely, that you are the resurrection and the life; but I do believe this, ***I believe that you are the Christ, the Son of the living God***. Augustine,[38] on the other hand, says that Martha answers this way because it gives the reason for all that our Lord had said. It is as though she were saying: Whatever you say about your power and the effect of salvation, I believe it all; because I believe something more, which is the root of all these things, that is, ***that you are the Christ, the Son of the living God***.

1520. Martha's profession is complete, for she professes Christ's dignity, his nature and his mission, that is, to be made flesh. She professes his dignity, both royal and priestly, when she says, ***you are the Christ***. Now "Christ" means "anointed." And kings and priests are anointed. Consequently, Christ is king and priest.[39] So the angel said: "To you is born this day in the city of David a Savior, who is Christ the Lord" (Lk 2:11). Furthermore, he is a "Christ" in a unique way, for others are anointed with a visible oil, but he is anointed with an invisible oil, that is, with the Holy Spirit, and more abundantly than others: "God, your God, has anointed you with the oil of gladness above your fellows" (Ps 44:8). Indeed, he was anointed above his fellows "for it is not by measure that he gives the Spirit" (3:34).[40]

Then she professes that Christ's nature is divine and equal to the Father; she says, ***the Son of the living God***. In calling him uniquely the Son of the living God, she affirms the truth of his sonship: for he is not the true Son of God unless he is of the same nature as his Father. Thus

---

36. See *ST* II-II, q. 3, a. 2; II-II, q. 6, a. 1.
37. *Hom. in Io.* 62. 3; PG 59, col. 346; cf. *Catena aurea*, 11:17–27.
38. *Tract. in Io.* 49. 15; PL 35, col. 1753–54; cf. *Catena aurea*, 11:17–27.
39. See *ST* III, q. 22, a. 1; III, q. 31, a. 2.
40. See *ST* III, q. 7, a. 13.

it is said of Christ: "That we may be in his true Son, Christ. This is the true God and eternal life" (1 Jn 5:20).[41]

She professes the mystery of his mission when she says, *he who is coming into the world*, by assuming flesh. Peter professed the same: "You are the Christ, the Son of the living God" (Matt 16:16); and Christ says, "I came from the Father and have come into the world" (16:28).

LECTURE 5

28 When she had said this, she went and called her sister Mary, saying quietly, "The Teacher is here and is calling for you." 29 And when she heard it, she rose quickly and went to him. 30 Now Jesus had not yet come to the village, but was still in the place where Martha had met him. 31 When the Jews who were with her in the house, consoling her, saw Mary rise quickly and go out, they followed her, supposing that she was going to the tomb to weep there. 32 Then Mary, when she came where Jesus was and saw him, fell at his feet, saying to him, "Lord, if you had been here, my brother would not have died." 33 When Jesus saw her weeping, and the Jews who came with her also weeping, he was deeply moved in spirit and troubled [himself]; 34 and he said, "Where have you laid him?" They said to him, "Lord, come and see." 35 Jesus wept. 36 So the Jews said, "See how he loved him." 37 But some of them said, "Could not he who opened the eyes of the blind man have kept this man from dying."

1521. The Evangelist, after describing Martha, now describes Mary. First, he mentions how she was called; secondly, her meeting with Christ; and thirdly, the devotion she showed him (v. 32).

1522. Mary was called by Martha, who had been consoled and instructed by Christ, as she did not want her sister to miss such consolation. *When she had said this*, the previous words, to the Lord, *she went and called her sister Mary, saying quietly, The Teacher is here and is calling for you*. She called her sister quietly: "The words of the wise heard in quiet . . ." (Ecc 9:17). She did this because a number of Jews were with her sister, as has been said; and perhaps there were some among them who did not like Jesus, or would have left, or who, if they had heard what Martha said, would not have followed her. As for the mystical sense, we may understand that one more efficaciously calls upon Christ in quiet or in private: "In quietness and in trust shall be your strength" (Is 30:15).

1523. There is a problem about her saying, *the Teacher is here and is calling for you*. This seems to be false, because our Lord did not tell

---

41. See *ST* I, q. 34, a. 1, ad 1.

Martha to call Mary. Augustine[42] says that the Evangelist omitted this detail from his account for the sake of brevity, for perhaps our Lord did tell Martha to call her. However, others say that Martha considered the very presence of Christ as a call. Martha was thinking: If he is here, it would be inexcusable for one not to go to meet him.

1524. Next, the Evangelist describes Mary going to meet Christ. He does three things about this: first, he mentions her promptness; secondly, the place where she meets Christ; and thirdly those who came with her (v. 31).

1525. Mary went to Christ promptly, not delaying on account of her sorrow, or hesitating because of those who were with her. But **when she heard it, she rose quickly** from the house where she was **and went to him**, Jesus. It is clear from this that Martha would not have arrived before Mary if Mary had been immediately told of Jesus' coming. Further, this furnishes us with the example that we are not to delay when called to Christ: "Do not delay to turn to the Lord, nor postpone it from day to day" (Sir 5:7); "I will hear him as a teacher" (Is 50:4).

1526. Mary meets Christ at the same place where Martha had spoken to him; **Now Jesus had not yet come to the village, but was still in the place where Martha had met him**. The Evangelist mentions this so that we do not think that Mary's trip was unnecessary, for Christ could have reached her village just as quickly as Martha did. But Christ remained where he was so as not to appear to be thrusting himself into a miracle. Yet once he is asked and prompted, he does perform a miracle, once they realize that Lazarus is dead, and so the miracle cannot be denied. We can also understand from this that when we wish to have the advantage of Christ we should go to meet him, and not wait until he accommodates himself to us; rather, we should accommodate ourselves to him: "They shall turn to you, but you shall not turn to them" (Jer 15:19).

1527. Those who followed Mary are described when the Evangelist says, **the Jews who were with her in the house ... followed her**. The reason they followed her is given when he says, **supposing that she was going to the tomb to weep there**. They thought that her action was inspired by her grief, since they had not heard what Martha had said to her. This was a commendable thing for the Jews to do, for as Sirach (7:34) says: "Do not fail those who weep." Still, that they did follow Mary was an effect of divine providence, and it was, as Augustine[43] says, so that with all these present when Lazarus was raised, this great miracle of raising one who had been dead for four days would have many witnesses.

1528. Then when he says, **then Mary, when she came where Je-**

---

42. *Tract. in Io.* 49. 16; PL 35, col. 1754; cf. *Catena aurea*, 11:17–27.
43. Ibid., 49. 17, col. 1754; cf. *Catena aurea*, 11:28–32.

sus was and saw him, fell at his feet, we see Mary's devotion to Jesus. First, we see the devotion she showed by her actions and secondly, the devotion she showed by her words.

1529. In regard to the first, notice her security and humility. She is secure because, contrary to the orders of the leaders that no one profess Christ, she is neither shamed by the crowd nor does she show any regard for the Jews' mistrust of Christ. Even though some of Christ's enemies are present, she runs to him: "The righteous are bold as a lion" (Pr 28:1).

She shows her humility because *she fell at his feet*, which was not said about Martha: "Humble yourselves therefore under the mighty hand of God, that in due time he may exalt you" (1 Pet 5:6); "Let us worship at his footstool" (Ps 131:7).

1530. She shows her devotion in words when she says to him, *Lord, if you had been here, my brother would not have died*. For she believed that he was the life, and where he was there would be no place for death: "What fellowship has light with darkness?" (2 Cor 6:14). It is like saying, says Augustine: "As long as you were present with us, no sickness or infirmity dared to appear among those with whom Life was a guest. O faithless fellowship! While you were still living in the world, your friend died. If a friend dies, what will an enemy suffer?"[44]

1531. Next (v. 33), Christ's feelings are presented. Christ did not answer Mary in the same way that he answered Martha; because of the crowd which was present he did not say anything, but showed his power by his actions. First, we see Christ's affection for Mary; secondly, the remarks of the Jews about Christ's affection (v. 36). Concerning the first, the Evangelist does three things. First, he mentions the affection present in the heart of Christ; secondly, how he expressed it in words (v. 34); and thirdly, how he revealed it by his tears (v. 35).

1532. With regard to the first, he says, *When Jesus saw her weeping* ... We should note here that Christ is truly divine and truly human. And so in his actions we find almost everywhere that the divine is mingled with the human, and the human with the divine.[45] And if at times something human is mentioned about Christ, something divine is immediately added. Indeed, we read of no weakness of Christ greater than his passion; yet as he hangs on the cross divine events are manifested: the sun is obscured, rocks are rent, the bodies of the saints that had been asleep arise. Even at his birth, as he lay in the manger, a star shines in the heavens, the angels sing his praises, and the Magi and kings offer gifts. We have a similar situation here: for Christ ex-

---

44. The sermon Aquinas cites here, *Serm. de Verbis Domini* 96 (App.); PL 39, col. 1929–31, comes from a medieval collection of sermons attributed to Augustine but generally considered inauthentic; cf. *Catena aurea*, 11:28–32.

45. See *ST* III, q. 16, aa. 1, 4.

periences a certain weakness in his human affections, becoming disturbed over the death of Lazarus. We read, *he was deeply moved in spirit and troubled himself.*

1533. In regard to this disturbance, we should note his compassion; secondly, his discernment; and thirdly, his power. There is compassion for a right reason, for one is rightly troubled by the sadness and the evils which afflict others. About this the Evangelist says, **When Jesus saw her weeping.** "Rejoice with those who rejoice, weep with those who weep" (Rom 12:15).

1534. There is discernment, because Jesus is troubled in harmony with the judgment of reason. Thus the Evangelist says that **he was deeply moved in spirit,** that is, observing the judgment of reason. In the Scriptures the spirit is also called the mind or reason, as in Ephesians (4:23): "Be renewed in the spirit of your minds." Sometimes these emotions of the sensitive part are neither evoked by the spirit, nor preserve the moderation of reason; rather, they go against it. But this did not happen in Christ because he was deeply moved in spirit.[46]

But what does it indicate to say that he was deeply moved in spirit *(fremuit spiritu)*? It seems that it indicates anger: "A king's wrath is like the growling *(fremitus)* of a lion" (Pr 19:12). It also seems to indicate indignation or resentment, according to Psalm 111 (v. 10): "He gnashes *(fremet)* his teeth and melts away." I answer that Christ's being deeply moved indicates a certain anger and resentment of the heart. For all anger and resentment are caused by some kind of pain and sadness. Now there are two things involved here: the one about which Christ was troubled was death, which was inflicted upon the human race on account of sin; the other, which he resented, was the cruelty of death and of the devil. Thus, just as when one wants to repel an enemy he is saddened by the evils inflicted by him, and indignant at the very thought of him, so too Christ was saddened and indignant.[47]

1535. There was power here because Christ troubled himself by his own command. Sometimes such emotions arise for an inappropriate reason, as when a person rejoices over something evil, or is saddened over what is good: like they "who rejoice in doing evil and delight in the perverseness of evil" (Pr 2:14). But this was not the case with Christ; thus he says, **When Jesus saw her weeping ... he troubled himself.** And sometimes such emotions arise for a good reason, but are not moderated by reason. So he says, *he was deeply moved in spirit.* Further, although these emotions are moderated, they sometimes spring up before the judgment of reason, as when they are sudden. This was not the case with Christ either, because every movement of his sensitive appetite was according to the control and command of reason.

---

46. See *ST* III, q. 15, a. 4.
47. See *ST* III, q. 15, aa. 6, 9.

Thus he says, ***he troubled himself*** (*turbovit semetipsum*). This was like saying: He took on this sadness by a judgment of reason.

But how does this agree with the statement of Isaiah (42:4): "He will not be sad nor troubled"? I answer that this refers to a sadness which precedes the judgment of reason and is immoderate. Christ willed to be troubled and to feel sadness for three reasons. First, to show the condition and the truth of his human nature. Secondly, so that by controlling his own sadness, he might teach us to moderate our own sadness. The Stoics had taught that a wise man is never sad. But it seems very inhuman not to be sad at the death of another. However, there are some who become excessively sad over the evils which afflict their friends. Now our Lord willed to be sad in order to teach us that there are times when we should be sad, which is contrary to the opinion of the Stoics; and he preserved a certain moderation in his sadness, which is contrary to the excessively sad type.[48] Thus the Apostle says: "But we would not have you ignorant, brethren, concerning those who are asleep, that you may not grieve as others do who have no hope" (1 Th 4:13). "Weep for the dead, for he lacks the light" (Sir 22:11), and then it continues, "Weep less bitterly for the dead, for he has attained rest." The third reason is to tell us that we should be sad and weep for those who physically die: "I am utterly spent and crushed" (Ps 37:9).

1536. Then our Lord shows the emotion in his own heart by words; he says, ***Where have you laid him?*** Was our Lord really ignorant of the place where he had been buried? It seems not, for just as in his absence he knew, because of his divinity, of Lazarus' death, so in the same way he knew where his tomb was. Why did he ask about something he already knew? I answer that he did not ask as though he did not know, but upon being shown the tomb by the people, he wanted them to admit that Lazarus had died and was buried. In this way he could prevent the miracle from being doubted.

There are also two mystical reasons for this. One is that a person who asks a question does not seem to know the things he asks about. Now, Lazarus in his tomb signifies those who are dead in their sins. And so our Lord presents himself as ignorant of where Lazarus is to have us understand that he does not, in a way, know sinners, according to: "I never knew you" (Matt 7:23); and in Genesis God said to Adam, "Where are you?" (3:9). The other reason is that if anyone rises from sin to the state of divine righteousness, it is due to the depths of divine predestination, the depths of which we are ignorant: "For who has known the mind of the Lord, or who has been his counselor?" (Rom 11:34); "For who among them has stood in the council of the

---

48. See *ST* III, q. 15, a. 6.

Lord to perceive and hear his word" (Jer 23:18).[49] And so our Lord, implying this, acts as one who does not know, since we also do not know this. Thus our Lord's question is given, and the answer of the people, when the Evangelist says, **They said to him, Lord, come and see.** *Come*, by showing mercy; *and see*, by giving your attention: "Consider my affliction and my trouble, and forgive all my sins" (Ps 24:18).

1537. Next, our Lord reveals his emotion with tears; the Evangelist says, **he wept.** Now his tears did not flow from necessity, but out of compassion and for a purpose. Christ was a well-spring of compassion, and he wept in order to show us that it is not blameworthy to weep out of compassion: "My son, let your tears fall for the dead" (Sir 38:16). He wept with a purpose, which was to teach us that we should weep because of sin: "I am weary with my moaning; every night I flood my bed with tears" (Ps 6:7).

1538. The Evangelist mentions the remarks that were made about Christ's affection when he says, **So the Jews said, See how he loved him!** First, he mentions those who sympathize with Christ's affection; secondly, those who doubted his previous miracle (v. 37).

The Evangelist infers that some sympathize with Christ's affection when he says, **So the Jews said**, after Christ showed his affections by his words and tears, **See how he loved him!**: for love is especially manifested when people are afflicted: "A brother is born for adversity" (Pr 17:17). As for the mystical sense, we understand by this that God loves us even when we are sinners, for if he did not love us he would not have said: "For I came not to call the righteous, but sinners" (Matt 9:13). So we read in Jeremiah (31:3): "I have loved you with an everlasting love; therefore I have continued my faithfulness to you."

1539. Those who doubted his previous miracle were from the group which envied Christ. The Evangelist says, **But some of them**, the Jews, **said, Could not he who opened the eyes of the blind man have kept this man from dying?** It was the same as saying: If he loved him so much that he now weeps over his death, it seems that he did not want him to die, for sadness concerns things that we do not want. So, if he died against Christ's wishes, it seems that Christ was not able to prevent his death; and all the more it seems that he could not open the eyes of the man born blind. Or, one could say that the Jews were speaking out of wonder or astonishment, as Elisha spoke when he said, "Where is the Lord, the God of Elijah?" (2 Kings 2:14); and David in "Lord, where is thy steadfast love of old?" (Ps 88:50).

---

49. See *ST* I, q. 23, a. 5, ad 3.

LECTURE 6

38 Then Jesus, deeply moved again, came to the tomb; it was a cave, and a stone lay upon it. 39 Jesus said, "Take away the stone." Martha, the sister of the dead man, said to him, "Lord, by this time there will be an odor, for he has been dead for four days." 40 Jesus said to her, "Did I not tell you that if you would believe you would see the glory of God?" 41 So they took away the stone. And Jesus lifted up his eyes and said, "Father, I thank thee that thou hast heard me. 42 I knew that thou hear me always, but I have said this on account of the people standing by, that they may believe that thou didst send me." 43 When he had said this, he cried with a loud voice, "Lazarus, come out." 44 [Immediately] the dead man came out, his hands and feet bound with bandages, and his face wrapped with a cloth. Jesus said to them, "Unbind him, and let him go."[50]

1540. The Evangelist, after having given certain preambles to the raising of Lazarus, now presents the raising itself. He considers four things: first, Christ's arrival at the tomb; second, the removal of the stone (v. 39); third, Christ's prayer; and fourth, the actual raising of the dead Lazarus (v. 43).

1541. In regard to the first he says, **Then Jesus, deeply moved again, came to the tomb.** The Evangelist is careful to frequently mention that Christ wept and was deeply moved because, as Chrysostom[51] says, he will later show the power of his divinity. And so he affirms that Christ experienced the weaker and humbler marks of our nature so that we do not doubt the reality of his human nature. And just as John shows his divine nature and power more explicitly than the other Evangelists, so he also mentions his weaker aspects, and other such things which especially reveal the affections of Christ's human nature.

As for the mystical sense, he was deeply moved in order that we might understand that those who rise from sin should continue to weep without interruption, according to: "All the day I go about mourning" (Ps 37:7).

Or, one could say that while Christ was deeply moved before due to the death of Lazarus, he is deeply moved now because of the unbelief of the Jews. Thus the Evangelist mentioned their doubt about his previous miracle, when they said, "Could not he who opened the eyes of the blind man have kept this man from dying." Indeed, he was deeply moved with compassion and pity for these Jews: "He saw a great throng; and he had compassion on them" (Mt 14:14).

---

50. St. Thomas refers to Jn 11:41 in *ST* III, q. 21, a. 3; q. 43, a. 1; q. 43, a. 2, obj. 2; Jn 11:42: III, q. 21, a. 1, ad 1; q. 21, a. 3, ad 1; q. 43, a. 2, ad 2.
51. *Hom. in Io.* 63. 1; PG 59, col. 350; cf. *Catena aurea*, 11:33–41.

1542. The Evangelist next mentions the removal of the stone; and he does four things about this. First, he describes the stone; secondly, he mentions the order of Christ to remove it; thirdly, he adds the objection to taking away the stone; fourthly, he states that the order was carried out.

1543. The stone is described as being over the tomb; he says, *it was a cave, and a stone lay upon it*. Note that in those regions they had certain cavities in the form of caves that were used as human burial places, and in them they could bury many bodies over the course of time. So they have an entrance which they could close and open with a stone when necessary. Thus we read, *a stone lay upon it*, i.e., over the entrance to the cave. We read the same in Genesis (chap. 23) when Abraham purchased a field and a cave for the burial of his wife Sarah.

In the mystical sense, the cave signifies the depths of sin, of which it is said: "I have come into deep waters, and the flood sweeps over me" (Ps 68:3). The stone laid upon the cave signifies the Law, which was written on stone, and which did not take away sin, but held them in sin, because they sinned more gravely in acting against the Law.[52] Thus we read in Galatians (3:22): "The scripture consigned all things to sin" (Gal 3:22).

1544. Then when he says, **Jesus said, Take away the stone**, he gives Christ's order to remove the stone. One might ask: Since it is a greater thing to raise the dead than to remove a stone, why did not Christ also use his power to remove the stone? Chrysostom[53] says that this was done in order to secure greater certitude about this miracle, that is, to make them such witnesses to the miracle that they could not, like they did in the case of the blind man, say and maintain that this was not the same person.

As for the mystical sense, according to Augustine,[54] the removing of the stone signifies the removal of the weight of the legal observances from Christ's faithful who came into the Church from the Gentiles, for some wanted to impose these observances on them. Thus St. James says: "For it has seemed good to the Holy Spirit and to us to lay upon you no greater burden than these necessary things" (Acts 15:28); and Peter says in the same work: "Why do you make trial of God by putting a yoke upon the neck of the disciples which neither our fathers nor we have been able to bear" (Acts 15:10). Concerning this our Lord says, **Take away the stone**, i.e., the burden of the Law, and preach peace.

Or, the stone signifies those in the Church who live wickedly, and so are a scandal to those who would believe, because they hinder their conversion. We read about this stone in Psalm 90 (v. 12): "Lest you

---

52. See *ST* III, q. 1, a. 5.
53. *Hom. in Io.* 63. 2; PG 59, col. 350–51; cf. *Catena aurea*, 11:33–41.
54. *Tract. in Io.* 49. 22; PL 35, col. 1756; see also *De div. quaest. 83*, q. 65; PL 40, col. 60; cf. *Catena aurea*, 11:33–41.

dash your foot against a stone." This is the stone that our Lord orders removed: "Remove every obstruction from my people's way" (Is 57:14).

1545. Next, we see Martha's objection. First, we see what she said; secondly, the words of Christ's answer.

1546. The Evangelist mentions Martha's words when he says, **Martha, the sister of the dead man, said to him, Lord, by this time there will be an odor, for he has been dead four days.** As for the literal sense, this happened in order to show the truth of the miracle, as his members were already beginning to corrupt and dissolve. As for the mystical sense, one who habitually sins is said to smell, that is, the foul odor of his reputation is spread abroad by his sins. For just as good works spread a good odor, as the Apostle says—"We are the aroma of Christ to God" (2 Cor 2:15)—so from evil works there arises an evil odor and a stench. Such a person is aptly described in terms of "four days," for he is pressed by the weight of earthly sins and sensual desires, and earth is the last of the four elements: "The stench and foul smell of him will rise" (Jl 2:20).

1547. Christ answers her, saying, **Did not I tell you that if you would believe you would see the glory of God?** Here our Lord seems to reprove Martha for not remembering what Christ had said to her: "He who believes in me, though he die, yet shall he live." For Martha was not certain that Christ could raise a person who had been dead four days. Although Christ had recently raised certain dead persons, this seemed impossible to believe of her brother because of the long time he had been dead. And so our Lord said, **Did not I tell you that if you would believe you would see the glory of God?** that is, the raising of your brother, by which God will be glorified.

Although our Lord had said to his apostles before that this miracle would be for his glory, saying, "so that the Son of God may be glorified by means of it" (11:4), that is, by means of this death, he now says to Martha that this miracle will be for the glory of God. The reason for this is that the glory of the Father and of the Son and of the Holy Spirit is the same. However, he did not mention the glory of the Son here so as not to excite the Jews who were present and ready to dispute him.

1548. These words of our Lord suggest two fruits of our faith. The first is the performing of miracles, which is due to faith: "If you have faith as a grain of mustard seed, you will say to this mountain, 'Move hence to yonder place,' and it will move; and nothing will be impossible to you" (Matt 17:19). The Apostle also says: "If I have all faith, so as to remove mountains" (1 Cor 13:2); and in Mark (16:20) we read: "And they went forth and preached everywhere, while the Lord worked with them and confirmed the message by the signs that attended it." Now this working of miracles is for the glory of God; thus he says, **if you would believe you would see the glory of God.**[55]

---

55. See *ST* II-II, q. 178, a. 1.

The second fruit is the vision of eternal glory, which is due as a reward to faith; thus he says, **you would see the glory of God**: "If you do not believe, you will not understand," as we read in Isaiah (7:9), in an alternate version; and in 1 Corinthians it is said: "For now we see in a mirror dimly," by faith, "but then face to face."

1549. Next, the Evangelist mentions that the command was carried out, saying, **So they took away the stone**. We may consider here, according to Origen,[56] that the delay in removing the stone was caused by the sister of the deceased. Consequently, the raising of her brother was delayed as long as she detained Christ with her talk; but as soon as the command of Christ was obediently carried out, her brother was raised. And we can learn from this not to interpose anything between the commands of Christ and their execution if we desire the effect of salvation to follow at once: "As soon as they heard of me they obeyed me" (Ps 17:45).

1550. Then he considers the prayer of Christ, in which he gives thanks. The Evangelist mentions four things in this regard. First, he mentions his way of praying; secondly, the efficacy of his prayer; thirdly, he excludes Christ's need to pray; and fourthly he mentions the usefulness of his prayer.

1551. Christ's way of praying is appropriate, because **Jesus lifted up his eyes**, that is, he lifted up his understanding, directing it in prayer to the Father above. As for us, if we wish to pray according to the example of Christ's prayer, we have to raise the eyes of our mind to him by turning them from the memories, thoughts and desires of present things. We also lift our eyes to God when we do not rely on our own merits, but hope in his mercy alone: "To thee I lift up my eyes, O thou who art enthroned in the heavens! Behold, as the eyes of servants look to the hand of their master, as the eyes of a maid to the hand of her mistress, so our eyes look to the Lord our God, till he have mercy upon us" (Ps 122:1–2); and "Let us lift up our hearts and hands to God in heaven" (Lam 3:41).[57]

1552. He mentions the efficacy of this prayer when he says, **Father, I thank thee that thou hast heard me**. Here we have a sign that God is quick to give, as we read: "Lord, thou wilt hear the desire of the meek" (Ps 9:38), so that he hears our desires even before they are put into words: "He will surely be gracious to you at the sound of your cry; when he hears it, he will answer you" (Is 30:19); and again in the same book: "While they are yet speaking I will hear" (65:24). Therefore, with much more reason we can think that God the Father, anticipating the prayer of our Lord, the Savior, would have heard him: for the tears which Christ shed at the death of Lazarus acted as a prayer.

---

56. *Comm. in Io.* XXVIII. 3, nos. 14–22; PG 14, col. 684A–85A; cf. *Catena aurea*, 11:33–41.

57. See *ST* II-II, q. 83, a. 3, ad 3; III, q. 21, a. 1.

By giving thanks at the beginning of his prayer, Christ gives us the example that when we pray, we should thank God for the benefits we have already received before asking for new ones: "Give thanks in all circumstances" (1 Thes 5:18).

1553. If the phrase, *that thou hast heard me*, is interpreted as applying to Christ insofar as he is human, there is no difficulty: for as having a human nature Christ is less than the Father and, accordingly, it is appropriate for him to pray to the Father and be heard by him. But if, as Chrysostom[58] wants, it is applied to Christ as God, then there is a problem: for as God, it is not fitting that he pray or be heard, but rather that he hear the prayers of others. Consequently, it should be said that one is heard when his will is fulfilled. Now the will of the Father is always fulfilled, because "He does whatever he pleases" (Ps 113:11). Therefore, since the will of the Father is the same as the will of the Son, whenever the Father fulfills his own will, he fulfills the will of the Son. Thus, the Son says, as Word, *that thou hast heard me*, i.e., that you have done those things which were in your Word to be done. For he spoke and they were done.[59]

1554. Christ's need to pray is excluded when he says, *I knew that thou hear me always*. Here our Lord vaguely shows his own divinity. As if to say: In order that my will be done I do not need prayer, because from eternity my will has been fulfilled: "In all things he was heard for his reverence" (Heb 5:7). *I knew* with certitude *that thou hear me*, the Word, *always*: because whatever you do, these things are in me to be done.

1555. Again, *thou hear me* in my human nature *always*, because my will is always conformed to your will. *But I have said this on account of the people standing by, that they may believe that thou didst send me*. We understand from this that our Lord did and said many things for the benefit of others: "For I have given you an example, that you also should do as I have done to you" (13:15). For every action of Christ is a lesson for us. In particular, Christ wanted to show by his prayer that he was not separated from the Father, but recognized him as his principle. And so he added, *that they may believe that thou didst send me*: "And this is eternal life, that they know thee the only true God, and Jesus Christ whom thou has sent" (17:3); "God sent forth his Son, born of woman, born under the law" (Gal 4:4). And this is the benefit coming from his prayer.

1556. Now the Evangelist considers the raising of Lazarus; and he does three things. First, he mentions the voice of the one awakening him; secondly, the effect of his voice (v. 44); and thirdly, the command to unbind the one awakened.

---

58. *Hom. in Io.* 64. 2; PG 59, col. 357; cf. *Catena aurea*, 41–46.
59. See *ST* III, q. 21, a. 4.

1557. The voice of the one awakening Lazarus is described as loud: **When he had said this**, that is, Jesus, **he cried with a loud voice**. As for the literal sense, this was done to refute the error of certain Jews and of the Gentiles that the souls of the dead lingered in the tombs with their bodies. So, **he cried with a loud voice**, as though summoning from afar the soul which was not present in the tomb.

Or, and this is a better explanation, it might be said that Christ's voice is described as loud because of its great power: for its power was so great that it raised Lazarus who had been dead four days, just as one asleep is roused from sleep: "He gave power to his voice" (Ps 67:34). Further, this loud voice represents that loud voice which will sound at the general resurrection and by which all will be roused from their graves: "At midnight there was a cry" (Mt 25:6).

He cried out, I say, saying, **Lazarus, come out**. He called him by his own name because such was the power of his voice that all the dead without distinction would have been awakened if he had not limited it to one by mentioning his name, as Augustine[60] says when speaking of the Word of the Lord. Again, we understand from this that Christ calls sinners to come out from living in sin: "Come out of her, my people" (Rev 18:4). We are also called to let our sins come out of concealment by revealing them in confession: "If I have concealed my transgressions from men" (Job 31:33).

1558. Then (v. 44), the effect of this voice is given: first, the resurrection of the dead man; secondly, his condition. The resurrection of the dead man was immediately after our Lord's command: **immediately the dead man came out**. For such was the power of Christ's voice that it gave life without any delay, as will happen at the general resurrection when the dead will rise in the twinkling of an eye when they hear the sound of the trumpet: "And the dead in Christ will rise first" (1 Thes 4:16). For Christ's mission was already being anticipated, as it was stated above: "The hour is coming, and now is, when the dead will hear the voice of the Son of God, and those who hear will live" (5:25). In this way what our Lord said was fulfilled: "I go to awake him" (11:11).

As to the condition of the one rising, he is described as having **his hands and feet bound with bandages**, with which the people of ages past wrapped their dead, **and his face wrapped with a cloth**, in order to hide his gruesome appearance. He was commanded to rise bound and wrapped to provide a greater proof of the miracle.

1559. When Jesus says, **Unbind him and let him go**, he orders that he be unbound so that those who do this may be more reliable witnesses to the miracle and have it more forcefully impressed on their

---

60. See *Serm. de Verbis Domini* 96 (App.); PL 39, col. 1929–31; cf. *Catena aurea*, 11:41–46.

memory. Furthermore, when they approach and touch him, they can see that it really is he. He adds, *and let him go*, to show that this miracle is not an illusion: for at times certain magicians have seemed to raise the dead, but those who were raised could not live as they formerly had because their raising was not real but illusory.

1560. Augustine gives a mystical explanation to this entire verse beginning at **The dead man came out**. He does this in two ways, depending on two ways of coming out. The sinner comes out when by repenting he passes from the practice of sin to the state of righteousness: "Come out from them, and be separate from them" (2 Cor 6:17). However, his hands are bound with bandages, i.e., with carnal desires, because, although he is rising from his sins, he cannot escape such annoyances as long as he lives in the body. Thus the Apostle says: "I of myself serve the law of God with my mind, but with my flesh I serve the law of sin" (Rom 7:25). His face being wrapped with a cloth signifies that in this life we cannot have full knowledge of God: "For now we see in a mirror dimly, but then face to face" (1 Cor 12:12). Christ commands them to unbind him and let him go because after this life all the veils are lifted from those who rise from sin, so that they may contemplate God "face to face" (1 Cor 12:12). Then we will be unbound from the corruptibility of the flesh which is like a chain binding and weighing down the soul and keeping it from full and clear contemplation: "Loose the bonds from your neck, O captive daughter of Zion" (Is 52:2).[61] This is one way to come out in a spiritual manner, and is given by Augustine[62] in his work, *The Book of Eighty-Three Questions*.

Another way to come out is by confession, about which it is said: "He who conceals his transgressions will not prosper, but he who confesses and forsakes them will obtain mercy" (Pr 28:13). One comes out in this way by leaving his secret sins by disclosing them in confession. Now that one confesses is due to God calling him with a loud voice, that is, by grace. And the one who confesses, as still guilty, is the dead person still wrapped in bandages. In order for his sins to be loosed, the ministers are commanded to loose him and let him go. For the disciples loose those whom Christ by himself vivifies inwardly, because they are absolved, being vivified by the ministry of the priests: "Whatever you loose on earth shall be loosed in heaven" (Matt 16:19).[63]

1561. Some who consider this mystery say that just as Christ by himself vivified Lazarus, and once he was vivified he was ordered to be loosed by the disciples, so God vivifies a soul from within by grace by remitting its guilt and absolving it from the debt of eternal pun-

---

61. See *ST* I, q. 12, aa. 2, 12–13.
62. *De div. quaest. 83*, q. 65; PL 40, col. 60; cf. *Catena aurea*, 11:41–46.
63. See *ST* III, q. 90, aa. 2, 4.

ishment; but priests, by the power of the keys, absolve in regard to the temporal punishment. But this position attributes too little to the keys of the Church. For it is proper to the sacraments of the New Law that in them grace is conferred. But the sacraments exist in the administration of the ministers: Thus, in the sacrament of penance, contrition and confession behave materially on the part of the one receiving the sacrament; but the causative power of the sacrament lies in the absolution of the priest, by the power of the keys, through which he somehow applies the effect of our Lord's passion to the one he absolves so that he obtains remission. Therefore, if the priest only absolved the punishment, the sacrament of penance would not confer a grace by which guilt is remitted; and consequently it would not be a sacrament of the New Law. Therefore, one must say that just as in the sacrament of baptism, the priest, by pronouncing the words and washing outwardly, exercises the ministry of baptism, while Christ baptizes inwardly, so the priest, by the power of the keys, outwardly administers the ministry of absolution, while Christ remits the guilt by grace.[64]

1562. Yet a difficulty arises from the fact that those who usually come for baptism are children who have not been justified before baptism, but obtain the grace of remission in baptism, whereas those who come for absolution are adults, who usually have obtained the remission of their sins beforehand by contrition; consequently, the absolution that follows seems to contribute nothing to the remission of sins.

If this matter is carefully considered as affecting adults, in both cases it will be seen that there is a perfect parallel. For it happens that certain adults having a desire to be baptized obtain the remission of their sins by the baptism of desire before they actually receive the sacrament of baptism; and yet the baptism which follows, so far as what it is of itself is concerned, effects the remission of sins, although it does not so function in a person whose sins are already remitted, but he obtains only an increase of grace. However, if an adult was not perfectly disposed before baptism to obtain the remission of his sins, still in the very act of being baptized he obtains their remission by the power of baptism, unless he places some obstacle to the Holy Spirit by his insincerity. The same must be said of penance. For if a person was fully contrite before the absolution of the priest, he obtains the remission of his sins by having the desire to subject himself to the keys of the Church, without which there would not be true contrition. But if there was not beforehand a full contrition sufficient for remission, he obtains the remission of his guilt in the absolution, unless he puts an obstacle to the Holy Spirit.[65] And the same is true in the Eucharist and in the Anointing of the Sick, and in the other sacraments.

---

64. See *ST* III, q. 84, a. 7.
65. See *ST* III, q. 86, a. 1.

LECTURE 7

45 Many of the Jews therefore, who had come with Mary [to Mary and Martha] and had seen what he did, believed in him; 46 but some of them went to the Pharisees and told them what Jesus had done. 47 So the chief priests and the Pharisees gathered the council and said, "What are we to do? For this man performs many signs. 48 If we let him go on thus, every one will believe in him, and the Romans will come and destroy both our place and our nation." 49 But one of them, Caiaphas, who was high priest that year, said to them, "You know nothing at all; 50 you do not understand that it is expedient for you that one man should die for the people, and that the whole nation should not perish." 51 He did not say this of his own accord, but being high priest that year he prophesied that Jesus should die for the nation, 52 and not for the nation only, but to gather into one the children of God who are scattered abroad. 53 So from that day on they took counsel how to put him to death.[66]

1563. After describing the death and resurrection of Lazarus, the Evangelist now sets forth the effect of his resurrection. First, its effect on the people; secondly, its effect on their leaders (v. 47).

1564. He does two things concerning the first. First, he says that certain ones among them believed, **Many of the Jews therefore, who had come to Mary and Martha** to console them, **and had seen what he did, believed in him.** And no wonder, because such a miracle had not been heard of from the beginning of time, that is, that one dead four days in the tomb should be raised to life. Also, our Lord had said that he would perform this miracle for those standing by, so that they might believe in him. And so his words were not empty, but many believed because of the miracle they saw: "Jews demand signs" (1 Cor 1:22).

1565. Secondly, he mentions that some were spreading news of the miracle, saying, **but some of them went to the Pharisees and told them what Jesus had done.** This can be understood in two ways. In one way, they told the chief priests what Jesus had done in order to soften them towards Christ and to reproach them for conspiring against Jesus, who had worked such marvels. In another way, and this is better, they told them these things in order to incite them against Christ: for they were unbelievers and were scandalized at the miracle. This is clear from the way the Evangelist describes it, for after saying that **many of the Jews ... believed in him**, he adds in contrast, **but some of them went to the Pharisees.** These are the ones of whom we read: "Though he had done

---

66. St. Thomas refers to Jn 11:47 in *ST* III, q. 43, a. 1, *sed contra*.; Jn 11:50: *ST* III, q. 50, a. 1, s. c.; Jn 11:51: *ST* II-II, q. 173, a. 4, s. c.

so many signs before them, yet they did not believe in him ... For they loved the praise of men more than the praise of God" (12:37, 43).

1566. Next (v. 47), the Evangelist mentions the effect of the miracle on the leaders. First, we have their evil conspiracy against Christ; secondly, we see how Christ escaped it (v. 54). He does three things concerning the first. First, he mentions the gathering of the council; secondly, the problem that confronted them (v. 47); and thirdly, their solution of this problem (v. 49).

1567. In regard to the first, three things are mentioned about the wickedness of the chief priests. First of all, their status: for they were not the common people, but **the chief priests and the Pharisees**.[67] Chief priests, because they were in charge of sacred matters; and they were Pharisees because they had the appearance of religion. Thus was fulfilled what was stated in Genesis (49:5): "Simeon and Levi are brothers; weapons of violence are their swords": for the founders of the sect of the Pharisees were descended from Simeon, and the chief priests were clearly from the tribe of Levi.

Secondly, we see that their wickedness was deliberate; thus he says, they **gathered the council** in order to make their plans: "O my soul, come not into their council" (Gen 49:6); "Blessed is the man who walks not in the counsel of the wicked" (Ps 1:1). But we also read: "No counsel can avail against the Lord" (Pr 21:30).

Thirdly, we see their evil intention, because it was against Jesus, i.e., the Savior: "All who hate me whisper together about me; they imagine the worst for me" (Ps 40:8); "Come, let us make plots against Jeremiah" (Jer 18:18).

1568. Now (v. 47b), he mentions their problem: first, he gives the reason for this problem; secondly, the core of the problem (v. 48).

1569. It was the miracles of Christ that raised their problem; so they said, **What are we to do? For this man performs many signs**. They were blind, for they still called him a man after such a great demonstration of his divinity. As he himself said: "The works which the Father has granted me to accomplish, these very works which I am doing, bear me witness" (5:35). In truth, they were no less foolish than the blind because they wondered what they should do, whereas there was nothing for them to do but believe: "What signs do you do, that we may see, and believe you?" (6:30). See how many signs he did work! Even they said, **this man performs many signs**: "Their wickedness blinded them" (Wis 2:21).[68]

1570. The root of their problem was that they feared the losses that would follow. The Evangelist mentions two things referring to this. First, their loss of spiritual leadership. He says about this, **If we let him**

---

67. See *ST* III, q. 47, a. 5.
68. See *ST* II-II, q. 15, aa. 1, 3; III, q. 43, a. 4.

go on thus, every one will believe in him. This, of course, would be the best for all concerned, because it is faith in Christ that saves and leads to eternal life: "But these are written that you may believe . . . and that believing you may have life in his name" (20:31). But in relation to their wicked intention this was terrifying to them, for they believed that no one who believed in Christ would obey them. And so, because of their ambition, they backed away from salvation and took others with themselves: "But Diotrephes, who likes to put himself first does not acknowledge my authority" (3 Jn 9).

1571. Secondly, he mentions their ambition for temporal possessions when he says, *and the Romans will come and destroy both our place and our nation*. This seems to follow from the other, as Augustine[69] says, for if all believed in Christ, there would be no one left to defend the temple of God against the Romans, because they would have abandoned the holy temple and the laws of their fathers, as they thought the teaching of Christ was directed against these. But this does not really seem to have much bearing on the issue, since they would still be subject to the Romans and would not be planning to war against them. Thus, it seems better to say, with Chrysostom,[70] that they said this because they observed that Christ was being honored by the people as a king. And because the Romans had ordered that no one could be king unless they had appointed him, they were afraid that if the Romans heard that they were regarding Christ as a king, they would look upon the Jews as rebels. Then they would move against them and destroy their city and nation: "Every one who makes himself a king sets himself against Caesar" (19:12).

1572. Notice their pitiable state, for they fear nothing but the loss of temporal things, and do not think of eternal life: "The fountain of Jacob alone, in a land of grain and wine" (Dt 33:28).[71] But as we read in Proverbs (10:24): "What the wicked dreads will come upon him"; and so after our Lord's passion and glorification, the Romans overcame and displaced them, taking their land and nation.

1573. The Evangelist sets down the resolution of the problem when he says, *But one of them, Caiaphas, who was high priest that year, said to them*. First, we have the decision; secondly, the explanation of the decision (v. 51); and thirdly, its acceptance by the assembly (v. 53). Concerning the first he does two things. First, he describes the one making the decision; secondly, he gives the words of the decision.

1574. The one making the decision is described by his name and office. By his name, that is, *Caiaphas*. This name was appropriate to his wickedness for it means, first of all, "investigator," and it attests to his

---

69. *Tract. in Io.* 49. 26; PL 35, col. 1757; cf. *Catena aurea*, 11:47–53.
70. *Hom. in Io.* 64. 3; PG 59, col. 359; cf. *Catena aurea*, 11:47–53.
71. See *ST* II-II, q. 125, a. 2.

presumption: "He who is a searcher of majesty shall be overwhelmed by glory" (Pr 25:27). For he was presumptuous when he said, "I adjure you by the living God, tell us if you are the Christ, the Son of God" (Matt 26:63). Secondly, it means "sagacious," which testifies to his cunning, because he strove to procure the death of Christ. Thirdly, it means "vomiting," which attests to his foolishness: "Like a dog that returns to his vomit" (Pr 26:11).

He is described by his office, namely, as **high priest that year**. Here we should note, as stated in Leviticus (chap. 8), that the Lord appointed one high priest, at whose death another was to succeed and was to exercise the office of high priest throughout his life. But later, as ambition and quarrels grew among the Jews, it was agreed that there should be a number of high priests, and that all who had attained to this office would exercise it in turn, year by year. (And sometimes they obtained this office by money; as Josephus says.) And to indicate this situation he says of the time, **that year**.

1575. Next (v. 49b), the Evangelist gives the words of the one making the decision, who first reproaches them for their sluggishness, saying, **You know nothing at all; you do not understand**. This was like saying: You are sluggish and you understand this affair even more sluggishly. And so, secondly, he reveals his wickedness, saying, **it is expedient for you that one man should die for the people**.

These words have one meaning according to the intention of Caiaphas, and another according to the explanation of the Evangelist. In order to explain them according to the evil intention of Caiaphas, we should note that, as mentioned in Deuteronomy (13:1), the Lord had commanded: "If a prophet arises among you, or a dreamer of dreams . . . and if he says, 'Let us go after other gods,' . . . that prophet or that dreamer of dreams shall be put to death." And so, according to this law, Caiaphas believed that Christ would turn the people from the worship of God: "We found this man perverting our nation" (Lk 23:2). Thus he says, **You know nothing at all**, that is, the Law. **You do not understand that it is expedient for you that one man**, this man, **should die**, so that the whole nation is not deceived. This is like saying: The welfare of one man must be ignored for the public good. Thus Deuteronomy (13:5) continues: "So you shall purge the evil from the midst of you." "Drive out the wicked person from among you" (1 Cor 5:13).[72]

1576. But the Evangelist explains this another way, saying, **He did not say this of his own accord**. He mentions three things: first, the author of these words; secondly, their correct meaning (v. 51b); and thirdly, the Evangelist adds to the words of Caiaphas (v. 52).

1577. In regard to the first we should note that because one might suppose that Caiaphas spoke these words by his own impulse, the

72. See *ST* II-II, q. 64, a. 2.

Evangelist rejects this, saying, **He did not say this of his own accord**. By this he lets us understand that at times a person does speak of his own accord. For a human being is what is the chief thing in him; but this is the intellect and reason. Thus a human being is what he is because of reason. Therefore, when a human being speaks from his own reason, he speaks of his own accord. But when he speaks under a higher and external impulse he does not speak of his own accord. Now this happens in two ways. Sometimes one is moved by the divine Spirit: "It is not you who speak, but the Spirit of your Father speaking through you" (Matt 10:20). But sometimes one is moved by a wicked spirit, as those who rave. And both of these are sometimes said to prophesy. That those who are moved by the Holy Spirit prophesy is asserted in 2 Peter (1:21): "No prophecy ever came by the impulse of man, but men moved by the Holy Spirit spoke from God." Again, that those moved by a wicked spirit prophesy is found in Jeremiah (29:26): "The Lord has made you a priest instead of Jehoiada the priest, to have charge in the house of the Lord over every madman [one who raves] who prophesies."[73]

Note also that at times some may speak by an impulse of the Holy Spirit or of an evil spirit in such a way that they lose the use of reason and are somehow seized. At other times, the use of reason can remain and they are not seized. When the sense powers are overflowing due to a higher impression, the reason is hindered, and disturbed and seized. An evil spirit has the power of affecting the imagination, since it is a power united to a physical organ. And such an evil spirit can so affect the imagination by a strong impression that as a result the reason is hindered; yet it is not forced to consent. This is the condition of those seized by an evil spirit.

1578. We have to decide, therefore, whether Caiaphas spoke these words by the impulse of the Holy Spirit or of an evil spirit. It seems that he did not speak by the impulse of the Holy Spirit, for the Holy Spirit is the spirit of truth (cf. Jer 15), and the wicked spirit is the spirit of lying: "I will go forth, and will be a lying spirit in the mouth of all his prophets" (1 Kg 22:22). But it is obvious that Caiaphas spoke a lie, saying, **it is expedient for you that one man should die**. Therefore, he did not speak by an impulse of the Holy Spirit, as it seems, but he prophesied by the impulse of a raving wicked spirit.

However, this does not seem to agree with the words of the Evangelist, for if it were such John would not have added, **who was high priest that year**. He mentions the dignity of Caiaphas in order to suggest that he spoke by an impulse of the Holy Spirit to speak truths about the future for the precise benefit of their subjects. Apropos of what is said in opposition to this, namely, that the statement, **it is ex-**

---

73. See *ST* II-II, q. 172, aa. 1, 5–6.

pedient for you that one man should die for the people, is false, this can be answered this way. The death of Christ considered in itself was expedient for all, even for those who killed him: "who is the savior of all men, especially of those who believe" (1 Tim 4:10); "So that by the grace of God he might taste death for every one" (Heb 2:9). In another way, one can take *it is expedient for you* as meaning "for the people." Hence the Evangelist, where Caiaphas says *that one man should die for the people*, uses below the words *for the nation*.

1579. The words of the Evangelist seem to indicate that he was a prophet, since he says, *he prophesied*; for if a person prophesies, it follows that he is a prophet. According to Origen,[74] however, it does not follow that every one who prophesies is a prophet; but if one is a prophet, he does prophesy. For sometimes an act is granted to a person, but not the state to which it is appropriate: for example, not every one who does something just is just, but one who is just does just things.

Furthermore, it should be noted that two acts concur in order that someone prophesy: namely, seeing—"He who is now called a prophet was formerly called a seer" (1 Sam 9:9)—and announcing—"He who prophesies speaks to men for their upbuilding and encouragement" (1 Cor 14:3). Now it sometimes happens that a person has both, and yet is not properly speaking a prophet: for sometimes a person has a prophetic vision, as Nebuchadnezzar and Pharaoh, and similarly announces the vision to others; yet they cannot be called prophets because they lack something, namely, an understanding of the vision, which is necessary in a vision, as stated in Daniel (10:1): "A word was revealed to Daniel . . . and he understood the word: for there is need of understanding a vision." Caiaphas, however, although he did not have a prophetic vision, did announce a prophetic matter insofar as he announced the benefit of Christ's death. For sometimes the Holy Spirit moves one to all that pertains to prophecy, and sometimes to something only.[75] In the case of Caiaphas, he enlightened neither his mind nor his imagination. Consequently, his mind and imagination remained intent on evil; yet he moved his tongue to tell the manner in which the salvation of the people would be accomplished. Thus, he is not called a prophet except insofar as he performed a prophetic act in announcing, his imagination and reason remaining fixed in the contrary. It is clear from this that he was no more a prophet than was Balaam's donkey.

1580. When the Evangelist says, *and not for the nation only, but to gather into one the children of God who are scattered abroad*, the Evangelist adds to the words of the high priest, and says that Jesus was

---

74. *Comm. in Io.* XXVIII. 13, nos. 98–106; PG 14, col. 705D–8C; cf. *Catena aurea*, 11:47–53.
75. See *ST* II-II, q. 171, a. 2; II-II, q. 173, a. 4.

to die not only for the nation of the Jewish people, as Caiaphas said—"So Jesus also suffered outside the gate in order to sanctify the people through his own blood" (Heb 13:12)—but he adds, even for the whole world. Thus he added, *to gather into one the children of God who are scattered abroad.*

Here one must guard against the error of the Manichees, who said that certain souls are the divine substance and are called the children of God, and that God came to gather together these children into one. This is erroneous because it is stated in Ezekiel (18:4): "All souls are mine," that is, by creation. Consequently, the statement, *to gather into one the children of God who are scattered abroad,* does not mean that they have already received the spirit of adoption, because, as Gregory[76] says, they were as yet neither his sheep nor children of God by adoption. Rather it should be taken according to predestination. It is as though he were saying: *to gather into one,* namely, into the unity of the faith—"And I have other sheep, that are not of this fold; I must bring them also . . . so there shall be one flock, one shepherd" (10:16); "The Lord builds up Jerusalem; he gathers the outcasts [the dispersed] of Israel" (Ps 146:2)—*the children of God,* predestined from eternity—"For those whom he foreknew he also predestined to be conformed to the image of his Son, in order that he might be the first-born of many brethren" (Rom 8:29), the brethren, that is, *who are scattered abroad* in diverse ceremonies and nations.[77]

1581. Then when he says, *So from that day on they took counsel how to put him to death,* the Evangelist sets down the agreement among the Jews on the death of Christ. But did they not previously think of putting him to death? It seems so, because before in many places it is stated that the Jews sought to kill him. I answer that they previously did have some desire to kill him, but *from that day on,* incited to anger by the words of Caiaphas, they ended with a firm proposal to kill him "For their feet run to evil" (Pr 1:16).

LECTURE 8

54 Jesus therefore no longer went about openly among the Jews, but went from there to the country near the wilderness, to a town called Ephraim; and there he stayed with the disciples. 55 Now the Passover of the Jews was at hand, and many went up from the country to Jerusalem before the Passover, to purify themselves. 56 They were looking for Jesus and saying to one another as they stood in the temple, "What do you think? That he will not come to the feast?" 57 Now the chief

---

76. See *XL hom. in Evang.* 4. 1; PL 76, col. 1089–90.
77. See *ST* III, q. 24, a. 4.

priests and the Pharisees had given orders that if any one knew where he was, he should let them know, so that they might arrest him.

1582. Here the Evangelist sets down how Christ escaped from their malice: first, the way he escaped; secondly, the effect this had on the people of making them question (v. 56).

1583. The way he escaped was to hide himself and leave the presence of the Jews: for after their plan, he moved more cautiously and **no longer went about openly among the Jews**. He did not withdraw to a populated city, but into a remote region, a **country near the wilderness, to a town called Ephraim; and there he stayed with his disciples**.

1584. But did he lack the power by which, if he had wished, he could have lived publicly among the Jews and they would not do anything to him? Of course not. He did not do this because he did not have the power, but as an example for the disciples. This shows that it is not a sin if his faithful withdraw from the sight of their persecutors, choosing rather to evade the fury of the wicked by hiding, than kindle it more by showing themselves: "When they persecute you in one town, flee to the next" (Matt 10:23).[78]

Moreover, Origen[79] says that no one should place himself in danger; but when dangers are immediately threatening, it is very praiseworthy not to run from professing Christ or not to refuse to suffer death for the sake of the truth. No one should place himself in danger for two reasons. First, because it is very presumptuous to place oneself in danger, both on account of a lack of experience of one's own virtue, which is sometimes found to be fragile, and on account of the uncertainty about the outcome; "Let any one who thinks that he stands take heed lest he fall" (1 Cor 10:12). Secondly, lest by presenting ourselves to our persecutors, we give them the occasion to be more wicked and culpable: "Give no offense to Jews or to Greeks or to the church of God" (1 Cor 10:32).

1585. Now the effect of his leaving, that the people questioned, is set down: first, the occasion for their questioning; secondly, their questioning; and thirdly, the reason for their questioning.

1586. Two occasions for their questioning and wondering are mentioned. The first was the nature of the time, because the **Passover of the Jews was at hand**, when the flight of the Hebrews out of Egypt was recalled: "It is the Lord's Passover" (Ex 12:11). He adds, **of the Jews**, because they celebrated their Passover in an unholy and unbecoming way: for when one celebrates the Passover in a devout way it is called the Passover of God: "Your assemblies I will not abide," as we read in Isaiah (1:13).

---

78. See *ST* II-II, q. 126, a. 2, ad 1.
79. *Comm. in Io.* XXVIII. 23, nos. 192–94; PG 14, col. 728C–29A; cf. *Catena aurea*, 54–57.

CHAPTER 11

The second occasion was the gathering of the people, *and many went up from the country to Jerusalem.* For as we see from Exodus (chap. 23), the children of Israel were to present themselves to the Lord three times a year on the three festivals, and the foremost of these was the Passover. And so a great number traveled to Jerusalem, where the temple was located. But because it was not yet actually the Paschal time, when they were obliged to go, the Evangelist tells why they went then, adding, *before the Passover, to purify themselves.* For no one dared to eat the lamb if he was unclean, and so they went before the Passover so that, by purifying themselves in the meantime, they could fittingly eat the lamb on the Passover. This gives us an example that we should purify ourselves during Lent by fasts and good works, so that on the Passover we might receive the body of our Lord in a fitting manner.[80]

1587. The reason for their questioning is mentioned as due to Christ's absence: *they were looking for Jesus,* not to honor him, but to kill him, *and saying to one another as they stood in the temple, what do you think? That he will not come to the feast?* But note that when a festival day is celebrated in a holy manner, Christ is always present: "For where two or three are gathered in my name, there am I in the midst of them" (Matt 18:20). And so let us, when we gather together in the house of God, seek Jesus by consoling each other and by praying that he come to our festival day. But Jesus does not come when a feast is not celebrated in a holy manner: "Your new moons and your appointed feasts my soul hates" (Is 1:4).

1588. He adds the reason for their questioning and for the absence of Jesus, saying, the chief priests and the Pharisees had given orders that if any one knew where he was, that is, Jesus, he should let them know, so that they might arrest him, to kill him. "You will seek me and die in your sin" (8:21). As Augustine[81] says, we who know where Christ is, that is, at the right hand of the Father, should tell them so that they may truly apprehend him by faith.[82]

---

80. See *ST* I-II, q. 102, a. 5, ad 3, 4.
81. *Tract. in Io.* 50. 4; PL 35, col. 1759; cf. *Catena aurea,* 11:54–57.
82. See *ST* III, q. 58, a. 1.

CHAPTER 12

LECTURE 1

1 Six days before the Passover, Jesus came to Bethany, where Lazarus was, whom Jesus had raised from the dead. 2 There they made him a supper; Martha served, and Lazarus was one of those at the table with him. 3 Mary took a pound of costly ointment of pure nard and anointed the feet of Jesus and wiped his feet with her hair; and the house was filled with the fragrance of the ointment. 4 But Judas Iscariot, one of his disciples (he who was to betray him), said, 5 "Why was this ointment not sold for three hundred denarii and given to the poor?" 6 This he said, not that he cared for the poor but because he was a thief, and as he had the money box he used to take what was put into it.[1]

1589. So far the Evangelist has been showing the power of Christ's divinity by what he did and taught during his public life. Now he begins to show the power of his divinity as manifested in his passion and death.

First, he treats of Christ's passion and death; secondly, of his resurrection (chap. 20). The first is divided into three parts: in the first he states what caused or occasioned Christ's passion and death; in the second, how Christ prepared his disciples, since his death involved his physical separation from them (chap. 13); in the third, he describes his passion and death (chap. 18).

Now there were two things which caused or occasioned the passion of Christ: the glory of Christ, which aroused the envy of the Jews, and their disbelief, which blinded them. So first, he treats of the glory Christ received; secondly, of the unbelief of the Jews (v. 37). In regard to the first he does two things: first, he shows how Christ received glory from other people; secondly, how he received glory from God (v. 27). Concerning the first he does three things: first, he shows how Christ received glory from his intimate friends; secondly, from the crowd of the Jewish people (v. 9); thirdly, from the Gentiles (v. 20). Concerning the first he does two things: first, he shows the glory Christ received by being ministered to by his friends; secondly, how this kindled the indignation of the one who was to betray him (v. 4). In regard

---

1. St. Thomas refers to Jn 12:6 in *ST* II-II, q. 55, a. 7, obj. 3; q. 188, a. 7.

to the first he does three things: first, he describes the time; secondly, the place (v. 1); and thirdly, the kindness shown to Christ (v. 2).

1590. He says first, what we have already stated: that before the Passover Christ went into a region near the wilderness, and since the feast was drawing near, the Jews began to look for him. Thus, when the paschal season was at hand, during which the symbolic lamb was immolated, he, as the true lamb, came to the place where he would suffer and of his own free will be immolated for the salvation of the world: "He was offered because it was his own will," as we read in Isaiah (53:7).[2]

The Evangelist says Christ came there *six days before the Passover*, to inform us that by the day of the Passover he did not mean the fourteenth day of the first month (when according to the twelfth chapter of Exodus, the Passover lamb was slain in the evening), but the fifteenth day. This entire day was festive, and that year it fell on the Friday our Lord suffered. Thus the sixth day before the Passover was the first day of the week, i.e., the Palm Sunday on which our Lord entered Jerusalem. Consequently, Christ came to Bethany on the previous day, that is, on the Sabbath. This is what he means by the phrase, *six days before the Passover*.

1591. This number is very appropriate to the mystery to be enacted. First of all, because of the number itself, for six is a perfect number. For God completed the works of creation in six days. For this reason it was appropriate that it should take six days to accomplish the work of the passion, which would restore all things: "to reconcile all things, whether on earth or in heaven, making peace by the blood of his cross" (Col 1:20); "God was in Christ reconciling the world to himself" (2 Cor 5:19).

Secondly, it is appropriate to the mystery, considering its foreshadowing. For Exodus (chap. 12) commanded that on the tenth day of the first month every man was to take a lamb for his household and keep it for the sacrifice. Thus it was also on the tenth day of the first month, i.e., on the sixth day before the fifteenth day, that our Lord decided to enter Jerusalem, drawing near to the place where he would be sacrificed. This is clear from what follows: "The next day a great crowd who had come to the feast heard that Jesus was coming to Jerusalem. So they took branches of palm trees and went out to meet him" (12:12).

1592. Then when he says, *Jesus came to Bethany*, the place is mentioned. Bethany was a village near Jerusalem, and it means the "house of obedience." This also is appropriate to the mystery. First, as regards a reason for the passion: "He became obedient unto death" (Phil 2:8).[3]

---

2. See *ST* III, q. 73, a. 6.
3. See *ST* III, q. 47, a. 2.

Secondly, with respect to the fruit of the passion, which is obtained only by those who obey Christ: "He became the source of eternal salvation to all who obey him" (Heb 5:9).

It is significant that he added, **where Lazarus was, whom Jesus had raised from the dead**, because in the house of obedience those who are spiritually dead are raised to life by being restored to the way of righteousness: "By one man's obedience many will be made righteous" (Rom 5:19). According to the literal sense, however, this was written to show that Christ came to Bethany in order to revive the memory of the resurrection of Lazarus: "He has caused his wonderful works to be remembered; the Lord is gracious and merciful" as we read in the Psalm (110:4).

1593. Then when he says, **there they made him a supper**, he mentions the kindness shown to Christ by his friends: first, by his friends in general; secondly, in particular. **Martha served**, etc.

1594. It was also appropriate to this mystery that they served him a supper there, at Bethany, because the Lord is spiritually refreshed in the house of obedience since our obedience pleases him, according to: "Behold, I stand at the door and knock; if any one hears my voice and opens the door, I will come in to him and eat with him, and he with me" (Rev 3:20).[4]

1595. Next he mentions the three people who attended or sat with Jesus: Martha, Lazarus and Mary. Martha signifies the prelates who are appointed to serve in the churches: "This is how one should regard us, as servants of Christ and stewards of the mysteries of God" (1 Cor 4:1). Thus we read that **Martha served**: "Martha was busy with much serving" (Lk 10:40). Lazarus, who had been raised to life, signifies those who have been brought from sin to the state of righteousness by the ministry or service of the prelates; and they, alone with the other righteous, feast spiritually with the Lord. Thus he says, **and Lazarus was one of those at table with him**: "Let the just feast and rejoice before God and be delighted with gladness" (Ps 67:4). Mary signifies the contemplatives, for we read in Luke (10:39): "Mary sat at the Lord's feet and listened to his teaching."[5]

1596. Three things are mentioned about Mary's kindness: first, the ointment she used; secondly, the kindness she offered; thirdly, its effect.

With regard to the ointment, three things are noted. First, the amount, and it was a large amount, **a pound** of ointment: "If you have many possessions, make your gift from them in proportion" (Tb 4:8). Secondly, its matter, for it was made of **nard**: "While the king was on his couch, my nard gave forth its fragrance" (Sg 1:11). Recall that nard is a short black aromatic herb; and the ointment which is made

---

4. See *ST* II-II, q. 104, a. 3.
5. See *ST* II-II, q. 182, a. 1.

from it has a fragrance which has the power to give strength and comfort. Thirdly, its composition is noted, for the nard is described as *pisticus*. According to Augustine,[6] the word *pisticus* is taken from the place where nard originates. However, it is better to interpret this word as meaning "true" or "pure," that is, as not adulterated: for *pistis* in Greek is the same as our *fides* [truthful, honest]. He adds that it was **costly**, because it was made from nard, which is used in costly ointments, and perhaps other expensive ingredients were added to it. This teaches us that we should offer to God those things we regard as most precious: "I will offer to thee burnt offerings of fatlings, with the smoke of the sacrifice of rams" (Ps 65:15); "Cursed be the cheat who has a male in his flock, and vows it, and yet sacrifices to the Lord what is blemished" (Mal 1:14).

See Mary's humility, for she fell down at the feet of Jesus **and anointed the feet of Jesus**, according to, "Let us worship at his footstool" (Ps 131:7). Secondly, see her devotion, for she **wiped his feet with her hair**, in this way making an offering of herself: "Yield your members to God as instruments of righteousness" (Rom 6:13).[7]

He mentions the effect of her ministering when he says, **and the house was filled with the fragrance of the ointment**. This tells us of the goodness of this ointment, which filled the entire house: "We will run after thee to the odor of thy ointments" (Sg 1:3).

1597. The question is raised as to whether this woman is the same woman who anointed our Lord as mentioned in Luke (7:37), Matthew (26:7) and Mark (14:3). We learn from Jerome[8] and Chrysostom[9] that many think that the sinful woman mentioned by Luke is not the sister of Lazarus, Mary, who is said [in John] to have anointed the Lord. Origen[10] adds that [in John] she is also not the woman of whom Matthew and Mark speak, but they were speaking of some other woman. He gives three reasons for this opinion. The first is based on the time: for the woman in John anointed the Lord six days before the Passover, while the woman mentioned by Matthew and Mark did so some time during the two days preceding the Passover. For Matthew prefaces his account by stating that the Lord said: "You know that after two days the Passover is coming" (Matt 26:2); and in Mark we read: "It was now two days before the Passover and the feast of the Unleavened Bread" (Mk 14:1). The second reason is based on the place: for in Matthew and Mark the woman is said to have anointed the Lord in the house of Simon the leper, but in John she seems to be in the house of Martha, for we read that Martha was serving the guests. And Augustine agrees

---

6. *Tract. in Io.* 50. 6; PL 35, col. 1760; cf. *Catena aurea*, 12:1–11.
7. See *ST* II-II, q. 82, a. 1.
8. *Comm. in Matt.* 4. 26. 7; PL 26, col. 191.
9. *Hom. in Io.* 62. 1; PG 59, col. 342; cf. *Catena aurea*, 11:1–5.
10. *Comm. in Matt.* 77; PG 13, col. 1721–22.

with this. The third reason is from the action itself: for the woman in Matthew and Mark anointed the head of our Lord, while the one in John anointed his feet.

On the other hand, Augustine[11] and Gregory[12] claim that the four Evangelists are speaking of one and the same woman, but that she anointed our Lord twice. The first time, mentioned by Luke, was at the beginning of her conversion, some time during the middle of Christ's public life. The second time, mentioned by the other three Evangelists, was a few days before Christ's passion. Thus the same act is mentioned here in John and in Matthew and Mark.

As for the discrepancy in the time, Augustine says that John preserved the historical order, while Matthew and Mark merely remembered that it took place just prior to Judas' betrayal, which was believed to have been occasioned by this event. As for the argument based on the difference of place, there is no reason why the house of Simon the leper could not be the house of Mary and Martha, since Simon might have been the head of the house. He is called a leper because at one time he was a leper, but was cured by Christ. As far as the act itself is concerned, Augustine says that the woman anointed both the head and feet of Jesus.

1598. If the objection is raised that according to Mark she broke the alabaster jar and poured ointment on the head of Jesus, one might answer this in two ways. First, that it was broken in such a way that some remained for anointing his feet; secondly, she could have anointed his feet first, and then, breaking the jar, poured the rest on his head.

1599. Mystically, the pound Mary used denotes the work of justice, for it belongs to justice to weigh things and give pound for pound: "Their weight shall be equal" (Ezek 45:11). Now four other virtues must be added if the work of justice is to be perfect. First, compassion: and so he says, **ointment**, which, because it is soothing, represents mercy: "For judgment is without mercy to one who has shown no mercy" (James 2:12). Secondly, humility is needed: so he says, **nard**, which, since it is a small herb, signifies humility: "The greater you are, the more you must humble yourself" (Sir 3:18). Thirdly, faith is needed: thus he says, **pure** (*pisticus*), that is believing (*fidelis*): "The righteous shall live by his faith" (Hab 2:4). Fourthly, charity must be present: so he says, **costly**, for charity alone pays the price for eternal life: "If I give away all I have ... but have not love, I gain nothing" (1 Cor 13:3).[13]

The works of justice anoint both the feet and head of Jesus. By his feet we understand the mystery of his humanity; and by his head, his divinity, according to: "The head of Christ is God" (1 Cor 11:3).

---

11. *De cons. Evang.* 2. 79; PL 34, col. 1154–55; cf. *Catena aurea*, 12:1–11.
12. *Ep. V ad Theoc.*; PL 77, col. 449C.
13. See *ST* II-II, q. 184, a. 3.

Thus one who venerates the divinity and humanity of Christ is said to anoint his head and feet.

Or, we can take the head as indicating the very person of Christ, according to: "He has made him the head over all things for the church" (Eph 1:22).[14] Then the feet are Christ's faithful, of whom we read: "As you did it to one of the least of these my brethren, you did it to me" (Matt 25:40); "How beautiful upon the mountains are the feet of him who brings good tidings, who publishes peace" (Is 52:7). Thus, one who honors Christ himself, anoints the head of Christ; and one who serves his faithful anoints our Lord's feet.

Again, because the hair is produced from what is superfluous in the body, one dries the Lord's feet with his hair when he takes what he has in surplus and relieves the needs of his neighbor: "Give that which remains as alms" (Lk 11:41). Thus Augustine[15] says: "If you have a surplus of anything, give it to the poor and you have dried the feet of the Lord."[16]

The fact that the house was filled with the fragrance of the ointment signifies that because of the works of justice, the Church enjoys and is filled with a good name: "We are the aroma of Christ" (2 Cor 2:15).

1600. Next (v. 40), the Evangelist describes the traitor's indignation at this. He does two things concerning it: first, he shows his indignation; secondly, how it was curbed (v. 7). Concerning the first he does three things: first, he describes the traitor; secondly, he mentions what he said; and thirdly, he states that his intention was evil (v. 6).

1601. The traitor is portrayed in three ways. First, his dignity is given when he says, **one of his disciples**. This teaches us that no one should presume on himself no matter to what dignity he has been raised: "His angels he charges with wickedness" (Job 4:18). Secondly, his name, **Judas Iscariot**. The name "Judas" means "professing," to indicate to us that in addition to a way of professing that is virtuous—"Man professes with his lips and so is saved" (Rom 10:10)—there is a way of professing that is blameworthy and mercenary—"He will profess you [that is, profess your praises] when you have done good to him" (Ps 48:19). Thirdly, his crime is mentioned, **he who was to betray him**: "Even my bosom friend in whom I trusted, who ate of my bread, has lifted his heel against me" (Ps 40:10).

1602. Then he gives the traitor's words, from which we see that he had died spiritually from the aroma of the ointment, according to: "For we are the aroma of Christ . . . to one a fragrance from death to death, to the other a fragrance from life to life" (2 Cor 2:15). Judas was displeased because the ointment was not sold but poured out as an act of

---

14. See *ST* III, q. 8, a. 6.
15. *Tract. in Io.* 50. 6; PL 35, col. 1760; cf. *Catena aurea*, 12:1–11.
16. See *ST* II-II, q. 32, a. 1.

homage to Christ. Thus Judas says, **Why was this ointment not sold for three hundred denarii?** But as we read in 2 Corinthians (11:14), the ministers of Satan disguise themselves as angels of righteousness. Thus Judas hid his evil under the cloak of piety, saying, **and given to the poor**: "His heart will work iniquity to practice hypocrisy and speak to the Lord deceitfully" (Is 32:6).

1603. The Evangelist unmasks the deceit when he adds, **This he said, not that he cared for the poor but because he was a thief.** For he was not interested in helping the poor—"The hearts of the wicked are cruel" (Pr 12:10)—**but because he was a thief**, and accustomed to stealing, he was pained that the use of the ointment had deprived him of an opportunity to steal, and it was this avarice that led to the betrayal, for we read: "Nothing is more wicked than the covetous man" (Sir 10:9); and "The thief comes only to steal and kill and destroy" (10:10). He had the opportunity to steal for **he had the money box**, that is, he was in charge of our Lord's purse, and **he used to take what was put into it**, i.e., whatever was donated by the faithful for Christ's use and for the poor he carried as a duty, but carried off as a thief.

1604. Two things can be noted here. First, that Christ lived on alms as a poor person: "As for me, I am poor and needy" (Ps 39:18). Secondly, it is not opposed to perfection to keep alms in a money box. Thus what we read in Matthew (6:34), "Do not be anxious about tomorrow," does not forbid one from saving for tomorrow, since our Lord did this very thing, and he is the supreme model of perfection.[17]

1605. One might ask why our Lord, since he knew that Judas was a thief, entrusted him with the money box? This can be answered in three ways. First, according to Augustine,[18] Christ did this so that his Church would be patient when it was robbed; for one is not good if he cannot endure those who are evil. Thus we read: "As a lily among brambles, so is my love among maidens" (Sg 2:2). Secondly, our Lord entrusted him with the money box to lessen his danger of final damnation, because he could then satisfy his greed from the money box. But as it is said: "He who loves money will not be satisfied with money" (Ecc 5:10). Thirdly, according to others, he did this in order to teach us that spiritual things should be entrusted to those who are more worthy, and temporal things should be entrusted to the less worthy. Thus the apostles said: "It is not right that we should give up preaching the word of God to serve tables" (Acts 6:2), and they entrusted this work to one of the deacons.

1606. But why does it say here that only Judas said this when the ointment was poured out, while Matthew says that the disciples said this? One reply is that Matthew uses the plural for the singular, as he

---

17. See *ST* II-II, q. 187, a. 5; II-II, q. 187, a. 7.
18. *Tract. in Io.* 50. 10; PL 35, col. 1762; cf. *Catena aurea*, 12:1–11.

also did in "Those who sought the child's life are dead" (2:20). Or, one might answer that Judas was the first to grumble and that this incited the others to say the same, although not from the same motive.

LECTURE 2

7 Jesus said, "Let her alone, let her keep it for the day of my burial. 8 The poor you always have with you, but you do not always have me." 9 When the great crowd of the Jews learned that he was there, they came, not only on account of Jesus but also to see Lazarus, whom he had raised from the dead. 10 So the chief priests planned to put Lazarus also to death, 11 because on account of him many of the Jews were going away and believing in Jesus.

1607. Having narrated the traitor's indignation at the kindness shown by the woman, the Evangelist now shows how our Lord put a stop to it. First, our Lord answers the unjust criticism Judas spoke against the woman; secondly, he rejects the spiritual reason Judas pretended to have (v. 8).

1608. He says, **Let her alone**, i.e., do not stop her. For it is well known that many good works are done which if our advice had been sought before they were done, we would not have advised that they be done, because something better could possibly have been done. Yet after they are begun, so long as they are good, they should not be stopped. Thus, as Chrysostom[19] says, before the woman had poured out the ointment, Jesus would perhaps have preferred that it be given to the poor, but now that it was done, he held back those who were trying to stop her, saying, **Let her alone**: "Do not prevent one who is able from doing good. If you are able, you also do good," as we read in Proverbs (3:27).

He adds, **let her keep it for the day of my burial**, foretelling both his approaching death and the kindness this woman was ready to do for him in his tomb if he had not precluded it by rising so soon, for as we read in Mark's Gospel (16:1): "Mary Magdalene," along with other women, "bought spices, so that they might go and anoint him." This is why he said, **let her keep it for the day of my burial**, not the identical ointment she used, but ointment of the same kind, in general or particular, or even a similar service. It is as though he were saying: Do not stop her from doing for me while I am alive what she will be unable to do for me when I am dead. For, as I said, she was prevented by the resurrection of Christ occurring so quickly. This is expressed in a

---

19. The comment that Aquinas attributes here to Chrysostom does not appear in either the *Catena aurea* or in Chrysostom's commentary on John chapter 12.

clearer way in Mark (14:8): "She has anointed my body beforehand for burying."

1609. But did she have foreknowledge of Christ's death? Not at all: for she did not understand what she was doing. Rather, she was moved to do it by a certain inner urge. It often happens that people are moved to do things that they do not understand, as in the case of Caiaphas, the high priest, who said, "You know nothing at all; you do not understand that it is expedient for you that one man should die for the people" (11:49). Things of this sort are called presages, because they take place before the event.

1610. Then when he says, *the poor you always have with you*, he rejects the spiritual reason which Judas feigned when he said: "Why was this ointment not sold for three hundred denarii and given to the poor." Our Lord answered, *the poor you always have with you*. Here it might be remarked that sometimes one should do what is less needful if the opportunity remains for doing what is more needful. Thus, although it was more needful that this ointment be given to the poor rather than having it used to anoint the Lord's feet, nevertheless, because there was still opportunity to do the former, since we always have the poor with us, our Lord allowed what was less needful.

In the statement that *the poor you always have with you*, we are led to understand the fellowship the rich should have toward the poor: "Make yourself companionable to the poor" (Sir 4:7).

1611. *But you do not always have me*. Yet we read in Matthew (28:20): "I am with you always, to the close of the age." Augustine[20] gives this reply. When our Lord said, *but you do not always have me*, he was speaking of his bodily presence, that is, as he appeared and in the form in which he would ascend into heaven: "Again, I am leaving the world" (16:28). But he is always with us as present in his divinity; and he is also present sacramentally in the Church.

Another explanation would be this. When our Lord said this he was thinking of the presence of his divinity. Now some seem to possess Christ spiritually, either in the sacrament or in professing the faith; yet they will not always possess him because they belong to the Church only nominally, and not by merit. These are the servants. But the children will always possess him because "the son continues for ever" (8:35). Thus he said to Judas, *but you do not always have me*, because you have made yourself unworthy of this.

As Chrysostom[21] says, our Lord was rebuking Judas when he said this: for by being annoyed that this respect was shown to Christ, he seemed to consider Christ's presence as a burden. So Christ said, *you*

---

20. *Tract. in Io.* 50. 13; PL 35, col. 1763; cf. *Catena aurea*, 12:1–11.
21. *Hom. in Io.* 65. 2; PG 59, col. 363; cf. *Catena aurea*, 12:1–11.

do not always have me. This was like saying: I am a burden to you; but wait awhile, and I will be leaving.

1612. Next (v. 9), the Evangelist shows how Jesus was honored by many of the Jews; first, by the crowd that went to see him there; secondly, by the crowd which meet him on his way to Jerusalem (v. 12). In regard to the first he does two things: first, he shows the eagerness of those who came to see him; secondly, he shows the vehemence of the Pharisees aroused by their envy (v. 10).

1613. The first part is divided into two parts: first, he states that a crowd came to him; secondly, he gives the reason why they came. As to the first, he says, **When the great crowd of the Jews learned that he was there, they came**, to Bethany. This was in keeping with our Lord's invitation: "Come to me, all who labor and are heavy laden, and I will give you rest" (Matt 11:28). And so, when we know where Jesus is, we should go to him quickly.

Now there were two reasons why they came. The first was to enjoy the sight and teaching of Christ. Secondly, they came *to see Lazarus*. And they came to see Lazarus for two reasons. First, because of the extraordinary miracle accomplished on Lazarus, that is, his being raised back to the living after four days in the tomb; and the people desired to see this: "Your works are wonderful, and my soul knows them well," that is, it attempts to understand them (Ps 138:14). Secondly, they came because they hoped they would learn something about the other life from Lazarus, for man has an inborn desire for knowledge of this kind, in spite of what the foolish say: "For they reasoned unsoundly, saying to themselves, 'Short and sorrowful is our life, and there is no remedy when a man comes to his end, and no one has been known to return from Hades'" (Wis 2:1). But here he is! Lazarus, whom he raised from the dead, has resumed from the lower world.

1614. Then the Evangelist describes the vehemence of the Pharisees in their envy, when he says, **So the chief priests planned to put Lazarus also to death**. In this they were opposing God: for God had raised him to life, and they wanted to kill him: "Running stubbornly against him" (Job 15:26). Then the reason for their vehemence is stated, because on account of him many of the Jews were going away and believing in Jesus.

1615. But since Christ had cured many people, such as the paralytic and the man born blind, why did they want to kill only Lazarus? Chrysostom[22] gives four reasons. First, because this miracle was more evident, it was performed before many people, and it was absolutely astounding to see a man dead for four days walking and speaking. The second reason was that Lazarus was a well-known person, while

---

22. Ibid., 66. 1, col. 365–66; cf. *Catena aurea*, 12:1–11.

the blind man was unimportant, so much so that they even expelled him from the temple. The third reason was because this miracle was accomplished near the time of a great feast, and all the Jewish people who had come for the feast disregarded the solemnities and went to Bethany. The fourth reason was that in the other miracles they could accuse Christ of breaking the Sabbath, and in this way alienate the people from him; but this time that way was closed. And so because they could find no reason to attack Jesus, they attacked Lazarus as the best way to conceal the miracle: "Their feet run to evil and they make haste to shed blood" (Pr 1:16).

LECTURE 3

12 The next day a great crowd who had come to the feast heard that Jesus was coming to Jerusalem. 13 So they took branches of palm trees and went out to meet him, crying, "Hosanna! Blessed is he who comes in the name of the Lord, even the King of Israel!" 14 And Jesus found a young ass and sat upon it; as it is written, 15 "Fear not, daughter of Zion; behold, your king is coming, sitting on an ass's colt!" 16 His disciples did not understand this at first; but when Jesus was glorified, then they remembered that this had been written of him and had been done to him. 17 The crowd that had been with him when he called Lazarus out of the tomb and raised him from the dead bore witness. 18 The reason why the crowd went to meet him was that they heard he had done this sign. 19 The Pharisees then said to one another, "You see that you can do nothing; look, the world has gone after him."

1616. Here we see the fervor of the crowd which went to meet Christ. First, they go to meet Christ; secondly, we have the reaction of the Pharisees (v. 19). Concerning the first the Evangelist does three things: first, he mentions their going out; secondly, he tells of our Lord's entrance (v. 14); and thirdly, he states why the crowd went out to him.

1617. He mentions four things concerning the crowd which went out to the Lord. First, the time they went out, **the next day**, that is, the day following the one he meant when he said, "six days before the Passover"; in other words, the tenth day of the month. This is in keeping with the figure in Exodus (12:3), where we read that the Paschal lamb which was to be immolated on the fourteenth day in the evening should be procured on the tenth day of the month.

1618. Secondly, the ones who went out are described, **a great crowd who had come to the feast**. They signify the multitudes of the people who would be converted to Christ: "Let the assembly of the people be gathered about thee" (Ps 7:8). He says **to the feast**, because believers

CHAPTER 12

are converted to Christ so that they may come to the feast day of the heavenly Jerusalem: "Many will come from east and west and sit at table with Abraham, Isaac, and Jacob in the kingdom of heaven" (Matt 8:11).

1619. Thirdly, the Evangelist mentions their motive for going out, which was that they heard that Jesus was coming: he says that they **heard that Jesus was coming to Jerusalem**. For all the faithful are converted to Christ through what they hear about the faith: "Faith comes from what is heard, and what is heard comes by the preaching of Christ" (Rom 10:17); "And the children of Israel heard that the Lord had visited the children of Israel; and the peoples believed," as we read in Exodus (4:31).

1620. Fourthly, he mentions how they conducted themselves. And first of all, what they did: **they took branches of palm trees**. Now the palm, since it retains its freshness, signifies victory. Thus in antiquity it was conferred upon conquerors as a symbol of their victory. Again, we read in Revelation (7:9) of the conquering martyrs that they held "palm branches in their hands." And so the branches of palm trees were given as praise, signifying victory, because our Lord was to conquer death by dying and to triumph over Satan, the prince of death, by the victory of the cross. **And went out to meet him**: "Prepare to meet your God, O Israel!" (Amos 4:12).

1621. Secondly, the Evangelist mentions what they said: **they shouted out Hosanna! Blessed is he who comes in the name of the Lord, the King of Israel!** Here they combine both petition and praise. There is petition when they say, **Hosanna**, that is "Save us, I implore you." It is like saying: *hosy*, which means "save," and *anna*, which means "implore." According to Augustine,[23] this is not a word, but rather an exclamation of one praying. And it is quite proper that they should ask the Lord Jesus for salvation, because we read in Isaiah (35:4): "Behold your God . . . He will come and save you"; "Stir up thy might, and come to save us!" (Ps 79:3).

1622. They praise him for two things: for his coming and for the power of his reign or kingdom. They praise his coming when they say, **Blessed is he who comes in the name of the Lord**. Note that to bless is to speak good things. Now God blesses us in one way, and we bless God in another way. For when God blesses us he makes us good, since for God to speak is to do: "For he commanded [that is, spoke], and they were created" (Ps 148:5). But when we bless God, we profess his goodness: "We bless you from the house of the Lord" (Ps 117:26); "Blessed be every one who blesses you!" (Gen 27:29). Therefore, **Blessed is he who comes in the name of the Lord**, for Christ worked in the name of God, because every thing he did he directed to the glory of God.

---

23. *Tract. in Io.* 51. 2; PL 35, col. 1764; cf. *Catena aurea*, 12:12–19.

Now because both the Father and the Son are the Lord, the phrase, *in the name of the Lord*, can be understood in two ways. In one way, *Blessed is he who comes in the name of the Lord*, means blessed is he who comes in his own name, as Lord: "The Lord is our ruler" (Is 33:22). Moses did not come in the name of the Lord in this way, because he came as a servant: "Now Moses was faithful in all God's house as a servant, to testify to the things that were to be spoken later" (Heb 3:5). According to Augustine,[24] the better interpretation would be to say that *in the name of the Lord* means in the name of the Father. For Christ's words direct our minds to this: "I have come in my Father's name" (5:45). Further, there are two ways in which Christ is said to have come in the name of the Father. First, he came as the Son, which implies the Father; secondly, he came to manifest the Father: "I have manifested thy name to the men whom thou gave me" (17:6).[25]

1623. The people praise the power of his reign when they say, *the King of Israel!* Literally, the Jews believed that he had come to reign over them temporally, and ransom them from subjection to the Romans. That is why they hailed him as a king: "He shall reign as king and deal wisely" (Jer 23:5); "Behold, a king will reign in righteousness, and princes will rule in justice" (Is 32:1).

1624. We should note that the above words can be gathered from the Psalms. For when the Psalm says, "The stone which the builders rejected" (Ps 117:22), it then continues on, "Save us, we beseech thee, O Lord! . . . Blessed is he who enters in the name of the Lord!" (v. 25–26). And there Jerome, according to the meaning of the Hebrew, translated hosanna as "blessed." But what the people added, *the King of Israel*, is not in the psalms. Instead, the Psalm says: "The Lord is God, and he has given us light" (v. 27). In saying this, the people, due to their blindness, have lessened his praise: for the Psalm praises our Lord as God, but they praised him as a temporal king.

1625. When the Evangelist says, *and Jesus found a young ass and sat upon it*, he describes our Lord's coming: first, he tells how he came; secondly, he mentions a prophecy (v. 15); and thirdly, he describes the state of mind of the disciples in regard to this event (v. 16).

1626. It should be noted in regard to the first point, that John the Evangelist wrote his Gospel after all the others. And so, after carefully noting what these had written, he merely summarized what they had already mentioned, but filled in what they had omitted. Therefore, since the other Evangelists had already told how the Lord sent two of his disciples to bring the ass, John contents himself with mentioning briefly that *Jesus found a young ass and sat upon it*.

Here it should be pointed out that Christ's actions are in a way mid-

---

24. Ibid., 51. 3, col. 1765; cf. *Catena aurea*, 12:12–19.
25. See *ST* III, q. 47, a. 3, ad 1.

CHAPTER 12   273

way between the events of the Old Testament and of the New Testament. Thus the crowds praised him, both the one which went before him, and the one which followed him, because Christ's actions are the rule and exemplar of the things that are done in the New Testament, and they were prefigured by the fathers of the Old Testament.

The young ass is an awkward animal, and signifies the Gentiles. Christ sat upon it to signify that he would redeem the Gentiles: "I will give you as a light to the nations, that my salvation may reach to the end of the earth" (Is 49:6); "Happy are you who sow beside all waters, who let the feet of the ox and the ass range free," that is, thus uniting the Jews and the Gentiles in one faith.

Now Matthew wrote his Gospel for the Jews, and so he made mention of a she-ass. This she-ass signifies the synagogue of the Jews, which was like a mother to the Gentiles in spiritual matters, because "out of Zion shall go forth the law, and the word of the Lord from Jerusalem" (Is 2:3). The other Evangelists, however, wrote their Gospels for the Gentiles, and so they mention the young colt of the she-ass.

1627. When the Evangelist says, *as it is written, Fear not, daughter of Zion!* he cites the prophecy which was written in Zechariah (9:9). First, he reassures them; secondly, he promises a kingly majesty; and thirdly, he adds the benefit which the king will bring.

He reassures them when he says, **Fear not, daughter of Zion**. Zion was the fortress in Jerusalem where the king lived. The daughter of Zion, therefore, would be the people of Jerusalem and of Judea who were subject to the king of Jerusalem. Thus the Jews are being told, **Fear not**, because the Lord is your defender: "Who are you that you are afraid of man who dies, of the son of man who is made like grass?" (Is 51:12); "The Lord is the defender of my life; of whom shall I be afraid?" (Ps 26:1). Here the Evangelist is driving out their worldly and servile fear.[26]

He promises them a kingly majesty, saying, **behold, your king is coming**: "For to us a son is given" (Is 9:6); "Upon the throne of David, and over his kingdom" (9:7). He says, *your king*, that means, taking flesh from you, for "It is not with angels that he is concerned, but with the descendants of Abraham" (Heb 2:16). Again, *your king*, that is, for your benefit. Thus he adds, *is coming*, to you: "Would that even today you knew the things that make for peace! But now they are hid from your eyes" (Lk 19:42). But when they resisted, they hindered their own good.

The king comes to you, I say, not to harm you, but to set you free; thus he adds, *sitting on an ass's colt!* This signifies the mercy of the king, which is most welcome to his subjects: "His throne is upheld by mercy" (Pr 20:28). This is just the opposite to "A king's wrath is like

---

26. See *ST* II-II, q. 19, aa. 3–4.

the growling of a lion" (Pr 19:12). He is saying in effect: He is not coming as a haughty king—which would make him hateful—but with gentleness: "If they make you master of the feast, do not exalt yourself" (Sir 32:1). Therefore, have no fear that the king will oppress you. Now the Old Law was given in fear, because the Law produced slaves. This phrase also signifies the power of the king, because by coming with humility and in weakness he attracted the entire world: "The weakness of God is stronger than men" (1 Cor 1:25).

1628. Then when he says, *his disciples did not understand this at first*, he describes the state of mind of the disciples regarding this prophecy. And he admits his own ignorance and that of the disciples, for as we read: "The just person is the first to accuse himself" (Pr 18:17). So he says, *his disciples did not understand this*, what was predicted, *at first*, that is, before the passion. *But when Jesus was glorified*, i.e., when he showed the power of his resurrection, *then they remembered that this had been written of him and had been done to him*. The reason they knew only after he had been glorified was because it was then that they received the power of the Holy Spirit, which made them wiser than all the wise: "The breath of the Almighty makes a man understand" (Job 32:8).[27] But the Evangelist says this for this reason, to show that what happened had not been carefully attended to by the disciples.

1629. Then he mentions why the crowd went to meet Jesus, which was to bear witness. This was done by *the crowd that had been with him*, at the resurrection of Lazarus, *when he called Lazarus out of the tomb . . . The reason why the crowd went to meet him was that they heard he had done this sign*. "For Jews demand signs" (1 Cor 1:22). Now this was a clearer and more marvelous sign than the others; thus Christ made it the last in order to impress it more forcefully on their memory.

1630. Then when the Evangelist says, *The Pharisees then said to one another*, he describes the reaction of the Pharisees, who were enraged because their plans had been frustrated. Thus they say, *You see that you can do nothing*. The Pharisees said this out of envy, as if to say: We are not having any effect, that is, in our evil intentions; we have failed to check him.

But why were they maddened at the blind crowd? Because *the world has gone after him* through whom the world was made. This was a sign that the whole world would follow him: "We shall live in his sight. We shall know and we shall follow the Lord" (Hos 6:3).

Chrysostom,[28] however, thinks that these words were said by the Pharisees who believed, but they were spoken privately for fear of

---

27. See *ST* II-II, q. 45, aa. 5–6.
28. *Hom. in Io.* 66. 2; PG 59, col. 367; cf. *Catena aurea*, 12:12–19.

the Jews. And they said this to stop the persecution of Christ. It is as though they were saying: No matter what snares you lay, he will grow in stature and his glory will increase. Why then not stop your plotting? This is practically the same as the advice of Gamaliel in the Acts (5:34).

LECTURE 4

20 Now among those who went up to worship at the feast were some Greeks [Gentiles]. 21 So these came to Philip, who was from Bethsaida in Galilee, and said to him, "Sir, we wish to see Jesus." 22 Philip went and told Andrew; Andrew went with Philip and they told Jesus. 23 And Jesus answered them, "The hour has come for the Son of man to be glorified. 24 Truly, truly, I say to you, unless a grain of wheat falls into the earth and dies, it remains alone; but if it dies, it bears much fruit. 25 He who loves his life loses it, and he who hates his life in this world will keep it for eternal life. 26 If any one serves me, he must follow me; and where I am, there shall my servant be also; if any one serves me, the Father will honor him."[29]

1631. Having described the glory Christ received from the helpfulness of his friends and from the devotion of the crowd, the Evangelist now describes the glory Christ received from the devotion of the Gentiles. First, the devotion of the Gentiles is mentioned; secondly, this devotion is reported (v. 22); and thirdly, we see the prediction of Christ's passion (v. 23). Concerning the devotion of the Gentiles, two things are set forth: first, their devotion to the sacraments of the Old Law; secondly, their devotion to Christ (v. 21).

1632. The devotion of the Gentiles to the sacraments of the Old Testament is shown by the fact that they visited the temple. Thus he says, **Now among those who went up**, to Jerusalem, **to worship at the feast were some Gentiles**. He is saying in effect: Not just the Jews, but the Gentiles, also, honored Christ. According to a Gloss,[30] the reason why they went up to Jerusalem was because they were proselytes, who had been converted to the Jewish rite by the preaching of those Jews who were scattered throughout the world, and who strove to convert whomever they could: "You traverse sea and land to make a single proselyte" (Mt 23:15). And so, in keeping with the Jewish rite, they went up with the others.

29. St. Thomas refers to Jn 12:24 in *ST* III, q. 74, a. 3, s. c.; Jn 12:24–25: *ST* III, q. 46, a. 2, obj. 1.
30. This comment does not appear in the *Glossa Ordinaria* or in the *Catena aurea* for Jn 12:20. It is Chrysostom who makes brief reference to the Gentiles coming up to the feast in order to be made proselytes: *Hom. in Io.* 66. 2; PG 59, col. 367; cf. *Catena aurea,* 12:20–26.

But a better reason is given by Chrysostom,[31] namely, that as we read in Maccabees (3:2), the temple of God in Jerusalem was held in such esteem by all the people and rulers throughout the world that they considered it an honor to glorify the temple with the finest gifts. And so it happened that on the feast days even many Gentiles would go up to Jerusalem. An example of this is mentioned in the Acts (8:27), where it tells of a eunuch, a minister to Queen Candace of Ethiopia, who had come to Jerusalem to worship. Thus Isaiah says: "My house shall be called a house of prayer for all peoples" (Is 56:7). The fact that these Gentiles came to the temple out of devotion prefigured the conversion of the Gentiles to the faith.

1633. The devotion of the Gentiles to Christ is shown by their desire to see him; for the Evangelist says, *So these*, that is, the Gentiles, *came to Phillip*. Here we should note that Christ personally preached only to the Jews: "For I tell you that Christ became a servant to the circumcised to show God's truthfulness, in order to confirm the promises given to the patriarchs" (Rom 15:8); but he preached to the Gentiles through the apostles. "And I shall send of them that shall be saved to the Gentiles ... and they shall declare my glory to the Gentiles" (Is 66:19); "Go therefore and make disciples of all nations" (Mt 28:19). This was now being indicated beforehand inasmuch as the Gentiles who wanted to see Christ did not come to him first, but to one of his disciples, to Philip. And this was fitting, because Philip was the first to preach to those who were not of the Jewish rite, namely, to the Samaritans, as we see from the Acts (8:5): "Philip went down to the city of Samaria, and proclaimed to them the Christ."

This was also fitting because of his name: for "Philip" means the "mouth of the lantern." Now preachers are the mouth of Christ: "If you utter what is precious, and not what is worthless, you shall be as your mouth" (Jer 15:19); and Christ too is the lantern: "I have given you as a light to the nations" (Is 42:6). It was also appropriate to him because of his home: for Philip *was from Bethsaida*, which means "hunting," and preachers hunt for those whom they convert to Christ: "I will send for many hunters, and they shall hunt them" (Jer 16:16). Again, it was appropriate because Bethsaida was *in Galilee*, which means "transmigration," and the Gentiles, by the preaching of the apostles, were transmigrated from the gods of paganism to the state of believers: "Therefore, son of man, prepare for yourself an exile's baggage, and go into exile by day in their sight," as we read in Ezekiel (12:3).

These Gentiles approached Philip and expressed their desires, saying, *we wish to see Jesus*. This signifies that those Gentiles who had not seen Christ in the flesh but who had been converted to the faith by the

---

31. *Hom. in Io.* 66. 2; PG 59, col. 367.

ministry of the apostles, desired to see him glorified in heaven: "All the earth desired to see the face of Solomon" (1 Kg 10:24).

1634. Then when he says, *Philip went and told Andrew; Andrew went with Philip and they told Jesus*, the news of the Gentiles' devotion is carried to Christ. In this action a definite order is being followed, because "the things that are from God are set in order" (Rom 13:1). Now it belongs to the divine order that lower things be led back to God through those that are higher, and since Andrew outranked Philip among the apostles, because he was converted before him, Philip did not wish to bring these Gentiles to Christ by himself, but through Andrew, perhaps remembering that the Lord had said: "Go nowhere among the Gentiles" (Mt 10:5). And this is what he says, *Philip went and told Andrew; Andrew went with Philip and they told Jesus*. This teaches us that all things should be done with the advice of those in authority. Thus, even Paul went up to Jerusalem and conferred with the apostles about the Gospel which he was preaching among the Gentiles (Gal 2:2).

Furthermore, from their names we can gather two things which are necessary for preachers if they are to lead others to Christ. The first is clear, orderly speech; and this is indicated by Philip's name, which means the "mouth of the lantern." The second is virtue, manifested in good actions; and this is indicated by Andrew's name, which has the meaning of "strength." "By the word of the Lord the heavens were made, and all their strength by the breath of his mouth" (Ps 32:6).

1635. Then, the passion of Christ is foretold: first, Christ foretells that the time of his passion is near; secondly, he intimates that his passion is necessary (v. 24); and thirdly, he mentions the necessity for others to suffer (v. 25).

1636. He says, *The hour has come for the Son of man to be glorified*. Here it should be noted that our Lord, seeing these Gentiles hastening to see him, and understanding that in them the conversion of the Gentiles was somehow beginning, foretold the imminence of his passion, somewhat like a person who sees a wheat field growing white says that the hour has come to use the sickle for the harvest" (4:35). This is the way the Lord speaks here. Since the Gentiles want to see me, he says, *The hour has come for the Son of man to be glorified*.

1637. Now there were three events where he was glorified. First, in his passion: "Christ did not exalt [glorify] himself to be made a high priest," on the altar of the cross, "but was appointed by him who said to him, 'Thou art my Son, today I have begotten thee,'" as we read in Hebrews (5:5). In reference to this he says, *The hour has come for the Son of man to be glorified*, that is, to suffer, because the Gentiles will not be converted to him before his passion. Indeed, in his passion he was glorified both with visible signs, such as the sun becoming dark, the rendering of the temple curtain and so forth, and with invisible signs, such as the victory by which in himself he overcame the powers of darkness, as stated in Colossians (2:15). Earlier he had said, "My hour has not yet come" (2:4), because the devotion of the Gentiles had not been as keen as it was now.

Secondly, he was glorified in his resurrection and ascension. For it was necessary for Christ to first rise and ascend into heaven, and thus glorified, to send the Holy Spirit upon the apostles, through whom the Gentiles were to be converted: "For as yet the Spirit had not been given, because Jesus was not yet glorified" (7:39); Christ "ascended to the heights: he captured his spoil" (Ps 67:19).[32]

Thirdly, he was glorified by the conversion of the Gentiles: in Philippians (2:11) we read, "Every tongue will confess that the Lord Jesus Christ is in the glory of God the Father."

1638. Then when he says, *I say to you*, he intimates the necessity of his passion: first, he suggests its necessity; secondly the benefit it brings (v. 24b).

1639. The necessity for Christ's passion is caused by the conversion of the Gentiles, which cannot take place unless the Son of man is glorified through his passion and resurrection. And this is what he asserts, **Truly, truly, I say to you, unless a grain of wheat falls into the earth and dies, it remains alone**. In regard to the literal sense of this text, it should be noted that we use a grain of wheat either for bread or as a seed. In this text, we should understand that the wheat is taken as a seed, and not as the wheat used for bread, for in the latter case it would never grow and bear fruit. He says, **dies**, not because it loses its strength, but because it is then changed into something else: "What you sow does not come to life unless it dies" (1 Cor 15:36). Now just as the word of God, so far as it is clothed in a sound that can be heard, is a seed planted in a person's soul to produce the fruit of good works—"The seed is the word of God" (Lk 8:11)—so the Word of God, clothed in flesh, is a seed sent into the world to bring forth a great harvest; thus it is also compared to a grain of mustard seed, in Matthew (13:31).

So Christ is saying: I have come as a seed, to bear fruit; and so I truly say to you, **unless a grain of wheat falls into the earth and dies, it remains alone**, that is, unless I die, the fruit of the conversion of the Gentiles will not follow. He compares himself to a grain of wheat because the reason he came was to refresh and nourish our spirits, which is principally done by bread made from wheat: "bread to strengthen man's heart" (Ps 103:15); "The bread which I shall give for the life of the world is my flesh" (6:51).

1640. But were the Gentiles to be converted only through the death of Christ? Considering God's power, they could have been converted without it; but according to God's decree they were to be con-

---

32. See *ST* III, q. 57, a. 6.

verted through the death of Christ as the more fitting way: "Without the shedding of blood there is no forgiveness of sins," as is said in Hebrews (9:22); "If I do not go away, the Counselor will not come to you" (16:7).[33]

1641. The benefit produced by Christ's passion is given when he says, **but if it dies, it bears much fruit.** He is saying in effect: Unless this seed falls into the earth by the humiliation of the passion—"He humbled himself and became obedient unto death" (Phil 2:8)—there is no benefit, because **it remains alone. But if it dies**, that is, is put to death and slain by the Jews, **it bears much fruit.**

The first of these fruits is the remission of sin: "This is all the fruit, that sin is taken away" (Is 27:9). Truly, this fruit was brought forth by the passion of Christ: "For Christ also died for sins once for all, the righteous for the unrighteous, that he might bring us to God" (1 Pet 3:18). The second of these fruits is the conversion of the Gentiles to God: "I appointed you that you should go and bear fruit and that your fruit should abide" (15:16). This fruit, too, was brought forth by the passion of Christ: "And I, when I am lifted up from the earth, will draw all men to myself" (12:32). A third fruit is the fruit of glory: "The fruit of good labors is renowned [i.e., glorious]" (Wis 3:15); "He who reaps receives wages, and gathers fruit for eternal life" (4:36). And again, the passion of Christ produced this fruit: "We have confidence to enter the sanctuary by the blood of Jesus, by the new and living way which he opened for us through the curtain, that is, through his flesh" (Heb 10:19–20).[34]

1642. Then he mentions the necessity for others to die, those who expose themselves to suffering for the love of Christ. First, he states the necessity for their death; secondly, he encourages us to do this (v. 26). Concerning the first he does two things: first, he states the necessity of dying for the sake of Christ; secondly, he mentions the benefit this death brings (v. 25).

1643. Now every one, as a matter of fact, loves his own life, but some love it absolutely, without qualification, and others love it partially, in a qualified way. To love someone is to will good to that person; so, to love one's own life is to will good to it. Therefore, one who wills what is good without qualification to his own life, loves it unqualifiedly; while one who wills his life some partial good loves it in a qualified way. Now the unqualified goods of life are those which make a life good, namely, the highest good, which is God. Thus, one who wills the divine and spiritual good to his life, loves it unqualifiedly; while one who wills it earthly goods, such as riches, honors and pleasures, and things of that sort, loves it in a qualified way.[35] "He who

---

33. See *ST* III, q. 46, a. 1.
35. See *ST* II-II, q. 25, aa. 4–5.
34. See *ST* III, q. 49, aa. 1, 5.

loves sin hates his own life" (Ps 10:6); "If you allow your soul to take pleasure in base desire, it will make you the laughingstock of your enemies" (Sir 18:31).

1644. This passage, therefore, can be understood in two ways. In one way, as saying, *he who loves his life* unqualifiedly, that is, in regard to eternal goods, *loses it*, that is, exposes it to death for Christ. But this is not the true sense. Accordingly it means, *he who loves his life*, in a qualified way, that is, in regard to temporal goods, *loses it*, unqualifiedly: "For what will it profit a man, if he gains the whole world and forfeits his life?" (Mt 16:26). That this is the true meaning is shown from the statement which follows: *he who hates his life in this world will keep it for eternal life*. Therefore, *he who loves his life*, in this world, that is, as to worldly goods, *loses it* as to eternal goods: "Woe to you that laugh now, for you shall mourn and weep," as we read in Luke (6:25); "Son, remember that you in your lifetime received your good things, and Lazarus in like manner evil things; but now he is comforted here, and you are in anguish" (Lk 16:25).

1645. The benefit produced by this death is asserted when he says, *and he who hates his life in this world*, that is, he who denies his own life's present goods, and endures, for God, things that seem evil in this world, *will keep it for eternal life*: "Blessed are those who are persecuted for righteousness' sake, for theirs is the kingdom of heaven" (Mt 5:10); "If any one comes to me and does not hate his own father and mother . . . yes, and even his own life, he cannot be my disciple," as we read in Luke (14:26).[36]

Note that what was said above about the grain of wheat is in keeping with this teaching. For just as Christ was sent into the world as a seed that was to bear fruit, so whatever temporal goods are given to us in this life by God are not given to us as fruit, but rather that by their means we may obtain the fruit of an eternal reward. Indeed, our very life is a temporal gift from God to us. Therefore, anyone who exposes it for Christ bears much fruit. Such a one, therefore, hates his own life, that is, he exposes his own life, and sows, for the sake of Christ, to gain life everlasting: "He that goes forth weeping, bearing seed for sowing, shall come home with shouts of joy, bringing his sheaves with him" (Ps 125:6). And the same is true of those who risk their wealth and other goods for the sake of Christ, and share them with others, to obtain life everlasting: "He who sows bountifully will also reap bountifully" (2 Cor 9:6).[37]

1646. Now because it seems difficult for one to hate his own life, our Lord encourages us to do this, saying, *If any one serves me, he*

---

36. See *ST* II-II, q. 26, a. 7; II-II, q. 184, aa. 2–3.
37. See *ST* II-II, q. 184, a. 2.

must follow me. First, his encouragement is given; secondly, the reason for this encouragement (v. 26b).

1647. In regard to the first he does three things. First, he describes his faithful; secondly, he urges them to imitate him; thirdly, he indicates the reward of those who imitate him.

Observe, in regard to the first, the dignity of Christ's faithful, for they are the ministers or servants of Christ: "Are they ministers of Christ? So am I" (2 Cor 11:23). Thus, those serve Christ who seek the things of Christ; but those who seek their own advantage are not servants of Christ, but servants of themselves: "They all seek after their own interests, not those of Jesus Christ" (Phil 2:21). Priests are servants inasmuch as they administer the sacraments to the faithful: "This is how one should regard us, as servants of Christ and stewards of the mysteries of God" (1 Cor 4:1). Again, every one of the faithful who keeps the commandments of Christ is his servant: "Let us act in all circumstances as God's ministers" (2 Cor 6:4).[38]

In regard to the second, observe the glory and grandeur of the faithful of Christ, for he says, *he must follow me*. This is like saying: We follow our masters, whom we serve. Therefore, *If anyone serves me, he must follow me*, so that just as I undergo death so that I might bear much fruit, so also my servant. Now to follow Christ is a great glory: "It is a great glory to follow the Lord" (Sir 23:38); "My sheep hear my voice, and I know them, and they follow me" (10:27).[39]

In regard to the third, note the beatitude of the faithful, for *where I am*, not only in the place, but also as regards the sharing of glory, *there shall my servant be also*: "Wherever the body is, there the eagles will be gathered together" (Mt 24:28); "He who conquers, I will grant him to sit with me on my throne" (Rev 3:21).[40]

1648. The reason for this encouragement is given when he says, *if any one serves me, the Father will honor him*, for the Father honors anyone who serves Christ. Now above we have read: "that all may honor the Son, even as they honor the Father" (5:23). Thus, it is the same to honor the Son and to honor the Father. But the Father says, "Those who honor me, I will honor" (1 Sam 2:31). Thus, the Father of Jesus will honor one who ministers to Jesus, not seeking his own, but the things of Jesus Christ. Jesus did not say, "I will honor him," but *the Father will honor him*, because these people did not think at this time that he was equal to the Father.

Or, it might be said that Jesus said this to show how intimately his servants are related to him, inasmuch as they will be honored by the same one who honors the Son. For the honor the Son has by his na-

38. See *ST* III, q. 82, a. 1, ad 2.
39. See *ST* III, q. 45, a. 1.
40. See *ST* III, q. 58, a. 4, ad 2, 3.

ture, they will have by grace. So Augustine[41] says: "An adopted son can receive no greater honor than to be where the only Son is." "For those whom he foreknew he also predestined to be conformed to the image of his Son, in order that he might be the first-born among many brethren" (Rom 8:29).[42]

LECTURE 5

27 *"Now is my soul troubled. And what shall I say? 'Father, save me from this hour?' No, for this purpose I have come to this hour. 28 Father, glorify thy name." Then a voice came from heaven, "I have glorified it, and I will glorify it again." 29 The crowd standing by heard it and said that it had thundered. Others said, "An angel has spoken to him." 30 Jesus answered, "This voice has come for your sake, not for mine. 31 Now is the judgment of this world, now shall the ruler of this world be cast out; 32 and I, when I am lifted up from the earth, will draw all men to myself." 33 He said this to show by what death he was to die.*[43]

1649. Above, we saw the glory shown to Christ by various types of people; here the Evangelist considers the glory shown to Christ by God. First, he mentions that Christ asked for glory; secondly, the promise of glory is made (v. 28b). Concerning the first he does two things. First, the interior state of Christ is given; secondly, he mentions the request made by Christ.

1650. Note, in regard to the first, that it seems incongruous for Christ to be saying, **Now is my soul troubled**, for he had urged his faithful to hate their own lives in this world; but with his own death near at hand, we hear the Lord himself saying, **Now is my soul troubled**. This leads Augustine[44] to say: "O Lord, You command my soul to follow. But I see your own soul troubled. What support shall I seek, if the rock crumbles?" Thus we must first examine this troubled state of Christ, and secondly, why he willed to undergo it.

1651. As to the first, we should note that, properly speaking, a thing is said to be troubled when it is greatly agitated. Hence when the sea is very agitated it is said to be troubled. And so whenever a thing oversteps the bounds of its repose and tranquility, it is said to be troubled. Now in the human soul there is a sentient area and a rational area. The sensitive area of the soul is troubled when it becomes

---

41. *Tract. in Io.* 51. 11; PL 35, col. 1767.
42. See *ST* III, q. 23, a. 4; III, q. 24, a. 3.
43. St. Thomas refers to Jn 12:31 in *ST* III, q. 44, a. 1; q. 49, a. 2, s. c.; Jn 12:32: *ST* III, q. 46, a. 4; q. 49, a. 2, s. c.
44. *Tract. in Io.* 52. 2; PL 35, col. 1769; cf. *Catena aurea*, 12:27–33.

strongly affected by certain movements. For example, when it is contracted by fear, raised up by hope, dilated by joy, or otherwise affected by one or other of the emotions. Sometimes this perturbation remains within the bounds of reason, and sometimes it exceeds the bounds or reason, namely, when the reason itself is troubled. And although this latter condition quite often occurs in us, it is not found in Christ, since he is the Wisdom of the Father.[45] Indeed, it is not found in any wise person; thus the Stoic tenet that one who is wise is not troubled, that is, in his reason.

Accordingly, the meaning of **Now is my soul troubled**, is this: My soul is affected by the emotions of fear and sadness in its sentient part; but these emotions do not trouble my reason, and it does not abandon its own order. "He began to be greatly distressed and troubled" (Mk 14:33).

Such emotions, however, exist in us otherwise than in Christ. In us, they arise from necessity, insofar as we are moved and affected from without, as it were. But in Christ, they are not from necessity, but from the command of reason, since there was never any emotion in him except that which he himself aroused. For in Christ the lower powers were subject to his reason so perfectly that they could not act or undergo anything except what reason appointed for them.[46] Thus as was said above (11:33): "he was deeply moved in spirit and troubled himself"; "You have moved the earth," that is, human nature, "and troubled it" (Ps 59:4). And so the soul of Christ was troubled in such a way that its perturbation was not opposed to reason, but according to the order of reason.

1652. In regard to the second point, note that Christ willed to be troubled for two reasons. First, to show us a doctrine of the faith, that is, the truth of his human nature. Accordingly, as his passion was drawing near, he did everything in a human way. Secondly, he wanted to be an example for us. For if he had remained unmoved and had felt no emotions in his soul, he would not have been a satisfactory example of how we should face death. And so he willed to be troubled in order that when we are troubled at the prospect of death, we will not refuse to endure it, we will not run away: "For we have not a high priest who is unable to sympathize with our weakness, but one who in every respect has been tempted as we are, yet without sinning" (Heb 4:15).[47]

1653. The relationship of this with what came before is clear. He encouraged his disciples to suffer when he said: "He who hates his life in this world will keep it for eternal life." But some might say to him:

---

45. See *ST* III, q. 15, a. 4.
46. Ibid.
47. See *ST* III, q. 15, a. 6, ad 4; III, q. 15, a. 7, ad 1.

"Lord, you can calmly discuss and philosophize about death because you are above human sorrows, and death does not trouble you." It was to counter this that he willed to be troubled. This disturbance in Christ was natural: for just as the soul naturally loves union with its body, so it naturally shrinks separation from it, especially since the reason of Christ allowed his soul and its inferior powers to act in their own proper way.[48]

1654. Again, when he said, **Now is my soul troubled**, he refuted the error of Arius and Apollinarius. For they said that Christ did not have a soul, and in place of his soul they substituted the Word.

1655. Then our Lord makes his petition for glory, saying, **And what shall I say? Father, save me from this hour** [understood here not as a question, but as a petition]. Here our Lord takes upon himself the emotions of one who is troubled. And acting as one troubled, he does four things in his petition. First, he poses a question, as one does when deliberating about what is to be done; secondly, he makes a request which arises from a certain inclination; thirdly, he rejects this inclination for a particular reason; and fourthly, he makes another request that arises from a different inclination.

1656. He poses this question as one does when in doubt, because it is natural to deliberate about what to do when one is perplexed. So the Philosopher[49] says in his *Rhetoric* that fear makes a person take counsel. Thus, after mentioning that he is troubled, Christ at once adds, **And what shall I say?** It is the same as saying: "What shall I do in my trouble." Something like this is met in Psalm 54 (v. 6): "Fear and trembling came upon me," and then follows, "O that I had wings like a dove! I would fly away and be at rest" (v. 7). For both the perplexed and the emotionally disturbed are weighed down and look for help to relieve themselves.

1657. He makes his petition, arising from a certain inclination, because when one is hesitant about what he should do, he ought to turn to God: "We do not know what to do, but our eyes are upon thee" (2 Chr 20:12); "I have lifted up my eyes to the mountains from whence help will come to me" (Ps 120:1). And so, turning to the Father, he says, **Father save me**, that is, from the sufferings which await me at the hour of my passion: "Save me, O God! For the waters have come up to my neck" (Ps 68:1). According to Augustine,[50] what our Lord says here—**Now is my soul troubled** and **Father, save me**—is the same as what he says in Matthew (26:38): "My soul is very sorrowful, even to death."

1658. Note that this petition is not made as though it arose from the

---

48. See *ST* III, q. 18, a. 5; III, q. 21, a. 2.
49. Aristotle, *Rhetoric*, II. 5. 14.
50. *Tract. in Io.* 52. 3; PL 35, col. 1770.

inclination of reason; rather, reason is speaking as an advocate of the natural inclination not to die. And so in this petition reason is pointing out the impulse of a natural inclination.[51]

This explanation solves a question which is frequently raised. For we read: "In all things he was heard for his reverence" (Heb 5:7); and yet in this case, Christ was not heard. The answer to this is that Christ was heard in those matters in which his petition came from reason itself and which he intended to be granted.[52] But the petition he made here did not come from reason, nor was it intended to be granted, rather, it expressed a natural inclination. Thus Chrysostom[53] reads it as a question, that is, as: *And what shall I say?* Shall I say, *Father, save me from this hour?* It is the same as saying: "No! I will not say this."

1659. Yet Christ rejects this petition, which arose from an inclination of the natural appetite, when he says, *No, for this purpose I have come to this hour.* It is the same as saying: It is not right that I be freed from this time of suffering, because I came to suffer; and not as compelled by the necessity of fate or forced by the violence of men, but by willingly offering myself: "He was offered because it was his own will" (Is 53:7); "No one takes it," my life, "from me, but I lay it down of my own accord" (10:18).[54]

1660. Now his reason proposes its own petition when he says, *Father, glorify thy name. Thy name* can be understood in two ways. First, it can mean the Son himself. For a name (*nomen*)—which comes from the word for knowledge or being known (*notitia*)—is like a sign (*notamen*). Thus a name is what manifests a thing. Now the Son manifests the Father: "Father . . . I have manifested thy name" (17:6). We read of this name: "Behold, the name of the Lord comes from far" (Is 30:27). So the meaning in this: *Father, glorify thy name*, that is, your Son: "And now, Father, glorify thou me in thy own presence with the glory which I had with thee before the world was made" (17:5). Or, the name of the Lord indicates the knowledge which men have of the Father, then the meaning is, *Father, glorify thy name*, that is, do what is for the glory of your name. Yet it comes to the same thing, because when the Son is glorified the name of the Father is glorified. He says this because the Son was going to be glorified by his passion: "He became obedient," to the Father, "unto death, even death on a cross. Therefore, God has highly exalted him" (Phil 2:8).[55]

He is saying here in effect: By the desire of nature I ask to be saved, but my reason asks that your name be glorified, that is, that the Son suffer, because it was by the passion of Christ that men were to receive their knowledge of God and glorify him. For before the passion God

---

51. See *ST* III, q. 18, a. 6.
53. *Hom. in Io.* 67. 1; PG 59, col. 371.
55. See *ST* III, q. 49, a. 6.
52. See *ST* III, q. 21, a. 4.
54. See *ST* III, q. 47, a. 1.

was known only in Judea, and his name was great in Israel; but after the passion, God's name was glorified even among the Gentiles.

1661. Then when the Evangelist says, **Then a voice came from heaven**, the promise of glory is given. First, the voice promising glory is heard; secondly, the crowd expresses its opinion (v. 29); lastly, the meaning of the voice is explained (v. 30).

1662. With regard to the first, he says, **Then a voice came from heaven**. This is the voice of God the Father. It was the same voice that was heard when Christ was baptized, "This is my beloved Son" (Mt 3:17), and at his transfiguration (Mt 17:5). Although every voice of this kind was formed by the power of the entire Trinity, this was specifically formed to represent the person of the Father; thus it is referred to as the voice of the Father.[56] In a similar manner the dove was formed by the entire Trinity to signify the person of the Holy Spirit.[57] And again, the body of Christ was formed by the entire Trinity, but specifically assumed by the person of the Word because it had been formed to be united to him.[58]

This voice, then, does two things. First, it reveals the past, when saying, *I have glorified it*, that is, I have begotten you as glorious from all eternity, because the Son is a certain glory and splendor of the Father: "For she [Wisdom] is a reflection of eternal light, a spotless mirror of the working of God" (Wis 7:26); "He reflects the glory of God and bears the very stamp of his nature" (Heb 1:3). Or, *I have glorified it* at your birth, when the angels sang: "Glory to God in the highest" (Lk 2:14) and in the miracles the Father performed through him.

Secondly, the voice foretells what is to come: *and I will glorify it again*, in the passion, in which Christ triumphed over the devil, and in the resurrection and the ascension, and in the conversion of all the world: "The God of Abraham and of Isaac and of Jacob, the God of our fathers, glorified his Son Jesus" (Acts 3:13).

1663. Next we see the opinion of the crowd, which was wondering about the voice: *The crowd standing by heard it and said*. In this crowd, as in every other, some were dull and slow to understand, and others were more perceptive; yet all of them failed to identify the voice. Those who were slow and carnal only heard it as a sound; so they said *that it had thundered*. Still, they were not entirely mistaken, for the Lord's voice was thunder, both because it had an extraordinary meaning, and because it contained very great things: "How small a whisper do we hear of him! But the thunder of his power who can understand?" (Job 26:14); "The voice of your thunder" (Ps 76:19).

Those who were keener discerned that the sound was a voice, pro-

---

56. See *ST* III, q. 39, a. 8; III, q. 45, a. 4.
57. See *ST* III, q. 39, a. 7.
58. See *ST* III, q. 2, a. 2; III, q. 31, aa. 1–3.

nouncing words and having a meaning; so they said someone was speaking. But because they thought that Christ was merely human they erred, attributing these words to an angel. So they said that, *an angel has spoken to him*. They were under the same error as the devil, who thought that Christ needed the help of the angels: thus he said: "He will give his angels charge of you" (Mt 4:6). But he did not need to be guarded and helped by angels; rather, he is the one who glorifies and guards the angels.[59]

1664. The voice is explained when he says, *Jesus answered*. First, he explains the voice; secondly, he mentions the answer given by the people (v. 34); and thirdly, our Lord's answer (v. 35). He does two things about the first: first he mentions the reason for the voice; and secondly, he adds its meaning (v. 31).

1665. It should be noted in regard to the first that they had said, *an angel has spoken to him*. Now an angel speaks by revealing something that will profit the one to whom he speaks, as is clear in Revelation (chap. 1) and in Ezekiel (chap. 1). And so to show that he did not need this voice or any revelation from an angel, our Lord says, *This voice has come for your sake, not for mine*, that is, it has not come to instruct me. For this voice mentioned nothing he did no know before, because "in him are hid all the treasures of wisdom and of knowledge" (Col 2:2), so that he knew all that the Father knew.[60] But *it has come for your sake*, that is, for your instruction. From this we can understand that many things relating to Christ were, in God's plan, allowed to take place not because Christ needed them, but for our sakes: "For whatever was written in former days was written for our instruction" (Rom 15:4).

1666. Then when he says, *Now is the judgment of this world*, he states the meaning of this voice. First, he mentions the judgment by which he would be glorified; secondly, the effect of this judgment (v. 31b); and thirdly, the way he will be glorified (v. 32).

1667. He says, *Now is the judgment of this world*. But if this is true, why do we expect that our Lord will come again to judge? The answer is that now he comes to judge with a judgment of distinction or discernment, by which he discerns his own from those who are not his: "For judgment I came into this world" (9:39). This is what he is speaking of when he says, *Now is the judgment of this world*. But he will come again to judge with the judgment of condemnation, for which he did not come the first time: "For God sent the Son into the world, not to condemn the world, but that the world might be saved through him" (3:17).

Or, we might say that there are two kinds of judgment. One is that which condemns the world; and this is not referred to here. The oth-

---

59. See *ST* I, q. 113, a. 4, ad 1.
60. See *ST* III, q. 10, a. 2.

er is the judgment which will be in favor of the world, insofar as the world is set free from servitude to the devil. This is the way the Psalm is understood: "O Lord! Judge those who wrong me; overthrow those who fight against me" (Ps 34:1). But this judgment and the judgment of distinction are the same, because by the very fact that the judgment is in favor of the world by casting out the devil, the good are distinguished from the wicked.

1668. The effect of this judgment is the casting out of the devil. So he says, **now shall the ruler of this world be cast out**, by the power of the passion of Christ. Thus the passion of Christ is his glorification; and this explains what he had said, **I will glorify it, insofar as the ruler of this world shall be cast out**, since Christ has the victory over the devil by his passion. "The reason the Son of God appeared was to destroy the works of the devil" (1 Jn 3:8).[61]

1669. A difficulty arises here on three points. First, because he says that the devil is the ruler or prince of this world. It was this that led the Manicheans to call him the creator and lord of everything that was visible. The answer is that the devil is called the ruler of this world not by a natural right, but by usurpation, insofar as worldly people, rejecting the true Lord, subject themselves to him: "The god of this world has blinded the minds of the unbelievers" (2 Cor 4:4). Thus, he is the ruler of this world insofar as he rules those who are worldly, as St. Augustine[62] says, and these are spread throughout the entire world.[63] For the word "world" is sometimes taken in a pejorative sense to mean those who love the world: "The world knew him not" (1:10). Yet sometimes it is taken in a good sense to indicate those who are good and live in the world in such a way that they are citizens of heaven: "God was in Christ reconciling the world to himself" (2 Cor 5:19).

1670. The second difficulty concerns the fact that the ruler of this world is said to be cast out. For if he had truly been cast out, he would no longer tempt us now as he did before; yet he continues to tempt us. Therefore, he was not cast out. Augustine[64] answers this by saying that although the devil may tempt those who have ceased to be of the world, he does not tempt them in the same way as he did before. For before he tempted and ruled them from within, but now he does so only from without. For as long as men are in sin, he rules and tempts them from within: "Let not sin therefore reign in your mortal bodies, to make you obey their passions" (Rom 6:12). And so he was cast out because the effect of sin in man is not [now] from within but from without.[65]

---

61. See *ST* III, q. 48, a. 4, ad 2 and 3; III, q. 49, a. 2.
62. *Tract. in Io.* 52. 6; PL 35, col. 1771; cf. *Catena aurea*, 12:27–33.
63. See *ST* III, q. 8, a. 7.
64. *Tract. in Io.* 52. 9; PL 35, col. 1772; cf. *Catena aurea*, 12:27–33.
65. See *ST* III, q. 49, a. 2, ad 2.

1671. Thirdly, there is a difficulty from the fact that he says, *now shall the ruler of this world be cast out*. For it seems to follow from this that he had not been cast out before the passion of Christ, and consequently, if he is cast out only when men are set free from sin, it seems that Abraham, Isaac and the other men of the Old Testament were not set free from sin. The answer, according to Augustine,[66] is that before the passion of Christ he had been cast out of individual persons, but not from the world, as he was to be later. For what formerly took place in only a few men, but now happens in many Jews and Gentiles who have converted to Christ, is recognized to have been accomplished by the passion of Christ.

Or, it might be said that the devil is cast out by the fact that men are set free from sin; but before the passion of Christ all the just had been set free from sin, although not entirely, because they were still kept from entering the kingdom.[67] In this respect, therefore, the devil had some right over them which was entirely taken away by the passion of Christ, when the fiery sword was removed, when Christ said to the man: "Today you will be with me in Paradise" (23:43).

1672. The form or manner of this passion would be by being lifted up; thus he says, *and I, when I am lifted up from the earth, will draw all men [all things] to myself*. In regard to this, Chrysostom[68] has the following example: If a tyrant, accustomed to oppress and rage against his subjects and cast them into chains, were in his madness to treat in the same way some one who was not subject to him and cast him into the same prison, then he would deserve that even his dominion over the others be taken from him. This is what Christ did against the devil. For the devil had some right over men because of the sin of the first parent; and so in some sense he could justly rage against them. But since he dared to try the same things with Christ, over whom he had no right, assailing him in whom he had no part, as the tempter, it was fitting that he be deprived of his dominion by the death of Christ.[69] *And I, when I am lifted up from the earth, will draw all things to myself*. First, he describes the manner of his death; secondly, the Evangelist explains it, saying, *he said this to show by what death he was to die*, for he would die by being lifted up on the wood of the cross.

1673. Here we should note that there are two reasons why the Lord willed to die the death of the cross.[70] First, because it is a shameful death: "Let us condemn him to a shameful death" (Wis 2:20). So Augustine[71] says: "The Lord willed to die in this way so that not even a

66. *Tract. in Io.* 52. 8; PL 35, col. 1772; cf. *Catena aurea*, 12:27–33.
67. See *ST* III, q. 49, a. 5.
68. *Hom. in Io.* 67. 3; PG 59, col. 373; cf. *Catena aurea*, 12:27–33.
69. See *ST* III, q. 49, a. 2.
70. See *ST* III, q. 46, a. 4.
71. See *Tract. in Io.* 52. 13; PL 35, col. 1774.

shameful death would keep a person from the perfection of righteousness."

Secondly, because such a death involves a lifting up; so our Lord says, **when I am lifted up**. Such a manner of death was in harmony with the fruit, the reason and the symbol of the passion. It was in harmony with its fruit, because it was by the passion that Christ was to be lifted up, exalted: "He became obedient unto death, even death on a cross. Therefore God has highly exalted him" (Phil 2:8). Thus the Psalmist said: "Be exalted, O Lord, in thy strength!" (Ps 20:14).

It harmonized with the reason for the passion, and in two ways: both with respect to men and with respect to the devil. With respect to men, because he died for their salvation. For they had perished, because they were cast down and sunk in earthly things: "They have set their eyes bowing down to the earth" (Ps 16:11). Thus he willed to die raised up in order to lift our hearts up to heavenly things. For in this way he is our way into heaven. With respect to the devils, it was fitting in the sense that those who exercised their principality and power in the air were trod under foot by him while he was raised in the air.

Finally, it harmonized with the symbol, because the Lord commanded that a bronze serpent be fashioned in the desert, as recorded in Numbers (21:9), and above: "And as Moses lifted up the serpent in the wilderness, so must the Son of man be lifted up" (3:14). And so thus lifted up *I will draw all things to myself*, through love "I have loved you with an everlasting love, therefore have I drawn you, taking pity on you" (Jer 31:3).

Furthermore, the love of God for men appears most clearly in the fact that he condescended to die for them: "God shows his love for us in that while we were yet sinners Christ died for us," as we read in Romans (5:8). By doing this he fulfilled the request of the bride: "Draw me after you, and we will run to the aroma of your perfume" (Sg 1:3).

1674. Here we may note that the Father draws and the Son also draws: "No one can come to me unless the Father who sent me draws him" (6:44). He says here, *I will draw all things*, in order to show that the same action belongs to both of them. And he says, *all things*, and not "all men," because not all men are drawn to the Son. *I will draw all things*, that is, the body and the soul; or all types of men, such as Gentiles and Jews, servants and freemen, male and female; or, all who are predestined to salvation.

Finally, we should note that to draw all things to himself is for Christ to cast out the prince of this world, for Christ has no fellowship with Belial, nor light with darkness (2 Cor 6:15).[72]

---

72. See *ST* I, q. 23, aa. 3–4; I, q. 105, a. 4.

LECTURE 6

34 The crowd answered him, "We have heard from the law that the Christ remains for ever. How can you say that the Son of man must be lifted up? Who is this Son of man?" 35 Jesus said to them, "The light is with you for a little longer. Walk while you have the light, lest the darkness overtake you; he who walks in the darkness does not know where he goes. 36 While you have the light, believe in the light, that you may become sons of light." When Jesus had said this, he departed and hid himself from them.[73]

1675. Having mentioned the promised glorification of the Lord and explaining the voice, the Evangelist now describes the doubt which prevailed among the crowd. First, they introduce the authority of the law; and secondly, they raise a problem based on it (v. 34).

1676. In regard to the first the Evangelist says, **The crowd answered him**, that is, the Lord, who was speaking of his death, **we have heard from the law**, and law is taken here for the entire Old Testament **that the Christ remains for ever.** This can be gathered from many passages of the Old Testament, especially from Isaiah (9:7): "Of the increase of his government and of peace there will be no end"; and in Daniel (7:14): "His dominion is an everlasting dominion, which shall not pass away, and his kingdom one that shall not be destroyed."

1677. Basing themselves on this authority, they formulate two doubts: one concerns a fact, and the other the person. As concerns the fact, they say, **How can you say that the Son of man must be lifted up?** But since Christ did not say that "the Son of man must be lifted up," but "and I, when I am lifted up," why do the Jews say that "the Son of man" must be lifted up? The answer to this is that the Jews were now accustomed to our Lord's words; thus they remembered that he called himself the Son of man. And so when he said, "And I, when I am lifted up," they took it to mean, "If the Son of man is lifted up," as Augustine[74] says. Or, one might answer that although Christ did not here mention the Son of man, yet earlier he had said: "The Son of man must be lifted up" (3:14).

1678. Yet it seems that their statement, **the Son of man must be lifted up**, is in no way opposed to the statement that **the Christ remains for ever.** The answer is that since our Lord was accustomed to speak to them in figurative language, they understood much of what was said in that way. And so they also suspected that when our Lord spoke of being lifted up, he was referring to death on the cross: "When you

---

73. St. Thomas refers to Jn 12:36 in *ST* I-II, q. 108, a. 1, s. c.
74. *Tract. in Io.* 52. 12; PL 35, col. 1773; cf. *Catena aurea*, 12:34–36.

have lifted up the Son of man, then you will know," as we read above (8:28). Or, it could be said that they understood it in this sense because they had already thought of doing that very thing. Thus it was not the sharpness of their understanding that gave them this interpretation of these words, but an awareness of their own wickedness.

1679. Note their wickedness, for they do not say: "We have heard from the law that the Christ does not suffer," because in many places of the law reference is made to his passion and resurrection: as "like a lamb that is led to the slaughter" (Is 53:7); "I have slept and taken my rest: and I have risen up" (Ps 3:6). Rather, they say, *the Christ remains for ever*. The reason for this is that the former would not have involved any opposition, since no obstacle to Christ's immortality arises from the mere fact of his suffering. In other words, as Chrysostom[75] says, they wished to show that he was not the Christ for the reason that *the Christ remains for ever*.

1680. They raise a question concerning his person when they say, *Who is this Son of man?* They ask this because it says in Daniel (7:13): "And behold, with the clouds of heaven there came one like a son of man, and he came to the Ancient of Days"; and by that Son of man they understood the Christ. It is as though they were saying: "You say the Son of man must be lifted up; yet the Son of man, whom we take to be the Christ, remains forever. So *Who is this Son of man?* If he does not remain for ever, neither is he the Christ." In this they deserve to be reprimanded for their dullness, because even though they had seen and heard so many great things, they still had doubts about his being the Christ: "He who tells a story to a fool tells it to a drowsy man" (Sir 22:9).[76]

1681. Then when he says, *Jesus said to them*, our Lord somewhat settles their doubt. First, he commends the good they had; and secondly, he encourages them to make progress (35b); thirdly, he explains his admonition (v. 36).

1682. Jesus said to them, *the light is with you for a little longer* (*Adhuc modicum lumen in vobis est*). This can be understood in two ways. In one way, according to Augustine,[77] so that "little" modifies "light." As if to say: "A little light is in you," insofar as it sees that the Christ remains for ever. For this is a truth, and every manifestation of the truth is a light infused by God.[78] Yet this light which is in you is "little," because even though you recognize the eternity of the Christ, you do not

---

75. *Hom. in Io.* 68. 1; PG 59, col. 374; cf. *Catena aurea*, 12:34–36.

76. See *ST* III, q. 42, a. 1; III, 43, a. 4.

77. *Tract. in Io.* 52. 13; PL 35, col. 1774. The Latin text used by Augustine and Aquinas allows for "little" to modify "light" because the noun "time" is absent; the Greek text used by Chrysostom has the noun "time" (*chronos*), demanding that "little" modify "time."

78. See *ST* I, q. 88, a. 3, ad 1.

believe in his death and resurrection. This shows that you do not have perfect faith. Thus, what was said to Peter applies also to them: "O man of little faith, why did you doubt?" (Mt 14:31).[79]

It is understood in another way by Chrysostom,[80] as meaning that **the light is with you for a little longer** time, that is, I, who am the light. It is the same as saying: I, the light, am among you for a brief time: "A little while, and you will see me no more" (16:16).

1683. And so he exhorts them to make progress in good. First, he gives his exhortation; secondly, he shows the danger threatening them unless they do make progress (v. 35b).

1684. He says: I say that you have a little light, but while you have it, **walk**, that is, move forward and make progress, so that you may understand that the Christ, in addition to his eternity, will also die and rise again. This is in keeping with the first explanation given above. Or, **walk while you have the light**, that is, while I am among you, make progress and be concerned with possessing me in such a way as never to lose me: "Blessed are the people . . . O Lord, who walk in the light of thy countenance" (Ps 88:16).

And do this **lest the darkness** of unbelief, ignorance and eternal damnation **overtake you** and prevent you from going any further. For a person is overtaken by darkness when he is totally sunk in unbelief; and they would be this way if they believed in the eternity of the Christ in such a way as to deny the humiliation of his death: "A man whose way is hid" (Job 3:23); "We are wrapped up in darkness" (Job 37:19).[81]

1685. The danger threatening them unless they do progress is mentioned when he says, **he who walks in the darkness does not know where he goes**. For light, whether exterior or interior, directs man. Exterior light directs him as to external bodily acts, while the interior light directs his will. One, therefore, who does not walk in the light, not perfectly believing in Christ, **but walks in the darkness, does not know where he goes**, that is, to what goal he is being led.[82] As we read in the Psalm (81:5): "They have neither knowledge nor understanding, they walk about in darkness." This is what happened to the Jews because they did not know what they were doing, but as people who were walking in the darkness they thought they were on the right road. And so they displeased God in the very things in which they believed they were pleasing him. Similarly, in the very things in which erring heretics believe they merit the light of truth and grace is the source of their being deprived of it: "There is a way which seems right to a man, but its end is the way to death" (Pr 14:12).

---

79. See *ST* II-II, q. 2, a. 7; II-II, q. 5, a. 4.
80. *Hom. in Io.* 68. 1; PG 59, col. 374; cf. *Catena aurea*, 12:34–36.
81. See *ST* II-II, q. 10, a. 1; II-II, q. 15, aa. 1–2.
82. See *ST* III, q. 46, a. 3.

1686. Then when he says, *while you have the light, believe in the light*, he explains what he said, namely, what it means to walk. This is explained in two ways, according to the two explanations given above. According to the first explanation: *while you have the light*, that is, while you have some knowledge and light of the truth, *believe in the light*, that is, in the complete truth, *that you may become sons of light*, that is, that you may be reborn in the truth: "We are not of the night or of darkness. So then let us not sleep" (1 Th 5:6).

Or, according to the other explanation: *while you have the light*, that is, me who am the light—"He was the true light which enlightens every man who comes into the world" (1:9)—*believe in the light*, that is, in me. In other words, make progress in the knowledge of me, *that you may become sons of light*, because from the fact that you believe in me you will be the children of God: "But to all who receive him, who believed in his name, he gave power to become children of God" (1:2).[83]

1687. *When Jesus had said this, he departed and hid himself from them*. Here the Evangelist tells what Jesus did, that he hid himself. When we read above (8:59) that Christ did this very thing, the reason was obvious, for they were taking stones to cast at him. But here there is no reason for his hiding given, such as that they took up stones or that they blasphemed him. Why then did he hide? The answer is that our Lord, seeing into their hearts, knew their rage and the evil they had planned, i.e., to kill him. And so in his desire to stop them he did not wait for them to act, but hid himself so their anger and envy would abate. In doing this he is an example to us that when the evil purposes of others are clear to us, we should flee before they can accomplish them. In addition, our Lord was showing by his actions what he had said by his words. For he just said, *Walk while you have the light, lest the darkness overtake you*. And by hiding himself he indicated what sort of darkness he means: "I will wait for the Lord, who is hiding his face from the house of Jacob" (Is 8:17).

LECTURE 7

37 *Though he had done so many signs before them, yet they did not believe in him;* 38 *it was that the word spoken by the prophet Isaiah might be fulfilled: "Lord, who has believed our report, and to whom has the arm of the Lord been revealed?"* 39 *Therefore they could not believe. For Isaiah again said,* 40 *"He has blinded their eyes and hardened their heart, lest they should see with their eyes and perceive with*

---

83. See *ST* III, q. 23, a. 3.

their heart, and turn for me to heal them." 41 Isaiah said this because he saw his glory and spoke of him.

1688. Above, the Evangelist gave many examples of Christ's glory, because of which the Jews sought to kill him out of envy. Now he deals with another of the occasions surrounding his passion, that is, the unbelief of the Jews. First, their unbelief is discussed; in the second place, it is reproved by our Lord (v. 44). Concerning the first he does two things: first, he reproves the unbelief of those who believed, but in secret (v. 42). As to the first, two things are done: first, he mentions the strange hardness of their unbelief; secondly, to show that it came about not without reason or by chance, he mentions a prophecy (v. 38).

1689. The Evangelist, as though at a loss to explain it, says that our Lord had done many miracles: such as changing water into wine, curing a paralytic, giving sight to a blind man, and raising a dead man to life: nevertheless, **though he had done so many signs before them, yet they did not believe in him**. They usually said: "What sign do you do, that we may see, and believe you?" (6:30). But now! The Evangelist says: **though he had done so many signs before them, yet they did not believe in him**. "If I had not done among them the works which no one else did, they would not have sin" (15:24). And so they could not say: "We do not see our signs" (Ps 73:9).[84]

1690. Then (v. 38), the testimony of the prophet on this point is cited. First, the prophecies are mentioned; secondly, it is shown that they refer to Christ (v. 41). He does two things about the first: he cites the prophecy foretelling their unbelief; secondly, he adds the prophecy foretelling the reason for their unbelief (v. 39).

1691. He says: I say that they did not believe in him **that the word spoken by the prophet Isaiah might be fulfilled**. Here we should note that in Sacred Scripture the word "that" sometimes indicates a cause, as in "I came that they may have light" (10:10). But at other times it just indicates a sequence of events, and signifies a future event; and that is how it is used here. These people did not believe, but it was not because Isaiah predicted this. Rather, Isaiah predicted this because they were not going to believe. And so this saying of Isaiah is fulfilled from the fact that they did not believe. "Everything written about me in the law of Moses and the prophets and the psalms must be fulfilled" (Lk 24:44); "Not an iota, not a dot, will pass from the law until all is accomplished" (Matt 5:18).[85]

1692. But if it was necessary that the saying of Isaiah be fulfilled, it seems that the Jews should be excused for not believing, for they could not act contrary to the prophecy. I answer that the prophecy

---

84. See *ST* III, q. 43, a. 4.
85. See *ST* II-II, q. 171, a. 6.

took account of their freedom. For God, knowing the future beforehand, foretold their unbelief in the prophecy, but he did not bring it about; for God does not force one to sin just because he already knows one's future sins.[86] And so our Lord, from whom nothing is hidden, predicted that the Jews would commit the sin which they did commit.

1693. Now the Evangelist states what the prophet said, **Lord, who has believed our report, and to whom has the arm of the Lord been revealed?** Here we should note that belief comes in two ways. Sometimes by instruction from another; and this is the usual way: "So faith comes from what is heard, and what is heard comes by the preaching of Christ" (Rom 10:17).[87] Sometimes it comes by a divine revelation; and this is the special way, spoken of by the Apostle: "For I did not receive it from man, nor was I taught it, but it came through a revelation of Jesus Christ" (Gal 1:12).

1694. Isaiah foretold that there would be few believers. First, as to those who would believe in the usual way, by instruction, he says, **Lord, who has believed our report?** This can be understood in two ways. In one way, the meaning is: *who has believed our report?* That is, what you reported to us, what we have heard from you. "We have heard tidings from the Lord" (Ob 1:1); "Let us hear what the Lord will speak" (Ps 84:9). It is like they were saying: "Lord, we have heard these things from you. But who will believe us when we tell what we have heard from you about your birth and passion?" This entire chapter of Isaiah (chap. 53) is speaking of these things.

Prophets are said to hear in order to suggest the way in which the prophets are instructed. By sight, a person receives an immediate knowledge of the thing seen, but by hearing he does not have an immediate knowledge of what he sees, but he gains his knowledge from certain signs of the thing. And so because the prophets did not immediately see the divine essence, but only certain signs of divine realities, they are said to hear. "If there is a prophet among you, I the Lord make myself known to him in a vision, I speak with him in a dream," by certain signs (Num 12:6).[88] The Son, however, eternally sees the divine essence itself: "No one has ever seen God; the only Son, who is in the bosom of the Father, he has made him known," as was said above (1:18). *Who has believed our report?* That is, who has believed in the things we have heard and preached? "What I have heard from the Lord of hosts, the God of Israel, I announce to you" (Is 21:10).

The second way of understanding *who has believed our report?* is to take it as meaning the things we report to them, what they have heard from us. "They hear what you say but they will not do it" as Ezekiel (33:31) says.

---

86. See *ST* I, q. 19, a. 8; I, q. 23, a. 6.
87. See *ST* III, q. 42, a. 4.
88. See *ST* II-II, q. 173, a. 1.

1695. As to the special way belief comes, by revelation, he says, *and to whom has the arm of the Lord been revealed?* The "arm" refers to the Son, through whom the Father does all things, just as we accomplish things through our arm. And if we accomplished things only through an interior word, then this word would be called our arm. And so the Son is called the arm of God not because God the Father has a human shape and a physical arm, but because "all things were made through him," the Son (1:3). "Have you an arm like God, and can you thunder with a voice like his?" (Job 40:9); "He has shown strength with his arm" (Lk 1:51).

1696. Here we should note that Sabellius misunderstood this passage and said that the Father and the Son are the same person; and Arius also did when he said that the Son is inferior to the Father. The reasons for this were that a person and his arm do not form two persons, but only one, and an arm is not equal to the person. The answer to this is that in expressions of this kind the similarities are not really adequate, for what we find in creatures does not perfectly represent what is in God. Thus Dionysius says that symbolic theology is not argumentative. Thus the Son is not called an arm as though he is the same person as the Father or inferior to the Father, but because the Father does all things through him.[89] When he says, *and to whom has the arm of the Lord been revealed?* it is like saying, only to a few, that is, to the apostles: "God has revealed to us through the Spirit" (1 Cor 2:10).

1697. When the Evangelist says, *therefore they could not believe*, he states the prophecy which foretold the reason for their unbelief. If we examine these words of the Evangelist they seem, if taken at their surface value, difficult to understand. First, because if it is said that *therefore they could not believe*, because Isaiah said this, the Jews seem to be excusable. For is it a sin for a person not to do what he cannot do? And what is more serious, the fault will be cast back on God, since he blinded their eyes. This could be accepted if it were said of the devil, as in 2 Corinthians (4:4): "The god of this world has blinded the minds of the unbelievers." But here it is said of our Lord, for Isaiah (6:1) says: "I saw the Lord seated on a high and lofty throne," and follows with "Blind the heart of this people and make their ears heavy, and shut their eyes, lest they see with their eyes and hear with their ears and understand with their heart and be converted and I heal them" (v 10).[90]

1698. To clarify this let us first explain the statement, *therefore they could not believe*. Here we should note that something is said to be impossible or said to be necessary in two ways: absolutely, and granted a certain presupposition. For example, it is absolutely impossible for a human being to be an ass; but granting a certain presupposition, it is

---

89. See *ST* I, q. 1, a. 9; I, q. 45, a. 6.
90. See *ST* I-II, q. 79, aa. 3–4.

impossible for me to be outside my house, presupposing, that is, that I remain within it sitting down. With this in mind, we may say that a person is excused if he does not do things that are absolutely impossible for him. But he is not excused if he does not do things that are impossible for him granting some presupposition. So, if someone has the evil intention of always stealing, and says that it is impossible for him not to sin as long as he continues with that intention, he is not excused: for this impossibility is not absolute, but based on a certain presupposition, for he can abandon his evil intention. So he says, **therefore they could not believe**, that is, because they had a will clouded over by their wickedness: "Can the Ethiopian change his skin or the leopard his spots? Then also you can do good who are accustomed to do evil" (Jer 13:23); "How can you do good things when you are evil?" (Mt 12:34). It is like one saying: "I can in nowise love him, because I hate him."

As to the second point, when we read that God blinds and hardens, we should not think that God puts malice into us or forces us to sin; but we should understand it as meaning that God does not infuse grace. Now he infuses grace because of his mercy, while the cause of his not infusing grace is due to us, insofar as there is something in us which opposes divine grace. As far as he is concerned: "He enlightens every man coming into this world" (1:9); "He desires all men to be saved" (1 Tim 2:4). But because we leave God, he takes his grace from us: "Because you have rejected knowledge, I reject you" (Hos 4:6), "Your destruction, O Israel, is from yourself; your help is only in me" (Hos 13:9). It is like a person who closes the shutters of his house, and someone says to him: "You cannot see because you lack the light of the sun." This would not be due to a failure of the sun, but because he shut out the light of the sun.[91] In the same way we read here that they could not believe, because God blinded them, that is, they were the cause why they were deprived of sight as in "their wickedness blinded them" (Wis 2:21).

1699. With these distinctions in mind, let us consider the words of this prophecy. It is found in Isaiah (6:10), not in these exact words, but with the same meaning. Three things are mentioned here: first, the hardening and blinding of the Jews; secondly, the effect of each of these; thirdly, their end.

1700. In regard to the first, note that our Lord brought people to the faith in two ways, by his miracles and his teaching. And so he rebukes them on both points: "If I had not done among them the works which no one else did, they would not have sin" (15:24); and again in (15:22): "If I had not come and spoken to them, they would not have sin; but now they have no excuse for their sin." For they had derided both.

---

91. See *ST* I-II, q. 79, a. 3.

Insofar as they did not give due consideration to Christ's miracles, he says, ***he has blinded their eyes***, that is, the eyes of their hearts, about which we read: "Having the eyes of your hearts enlightened" (Eph 1:18). For they should have understood that such miracles could only be done by divine power: "You see many things, but do not observe them" (Is 42:20); and again, "Who is blind but my servant? Or deaf, except he to whom I have sent my messengers?" (Is 42:19).[92]

Because they were not moved by the teaching of Christ, he adds, ***and hardened their heart***. That is very hard which is not melted by intense heat nor broken by divine blows. Now the words of Christ are "like fire . . . and like a hammer which breaks the rock in pieces" (Jer 23:29). Fire, indeed, because they inflame through love; and like a hammer because they terrify when they threaten, and break one by the revelation of the truth. And still the hearts of the Jews paid no attention to the words of Christ. Thus it is obvious that they were hardened: "His heart is hard as a stone" (Job 41:24); "He has mercy upon whomever he wills, and he hardens the heart of whomever he wills" (Rom 9:18).

1701. The effect of their becoming blind is mentioned when he says, ***lest they should see with their eyes***, that is, their spiritual eyes, and perceive the divinity of Christ: "They have eyes, but do not see" (Ps 113:13). In contrast, Luke says: "Blessed are the eyes which see what you see!" (Lk 10:23). The effect of their becoming hard of heart is mentioned when he says, ***lest they should perceive***, understand, ***with their heart***: "Because no one understands, they will perish forever" (Job 4:20); "He would not understand so that he might act well" (Ps 35:4). Here it should be noted that when he says, "lest they should see with their eyes and perceive with their heart," that is, "that they should not see with their eyes and perceive with their heart," the "that" does not indicate a cause, but merely the sequence of events.

1702. The end of their becoming blind and hard in heart is given when he says, ***and turn for me to heal them***. This can be understood in two ways, as Augustine[93] says in his work, *On Gospel Questions*. In one way, so that both parts are negative, and then the meaning would be: "And they do not turn to me and I do not heal them." For the way of salvation from sin is to turn to God: "Restore us to thyself, O Lord, that we may be restored! Renew our days of old!" (Lam 5:21). But to those who prove themselves unworthy to have their sins forgiven, God does not offer the gifts by which they might turn to him and be healed, as is obvious in the case of the non-chosen.

The other interpretation is to regard only the first part as negative and then the meaning would be: they were blinded and hard-

---

92. See *ST* III, q. 43, a. 4.
93. *Quaest. in Evang. sec. Matt* 1. 14; PL 35, col. 1372–73.

ened so they should not see or understand for a time, and so not seeing or understanding, that is, not believing in Christ, they would put him to death, but afterwards they would repent and turn to God and be healed. For now and then God permits us to fall into sin so that being humbled we may arise firmer in holiness.[94]

Each of these interpretations is verified in the case of some of the Jews: the first one in those who persisted to the end in their unbelief, and the second one in those who turned to Christ after his passion, namely, those with remorse in their hearts at the words of Peter, and who said to the apostles: "Brethren, what shall we do?" as we read in the Acts (2:37).

1703. Then (v. 41), the Evangelist shows that these words of Isaiah apply here. He says, **Isaiah said this because he saw his glory**, the glory of God. For when he saw the glory of God he saw at the same time that the Jews would be blinded, as is clear from, "I saw the Lord seated on a high and lofty throne" (Is 6:1), followed by, "Blind the heart of his people and make their ears heavy, and shut their eyes, lest they see with their eyes and hear with their ears and understand with their heart and be converted, and I heal them" (v. 10). And because it is fitting that one should testify about what he has seen—as we read in 1 John (1:1)—he adds, **and spoke of him**, that is, of Christ, whose glory he saw: "To him all the prophets bear witness" (Acts 10:43); "Which he promised beforehand through his prophets in the Holy Scriptures, the gospel concerning his Son" (Rom 1:2).[95]

1704. We read that Isaiah saw and said these things. As to the first, we should avoid the error of the Arians, who say that the Father alone is invisible to every creature, but that the Son was seen in the visions of the Old Testament. But since it is stated that "He who has seen me has seen the Father" (14:9), it is obvious that the Father and the Son are visible in one and the same way. And so Isaiah, seeing the glory of the Son, also saw the glory of the Father, and indeed of the entire Trinity, which is one God, seated upon a high throne before whom the seraphim cry out: Holy, Holy, Holy! This does not mean that Isaiah saw the essence of the Trinity; rather in an imaginary vision, with understanding, he expressed certain signs of this majesty, according to the saying in Numbers (12:6): "If there is a prophet among you, I the Lord make myself known to him in a vision, I speak with him in a dream."[96]

1705. As to the second thing, that Isaiah **spoke of him**: this excludes the error of the Manicheans, who said that there were no prophecies about Christ in the Old Testament, as Augustine[97] reports to us in his book *Against Faustus;* and it excludes the error of Theodore of Mop-

94. See *ST* I-II, q. 79, a. 4; I-II, q. 98, a. 4, ad 2.
95. See *ST* II-II, q. 174, a. 6.   96. See *ST* II-II, q. 173, a. 1.
97. *Con. Faust.* 4. 1; PL 42, col. 217.

suestia,[98] who said that all the prophecies of the Old Testament bore on some current event, but the apostles and evangelists appropriated them to the life of Christ, like things said about one event can be appropriated to another event. But all this is excluded by the statement, *and spoke of him*, just as Christ said of Moses that "he wrote of me" (5:46).

LECTURE 8

42 Nevertheless many even of the authorities believed in him, but for fear of the Pharisees they did not confess it, lest they should be put out of the synagogue: 43 for they loved the praise [glory] of men more than the praise [glory] of God. 44 And Jesus cried out and said, "He who believes in me, believes not in me but in him who sent me. 45 And he who sees me sees him who sent me. 46 I have come as light into the world, that whoever believes in me may not remain in darkness. 47 If any one hears my sayings and does not keep them, I do not judge him; for I did not come to judge the world but to save the world. 48 He who rejects me and does not receive my sayings has a judge; the word that I have spoken will be his judge on the last day. 49 For I have not spoken on my own authority; the Father who sent me has himself given me commandment what to say and what to speak. 50 And I know that his commandment is eternal life. What I say, therefore, I say as the Father has bidden [said to] me."[99]

1706. Above, the Evangelist described the failing of those who did not believe at all; here he explains the failing of those who believed in secret, because they were timid, faint-hearted. First, he mentions their dignity; secondly, their failing (v. 42); and thirdly, he suggests the root of this failing (v. 43).

1707. The dignity of those who believed in secret was great, for they were the authorities, and on this point he says, *many even of the authorities believed in him.* He is saying in effect: I said that although Jesus had done so many signs, still they did not believe in him; and although this was true for the majority, yet there were some who did believe in him, because *many even of the authorities*, of the people, *believed in him.* One of these was Nicodemus, who came to Jesus by night, as was said (chap. 3). Thus the words of the Psalm (46:10) were

---

98. Theodore of Mopsuestia (d. 428), the preeminent exegete of the Antiochene school, restricted the application of Old Testament prophecies to Christ, generally limiting them only to those that have the express warrant of the New Testament itself.

99. St. Thomas refers to Jn 12:43 in *ST* II-II, q. 132, a. 3; Jn 12:48: *ST* III, q. 59, a. 5, s. c.

fulfilled: "The princes of the peoples gather as their people of the God of Abraham"; and the statement of the Pharisees is proved false: "Have any of the authorities or of the Pharisees believed in him?" (7:48).

1708. The failing of these authorities is timidity, faint-heartedness; thus he says, **but for fear of the Pharisees they did not confess it**.[100] For as stated above, the Pharisees "agreed that if any one should confess him to be Christ, he was to be put out of the synagogue" (9:22). So, although they believed with their hearts, they did not profess him with their lips. Their faith, therefore, was insufficient, for as is said in Romans (10:10): "For a man believes with his heart and so is justified, and he confesses with his lips and so is saved." "Whoever is ashamed of me and my words, of him will the Son of man be ashamed" (Lk 9:26).

1709. The root of their failing is vanity, vainglory; so he says, **for they loved the glory of men more than the glory of God**.[101] By confessing Christ publicly they would have lost the glory of men, but won the glory of God. But they chose rather to be deprived of the glory of God than the glory of men: "How can you believe, who receive glory from one another and do not seek the glory that comes from the only God?" (5:44). "If I were still pleasing men, I should not be a servant of Christ" (Gal 1:10).[102]

1710. Now he shows how Christ rebuked the Jews for their unbelief: first, he shows their duty to believe; secondly, he mentions the fruit of faith (v. 46); thirdly, he warns the unbelievers about punishment (v. 47). But because vision comes after faith, with regard to the first, he treats of faith; and secondly, of vision (v. 45).

1711. As to the first he says, **And Jesus cried out**, both because of the importance of what he intended to say and because of their free will, to charge them with their sins: "Cry aloud, spare not, lift up your voice like a trumpet; declare to my people their transgression" (Is 58:1), and said, **He who believes in me, believes not in me but in him who sent me**. This seems to contain a contradiction, for he says, **he who believes in me believes not in me**. To understand this we should note first, according to Augustine,[103] that our Lord said this to distinguish his divine and human nature. For since the proper object of faith is God, we can indeed believe that a creature exists, but we should not believe in a creature (*in creaturam*) but in God alone (*in Deum*). Now in Christ there is a created nature and the uncreated nature. Therefore, the truth of faith requires that our faith be in Christ as having an uncreated nature.[104] And so he says, **he who believes in me**, that is, in my person, **believes not in**

---

100. See *ST* II-II, q. 125, a. 1. 101. See *ST* II-II, q. 132, a. 1.
102. See *ST* II-II, q. 3, a. 2.
103. *Tract. in Io.* 54. 2; PL 35, col. 1780–81; cf. *Catena aurea*, 12:44–50.
104. See *ST* III, q. 25, a. 2.

me, as a human being, **but in him who sent me**, that is, he believes in me as sent from the Father: "My teaching is not mine, but his who sent me" (7:16).

According to Chrysostom,[105] however, our Lord says this to suggest his origin. It is a way of speaking similar to a person drawing water from a stream and saying that this water is not from the stream but from the spring: for it does not originate from the stream. So our Lord says, **he who believes in me, believes not in me but in him who sent me**, as though to say: I am not the source of myself, but my divinity is from another, that is, from my Father. *So, he who believes in me, believes not in me*, except insofar as I am from the Father.

1712. Then when he says, **and he who sees me sees him who sent me**, he treats of vision. In regard to this we should note that just as the Father sent the Son to convert the Jews, so Christ also sent his disciples: "As the Father has sent me, even so I send you" (20:21). But no one of the disciples dared to say, nor should he, that one should believe in him [the disciple], although he could say that one should believe him (*crederetur ei*). For this could not take place without detracting from the One who sent him, because if someone believed in the disciple, they would cease to believe in the master. So the Jews could say on the same basis that since you have been sent from the Father, anyone who believes in you ceases to believe in the Father. Therefore, our Lord shows against this that one who does not believe in him, does not believe in the Father. This is his meaning when he says, **he who sees me sees him who sent me**.

The seeing which is referred to here is not a physical vision, but a consideration of the truth by the mind. And the reason why one who sees the Son also sees the Father is that the Father is in the Son by a unity of essence. For one thing is said to be seen in another either because they are the same, or they are entirely conformed. But the Father and the Son are the same in nature and entirely conformed: because the Son is the image of the Father and unlike in nothing, for "He is the image of the invisible God" (Col 1:15); "He reflects the glory of God and bears the very stamp of his nature" (Heb 1:3).[106] And so, just as one believes in the Father, so also he believes in me: "He who has seen me has seen the Father . . . Do you not believe that I am in the Father and the Father in me?" (14:9). It is as though he said: The reason why one who sees me sees the Father also, is that the Father is in me and I in the Father. Thus it is clear what faith should be: faith should be in Christ, as God, just as it is in the Father.[107]

1713. Next he shows the fruit of faith. First, he shows his own

---

105. *Hom. in Io.* 69. 1; PG 59, col. 377; cf. *Catena aurea*, 12:44–50.
106. See *ST* I, q. 35, a. 2.
107. See *ST* III, q. 25, a. 1.

worth and power when he says, *I have come as light into the world*. It has already been explained how Christ is a light: "He was the true light, which enlightens every man coming into this world" (1:9), and "I am the light of the world" (8:12). He also shows by this that he has the divine nature. For to be light is proper to God; others may give off light, that is participate in light, but God is light by essence: "God is light and in him is no darkness at all" (1 Jn 1:5).[108] But because he "dwells in unapproachable light, whom no man has ever seen" (1 Tim 6:16), we were unable to approach him. And so it was necessary that he come to us. This is what he says, *I have come as light into the world*, that is, I am the unapproachable light which rescues from error and disperses intellectual darkness: "I came from the Father and have come into the world" (16:28); "He came to his own" (1:11). And although the apostles are called light—"You are the light of the world" (Mt 5:14)—they are not light in the same way as Christ. For they are a light whose light has been given to them, even though in some way they also give light, that is, in their ministry.[109] Furthermore, none of the apostles could truly say, *I have come as light into the world*, because when they came into the world they were still darkness and not light, for in Job (37:19) it says: "We are wrapped in darkness."

1714. Secondly, he continues, *that whoever believes in me may not remain in darkness*. To become enlightened, therefore, is an effect of faith: "He who follows me will not walk in darkness" (8:12). *May not remain in darkness*: that is, the darkness of ignorance, of unbelief and eternal damnation. This shows that all are born in the darkness of sin: "For once you were darkness, but now you are light in the Lord," as we read in Ephesians (5:8). And in the darkness of ignorance: "A man whose way is hidden and God has surrounded him with darkness" (Job 3:23). And in the end, unless they turn to Christ, they will be brought to the darkness of eternal damnation. And so, he who does not believe in me remains in darkness: "Whoever is unbelieving in the Son will not see life; rather, the anger of God rests on him" (3:36).[110]

1715. Then he discloses the punishment of unbelievers, which they will incur through their condemnation at the judgment. First, he states that the judgment will be delayed; secondly, that there will be a judgment in the future (v. 48); and thirdly, he shows the cause of the judgment (v. 48b).

1716. As to the first he says, *If any one hears my sayings and does not keep them, I do not judge him*. Note that the ones to be made happy, beatified, are those who hear the word of God and keep it, believing it within in their hearts, and doing it without in their actions. But they who hear it but take no care to keep it, become more guilty: "For

---

108. See *ST* I, q. 3, a. 4.
109. See *ST* III, q. 26, a. 1.
110. See *ST* II-II, q. 15, a. 1.

it is not the hearers of the law who are righteous before God, but the doers of the law will be justified" (Rom 2:13); "But be doers of the word, and not hearers only" (Jas 1:22).[111] And so, *If any one hears my sayings and does not keep them, I do not judge him.*

But this seems to conflict with what was said above (5:22): "The Father . . . has given all judgment to the Son." Therefore, we should understand it as, *I do not judge him* at this time. It could be considered a weakness in him if he overlooked those who despised him. And so he says that such persons will be judged, although not now; for we read that "God will bring every deed into judgment" (Ecc 12:14), and "Flee from the face of iniquity, for the sword is the avenger of iniquity: and know that there is a judgment" (Job 19:29).

1717. He continues with the reason for the delay, saying for *I did not come to judge the world but to save the world.* Now the Son of God comes two times: one time he comes as Savior, and the next as judge. But since all were in sin, if he had come the first time as judge, he would have saved no one, because all were the children of wrath. And so it was fitting that he come first to save believers, and later to judge both believers and sinners.[112] This is what he is saying: I do not judge now, *for I did not come to judge the world but to save the world.* "God did not send his Son into the world to judge the world, but that the world might be saved through him" (3:17).

1718. Then when he says, *he who rejects me and does not receive my sayings has a judge*, he foretells the judgment to come. It is like saying: Although those who do not keep my word are not judged now, they will not go unpunished, whoever they are, because, *he who rejects me and does not receive my sayings* by believing them and acting according to them, *has a judge.* The reason for this is that if one does not receive the word of Christ, he scorns the word of God, whose Word is Christ, just like the one who does not obey the command of his master. "Flee from the face of iniquity; and know that there is a judgment" (Job 19:29); "For God will bring every deed into judgment" (Ecc 12:14); "Woe to you who scorn. Will not you yourselves also be scorned?" (Is 33:1); "They who despise me will be despised" (1 Sam 2:30).

1719. Then when he says, *the word that I have spoken will be his judge on the last day*, he assigns the cause of the judgment. And first, he mentions the cause of the judgment; secondly, the adequacy of this cause (v. 49).

1720. He says: I say that such a person has one that judges him. But who will that judge be? He says, *the word that I have spoken will be his judge on the last day.* According to Augustine,[113] this is the same as

---

111. See *ST* II-II, q. 4, a. 3.
112. See *ST* III, q. 59, a. 5.
113. *Tract. in Io.* 54. 6; PL 35, col. 1782–83; cf. *Catena aurea*, 12:44–50.

saying: I will judge him on the last day. For Christ revealed himself in his sayings, he announced himself. He, therefore, is the word that he spoke, for he spoke about himself: "Even if I do bear witness to myself, my testimony is true, for I know whence I have come and whither I am going" (8:14). It is like saying: What I have said to them and they have despised will judge them: "He is the one ordained by God to be judge of the living and the dead. To him all the prophets bear witness" (Acts 10:42).

1721. Then he shows the sufficiency of this cause, saying, *for I have not spoken on my own authority [of myself, ex meipso]*. So first he shows this from the origin of his sayings; secondly, from their dignity or value (v. 50). Concerning the first he does two things: first, he excludes a false notion: secondly, he states the truth.

1722. The false notion, of course, is that the Son works, or says, or is, merely of himself, and not from another: for this would be to say that the Son is not from the Father. And this is what he does say: I say that the word which I have spoken will judge them, *for I have not spoken of myself*: "The Son cannot do anything of himself" (5:19); "I do not speak of myself" (14:10). *Indeed, I have not spoken of myself*, is the same as "I was not born of myself but from the Father." He is saying in effect, I will judge him on the last day (appearing in the form of a servant): "He gave him the power to pass judgment, because he is the Son of man" (5:27). Yet I will not judge from human authority, that is, because I am the Son of man, but from divine authority, because I am the Son of God. Therefore, I will not judge of myself, but from the Father from whom I have the authority to judge.[114]

1723. He establishes the truth when he says, *the Father who sent me has himself given me commandment what to say and what to speak*. Unless this is appropriately understood, it can be the source of two errors. The first is that since the one commanding is greater than the one commanded, the Father is greater than the Son. Secondly, since what is given to someone was not possessed by him before it was given, and so was not known by him, it seems that if the Father gave a commandment to the Son it follows that the Son at some time did not have it, and so did not know it. As a result, something has been added to the Son, and so the Son is not truly God.

In answer to this we should note that all the divine commands are in the mind of the Father, since these commands are nothing other than the plans or patterns of things to be done. And so just as the patterns of all creatures produced by God are in the mind of the Father, and are called ideas, so the patterns of all things to be done by us are in his mind.[115] And just as the patterns of all things pass from the Fa-

---

114. See *ST* III, q. 59, a. 2.
115. See *ST* I, q. 14, a. 5; I, q. 15, a. 3.

ther to the Son, who is the Wisdom of the Father, so also the patterns of all things to be done. Therefore, the Son says, ***the Father who sent me has himself given me***, as God, ***commandment***, that is, by an eternal generation he has communicated to me ***what to say*** within ***and what to speak*** without, just as what we say (if we speak the truth) makes known what is in our minds.

1724. Chrysostom[116] explains all this differently, and more clearly. First of all (v. 47): ***If any one hear my sayings and does not keep them, I do not judge him***. Now one is said to be condemned in two ways: either by a judge or by the reason for the condemnation. For a murderer is condemned to be hanged both by the judge who passes sentence and by the murder he committed, which is the reason for his condemnation. He says, ***I do not judge him***, that is, I am not the reason for his condemnation, but he himself is: "Your destruction, O Israel is from yourself; your help is only in me" (Hos 13:9).[117] And the reason is: ***for I did not come to judge the world***, that is, I was not sent to condemn but to save.

But will not such a person be judged? He certainly will, because ***he who rejects me and does not receive my sayings has a judge***. He shows what that judge is when he says, ***the word that I have spoken***, and you have heard, will be his accuser and ***will be his judge on the last day***. "If I had not come and spoken to them, they would not have sin; but now they have no excuse for their sin" (15:22). He shows that the word that he spoke will judge them by saying, ***for I have not spoken of myself***. This is not said causally, but in a material sense, so that the meaning is: You say that your word will judge. But what is that word? It is the word that I have spoken, ***for I have not spoken of myself***; that is, it is the word from the Father that I have spoken, and what he gave me to say and speak. Otherwise, if I had spoken something in opposition to the Father, or something I had not received from the Father, and they had believed me, they would have an excuse. But because I have spoken as I have, it is certain that they have rejected not only me, but also my Father.

1725. According to this explanation, the statement, ***the Father who sent me has himself given me commandment what to say and what to speak***, shows the sufficiency of the basis of the judgment because of the dignity or value of the word. First, its dignity is given; secondly, the fact that the word was spoken. Its dignity is stated when he says, ***I know that his commandment is eternal life***. "This is the true God and eternal life" (1 Jn 5:20). For the Son himself is the commandment of the Father, or, he is eternal life. "If you would enter life, keep the commandments" (Mt 19:17).

---

116. *Hom. in Io.* 69. 2; PG 59, col. 379; cf. *Catena aurea*, 12:44–50.
117. See *ST* I, q. 19, a. 6, ad 1.

Therefore, because the Father has given me commandment, and this commandment is eternal life, and since I have come to lead men to eternal life, I accomplish the commandment of the Father in all that I do. This is what he is saying, **What I say, therefore, I say as the Father has said to me.** According to Chrysostom, whose explanation is clear, the meaning is: *what I say, therefore*, when preaching in public, *I say as the Father has said to me*, that is, insofar as I have received knowledge from him—understanding this was received by Christ as man.[118]

1726. But if, with Augustine,[119] we understand this to apply to Christ as God, how can the Father say something to him, since Christ is his Word? The answer is that the Father did not say anything to him as though he spoke by words to his only Word. Rather, the Father spoke to the Son by generating him, and giving him life in himself: "The Lord said to me, 'You are my son'" (Ps 2:7).[120]

118. See *ST* III, q. 9, aa. 1–3.
119. *Tract. in Io.* 54. 8; PL 35, col. 1784; cf. *Catena aurea*, 12:44–50.
120. See *ST* I, q. 27, a. 2.

INDEX

This index covers chapters 6–12 of Thomas Aquinas's commentary. References denote paragraphs of Aquinas's commentary.

active life, 1473, 1510
Alcuin, 1119n3, 1337n45
Ambrose, 1007, 1250, 1474
angels, 868, 895, 904, 1042, 1062, 1246, 1279, 1287, 1431, 1602, 1663
Anointing of the sick, 1562
Apollinarius, 1654
apostles, 861, 865, 938, 1000, 1015, 1081, 1093, 1391, 1398, 1418, 1469, 1491, 1633, 1634, 1696, 1705, 1713
Aristotle, 1402, 1656
Arius/Arians, 935, 978, 1278, 1290, 1355, 1451, 1456, 1654, 1696, 1704
Athanasius, 1406
Augustine, 855, 872, 879, 880, 884, 893, 895, 896, 904, 905, 915, 921, 923, 935, 938, 943, 944, 953, 966, 972, 973, 974, 976, 987, 991, 993, 997, 998, 1004, 1007, 1012, 1015, 1017, 1019, 1026, 1027, 1031, 1037, 1039, 1040, 1042, 1043, 1045, 1049, 1050, 1052, 1058, 1069, 1070, 1077, 1078, 1081, 1090, 1093, 1094, 1095, 1119, 1124, 1131, 1142, 1156, 1162, 1163, 1173, 1183, 1191, 1195, 1201, 1203, 1204, 1215, 1217, 1219, 1222, 1225, 1243, 1248, 1251, 1259, 1278, 1279, 1285, 1287, 1290, 1291, 1294, 1296, 1301, 1311, 1314, 1318, 1319, 1329, 1334, 1336, 1337, 1340, 1347, 1360, 1363, 1365, 1368, 1370, 1371, 1379, 1380, 1391, 1392, 1393, 1398, 1406, 1424, 1433, 1449, 1450, 1463, 1466, 1470, 1474, 1476, 1479, 1491, 1495, 1504, 1507, 1519, 1523, 1527, 1530, 1544, 1557, 1560, 1571, 1588, 1596, 1597, 1599, 1605, 1611, 1621, 1622, 1648, 1650, 1657, 1669, 1670, 1671, 1673, 1677, 1682, 1702, 1705, 1711, 1720, 1726

baptism, 964, 969, 1311, 1319, 1355, 1561–62

beatific vision, 921, 927, 947, 1062, 1170, 1271, 1287, 1370, 1548, 1647
Bede, 942
Bible. *See* Scripture
Blessed Virgin. *See* Mary
Body of Christ. *See* Church

causality: divine, 1301; meritorious, 1192, 1422
charity/love, 875–77, 879, 882, 887, 901, 946, 950, 969, 972, 976, 993, 1020, 1094–95, 1167, 1192, 1225, 1234, 1236, 1238, 1398–99, 1405, 1412, 1419, 1422, 1426, 1475, 1479, 1503, 1538–39, 1599, 1643, 1673
Christ: ascension, 874, 886, 1093, 1307–8, 1637, 1662; baptism, 898, 1469; emotions of, 1531–38, 1541, 1651–52; grace at work in, 862, 898, 1278; human knowledge, 868, 948, 1037, 1061–65, 1192, 1283–84, 1374, 1412, 1414, 1665, 1725; Lamb of God, 1469, 1590; as mediator, 1414; Messiah, 1004, 1269, 1520; passion and death, 841, 874, 961–64, 1012, 1019, 1023, 1075, 1096, 1166–67, 1170, 1173, 1191, 1227, 1287, 1308, 1416, 1421–22, 1425, 1474, 1490, 1532, 1561, 1578, 1589–92, 1620, 1628, 1635–41, 1647, 1652–53, 1657, 1660, 1668, 1671–73, 1678–79, 1694; as priest, 854, 1520; as prophet, 867–68, 984, 1098, 1329; resurrection, 841, 963, 1093–96, 1637; savior, 1124, 1188, 1479, 1552, 1567, 1717; second coming, 1667; Son of God, 897, 914, 923, 935, 944, 977, 990, 1004, 1037, 1062, 1143, 1149, 1157, 1176, 1227, 1257, 1265, 1277–78, 1355–58, 1439, 1451, 1461–62, 1478, 1520, 1717, 1722; Son of Man, 897–98, 914, 977, 989–91, 1037, 1192, 1274, 1278, 1357–58, 1465, 1637–39, 1677–80,

310   INDEX

Christ: Son of Man *(cont.)*
  1722; soul of, 959, 962, 1037, 1065,
  1176, 1415, 1650–54; teaching of,
  838, 843–44, 854, 944, 982, 984, 987,
  1003, 1010, 1028, 1034, 1036, 1053,
  1070, 1076, 1084, 1122, 1124, 1140,
  1193, 1198, 1357; transfiguration,
  1662; wisdom of God, 854, 914, 1035,
  1058, 1064, 1176, 1384, 1651, 1662,
  1723; Word of God, 895, 914, 936,
  1037, 1108, 1176, 1311, 1343, 1384,
  1460–61, 1639, 1718
Christology (divine and human in Christ),
  898, 910, 914, 923, 959, 973, 977, 980,
  990, 1004, 1012, 1027, 1052, 1059–60,
  1065, 1108, 1122, 1131, 1143, 1150,
  1161, 1179, 1183, 1192, 1236, 1286–
  87, 1310, 1358, 1393, 1415, 1422,
  1456, 1511, 1532–38, 1541, 1553–55,
  1599, 1651–52, 1711
Church: Body of Christ, 960, 972, 976,
  998; as bride, 935, 1673; catechumens, 1311, 1319; Christ as head,
  1434, 1599; of Jews and Gentiles,
  1626; militant, 1392, 1396; Peter
  as head, 1398; practices of, 969–70,
  1085; prelates/leaders, 1398, 1403,
  1406, 1595; teaching of, 1142; triumphant, 1392; unity of, 886–87, 960,
  969, 972, 1419
circumcision, 953, 1047–49
contemplation, 854, 882, 1311, 1391,
  1393, 1495, 1510, 1560
contemplative life, 1473, 1510, 1595
courage, 1052
covenant, 974, 1047, 1049, 1507
creation, 901, 1049, 1183, 1240, 1246,
  1296, 1580, 1591

death: physical, 914, 954, 1169, 1243,
  1273–75, 1477, 1495, 1501, 1517,
  1534–36; spiritual, 954, 1138, 1168–
  69, 1243, 1271, 1273–75, 1507, 1517
Dedication, feast of, 1433–35
deification, 972, 1258, 1459–61
devil, 850, 860, 923, 998, 1006, 1068,
  1093, 1176, 1208, 1217, 1240–52,
  1264–65, 1273, 1405–6, 1602, 1620,
  1662, 1663, 1667–73, 1697
Dionysius the Areopagite, 969, 1247,
  1311, 1696

eternal life, 895–900, 921, 927–28,
  950–51, 963, 969, 972, 975, 981, 989,
  1003, 1095, 1108, 1307, 1396, 1450,
  1517, 1570, 1599, 1645–46, 1725

Eucharist, 954, 960, 959, 962, 964,
  966–82, 1562
evil, 1007, 1016, 1040, 1053, 1067,
  1107, 1111, 1191, 1209, 1214, 1240–
  41, 1246–47, 1253, 1301, 1326, 1360,
  1374, 1395, 1399–402, 1477, 1502,
  1535, 1546, 1602, 1698

faith, 867, 882, 886–87, 901–4, 918–21,
  927, 936, 939, 940, 943, 944, 946,
  950, 972–73, 997, 1004, 1070, 1078,
  1114, 1161, 1179, 1191, 1193, 1195,
  1222–24, 1311, 1319, 1350, 1355–56,
  1396, 1447, 1470, 1504, 1511, 1517–
  18, 1548, 1570, 1599, 1682, 1708,
  1711–14
Father: activity of, 935–37, 1465, 1648;
  attributes, 947; in the Old Testament,
  1161; person of, 1154, 1451, 1662,
  1696; prayer to, 1551–55; proces-
  sions, 990, 1037, 1092, 1150, 1183,
  1236, 1308, 1311; relationship to the
  Son, 898, 918, 923–28, 977–80, 1037,
  1059, 1065, 1162, 1192, 1216, 1278,
  1414, 1461, 1466, 1520, 1622, 1712,
  1723; as source, 1183, 1192, 1237
fortitude. *See* courage
free will, 946, 1007, 1199–205, 1209–10,
  1246, 1390, 1692, 1711
friendship, 947, 1001–2, 1096, 1475,
  1494, 1510, 1589

Gentiles, 854, 1081, 1263, 1292, 1361,
  1416–19, 1469, 1483, 1544, 1626,
  1631–41, 1671
Gloss, 955, 1632
God: divine nature (essence), 927,
  977, 1065, 1179, 1187, 1192, 1450,
  1459–60, 1466, 1712; divine persons,
  1154, 1156, 1183, 1192, 1696; divine
  providence, 1477–78, 1527; love of,
  1004, 1094, 1673; works of, 843,
  1039, 1049, 1142, 1300–305, 1352,
  1441, 1465–66, 1591
good works, 895, 901–2, 921, 1222,
  1224–25, 1307, 1422, 1546, 1586,
  1608, 1639
grace, 937, 964, 997, 1063, 1090, 1093,
  1119–20, 1198–99, 1209, 1305–8,
  1311, 1363, 1371, 1412, 1418, 1422,
  1434, 1443, 1507, 1560–62, 1648,
  1698
Gregory the Great, 893, 1204, 1255,
  1260, 1264, 1287, 1290, 1292, 1302,
  1311, 1392, 1435, 1474, 1483, 1580,
  1597

happiness, 935, 1245, 1300, 1382, 1398
heaven, 872, 886, 909–10, 923, 939–40, 949, 953, 955, 980, 989, 990, 1078, 1176, 1611, 1669, 1673
hell, 1139, 1302, 1307
Helvidius, 1015
heresy/heretics, 887, 1037, 1143, 1240, 1366, 1395, 1405–6, 1685
Hilary of Poitiers, 898, 978, 1060, 1237, 1355, 1461, 1463, 1466
Holy Spirit: adoption, 1234, 1462, 1580; appropriation, 1662; baptism, 969, 1562; charity, 976, 1004, 1094–95, 1234; in Christ, 980, 1004, 1058, 1116, 1520; Eucharist, 993; gifts of, 1090, 1093–94; as God, 1156, 1547; grace of, 1090; indwelling, 976, 993, 1090; inspiration, 992, 1577–79; procession of, 1092, 1183; resurrection, 973; sin against, 1169; source of truth, 1037, 1250, 1371, 1628; unity of, 972
hope, 930, 950, 1095, 1179, 1191, 1205, 1444, 1472, 1495, 1651
humility, 860, 923, 1040, 1122, 1368, 1529, 1596, 1599, 1627

image of God, 947, 1164, 1258, 1466, 1580, 1648
Incarnation. *See* Christology
intellect, created, 950, 984, 1040, 1064, 1069, 1142, 1577
Israel, 1013, 1262, 1384, 1417, 1586, 1660

Jerome, 1030, 1089, 1474, 1597, 1624
Jews/Judaism, 840, 854, 868, 900, 905–7, 949, 966, 984, 1023, 1048–49, 1079, 1081, 1161, 1173, 1214, 1218, 1222, 1239–40, 1262–63, 1291, 1361, 1416–17, 1483, 1527, 1574, 1581, 1623, 1626, 1632, 1633, 1685, 1692, 1702, 1712
John Chrysostom, 840, 870, 884, 890, 898, 904, 923, 930, 943, 974, 988, 992, 1002, 1007, 1012, 1019, 1023, 1026, 1027, 1039, 1040, 1052, 1071, 1073, 1077, 1089, 1093, 1096, 1149, 1157, 1184, 1188, 1191, 1210, 1217, 1255, 1275, 1296, 1310, 1329, 1337, 1340, 1353, 1361, 1363, 1365, 1366, 1367, 1371, 1390, 1474, 1478, 1486, 1493, 1504, 1510, 1519, 1541, 1544, 1553, 1571, 1597, 1608, 1611, 1615, 1630, 1632, 1658, 1672, 1679, 1682, 1711, 1724, 1725
John of Damascus, 959

judgment, final, 870, 1050, 1131, 1152–54, 1185–86, 1269, 1360–61, 1447, 1667–68, 1715–19
justice, 845, 938, 1124, 1127–30, 1134, 1135, 1185, 1211, 1599
justification, 926, 1417

law: divine law, 1050; natural law, 1507; New Law, 846, 860, 880, 1131, 1199, 1507, 1561; Old Law (Law of Moses), 846, 854, 880, 1050, 1198, 1353, 1363, 1458, 1507, 1508, 1543, 1627, 1631, 1676
likeness. *See* image of God
love. *See* charity

Manicheanism, 860, 1142, 1176, 1240, 1246, 1251, 1279, 1384, 1580, 1669, 1705
Mary, 1015, 1055, 1058, 1357
mercy, 938, 1119, 1124, 1130, 1135–36, 1447, 1500, 1503, 1536, 1551, 1599, 1627, 1698, 1700
merit, 895, 1145, 1206, 1271, 1307, 1348, 1350, 1403, 1422, 1551, 1611
miracles, 843–44, 862, 883, 893, 904, 935, 1013, 1016, 1070, 1073, 1093, 1108, 1119, 1262, 1310, 1313, 1348–50, 1430, 1431, 1456, 1548, 1569, 1689, 1700

Nestorius, 1143, 1357

obedience, 1188, 1310, 1318, 1419, 1473, 1508, 1592, 1594
Origen of Alexandria, 1161, 1164, 1173, 1175, 1222, 1232, 1237, 1240, 1243, 1247, 1263, 1264, 1274, 1449, 1474, 1549, 1579, 1584, 1597

paganism, 1633
participation, 868, 871, 1065, 1145, 1179, 1183, 1187, 1370, 1384, 1459–61, 1713
Passover, 846, 1012, 1013, 1024, 1586, 1590, 1597, 1617
peace, 1039, 1508, 1544
penance, 1138, 1561–62
persecution, 879, 1012, 1292, 1390, 1406, 1469, 1483, 1584, 1630
Philosopher, the. *See* Aristotle
philosophy/philosophers, 854, 947, 1368
Photinus, 935
poverty, 849, 852, 1313, 1604, 1610
prayer, 849, 1348, 1431, 1511, 1550–55

predestination, 921, 925–26, 1007, 1373–74, 1412, 1417–18, 1443, 1446, 1536, 1580
priesthood, 961, 964, 970, 1560–62, 1647
Priscian, 1030
prophecy, 867, 1070, 1093, 1384, 1458, 1577–79, 1627–28, 1690, 1692, 1694, 1705
purgatory, 964

reason, 854, 1142, 1144, 1204, 1534–35, 1577, 1651, 1658
repentance, 1133, 1347, 1560, 1702
resurrection of the dead, 925, 928, 939, 973, 1360, 1514–17, 1557–58

sabbath, 870, 1012, 1023, 1042, 1048–49, 1262, 1321–22, 1326–29, 1590, 1615
Sabellius, 1037, 1154, 1237, 1451, 1696
sacraments, 865, 886, 914, 959–64, 969, 972–77, 992, 1138, 1363, 1434, 1561–62, 1611, 1631, 1632, 1647
sacrifice, 1208, 1292, 1350, 1591
saints, 870, 1019, 1020, 1021, 1022, 1393, 1406, 1431, 1434, 1449, 1474, 1532
salvation, 919, 920, 923, 925, 943, 970, 1049, 1081, 1088, 1179, 1215, 1263, 1313, 1374, 1414, 1416, 1519, 1549, 1570, 1579, 1590, 1621, 1673, 1674
Samaritans, 912, 1119, 1262–63, 1633
sanctification, 925, 986, 1094, 1461, 1463
scientia. See reason
Scripture: allegorical sense, 1311; authority of, 1101, 1246, 1273, 1366–67, 1371, 1457; fulfillment of, 1197, 1370, 1691; literal sense, 840, 852, 857, 884, 1107, 1310, 1469, 1487, 1546, 1557, 1592, 1639; mystical sense, 841, 848, 854, 856, 857, 861, 872, 874, 877, 1294, 1311, 1435, 1469, 1483, 1508, 1510, 1522, 1536, 1538, 1541, 1543, 1544, 1546, 1560, 1599; as the word of God, 1195, 1258, 1271
shepherds (pastors), 942, 1368–74, 1398–99, 1402–6, 1412–13
simony, 1368
sin: of the angels, 1242–46; forgiveness of, 843, 1138–39, 1363, 1641, 1671; mortal, 1274, 1307, 1507, 1513; original, 937, 1047, 1179, 1294, 1299, 1447, 1672; slavery to, 1203–5, 1207, 1209, 1326
Son of God. *See* Christ
soul, 843, 862, 901, 914, 923, 928, 972–74, 993, 1049, 1065, 1069, 1232, 1240, 1296–97, 1353, 1406, 1425, 1516–17, 1557, 1560–61, 1580

Tabernacles, feast of, 1013, 1026–27
temple, 982, 1034, 1119–20, 1163, 1292, 1433, 1435–37, 1571, 1632
testimony, 1108, 1147–51, 1156–57, 1349, 1470
Theodore of Mopsuestia, 1705
Theophylact, 1490
Trinity, 865, 1004, 1007, 1069, 1156, 1192, 1287, 1662, 1704
truth, 895, 935, 946, 1031, 1037, 1040, 1059, 1063, 1124, 1149, 1187–88, 1198–201, 1228, 1244–52, 1253–58, 1271, 1333, 1335, 1370, 1686

Valentinus, 990, 1176
virtue, 846, 880, 893, 1008, 1011, 1034, 1269, 1302, 1368, 1584, 1599, 1634

will: divine, 861, 927, 935, 938, 1039, 1163, 1700; human, 984, 1240, 1246, 1425, 1645
wisdom: divine, 846, 849, 857, 895, 946, 1088, 1142, 1229, 1271, 1357, 1391, 1511, 1665; human, 854
Word. *See* Christ
worship, 1081, 1350, 1433, 1632

Commentary on the Gospel of John: Chapters 6–12 was designed and typeset in Meridien by Kachergis Book Design of Pittsboro, North Carolina. It was printed on 55-pound Natural and bound by Versa Press of East Peoria, Illinois.

www.ingramcontent.com/pod-product-compliance
Lightning Source LLC
Chambersburg PA
CBHW032028290426
44110CB00012B/708